# YALE CLASSICAL STUDIES

## EDITED FOR THE DEPARTMENT OF CLASSICS

*by*

### NAPHTALI LEWIS

*Distinguished Professor (Emeritus) of Classical Studies,*
*The City University of New York;*
*sometime Visiting Professor of Classics,*
*Yale University*

## *VOLUME XXVIII*
## *PAPYROLOGY*

## CAMBRIDGE UNIVERSITY PRESS

### CAMBRIDGE

#### LONDON   NEW YORK   NEW ROCHELLE
#### MELBOURNE   SYDNEY

Published by the Press Syndicate of the University of Cambridge
The Pitt Building, Trumpington Street, Cambridge CB2 1RP
32 East 57th Street, New York, NY 10022, USA
10 Stamford Road, Oakleigh, Melbourne 3166, Australia

First published 1985

Printed in Great Britain by the
University Press, Cambridge

Library of Congress catalogue card number: 84-28591

*British Library Cataloguing in Publication Data*
Papyrology – (Yale Classical Studies; v. 28)
1. History, Ancient – Sources
2.   Manuscripts (Papyri)
1. Lewis, Naphtali   II. Series
930   D52

ISBN 0 521 30015 0

# Contents

v

## Contents

## Contents

# Plates

# Preface

This twenty-eighth volume of *Yale Classical Studies* celebrates the centenary of papyrology as a classical discipline. Not that the discipline sprang forth full-blown on any date certain. What is certain, however, is that, following upon the startling finds of masses of Greek papyri that began in the late 1870s, it was in the 1880s that there appeared the first publications of what has grown in a hundred years into a voluminous literature of papyrus texts and commentary, and of topical analysis and synthesis.

The state of the art today is reflected in the contents of the present volume. All of the principal facets of papyrological study are sampled here: there are editions and re-editions of texts, literary and documentary, including that relative rarity, a Latin papyrus; there are papers, ranging from brief occasional pieces to comprehensive studies, in the several areas of classical antiquity in which our knowledge has been so immeasurably enriched by the papyri – language, government (especially administration and taxation), social and economic history, private life, law. The Ptolemaic, Roman and Byzantine periods are all represented. And the interdisciplinary ramifications of the papyrus documents are also apparent in more than one of the articles herein.

The pioneering founders of papyrology impressed upon the discipline, as they created it, their stamp of friendly international co-operation, and happily that spirit continues to imbue the work of papyrologists to this day. The international quality of the discipline stands out readily enough in the names, languages and institutional affiliations of the contributors to this volume, and in the various collections to which papyri edited herein belong. What is not so readily apparent (except to papyrologists), and is also cause for continuing gratification, is that the contributors to this volume represent a continuum of three generations, the elderly retired (from teaching, that is, not from papyrological activity), the middle-aged and elderly who are still actively teaching, and their students, the young men and women of the rising generation, our hope and promise for the future.

A personal reminiscence may not be out of place by way of envoi. It was just over fifty years ago that a young graduate student, beginning to collect data for his doctoral dissertation, took the train to New Haven for a consultation. The consultant was Michael I. Rostovtzeff, who had a few years earlier come to Yale as professor of ancient history and had (*inter alia*) begun to build Yale's collection of Greek papyri. The visiting student was the undersigned. Rostovtzeff had just published, in *Yale Classical Studies* 3, a large group of clay seals of Seleucid date. From the impressions still visible on their backs, some of those seals had obviously been applied to documents written on papyrus. But was there any clue in those impressions to suggest that the papyri were of local rather than Egyptian manufacture? (The answer: *Non liquet.*) A third party was brought into the scrutiny and discussion, the late C. Bradford Welles, then Rostovtzeff's assistant, later to be his successor in the chair of ancient history. The room in which we sat and talked was then Rostovtzeff's office (complete with his stand-up desk), which also then housed Yale's nascent papyrus collection and papyrological library. The papyri, which have increased in numbers to become the second largest collection in the United States, have long since been moved to the Beinecke Rare Book and Manuscript Library. The room now serves the Department of Classics as the office of its chairman and as a meeting place for seminars. It is at the seminar table that I sit penning these words of nostalgia.

Let us not, however, close with mere retrospection. This volume, which acknowledges a century of achievement, also heralds the advent of a second century, one – it is to be hoped – of even greater attainments. *Quod bonum faustum felix fortunatumque sit!*

N. L.

# Ilias K 372–443 (*P. Berol.* 10570)

## GÜNTER POETHKE

Der von Otto Rubensohn 1905 für die Berliner Papyrus-Sammlung erworbene Text wurde erstmalig in *BKT* v 1, S.5 erwähnt ( = Pack² 864), fand dann als Π⁴⁶ Aufnahme in die Iliasausgabe von T. W. Allen und wurde zuletzt im Katalog der Ausstellung "Troja und Thrakien" vorgestellt.¹ Eine philologische Edition von ihm gab es bisher nicht.

Vorhanden sind sieben Fragmente eines Blattes eines Papyrus-kodex mit Resten der Partie K 372–443; allerdings sind von den Versen 392f., 406 und 428 keine Spuren mehr erkennbar. Die Mindestmasse des Blattes betragen 28 cm in der Höhe und 15,5 cm in der Breite; demnach ergibt sich ein Verhältnis der Höhe zur Breite von 2:1. Kodizes dieses schmalen Hochformates bilden eine umfangreiche Gruppe, auf die W. Schubart und E. G. Turner hinwiesen.² Eine Klebung ist etwa 4 cm vom linken Rand (Recto) bzw. etwa 2 cm vom rechten Rand (Verso) entfernt zu erkennen. Die Verszahl pro Seite beträgt 36, so dass der Gesang etwa 16 Seiten umfasste.

Der Schreiber bemüht sich um eine Buchschrift, doch ist der Einfluss der byzantinischen Geschäftsschrift sehr stark. Auffällig sind die häufig über die gedachten Zeilen ragenden senkrechten Hasten. Ausser den Anfangsbuchstaben der Verse werden β und κ vergrössert. Stilistisch am nächsten steht die von W. Schubart gegebene Probe aus dem Dioskoros-Papyrus *P. Cair. Masp.* 1 67067 von der Mitte des 6. Jahrhunderts.³ Gleiche Charakteristika zeigt das Fragment einer Manetho-Epitome aus dem 5. Jahrhundert, wenn auch das gesamte Schriftbild ausgeglichener wirkt.⁴ Somit wird man den in *BKT* v 1, S.5 für den Iliastext genannten

1. "Troja und Thrakien" (Berlin 1982) 50, Abb. 103–4.
2. W. Schubart, *Das Buch*,² 131; E. G. Turner, *The Typology of the Early Codex* (Philadelphia 1977) 20.
3. *Paläographie*, Abb. 100.
4. Abb. bei R. Seider, *Paläographie der griechischen Papyri* II, Abb. 61.

Zeitansatz "etwa 5. Jahrh. n. Chr." wohl mit der Feststellung erweitern müssen, dass die Schrift auch im 6. Jahrhundert möglich wäre.

Lesezeichen sind ziemlich regelmässig zu finden. Wo sie fehlen, können sie ursprünglich gestanden haben, da die Schrift an zahlreichen Stellen abgerieben ist. Der Schreiber verwendet alle drei Akzente (413 falsch τοῖ) und setzt sie bei Diphthong zuweilen auf dessen ersten Bestandteil; einmal bezeichnet ein waagerechter Strich die Längung des Vokals (429 δ]ῡο[ι). Ferner sind Spiritus lenis und asper, Apostroph, Trema über ι und υ, an Interpunktion der Punkt in mittlerer Zeilenhöhe sowie auf der Zeile anzutreffen.

Korrekturen fallen durch die schwarze Tinte auf, so in den Versen 377, 380, 385, 417, 420, 421. Iota adscriptum ist in Vers 438 an zwei Stellen nachgetragen; Akzente, Satzzeichen und möglicherweise ein Spiritus (435) wurden ergänzt.

Der Papyrustext weicht an einigen Stellen von der Vulgata ab; hervorzuheben sind die Verse 380 (χ' ὑμῖν) und 385 (τίφθ'). Bisher ist diese Partie der *Ilias* in Gänze auf Papyrus nur einmal auf einer aus mehreren Fragmenten bestehenden Rolle aus dem Anfang des 3. Jahrhunderts bekannt geworden.[5] Als Grundlage für den Textvergleich dienten die Ausgaben von W. Leaf (London 1900) und T. W. Allen (Oxford 1931).

Recto                                    Plate I

372 Ἡ̣ [ρ]α̣ κ̣[αι] ἐγχος αφηκ̣[εν] ἑκὼν δ[ημαρτα]νε φωτὸς·
     δ[ε]ξιτερόνδ' ὑπ[ε]ρ ὧμον εὔξου [δουρος α]κωκὴ
     ἐν γαιή ἐπάγη ὁ δ αρ' ἐστη τα[ρβησεν τε]
375 βαμβαίνων· ἀρα[βο]ς̣ δὲ δια στόμα γιγ[νετ οδοντων]
     χλωρὸς ὕπαι δ[ε]ίου[ς] τώδ' ασθμαίνοντ[ε κιχητην]
     χειρῶν 'δ''ἀψασθην· ὁ δὲ δακρύσας ἐπο[ς ηυδα]
     ζωγρ̄εῖτ' αυτα[ρ] εγὼν εμὲ λύσομαι· εσ[τ]ι̣ [γαρ ενδον]
     χαλκός τε χρυσός τε πολύκμητός τ̣ε ς̣ι̣[δη]ρ[ος]
380 τῶν χ' ὑμῖν χα[ρι]ʹσαιτο πατὴ[ρ α]περεισι [α]ʹποιν[α]
     ει κεν εμὲ̣ ζω̣ὸ̣ν πεπύθο[ιτ ε]πι νηυσιν [Α]χαιω[ν]
     τόνδ' απαμ̣ειβόμενος προσ[εφη] πολύμητ[ις Οδυσσευς]
     θαρσει μηδε τί το̣ι θαν[ατος] κ̣αταθύ[μιος εστω]
     αλλ' αγε μοι τοδε ειπὲ κ̣[αι ατρεκεως καταλεξον]
385 τιφθ' οὕτως επὶ νῆας απο [στρατου ερχεαι οιος]
     νύκτα δι ορφ[ναιη]ν̣' ὁτε θ' [ευδουσι βροτοι αλλοι]

5. Veröffentlicht von H. Maehler, W. Müller, G. Poethke, *APF* 24/25 (1976) 13–26 (zitiert hier als *P. Berol.* 11911).

[η τ]ι[να σ]υ[λησων] νεκύ[ων κατατεθνηωτων]
[η σ Εκτωρ προε]ηκε [διασκο]πιᾶσ[θαι εκαστα]
[νηας επι γλαφυ]ρὰς [η σ αυτον] θυμῷος ανηκε]
390  [τονδ ημειβετ]' επει[τα Δολων υ]πο δ [ετρεμε γυια]
[πολλησιν μ ατη]σι πα[ρεκ νοον ηγαγεν Εκτωρ]
[ος μοι Πηλειωνος αγαυου μωνυχας ιππους]
[δωσεμεναι κατενευσε και αρματα ποικιλα χαλκω]
[ηνωγει δε] μ [ιοντα θοην δια νυκτα μελαιναν]
395  [ανδρων δυ]σμ[ενεων σχεδον ελθεμεν εκ τε πυθεσθαι]
[ηε φυλασσον]τ[αι νηες θο]αι ως το [παρος περ]
[η ηδη χειρε]σσιν [υφ ημε]τερησι δ[αμεντες]
[φυξιν βουλ]εύοισ[θε μεταγ' σφισιν· ου[δ εθελοιτε]
[νυκτα φυλασσε]μ[εναι κα]ματω ἀδηκ[οτες αινω]
400  [τονδ επιμει]δ[ησας πρ]οσέφη πολύμητ[ις Οδυσσευς]
[η ρα νυ τοι με]γάλω[ν δωρων] ἐπεμαίετο θυ[μος]
[ιππων Αιακιδ]αο δα[ιφρονο]ς· όι δ' αλεγε[ινοι]
[ανδρασι γε θνητ]οι[σι δαμη]μεναι ἠδ' ο[χεεσθαι]
[αλλω γ η Αχιληι] τ[ον αθανατη τεκε μητηρ]
405  [αλλ αγε μοι] τ[οδε ειπε και ατρεκεως καταλεξον]
[που νυν δευρο κιων λιπες Εκτορα ποιμενα λαων]
[που δε οι ε]ν[τεα κειται αρηια που δε οι ιπποι]


Verso
[π]ῶς δαὶ τῷ[ν αλλων] Τρώων φυλακὰι τε και ευν'[αι]·
[ασσα τε μητιωσι] μετά σφισιν ἠ μεμάασιν
410  [αυθι μενειν παρα ν]ηὐσιν απόπροθεν. ἠε πόλινδε
[αψ αναχωρησ]ουσιν επει δαμάσαντο γ' Αχαιοὺς·
[τονδ αυτε π]ροσέειπε Δόλων Ευμήδεος υἱὸς·
[τοι γαρ εγω] τοῖ ταῦτα μαλ' ατρεκέως [κ]αταλέξω·
[Εκτω]ρ [με]ν μετα τοῖσιν ὃσοι βουληφόροι ἐισιν
415  [βου]λὰς [βο]υλεύει θέιου παρα σήματι Ἴλου
[νοσ]φιν απο φλοίσβου [φ]υλακὰς δ' ἅ[ς] είρεαι ἥρως.
[ου τις κε]κριμένη ρ[υετ]αι στρατὸν ουδε φυ'λ'άσ'σ'ει·
[οσσαι μεν] Τρώων π[υρος] εσχάραι· οἱσιν ανάγκη
[οι δ εγρηγο]γ'ρθασι φυ[λασσ]έμεναι τε κέλονται
420  [αλληλοις αταρ αυτε π]ολυκλητοι τ' επικουροι
[ευδουσι Τρωσιν γαρ επ]ιτραπέουσι φυλάσσειν·
[ου γαρ σφιν] π[αιδες σχε]δὸν είατα[ι ου]δε γυναίκες
[τονδ απαμει]βομ[ενος προσ]έφη [πολυμητις] Ο[δυ]σ[σευς]
[πως γαρ νυν Τ]ρώε[σσι μεμιγ]μένο[ι ιπποδαμοισιν]
425  [ευδουσ η απ]ανε[υθε διειπ]έ μ[οι οφρα δαειω]
[τονδ ημειβ]ετ' [επειτα Δολ]ων Ε[υμηδεος υιος]
[τοιγαρ εγω και ταυτα μαλ α]τρεκ[εως καταλεξω]
[προς μεν αλος Καρες και Παιονες αγκυλοτοξοι]
[και Λελεγες και Καυκωνες δ]ῦο[ι τε Πελασγοι]

3

430 [προς Θυμβρης δ ελαχον Λυκιοι Μυσ]οί τ [αγερωχοι]
[και Φρυγες] ι[ππ]ο̣[μαχοι και Μη]ο̣ν̣ε̣[ς ιπποκορυσται]
[αλλα τιη εμε] ταῦτα δ̣[ιεξερε]‵ε̣σθ[ε εκαστα]
[ει γαρ δη με]μ̣ατον Τρ[ωων κατ]αδῦν[αι ομιλον]
[Θρηικες οι]δ᾿ απάνε[υθε νεη]‵λυδες [εσχατοι αλλων]
435 [εν δε σ]φιν ῾Ρησος βασ̣ι[λεὺς π]α̣ις Η[ιονηος]
[του δη] καλλιστους ἵππ̣[ους ιδον] ἡδε [μεγιστους]
[λευ]κότεροι χιόνος· [θειειν δ] α̣νέμο[ισιν ομοιοι]
[αρμ]α̣ δε οἱ χρυσῶ‵ι᾿ τ[ε και αργ]υ̣ρ̣ω‵ι᾿ ευ [ησκηται]
[τευχεα δ]ε̣ χ[ρυ]σ̣εια [πελωρια] θαῦμα [ιδεσθαι]
440 [ηλυθ εχων τα μεν ου τι κατα]θ̣ν̣η̣τ̣ο̣ι̣[σιν εοικεν]
[ανδρεσσιν φορεειν αλλ αθαν]α̣τ̣ο̣ι̣σ̣ι̣ [θεοισιν]
[αλλ εμε μεν νυν νηυσι πε]λ̣α̣σ̣σ̣ε̣τον [ωκυποροισιν]
[ηε με δησαντες λιπετ] αυτ̣ο̣θ̣ι̣ νη[λει δεσμω]

372 ἑκών δ᾿ wie AB und einige andere Hss.: ἑκώνδ᾿ die übrigen    373
δ[ε]ξιτερόνδ᾿ wie die meisten Hss.: -ὸν δ᾿ AB und einige andere Hss. εὔξου wie
einige Hss.: εὔξόου Vulgata    374 *l.* γαίη    375 γίγ[νετ᾿ Pap.? γίνετ᾿ Hss.,
γείν- *P. Berol.* 11911    376 τώδ᾿ wie die meisten Hss.: τὼ δ᾿ B und einige
andere Hss.    377 δ᾿ kursiv in missglückter Ausführung vom Korrektor mit
daruntergesetztem Haken eingefügt    380 χ᾿ ὕμῖν (wie noch P[11]) vom
Korrektor über ausgelöschtes κ᾿ ὕμμιν (Vulgata) geschrieben: κ᾿ ὕμιν AB, einige
Hss. und *P. Berol.* 11911. ἀ]περείσι᾿ vielleicht auch möglich    382 τόνδ᾿ wie
die meisten Hss., so auch 390, 400, 412, 423, 426 zu erwarten: τὸν δ᾿ einige Hss.
Am linken Rand Tintenfleck oder Abdruck eines Buchstabens (Γ̂ ?)    385
τίφθ᾿ (wie einige Hss.) korrigiert über πῆ δ᾿ (Vulgata): andere Hss. ποῖ bzw.
ποῦ    386 ὀρφναίην wie die Vulgata: ἀμβροσίην drei Hss. und *P. Berol.*
11911    398 βουλεύοισθε ... ἐθέλοιτε auch P[7]: βουλεύοιτε ... ἐθέλοιτε Vulgata:
-ουσι ... -ουσι zahlreiche Hss.    408 δαὶ Ar. A und mehrere Hss.: δ᾿ αἱ
Vulgata und *P. Berol.* 11911    410 πόλινδε die meisten Hss.: πόλιν δὲ AB und
einige andere Hss.    413 καταλέξω Ar. Vulgata: ἀγορεύσω einige Hss. und
*P. Berol.* 11911    417 φυάσει Pap., wobei υ und α kräftig über frühere
Buchstaben gesetzt sind    420 πολύκλητοί τ᾿ ἐπίκουροι auch A und mehrere
Hss.: πολύκλ. γ᾿ ἐπ. *P. Berol.* 11911: πολύκλ. ἐπ. Vulgata: ἐπίκουροι vom
Korrektor    421 ἐ]πιτρ̣απέουσι: -τρ- aus Korrektur    429 *l.* δῖοί τε
435 ῾Ρῆσος: vom Korrektor über P Spiritus nachgetragen (oder nur Punkt?)
438 χρυσῶτ[ und αργ]ύρω‵ Pap.

4

# The ancient title of the *Ad Demonicum*

## SUSAN A. STEPHENS

The following two papyrus scraps – an end title and a book title – are the property of the Egypt Exploration Society; they are published here with the generous permission of the Society.

### I

P. Oxy. ined. 4B4/4a                                    Plate II (top)
5.0 × 6.5 cm

The first is written in a common type of informal round hand normally assigned to the second century A.D. There are some cursive affinities; note especially *kappa* and *nu*. The back is blank. The text, written along the fibres, can be reconstructed as follows:

[Ισοκρατους]
[Προς Δ]ημονικον
[Παρα]ινεσεις

It is most likely to have been written at the foot of the final column of a roll and to have been broken off; there are characteristic ornamental flourishes above and below the final letters of the two remaining lines. The title it preserves is found also in Harpocration as αἱ πρὸς Δημόνικον παραινέσεις (s.v. ἐπακτὸς ὅρκος)[1] and in one medieval manuscript, the cod. Parisinus ( = Y), as ʼΙσοκράτους παραινέσεις πρὸς Δημόνικον. I think it likely that a form of this title is also to be restored in P. Berol. 8935 ( = Pack² 1244) published in *APF* 27 (1980) 17, a late second- or early third-century roll for which the following lacunose end title survives:

ι[. . .]ρατους[
]η[.]ον[.]κον
]αραινε[

---

1. However, the speech is assigned to Isocrates Apolloniates, on whom see F. Blass, *Die Attische Beredsamkeit* II, 449–51. The authorship of the *Ad Demonicum* has often been called into question, see E. Drerup, *Isocratis Opera Omnia*, cxxxiv–cxli.

5

The editors, following E. Drerup, *Isocratis Opera Omnia*, 116 (apparatus), have restored this as ι[σοκ]ρατους [προς/ δ]η[μ]ον[ι]κον/ π]αραινεσ[ις], but the singular παραίνεσις, which occasionally appears in the manuscript tradition, does not seem to occur in the ancient sources.[2]

## II

P. *Oxy.* ined. 5B4/G(2–4)b                                    Plate II (bottom)
2.8 × 6.5 cm

The second scrap is written in a late Severe style assignable to the late third or early fourth century A.D. (compare, e.g., Turner, *Greek Manuscripts of the Ancient World* (Princeton 1971) pl. 70); the back is blank. Written along the fibres, the text reads:

]Ισοκρατους
]Παραινεσεις

*Prima facie* this is a book title or *sillybos* since the title appears to be complete. The edges, while frayed, have been cut, not broken, and there are no traces of ink either above or below the existing writing. While this may represent no more than a variant of the first title, it is also possible that it is intended to be generic, to include the first three speeches of the Isocratean corpus – *Ad Demonicum* (I), *Ad Nicoclem* (II), *Nicocles* (III) – classified by ancient grammarians as αἱ παραινέσεις. The clearest evidence for this usage is found in the so-called anonymous *Life* of Isocrates attributed to Zosimus, where the purpose and style of the three speeches is discussed.[3] Further, in a rhetorical treatise attributed to Hermogenes, the author finds it necessary to distinguish the *Ad Demonicum* as τῷ πρώτῳ λόγῳ τῶν παραινέσεων (ed. H. Rabe,

2. See Drerup's *descriptiones*, iv–xlii. Other manuscript titles for this speech include παραινετικὸς λόγος or simply πρὸς Δημόνικον. P. *Amh.* II 25 (= Pack² 1252), a first- or second-century papyrus roll of the *Ad Demonicum* that preserves only very broken initial letters of an end title – to judge from the layout – could also be restored as 'Ισ[οκράτους πρὸς]/ Δ[ημόνικον]/ Π[αραινέσεις].

3. Lines 57–82 in particular (cited from G. Mathieu's Budé, *Isocrate* I xxxiv–xxxv). This material is repeated in the hypothesis to the *Ad Demonicum*, lines 1–27 (p. 122). See also the hypothesis to *Evagoras* init. (*Isocrate* II 146). But note that in the hypothesis to the *Ad Nicoclem* (II 97: πρὸς τοῦτον γράφει πάλιν ὁ 'Ισοκράτης παραινέσεις, πῶς δεῖ βασιλεύειν ὀρθῶς), παραινέσεις without the article = 'counsel' or 'advice' and is used to describe only one speech.

p. 441.19–20). Similarly, in *P. Massiliensis* ( = Pack² 1254), a third-
or fourth-century papyrus of the *Ad Nicoclem*, which has the
following title, written in a second hand, at both the beginning
and the end of the text: Ἰσοκράτους παραινέσεων λόγος ΒΒ, the
plural must refer to the grammarians' classification.[4]

Unfortunately, other citations found in ancient sources are more
ambiguous. For example, entries in the Suda (s.v. ξυλλαβεῖν, from
*Ad D.* §3),[5] in Harpocration (s.v. παράκλησις from *Ad D.* §5) and
in Priscian (from *Ad D.* §20 and §34)[6] are all attributed to ταῖς
παραινέσεσιν, a circumstance which has led some scholars to
conclude that the plural παραινέσεις was the ancient name of the
*Ad Demonicum* (see, e.g., Drerup, lxxxviii), especially since passages
extracted from the other two speeches are never so identified. But
this may reflect nothing more than the source of the references,
determined in part by convenience; that is, passages from the *Ad
Demonicum* are as easily found in a roll in which it is the first of
three speeches (αἱ παραινέσεις) as in a roll in which it is the only
speech (πρὸς Δημόνικον), but the relative difficulty of finding
passages well into a long roll might have resulted in fewer or no
references from other parainetic speeches unless a roll containing
an individual speech was at hand. And, in fact, specific quotations
from the latter two speeches are infrequent.

The following explanation suggests itself: (1) originally αἱ
παραινέσεις served as the title for all three speeches. (2) Because
the *Ad D.* was more popular than its fellows – to judge from the
relative number of papyrus fragments and the references to each
found in ancient sources – the plural came to be most frequently
associated with only this one speech, a circumstance which has
naturally occasioned some confusion. (3) The plural in a context
of the *Ad Demonicum* alone necessitated a semantic shift (now no

4. B. Keil in *Hermes* 19 (1894) 637 translates this title as 'Isocratis suasoriarum
oratio; alter (sc. oratio) alterius (sc. classis Isocratearum).' It is based on his
observation that the first seven speeches in the archetype of the manuscript
tradition must have fallen into two groups – the first are encomia, the second
paraineses. The *Ad Nicoclem* therefore is the second speech of group two, so ΒΒ =
II 2. So also K. Ohly, *Stichometrische Untersuchungen* ( = Zentralblatt für
Bibliothekswesen, Beiheft 61) (Leipzig 1928) 73–74, and G. Pasquali, *Storia della
tradizione e critica del testo* (Florence 1962) 300.

5. This is thought to be from Caecilius, see *Fragmenta* 175.25 Offenloch.

6. *Grammatici Latini* II 354.9 Keil (for *Ad D.* §20), II 279.3 and 295.4 (for *Ad
D.* §34).

longer 'parainetic speeches' but 'exhortations' or 'advice'), and this probably led to the addition of πρὸς Δημόνικον as a clarification or, in some cases, to the substitution of a less ambiguous word.[7] (4) Finally, in the manuscript tradition, the plural in the title παραινέσεις πρὸς Δημόνικον has been reduced to the singular παραίνεσις, either through itacism or as an attempt at correction, so that it is once more generic, the equivalent of παραινετικὸς λόγος. If this explanation is correct, the unqualified Ἰσοκράτους Παραινέσεις used as a book title is perhaps more likely to refer to a collection of three speeches than to the *Ad Demonicum* alone, but certainty is impossible.

7. See above n. 3 and compare hypothesis to *Ad Demonicum*, line 42 (1 122), which uses the synonym ὑποθήκας. αἱ πρὸς Ν. ὑποθῆκαι appears as a title for the *Ad Nicoclem* in both the cod. Urbinas (= Γ) and in Harpocration (s.v. Θέογνις).

# Gnomology[1]

## WILLIAM BRASHEAR

*P. Berol.* 21166                          2nd–3rd c. A.D.

17.7 × 6 cm                             Plate III

Margins: right 2.5–3 cm, left 1 cm, upper 2.5 cm; an indeterminate amount missing from the bottom. One vertical *kollesis* 2.5 cm from the left edge.

The extremely lacunose papyrus, consisting almost exclusively of horizontal fibers (isolated sections of vertical fibers are visible on the back to the far right) has writing on both sides. The letters of the recto text (Menandrean *monostichoi*)[2] were written first in fine, light traces and then penned over in thicker, darker strokes that do not always coincide exactly with the first draft underneath. Since both scripts are equally facile and practiced and do not differ significantly from one another, one might assume that the same person penned the two versions here. However, from what we know of ancient calligraphical methods, the likelihood of a scribe sketching his own first draft – much as the modern day calligrapher pencils his – and later penning the final draft over it is so unlikely that one cannot escape the conclusion that two people – teacher and pupil – were at work here. The student, however, was no

1. H. Maehler, *Mus. Helv.* 24 (1967) 71 nn. 19, 21, cites the following references pertinent to the meaning of the word: J. W. B. Barns, *Class. Quart.* 44 (1950) 132ff.; O. Luschnat, *Gnomologium Vaticanum*, ed. L. Sternbach (Berlin 1963) viiif. (Anm. 3); on the origin and history: Horna, *R-E* Suppl. VI 78f.; Hense, *R-E* IX 2575ff.; O. Guéraud and P. Jouguet, *Un livre d'écolier* (Cairo 1938) xxiv–xxxi; J. W. B. Barns, *Class. Quart.* n.s. 1 (1951) 1ff.

2. The *sententiae* attributed to Menander have been preserved not only in Greek but also in Coptic (see Hagedorn and Weber, *ZPE* 3 (1968) 15–50), Arabic-Syriac (see S. Jäkel, ΜΕΝΑΝΔΡΟΥ ΓΝΩΜΑΙ ΜΟΝΟΣΤΙΧΟΙ, *Die Menandersentenzen gesammelt u. neu herausgegeben* (Diss. Hamburg 1957) 28; M. Ullmann, 'Die arabische Überlieferung der sog. Menandersentenzen', *Abh. f. d. Kunde d. Morgenlandes* 34.1 (Wiesbaden 1961); J. Kraemer, *Zeitschr. d. Deutschen Morgenländ. Gesellsch.* 106 (1956) 304ff.) and Old Slavic (see R. Führer, 'Zur slavischen Übersetzung der Menandersentenzen', *Beitr. Klass. Phil.* 145 (1982)).

9

neophyte but already an accomplished scribe in his own right, and it is furthermore quite to be expected that he would strive to make his calligraphy resemble his master's as much as possible.

The same advanced student may have penned the Menandrean *monostichoi* of *P. Iand.* v 77.[3] There are only two significant discrepancies in the paleography. *Rho* in the Berlin papyrus is always adorned at the bottom with a diagonal upstroke; in the Ianda papyrus it is left unadorned. The Berlin papyrus shows *iota* rising high above the other letters – more so than in the Ianda papyrus. Otherwise, the *ductus* of the other letters – *omega, kappa, mu* and *lambda*, for example – appears to be identical in both papyri. An almost identical hand is that of *P. Ryl.* 457.[4]

Kalbfleisch suggested in the *ed. prin.* that *P. Iand.* 77 was the '"Gesellenstück" eines Berufsschreibers'.[5] For at the end of the collection of sayings and written in a different hand is the comment κ[ε]χάρισται, indicating someone's – the teacher's? – approval of a work well done. Is it possible that the teacher who wrote his '*placet*' at the end of *P. Iand.* 77 also penned the first draft for *P. Berol.* 21166 or that *P. Iand.* 77 and *P. Berol.* 21166 once belonged to the same roll?

To try to determine the identity of two scripts, one of which is represented by a single word, the other of which is written over by another hand, is a risky undertaking, to say the least. Although identity cannot be absolutely established, the possibility that the same teacher penned both the first draft in *P. Berol.* 21166 and κεχάρισται in *P. Iand.* 77 cannot be rejected out of hand.

Even if both papyri (which show the same linear spacing and probably the same script) were written by one and the same student, they cannot have belonged to the same roll. Whereas the *sententiae* of *P. Iand.* v 77 all begin with *omega*, there is no evidence of alphabetizing in *P. Berol.* 21166. Furthermore, the upper margin of *P. Iand.* v 77 measures 1 cm, in contrast to the margin of 2.5 cm here. Finally, the Ianda papyrus shows no signs of being written over like the Berlin papyrus; it is a finished product, not a practice piece.

3. *P. Iand.* v 77 (see there Tafel XVI) = Kalbfleisch, *Hermes* 63 (1928) 100ff. = Pack[2] 1591 = S. Jäkel, *Menandri Sententiae* (Leipzig 1964) no. III = D. L. Page, *Greek Literary Papyri* 1 (London–New York 1942) no. 56.

4. K. and B. Aland, *Der Text des Neuen Testaments* (Stuttgart 1982) 94; *c.* A.D. 125.          5. *Op. cit.* (n. 3) 102.

Kalbfleisch dated the Ianda papyrus to the second century A.D.,[6] citing as parallel the script of Schubart, *P. Graec. Berol.* 30b, and as authority Schubart himself, who placed it 'ins 2./3. Jahrhundert...sicher nicht später als 3. Jahrhundert'. In the second and revised edition, i.e. *P. Iand.* v 77, Kalbfleisch reported Hunt's impression that it was more likely from the third century – hence the date assigned to the Berlin papyrus.

*P. Berol.* 21166 contains five lines of *sententiae*. The first two and most complete lines are attested in the *Comparatio Menandri et Philistionis* I 59, 60, most recently edited by S. Jäkel.[7] The first line presents no problems. The second is full of them. Various attempts have been made to emend them away, to wit:

(a) οὐ τῷ λόγῳ δὲ δεῖ † χρῆσθαι, ἀλλὰ τῷ τρόπῳ (Jäkel)

(b) οὐ τῷ λόγῳ πίστευσον ἀλλὰ τῷ τρόπῳ (Meyer, *Abh. Bayer. Akad. Wiss.* 19 (1892) 225–95)

(c) οὐ τὸν λόγον δ⟨ε⟩ῖ χρηστὸν {εῖ[ν]ạ[ι} ἀ]λλὰ τὼν τρόπον (*P. Berol.* 21166)

If the reading-restoration εῖ[ν]ạ[ι] is correct, it has all the earmarks of an interpolation made by someone (an apprentice scribe?) who could not resist giving δεῖ a complementary (and unnecessary – see *LSJ* s.v. δεῖ 1 3) infinitive despite the rules of meter. By excising it one arrives at a proper iambic trimeter.

The third and fourth lines are so damaged that so far no line of Menandrean gnomology has been found which seems compatible with the traces on the papyrus.

The verso text has likewise proved very resistant to attempts at decipherment. The hand is a different and a very cursive one.

Recto                                                  Plate III

   πολλῶν μὲν ὁ λόγος χρηστός, ὁ δὲ τρόπος κακός
⟦.⟧οὐ τὸν λόγον δ⟨ε⟩ῖ χρηστὸν {εῖ[ν]ạ[ι} ἀ]λλὰ τὼν τρόπον
  οσ ṭ . .ιγαμονκα.....[                  ]λουμενον
  .ṭιṣ[.. ].ιακατανται[.]..[
5   [        ]...[

6. *Ibid.*
7. *Op. cit.* (n. 3). The last addition to the sources for the *Comparatio* was made by A. Guida, *Rhein. Mus.* 116 (1973) 361, who identified *BKT* v 2, p. 123, lines 7–8 as *Comparatio* I 51–52.

Verso
traces
ηπερυσιπτηχειστιε‾ γραμματα
    ]. .

2 τόν

Line **2**. ε͙[ν]ạ[ι: Only the merest speck of ink remains which could belong to the uppermost tip of an *alpha*.

δ⟨ε⟩ῑ: Cf. *P. Iand.* v 77.1: μ{ε}ικρόν, 8 φρόνησ{ε}ις. This confusion, evident in both papyri, might be cited as additional evidence for the scribe's having written both texts, if the error were not so widespread a phenomenon of the times.

**4**. ητισ[ , γεισ[ , πεισ[ ?

The verso text is written directly on the horizontal fibres, i.e. damage to the text is not a result of loss of vertical fibres. To the right and left extend broad margins measuring 4 and 5.5 cm respectively. The third line contains two tachygraphic symbols or decorative strokes (?): ↘ ⁄.

# Euclid, *Elements* I, Definitions 1–10
## (*P. Mich.* III 143)

†SIR ERIC TURNER, DAVID H. FOWLER,
LUDWIG KOENEN, LOUISE C. YOUTIE

The republication of *P. Mich.* III 143 is an exercise in *amicitia papyrologorum*. When, early in 1981, D. H. Fowler wished to refer to the papyrus in a forthcoming book on Greek mathematics, he asked Sir Eric for his advice. On the basis of a photograph, the latter questioned the readings in lines 1, 2 (interlinear correction), 6, and 12, and suggested what, upon inspection by L. Koenen and L. C. Youtie, turned out to be the correct reading. The Michigan branch of our partnership straightened out some folds and improved the readings of a few additional lines (7, 18f., 20 (interlinear mark), 21, 23, 24, 26, and 27). Most of the corrections are trivial (except in lines 1, 18f., and 21), but they substantially reduce the number of scribal mistakes (see below, p. 15). Admittedly the text of this papyrus is only a private extract from the *Elements*, but its mistakes should no longer be characterized as 'not...excusable' and as resulting from 'carelessness, ignorance, or accident' (first edition). The text was clearly undervalued. Sir Eric therefore suggested that the four of us should join forces and re-edit the papyrus. He had volunteered to write the draft, but Fate did not permit him to do so; the remaining members of the team decided to complete the task. The various readings and the general evaluation of the text and its scribe had been discussed with Sir Eric in letters (partly to and from his hospital bed). Little had to be added.[1]

1. We regret that he could not give us his view on the reading of ç in the deleted interlinear correction of line 2, on the final evaluation of the mess in line 7, on the interlinear letter or mark in line 20, and on the reading in line 21. Nor can he be held responsible for most of the details of our evaluations of textual problems.

P. Mich. III 143 (Pack² 366)

Inv. 925                                      3rd c. A.D.

5.5 × 19.2 cm                                   Plate IV

The papyrus is written in a small, rather personal hand of the third century A.D.; comparable, though much more formal, is *P. Oxy.* XLVII 3366 written by a grammaticus, A.D. 253–60 (= P. Parsons in *P. Coll. Youtie* II 66 with pl. 22). The scribe of the Michigan papyrus used the back of a piece which had been cut from an official or business letter seemingly written somewhat earlier in the same century.² The small column of the text of Euclid (width of lines at the top 5 cm, at the bottom 4.6 cm; height of the column 12.6 cm) leaves a left margin of 0.3–0.5 cm; on the right side the writing reaches the very edge of the papyrus. The upper margin is 0.8 cm, the lower 5.5 cm. The latter measurement is taken below the *paragraphos* which appears 0.3 cm under the last line. There is no dash across the middle of the column about 1.2 cm below the writing – the first editor who claimed its existence was deceived by a fold (he presumably worked from a photograph). Five vertical folds, partly marked by slight damage, indicate that the papyrus was rolled, seemingly from left to right. As a result of humidity some ink has run and traces of ink appear where they should not. Many letters are blurred. There are no accents or diacritical marks. The writing is across the fibres.

It follows from the preceding description that this copy of

2. Extant are the right part of a column of the document, the following intercolumnium (about 1 cm wide), and halves of the first letters of the top three lines of the next column seemingly written by the same hand. At the top, the papyrus seems to be cut along the middle of the letters of the first line. The ink is somewhat faded and partly rubbed off, and there is not enough context to inspire reconstruction. Hence much of the transcript remains tentative. The writing is along the fibres.

| | | | |
|---|---|---|---|
| 1 | | ]. ερᾳψειδ[.]... | (perhaps ῥάψει, cf. line 4) |
| | | ]ει αἱρεῖ τοὺς δο- | (αἱρεῖ or αἴρει) |
| | | ]τε βούλει διδο- | |
| 4 | [ναι | ]χεις ποίηϲιν τῶν | |
| | | ].λᾳ. ὑποποι- | (λα or αδ or αλ) |
| | | ]ἰδίαι γεγραμμε- | (tentative reading) |
| | [ν- | ] ἐπὶ τῶν εἰδῶν | |
| 8 | | ].τα μεριϲμὸν | (κ]ατὰ possible) |
| | | ].εια..ε... | |
| | (after an enlarged interlinear space) | ]τη καλουμε- | (nom. or dat.) |
| | [νη (after double the interlinear space) | ] | |
| | | ]..τον κει | (ο: ε or ο; there is a bar on top of υ) |
| 12 | | π]ερι εμ.ϲ. υτοϲ | (ἐμοῦ does not fit) |

There are a few traces of ink in the space between lines 10 and 11, but they seem not to be writing.

definitions 1–10 from the *Elements* of Euclid[3] is an extract of a single page, a memorandum, but not part of a book-roll. The minute hand is not the sort of writing normally associated with persons learning to write. One might guess that the piece was written by a schoolmaster, a grammaticus, making sure he had the text which he wanted to dictate to his students or on which he intended to base his next lesson.[4] He made a number of mistakes: common iotacism in lines 7, 10 (in both cases επιφανια; the word is correctly spelled in 8f.), 16 (κιμενων), and 18f. (in combination with a more serious omission: εκ⟨τε⟩θι/cαι); simplification of μμ in lines 9, 17, and 20 (correctly spelled in 2, 3, 4, 14, 19, and 27f.); missing movable ν in 20, perhaps 7 (combined with another mistake; see nn. on 7 εcτ⟦.⟧ and ọ [= δ]); and another misspelling in line 23. Nevertheless the scribe cared for his spelling (see n. on 27f.). There is one new, perhaps genuine reading (lack of δέ in 7, see n.), and another variant deserves consideration (see line 21n.). Three further variants are remarkable though unauthentic: in lines 13–18 the syntax is simplified through transposition of the article (but see 13 and 16nn.); lines 18f. witness a striving for precision through the use of a shorter, technical wording (blurred by a scribal mistake; see above and n. on lines 18f.); and at the end of the present extract, the final relative clause is omitted, possibly with reason (see line 28n.).

It is of particular interest to compare the readings of the papyrus with those of the medieval codices. The manuscript tradition of the *Elements* is split into two main branches. Only the Vatican codex P represents the earlier tradition. All other codices derive from the recension made by Theon of Alexandria in the fourth century A.D., although, in detail, P has influenced individual readings of the Theonine tradition.[5] The Michigan papyrus once

3. On Euclid see the excellent pages in P. M. Fraser, *Ptolemaic Alexandria* I (Oxford 1972) 376, with notes in II.

4. *P. Oxy.* XLVII 3366, quoted above for the similarity of its handwriting, was written by a grammaticus. The first editor of the Michigan text, however, assumed that 'from appearance' the piece had not been written 'by a young child, but might well be the attempt of an older youth to reproduce from memory definitions imperfectly learned'.

5. In particular the Theonine codex F seems to show signs of being influenced by the pre-Theonine tradition which emerges in P. See J. L. Heiberg, *Hermes* 38 (1903) 52f. (in an evaluation of the text of *P. Fay.* 9 as reconstructed by him;

supports the correct reading of P against Theon (as do two Theonine manuscripts (bp); see n. on lines 25f.). In lines 27f., however, the papyrus agrees with some Theonine codices (γραμμή BVf^{m1}) and Proclus against other Theonine codices (Fbpf^{m2}) and P (εὐθεῖα). γραμμή must have been Theon's reading (see *ad loc.*) and represents what he found in older manuscripts not available to us. Hence it could even be the correct reading. We may further infer that P influenced Fbpf^{m2}. Mixed allegiances are characteristic for papyri of known authors and reflect the realities of a time before the split of the manuscript tradition into distinct recensions and families.

In summary, the scribal mistakes in the papyrus and its text as compared with the medieval tradition do not support the assumption that the piece was written from memory (see n. 4), and nothing contradicts the view that our 'schoolmaster' copied from an exemplar with some care. Therefore the text should be taken seriously and treated as a possible source for our knowledge of the tradition of the text of Euclid, if not for authentic readings.

Our efforts to place the papyrus fragment within the history of the text of Euclid's *Elements* are hampered by our lack of information on the manuscript tradition. J. L. Heiberg's admirable edition is based on only eight codices, of which merely six offer the text of Book I (denoted here by Heiberg's sigla).[6] Information on additional codices may be extracted from Heiberg's 'Paralipomena zu Euklid'.[7]

Only two other fragments from the *Elements* have hitherto been published (*P. Fay.* 9 = Pack² 367; *P. Oxy.* I 29 = Pack² 368); cognate in form and manner are a number of ostraca from Elephantine written by the same hand (*O. Berol.* 11999 etc.).[8] At least one more fragment from the *Elements* can be expected from

see below). On the two branches of the manuscript tradition see *ibid.* p. 46. For the sigla of codices see below, nn. 6 and 7.

6. Heiberg's edition was revised by E. S. Stamatis: *Euclidis elementa* (Leipzig 1969–77); the mss. used in Book I are P; BFVbp. The edition lists the parallels and quotations from ancient authors in a separate apparatus; for supplements see J. L. Heiberg, *Hermes* 38 (1903) 352ff. Appendix II of Heiberg–Stamatis' vol. I reprints *P. Mich.* III 143 (with an additional error in line 6); see also n. 9.

7. *Hermes* 38 (1903) 46–74, 161–201, 321–56. We have used information on Cod. Paris. gr. 2342 (p. 59), Cod. Laur. 28, 6 (= f), and Cod. Scorial. Y III 21 (pp. 178f.).

8. Published by J. Mau and W. Müller, *APF* 17 (1960) 1ff. = Pack² 2323; cf. P. Fraser, *Ptolemaic Alexandria* II, 558 n. 43.

the Oxyrhynchus collection.[9] A quotation of *Elements* I, *def.* 15 has been found in *P. Herc.* 1061 (Demetrios Lakon, περὶ γεωμετρίας).[10]

The reader who compares the present edition with its predecessor will notice a number of small divergences in details of readings which we thought need no discussion. The first edition's lines 13–29 became lines 12–28, because we did not count the interlinear correction above line 12 (our count) as a separate line.

For the actual reading of the papyrus the reader may inspect the diplomatic transcription, as, in the edited text, we did not indicate iotacistic misspellings and avoided accumulations of brackets. Pointed brackets (⟨ ⟩) are used both for omitted letters and for editorial corrections.

| | | |
|---|---|---|
| 1 cημειονεcτινουμεροc | *def.* 1 | cημεῖόν ἐcτιν οὗ μέροc |
| ⟦ϲ⟧ | | |
| ουθενγραμμηδεμηκος | *def.* 2 | οὐθέν· γραμμὴ ʼ⟦ϲ⟧ʼ δὲ μῆκος |
| απλατεςγραμμηςδεπερα | *def.* 3 | ἀπλατέc· γραμμῆc δὲ πέρα- |
| 4 τασημειαευθειαγραμμη | *def.* 4 | τα cημεῖα. εὐθεῖα γραμμή |
| εcτιcητιcεξιcουτοιcε | | ἐcτι⟨ν⟩ ἥτιc ἐξ ἴcου τοῖc ἐ- |
| φεαυτηccημειοιcκειται | | φ' ἑαυτῆc cημείοιc κεῖται. |
| επιφανιαεcτ⟦. ⟧ομηκ[ο]cκαι | *def.* 5 | ἐπιφάνειά ἐcτ⟨ιν⟩ ᾢ μῆκ[ο]c καὶ |
| 8 πλατοcμονονεχειεπι | *def.* 6 | πλάτοc μόνον ἔχει. ἐπι- |
| φανειαcδεπερατα ταγραμαι | | φανείαc δὲ πέρατα γραμ⟨μ⟩αί. |
| επιπεδοcεπιφανιαεcτιν | *def.* 7 | ἐπίπεδοc ἐπιφάνειά ἐcτιν |
| ητιcεξιcουταιcεφεαυ | | ἥτιc ἐξ ἴcου ταῖc ἐφ' ἑαυ- |
| ευθειαιcκειται | | |
| 12 τηcεπιπεδοcδεγωνι | *def.* 8 | τῆc 'εὐθείαιc κεῖται'. ἐπίπεδοc δὲ γωνί- |
| αεcτινενεπιπεδωδυ | | α ἐcτὶν ἐν ἐπιπέδῳ δύ- |
| ογραμμωναπτομενων | | ο γραμμῶν ἁπτομένων |
| αλληλωνκαιμηεπευ | | ἀλλήλων καὶ μὴ ἐπ' εὐ- |
| 16 θειαcκιμενωνηπροc | | θείαc κειμένων ἢ πρὸc |
| αλληλαcτωνγραμων | | ἀλλήλαc τῶν γραμ⟨μ⟩ῶν |
| κλιcιcοτανδεαιεκθι | *def.* 9 | κλίcιc. ὅταν δὲ αἱ ἐκ⟨τε⟩θεῖ- |
| cαιγραμμαιευθειαι | | cαι γραμμαὶ εὐθεῖαι |
| [].[] | | |
| 20 ωcιευθυγραμοcηγωνι | | ὦcι⟨ν⟩, εὐθύγραμ⟨μ⟩οc ἡ γωνί- |
| ακαλειcθωοτανδεευ | *def.* 10 | α καλείcθω. ὅταν δὲ εὐ- |
| θειαεπευθειανcταθει | | θεῖα ἐπ' εὐθεῖαν cταθεῖ- |
| ca⟦ν⟧τασεφεξοcγω | | ca τὰc ἐφεξ⟨ῆ⟩c γω- |

9. According to E. G. Turner in a letter (confirmed by P. Parsons). *P. Fay.* 9 and *P. Oxy.* I 29 were reprinted in Appendix II of Heiberg–Stamatis' edition (together with *P. Mich.* III 143, see n. 6). It may be noted that E. G. Turner would date *P. Oxy.* I 29 to the last quarter of the first or the first quarter of the second century A.D. (III-IV edd.).

10. J. L. Heiberg in *Oversigt over det Kong. Danske Videnskabernes Selskabs Forhandlinger* (1900) 155ff.; cf. *idem, Hermes* 38 (1903) 47; W. Crönert, *Kolotes und Menedemos (Stud. Pal.* 6, 1906) 111f.

24 νιαcιcαcαλληλαιcποι
ηορθηεκατερατωνι
cωνγωνιωνεcτιν <sub>μ</sub>
καιηεφεcτηκυιαγρα
28 μηκαθετοcκαλειται.

νίας ἴσας ἀλλήλαις ποι-
ῇ, ὀρθὴ ἑκατέρα τῶν ἴ-
cων γωνιῶν ἐcτιν,
καὶ ἡ ἐφεcτηκυῖα γρα‘μ΄-
μὴ κάθετος καλεῖται.

(1) A point is that which has no part; (2) a line is length without breadth, (3) and the limits of a line are points.

(4) A straight line is one which lies evenly with the points upon it.[11]

(5) A surface is that which has length and breadth only; (6) and the limits of a surface are lines.

(7) A plane surface is one which lies evenly with the straight lines upon it.[12] (8) A plane angle is the inclination of two lines to each other if, in

11. In spite of reservations we accept the standard translation; it is understood to say that the infinite straight line is 'without bias, i.e. without inclining one way or the other', and to express essentially the same thought as Plato's definition of the finite straight line (τὸ εὐθύ): οὗ ἂν τὸ μέcον ἀμφοῖν τοῖν ἐcχάτοιν ἐπίπροcθεν ᾖ (*Parm.* 137E), 'the middle of which stands in front of both ends', i.e. obscures the view of the ends: it does not swerve (T. L. Heath, *Euclid in Greek* (Cambridge 1920) 118ff.; idem, *The Thirteen Books of Euclid's Elements*[2] (Cambridge 1926; reprinted, Dover 1956) 166ff.). L. Koenen wishes to point out that the definition as given in the *Elements* is an attempt to define the straight line from a point of view analogous to the one used in Plato's preceding definition of the circular curve: cτρογγύλον γέ πού ἐcτι τοῦτο οὗ ἂν τὰ ἔcχατα πανταχῇ ἀπὸ τοῦ μέcου ἴcον ἀπέχῃ. The ἐξ ἴcου...κεῖται of the definition of the straight line in the *Elements* corresponds to the ἴcον ἀπέχῃ of the definition of the circular line in the *Parmenides*. This gives ἐξ ἴcου a spatial connotation (cf. δι' ἴcου in Plato, *Rep.* x 617B ('in the same distance'), and Euclid, *Elements* v *def.* 17, where the phrase is used in a sense abstracted from its spatial meaning ('δι' ἴcου, *ex aequali*, must apparently mean *ex aequali distantia*, at an equal distance or interval, i.e. after an equal number of intervening terms', Heath, *Euclid's Elements* ii 136)). Hence, L. K. understands the definition in the *Elements* as saying: 'A straight line is one which lies evenly with the distance between the points upon it'; between any of its points, the straight line is equal to the line marking the distance between these points. According to this interpretation, the definition in the *Elements* comes close to Archimedes' assumption of the finite straight line (*De sph. et cycl.* i, post 1, ed. J. L. Heiberg, Leipzig 1910) as τῶν τὰ αὐτὰ πέρατα ἐχουcῶν γραμμῶν ἐλαχίcτη (this is also modelled on parts of Plato's definitions, but assumes a different meaning) and to Proclus' interpretation of the definition in the *Elements*: δηλοῖ διὰ τούτου μόνην τὴν εὐθεῖαν ἴcον κατέχειν διάcτημα τῷ μεταξὺ τῶν ἐπ' αὐτῆς cημείων. ὅcον γὰρ ἀπέχει θάτερον τῶν cημείων θατέρου, τοcοῦτον τὸ μέγεθος τῆς εὐθείας τῆς ὑπ' αὐτῶν περατουμένης (p. 109, 8ff. Friedl., cf. 117, 1ff.); contra: e.g. Heath, *locc. citt.* (see above, this note); W. Frankland, *The First Book of Euclid's Elements with a Commentary* (Cambridge 1905) 4ff.; and, more recently, G. R. Morrow in his translation of Proclus' *Commentary on the First Book of Euclid's Elements* (Princeton 1970) 88 n. 45. See also C. Thaer, 'Euklid, Die Elemente', *Ostwalds Klass.* 235 (1933) 78.

12. The problems for translation and interpretation of the 7th definition are analogous to those in *def.* 4 (see n. 11), although even more difficult. The phrase

a plane, the lines touch one another without forming a straight line; (9) and whenever the lines described [cf. n. on line 18f.] are straight, the angle should be called a rectilinear one [cf. n. on line 21]; (10) but whenever a straight line stands upon a straight line and makes the adjacent angles equal to each other, each of the equal angles is a right angle, and the erect line is called a perpendicular.

Line **1.** μεροc: The upper part of ε is completely rubbed off; the extant foot of the letter, however, suits ε, not ο (μορ⟨ι⟩ον *ed. prin.*).

**2.** γραμμη‛[[c]]′: The interlinear letter is either c, ε, or ο. It is crossed out by a long, slightly ascending horizontal stroke. When the scribe proof-read the piece, he either thought of the start of the following definition beginning with the genitive γραμμῆc (see line 3) or his eye caught the initial word of the wrong sentence in his exemplar. As soon as he had made the correction, he continued to read and cancelled the correction after he had discovered that it was wrong.

**5.** εcτιc: Read ἐcτιν. This mistake may have been caused by the following ητιc.

**7.** επιφανια: ἐπιφάνεια δὲ mss. The definitions are arranged in groups by using δέ to connect the definitions within units: 1–3 point and line; 7–10 plane surface and plane angles; 11–12 acute and obtuse angles; 15–18 circle; 19–22 rectilinear figures. (In general, the same careful use of δέ and, occasionally, of other co-ordinating conjunctions can be observed in the definitions of the other Books. Cf. also the critical apparatus to v *def.* 15, p. 3, 7 H.-S.; *ibid. def.* 17a, p. 3 *in app. ad lin.* 17 (see also Heiberg, *Hermes* 38 (1903) 181ff.); vii *def.* 10, p. 104, 1; *ibid. def.* 13, p. 104, 6; xi *def.* 21.) Stating the same fact from the opposite point of view, we may say that the omission of δέ marks the beginning of a new group of definitions (1, here line 1; 7, here line 10; 11; 15; and 19) and unconnected single definitions (as *def.* 23, the final one of the series in Book 1, dealing with parallels). According to PBV, *deff.* 13

designed to define the one-dimensional straight line is changed as little as the author saw fit so as now to define the two-dimensional plane surface. In this context, ἐξ ἴcου assumes, according to L. K.'s interpretation, the meaning of extending over the same area. He translates: 'A plane surface is one which lies evenly with the space enclosed by the lines upon it.' According to Archimedes, the plane surface is the least of all surfaces which have the same boundaries. Cf. the commentaries quoted in n. 11.

(boundary) and 14 (figure) are also such unconnected single definitions: (ιγ′) ὅρος ἐστὶν ὃ τινός ἐστι πέρας. (ιδ′) cχῆμά ἐcτι τὸ ὑπό τινος ἤ τινων ὅρων περιεχόμενον. In Fbp, however, the two definitions are connected (cχῆμα δὲ τὸ...) and form a group, not without reason: the explanation of ὅρος in 13 prepares for the use of this word in *def.* 14; both together are needed for the following explanations regarding the circle and rectilinear figures. Similarly *def.* 1 (here lines 1f.) is needed for the following explanation of 'line' (*deff.* 2–3, here lines 2–4) and for this reason they are grouped together. By using δέ in *def.* 5, the tradition (so far as known) also groups *def.* 4 (straight line; here lines 4–6) together with *deff.* 5–6 (surface; here lines 7–9). The term 'straight line', however, is not used in the explanation of 'surface', but it recurs for the first time in *def.* 7 (plane surface, here lines 10–12) and then in the following definitions of this group (7–10). Hence it may be argued that *def.* 4 should be separated from *deff.* 5 and 6. In this view, the omission of δέ in line 7 makes sense and, far from being an obvious scribal error, may be authentic. It constitutes *deff.* 5–6 (here lines 7–9) as a separate group (surface), and makes *def.* 4 (straight line) an unconnected single definition although it could easily have been connected with the preceding group 1–3 (point and line). So far as we can determine from the available manuscript evidence, this was avoided, probably because of the fundamental differentiation of straight and curved lines implied in the rest of the definitions. The isolation of *def.* 4 may then have induced redactors and scribes to connect it with the following group by adding δέ in *def.* 5. For the difficult and controversial meaning of *def.* 4 and 7 see nn. 11 and 12.

ECT⟦.⟧: After τ the papyrus is marred by several holes, and some of the ink is rubbed off. The uncertain letter is small and looks roundish, rather ọ than ı̣. If the letter was ı̣, the scribe omitted movable ν; if it was ọ, he omitted ıν and wrote the ο (ὃ following ἐcτιν) twice. Be the letter ọ or ı̣, there appears a diagonal stroke reaching from the foot of τ to, or through, that letter. It probably indicates a deletion of the letter (cf. the deletions in lines 2 and 23). Alternatively the diagonal could belong to a letter of a previous error which was deleted by writing τ̣ across the traces. See also the following note.

ọ (= ὃ): The letter looks very much like ε̣, probably because some ink was rubbed off at its lower right side. To sum up the possibilities discussed here and in the preceding note, we might write ἐϲτ⟦.⟧⟨ιν⟩ ὅ (rather than ἐϲ⟨θ'⟩⟦.⟧ ὅ with an incomplete correction; cf. E. Mayser and H. Schmoll, *Grammatik* 1.1² (Berlin 1970) 134.2b) or paleographically more difficult, ἐϲτι⟨ν⟩ ὅ (τι written in corr.). The mss. read ἐϲτιν ὅ.

**9.** γραμ⟨μ⟩αί: For the spelling (also in line 17, cf. 20; for the correct spelling in other occurrences of the word see n. on lines 27f. and above, p. 15) cf. F. T. Gignac, *A Grammar of the Greek Papyri of the Roman and Byzantine Periods* 1 (Milan 1976) 157 (2a); Mayser-Schmoll, *Grammatik* 1.1², 188c; W. Crönert, *Mem. Gr. Herc.* 74.

**13 and 16.** The article ἡ (16) appears in the mss. collated by J. L. Heiberg (see n. 6) and in Hero, *Def.* 14, before ἐν ἐπιπέδῳ (13). The reading of the papyrus simplifies the syntax. It may be significant that in PF (cf. n. 5) one letter is erased before πρὸϲ (here line 16), i.e. precisely where the papyrus places ἡ. Before the erasure, the scribes probably repeated the article because, forgetting that the article was already placed before ἐν ἐπιπέδῳ, they seemingly felt a need for the article here. When rereading the entire sentence, they discovered the error and deleted the second ἡ. These assumptions seem to be more likely than their reversal. For, theoretically, the erasure in PF could indicate an original agreement between the pre-Theonine text and the papyrus (cf. above, pp. 15f, and below, n. on lines 25f.), and, in this case, ἐϲτὶν ἐν ἐπιπέδῳ δύο γραμμῶν ἁπτομένων ἀλλήλων καὶ μὴ...κειμένων ἡ...κλίϲιϲ would be the authentic reading. The ἡ after ἐϲτὶν (before ἐν ἐπιπέδῳ) would be Theonine. Either from the Theonine text or simply by scribal negligence, it could have been intruded into the same position in PF, and this duplication of the article could finally have led to the erasure of the ἡ before πρὸϲ.

**18f.** εκθι|ϲαι (read ἐκ⟨τε⟩θεῖ|ϲαι; not εκου|ϲαι = ἔχου|ϲαι as read in *ed. prin.*): περιέχουϲαι τὴν (εἰρημένην add. P) γωνίαν (cf. Hero, *Def.* περιέχουϲαι αὐτήν, *sc.* τὴν γωνίαν; Boeth., *Geom.* 374 *quae angulum continent*; Mart. Cap. 6, 710 {*ae*}*quae angulum intra se tenent*): τὴν γωνίαν περιέχουϲαι Procl. In the phrase as transmitted by the mss., τὴν γωνίαν refers to the preceding definition of γωνία (*def.* 8). Though the phrase is clear enough, a need for explicit precision was felt as is evidenced by the addition of εἰρημένην in P. The same purpose is served by the papyrus' shorter phrase ('the described lines' disposes of any need to repeat mention of the angle). ἐκτίθημι is a word much used in scientific prose; cf. e.g. Sextus Empiricus, *Adv. math.* VIII 303 ἐπὶ τοῦ μικρῷ πρόσθεν ἐκτεθέντος (sc. λόγου; ≃ *Pyr. Hypot.* II 137 ὁ προειρημένος λόγος; cf. K. Janáček's index) and Procl. *In I Eucl. elem. comm.*, p. 76, 4 Friedl. τὰς κοινὰς τῆς ἐπιστήμης ταύτης ἀρχὰς ἐκτιθέμενος. More specifically, the word refers to the ἔκθεσις (exposition), the second part of a mathematical πρόβλημα (proposition) which follows the πρότασις (enunciation of the proposition) and precedes the διορισμός (definition; see Procl. *loc. cit.* 203, 1ff. πᾶν δὲ πρόβλημα καὶ πᾶν θεώρημα...βούλεται πάντα ταῦτα ἔχειν ἐν ἑαυτῷ· πρότασιν, ἔκθεσιν, διορισμόν, κατασκευήν, ἀπόδειξιν, συμπέρασμα); the ἔκθεσις describes what is given (*ibid.* αὐτὸ καθ᾽ αὑτὸ τὸ διδόμενον ἀποδιαλαβοῦσα; cf. P. M. Fraser, *Ptolemaic Alexandria* I, 394f.). For this use of ἐκτίθημι see for example Procl. *ibid.* 207, 14 τοῖς ἐκτεθεῖσιν and 208, 20f. δεῖ δὴ ἐπὶ τῆς ἐκτεθείσης πεπερασμένης εὐθείας τρίγωνον ἰσόπλευρον συστήσασθαι. In *def.* 9 αἱ ἐκ⟨τε⟩θεῖσαι γραμμαί do not refer to a formal ἔκθεσις, but to the preceding description of the lines as forming an angle by touching each other though not being part of the same straight line; this use is comparable.

**20.** ὡσι⟨ν⟩: For the omission of the movable ν see above, p. 15 and n. on line 7 εϲτ⟦.⟧.

Interlinear [].[]: Above the little space between η and γ, a circle appears almost entirely filled with ink; in its middle a horizontal bar seems to exceed the circle to the right; possibly θ or a deleted ǫ, though ε, deleted or not, cannot be ruled out. There is a lacuna capable of accommodating two letters in front of the trace, and another lacuna of the size of about two letters follows the trace. Some fibres cross the second lacuna vertically; they exhibit no trace of ink, and it seems unlikely that a second letter followed. We have no explanation for this trace, whether it is indeed a letter or a mark.

**21.** καλείϲθω: To our knowledge this reading is unattested (καλεῖται mss., Hero, cf. Boet.). This imperative occurs, however, in definitions: I *def.* 22 τραπέζια καλείϲθω; II *def.* 2 γνώμων καλείϲθω; V *def.* 6 ἀνάλογον καλείϲθω; X *def.* 3 ἄλογοι καλείϲθωσαν; *ibid. def.* 4 ἄλογα καλείϲθω (in Theon's recension καλείϲθωσαν, followed by another ἄλογοι καλείϲθωσαν (thus also in Cod. Paris.

I. *P. Berol.* 10570 Recto

II. *P. Oxy.* inedd. 4B4/4a; 5B4/G (2–4) b

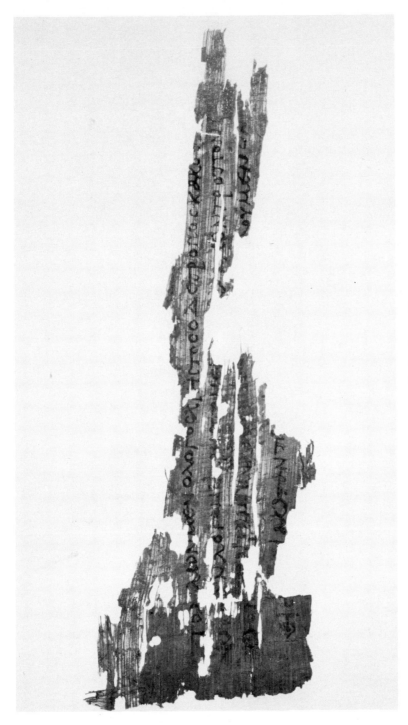

III. *P. Berol.* 21166

IV. *P. Mich.* III 143

V. *P. Mon. Gr.* inv. 329 + *P. Berol.* 21141 a. Recto b. Verso

VI. *P. Sorbonne* inv. 2407

VII. *P. Vindob.* G. 40589

VIII. *P. Bodleian* ined.

gr. 2342, see n. 7)); further *def. alt.* 1–4 and *def. tert.* 1–4. καλείcθω suits the style of the definitions, but as this form was used less frequently it was exposed to replacement by the more common καλεῖται. In the absence of any confirmation by mss., however, no case can be made for the correctness of καλείcθω in the present passage. The first edition read καλεῖcθαι which suits neither syntax nor extant traces and space.

**25f.** ὀρθή...γωνιῶν ἐcτιν: Thus (except for ἐcτι (see next note)) Pbp and most ancient attestations; ὀρθή ἐcτιν...γωνιῶν BFV and some attestations (see Heiberg's apparatus). The latter reading is Theonine, and the pre-Theonine version in b and p is probably due to P's influence. The papyrus' agreement with P confirms the correctness of this reading. See above, pp. 15f., and n. on lines 13 and 16.

**26.** ἐcτιν: ἐcτι Heiberg, presumably on the basis of manuscript evidence. The use of the movable ν may be deliberate and may mark punctuation before the following καί (but, of course, the addition of the ν could be casual).

**27f.** The interlinear μ at the end of the line is not a correction, rather the scribe ran out of space. It illustrates his general concern for spelling although, in other cases, he wrote γράμμα with a single μ (see above, line 9n.).

γραμμή is also the reading of BVf^m1 (for f, see n. 7) and Procl.; εὐθεῖα PFbpf^m2; (both readings are combined in Cod. Scorial (see also n. 7): εὐθεῖα γραμμή; om. Philop., Mart. Cap. 6, 710, see below). Only BVf^m1 and Proclus (also cf. 1 *def.* 19 (app. p. 3 on line 9 in H.-S.'s edition) where Procl. and Boet. wrote γραμμῶν instead of εὐθειῶν) seem to have retained Theon's reading while Fbpf^m2 submitted to the influence of P's tradition. For, as has correctly been stated by Heiberg (*Hermes* 38 (1903) 52), agreement between pre-Theonine papyri and some or all Theonine manuscripts against P indicates that this is Theon's reading. In the present case, Theon must have found γραμμή in the manuscripts he used, and both readings, γραμμή as well as εὐθεῖα, are pre-Theonine variants. Which is the correct reading, is less clear. εὐθεῖα is more precise than γραμμή; therefore the former reading could be the result of a search for greater precision. See above, pp. 15f.; and on the search for greater precision, cf. n. on lines 18f.

**28.** The definition continues ἐφ' ἣν ἐφέcτηκεν. The *paragraphos* on the left margin indicates that the scribe regarded his text as complete. The relative clause omitted in the papyrus clarifies the sense; it is, however, easily understood as implied. Cf. Mart. Cap. 6, 710 *et illa superstans perpendicularis dicitur, sed Graece* ΚΆΘΕΤΟC.

# Papyri of medical content

ANN ELLIS HANSON

The myth of Egypt as the cradle of civilized life surfaces not infrequently in ancient *Kulturgeschichte*, and this claim leaves its mark in a capsule history of ἰατρικὴ τέχνη which appears at the beginning of an anonymous treatise within the Galenic Corpus, 'Introduction, or the Doctor'.[1] The author's intention is to contrast medicine among the Greeks favorably with that among the Egyptians, and he begins by observing that the Greeks tend to attribute the invention of the various crafts to children of the gods. Hence Asklepios first learned medicine from his father Apollo and transmitted it to men: before Asklepios there was no ἰατρικὴ τέχνη. At the same time, the ancients had some experience of drugs and plants, he continues, citing among other Greeks Cheiron, the centaur, and the heroes he instructed. He claims a different use of plants and drugs for the Egyptians, appealing to Homer and the episode in *Odyssey* IV in which Helen mixes a euphoric drug from Egypt with wine she serves Menelaus and Telemachus; and he quotes the lines 'Egypt bears the greatest number of drugs, a grain-growing earth; / many are good when mixed and many

---

1. Εἰσαγωγὴ ἢ 'Ιατρός, XIV 674–797 Kühn, with ch. 1 on pp. 674–76. According to A. Issel, *Quaestiones Sextianae et Galenianae* (Marburg 1917) 16–55, the editor of the Aldine Galen of 1525 was the first to doubt Galen's authorship, basing his argument on the fact that Galen did not mention the work in discussions of his treatises. Issel bolsters that argument with examples of differences from Galenic use of technical terms, principles followed in hiatus, and method of citing titles of works. Issel notes as well the special attention paid to Egypt throughout and cautiously suggests that such attention may indicate the homeland of the author. He leaves the author anonymous, but labels him a follower of the Dogmatic sect, particularly devoted to Hippocrates, and a contemporary of Galen. For the Εἰσαγωγή as a type of medical handbook whose contents and arrangement were no doubt common in antiquity, see J. Kollesch, *Untersuchungen zu den pseudogalenischen Definitiones medicae* (Berlin 1973) 30–35.

For Egypt as setting for the origin of civilization, see, for example, the discussion of Diodoros' *Aegyptiaka* in T. Cole, *Democritus and the Sources of Greek Anthropology* (Cleveland 1967) 179–89.

harmful' (229–30). Among the Egyptians, he argues, advances in medicine come by accident, and it is this theme which dominates his treatment of medicine in Egypt. Dissection of corpses in mummification taught them something of surgery; the development of a treatment for cataract came from observing a goat who recovered its sight when a sea-rush was impaled in its afflicted eye, and the klyster, or enema, was invented from observing an ibis inject itself with Nile water.[2] A custom which Herodotus (I 197) attributed to the Babylonians, the placing of the sick in the streets so that those who suffered from the same diseases may instruct them and lead them to cure, is appealed to and said to be a custom of the Egyptians.[3] The author concludes that while experience lays the beginnings for τέχνη, it lacks logic and rational development, a deficiency common to the medical art among all barbarians.[4] By contrast, among the Greeks ἰατρικὴ τέχνη has been perfected, and he turns to consider that development of logical method and theory which he sees as beginning in the Greek world with Hippocrates.

The author's history of medicine naively discusses problems which continue to occupy those concerned with Greek papyri of medical content.[5] First, the relation of Greek medicine to the

2. The story of the ibis is apparently drawn by the author from a collection of discoveries made by animals which proved of use to man, converted by him to a new setting, that of showing that discoveries in Egyptian medicine were made by accident. The story is frequently mentioned: Cicero, *ND* II 126; Pliny, *NH* VIII 97; Plutarch, *Moralia* 381c and 974c; Aelian, *NA* II 35; Galen, *De venae sectione* 6 (XI 168.3–4 Kühn). See discussion by J. G. Griffiths, *Plutarch's De Iside et Osiride* (Cardiff 1970) 558.

The story remained in vogue and appears in volumes of emblemata, including that of Alciati, 1550: A. Henkel and A. Schöne, *Emblemata* (Stuttgart 1976) col. 793.

3. The same tale is told by Strabo about the mountaineers of Spain, and he notes that they behave 'in the same way as the Egyptians did in ancient times' (ὥσπερ οἱ Αἰγύπτιοι τὸ παλαιόν, III 155c). Editors have proposed emending to Ἀσσύριοι, to bring the passage in line with Strabo's later telling of the story as an Assyrian custom (XVI 746c) and closer to Herodotus – apparently without knowledge of this passage. The custom is cited without provenience by Maximus of Tyre VI 2 (67.11–17 Holbein), Servius on *Aeneid* XII 395, and Isidore, *Etym.* X 72.

4. Galen himself often contrasts λόγος and πεῖρα in his pharmacology: C. Fabricius, *Galens Exzerpte aus älteren Pharmakologen* (Berlin 1972) 36–43.

5. Students of medical papyri are well served by the recent review of published literary and sub-literary texts of medical content by M.-H. Marganne, *Inventaire*

Egyptian medical tradition: in specific, Greek pharmacology and its pharmacopoeia often resemble Egyptian antecedents. In some instances the debt may be a direct one: a strong case has recently been made for interaction and sharing between Egyptian herbal and medicinal information collected in temple libraries (with perhaps Memphis as ultimate source) and the works of Greek herbalists of Alexandria in the Ptolemaic and early Roman period.[6] The *Corpus Hippocraticum* also shares, among other things, birth prognoses, gynecological techniques, and pharmacopoeia with earlier Egyptian medical writings, yet the fact that broadly similar drugs, techniques and recipes can be documented widely among societies at similar stages of development, makes arguments for a direct line less convincing.[7] The *Corpus* antedates the period of easier exchange between Egyptian and Greek practitioners afforded at Alexandria, and pointing to individual items shared by widely contrasting medical traditions may not unravel the complex fabric of Greek medicine and its relation to its Medi-

---

*analytique des papyrus grecs de médecine* (Geneva 1981), with full bibliography of previous studies. But work continues and to her catalogue can be added, for example, *P. Laur.* IV 151, a recipe for a plaster for stomach complaint, copied in a second- or third-century hand, and corrections for several of the recipes in H. Harrauer and P. J. Sijpesteijn, *Medizinische Rezepte und Verwandtes* (Vienna 1981) no. 4, for which see J. C. Shelton, *ZPE* 45 (1982) 154 and n. 8; L. C. Youtie, *ZPE* 51 (1983) 71–74.

The most detailed study of doctors in Greco-Roman Egypt remains that by K. Sudhoff, *Ärtzliches aus griechischen Papyrus-Urkunden* in *Studien zur Geschichte der Medizin* V–VI (Leipzig 1909), although it is limited in scope and in need of an up-to-date replacement. In addition to other studies listed by M.-H. Marganne, nn. 3–7, p. ii, useful are: for the Ptolemaic period, P. M. Fraser, *Ptolemaic Alexandria* I (Oxford 1972) 338–76, on 'Medicine', which covers not only the medical scholars of the Museum and court physicians, but also medical practice in the *chora*; for the Roman period, N. Lewis, *Life in Egypt under Roman Rule* (Oxford 1983) 151–54; Lewis notes that much of the evidence shows physicians in mundane contexts, such as tax-paying, and only on rare occasions affords a glimpse of them at work.

6. E. A. E. Reymond, *A Medical Book from Crocodilopolis* I (Vienna 1976) 43–62. I have not seen M.-H. Marganne, 'Nouvelles perspectives dans l'étude des sources de Dioscoride', paper presented to the XXVII Congreso Internacional de Historia de la Medicina (Barcelona 1980).

7. References to ancient texts and scholarship on the question are collected in G. E. R. Lloyd, *Science, Folklore and Ideology* (Cambridge 1983) 65 n. 21, and 84 n. 100; see also pp. 201–2 for the suggestion that techniques and recipes, approximating those in the Corpus, are 'widespread, if not universal'.

terranean antecedents.[8] Recent study of Greek recipes found on papyri has, however, documented the conservatism in transmission which preserves recipes once they enter written tradition, maintaining a textual integrity of their own special kind from copy to copy, because of the logic which dominates the therapy.[9]

The author of the treatise likewise emphasizes the importance of individuals within the Greek tradition and the readiness to associate the name of an inventor with a discovery or a recipe.[10] As might be expected, the name of Hippocrates is mentioned often in medical papyri, and treatises from the *Corpus* are conspicuous for their frequent appearance among the assigned medical texts.[11] Considerable progress is also being made in the identification of papyrus fragments of medical writers whose works are lost to the

8. G. Harig, 'Bemerkungen zum Verhältnis der griechischen zur altorientalischen Medizin', in *Corpus Hippocraticum: Actes du colloque... de Mons* (Mons 1977) 77–94. D. Goltz, *Studien zur altorientalischen und griechischen Heilkunde, Therapie, Arzneibereitung, Rezeptstruktur* (Wiesbaden 1974), has found many points for comparison between Greek and Near Eastern treatments and pharmacology, yet she insists on many differences as well, in both form and content of recipes.

9. To the bibliography cited by Marganne, *op.cit.* (n. 5) nn. 2–4, p. iii, now add, e.g., I. Andorlini, 'P. Grenf. 1 52: note farmacologiche', *BASP* 18 (1981) 1–25; and 'Ricette mediche nei papiri', *Atti e Memorie dell' Acc. Toscana di Scienze e Lettere* 46 (1981) 31–81.

When I first published *P. Mich.* inv. 3243 = *SB* XIV 12074, I saw it as a list of medicinal ingredients. Marganne has included it as no. 120 in her inventory, suggesting, as I now think rightly, that the six ingredients (cinnamon, cassia, nard, myrrh, honey either from Crete or Theangela in Caria, saffron) are likely to constitute a recipe, although it remains less certain in my mind that the mark which appears more than two cm above the first item indicates quantity, a drachma, for the first four and/or the sixth ingredient. In combination, the ingredients produce a soothing matrix to which other, more active, substances may be added, for a throat medicine, or complaints of liver, kidney, or spleen: Galen, *De compositione medicamentorum* VI 6 (XII 933.13–34.3 Kühn), VII 2 (XIII 27.6–10, 52.6–15, 52.15–53.3 Kühn), VIII 7 (XIII 203.13–17 Kühn), VIII 8 (XIII 213.6–11 Kühn).

10. Galen also found the anonymity prevailing in traditions of *Kulturgeschichte* of Egypt noteworthy: *Adversus ea quae Iuliano* 1.2–3 (*CMG* V 10,3: 33.10–17 Wenkebach).

11. For references to Hippocrates, see Marganne, *op. cit.* (n. 5) 353. For papyri of treatises in the *Corpus*, see Marganne nos. 1, 2, 41, 44, 66, 67, 68, 81, 84, 97, 114, 135, 138, 152, 158, and see below pp. 30–39.

For the authority of the *Corpus*, beginning in Empiric circles in later Hellenistic times, in conjunction with the writing of commentaries on the treatises and the elevation of Hippocrates to founder of Greek medicine, see W. D. Smith, *The Hippocratic Tradition* (Ithaca 1979) 177–78, 204–15; for Galen's use of the *Corpus*, 61–176.

manuscript tradition, thus restoring some degree of life and medical reality to such as Heras, Cassius, Herodotos, and Kriton, beyond the quotations from their works by Galen and other references to them in Celsus and Pliny.[12]

The author also points, albeit chauvinistically, to Greek enthusiasm for defining the problems of medicine and establishing a methodology for development of the art, beginning, as he sees it, with Hippocrates, and continuing to his own time, presumably well into the second century A.D. The large number of *adespota* among medical papyri complement lists of names of doctors and medical writers in doxographies and historical accounts, giving a more vital sense of the vastness of medical writing that is lost and of the vigor with which medical studies were pursued between the *Corpus* and Galen. The diversity exhibited by the Greek papyri among medical genres suggests that their Greek, or Greco-Egyptian, readers were also a varied lot. The texts range from theoretical and technical treatises which would interest the more sophisticated medical scholar and practitioner at Alexandria[13] and the district capitals,[14] to the popular medical questions and useful collections of recipes which were likely to appeal to literate doctors in the *chora* as well.[15] Individual recipes, jotted on pieces of papyrus

12. E.g. M.-H. Marganne, 'Un fragment du médecin Hérodote: P. Tebt. II 272', *Proceedings of the XVIth International Congress of Papyrology* (Chico 1981) 73–78, and her 'Une étape dans la transmission d'une prescription médicale: P. Berl. Möller 13', in *Papyrologica Florentina* VII (Florence 1980) 179–83. See also I. Andorlini, 'L'apporto dei papiri alla conoscenza dei medici pregalenici', forthcoming in *Atti del XVII Congresso internazionale di papirologia* (Naples 1984); I am grateful to Dr Andorlini for sharing her work with me in advance of publication.

13. E.g. for the surgeons of Alexandria prior to Celsus, see the collection of their fragments and testimonia for their lives, all gleaned from the works of later writers preserved in the manuscript tradition: M. Michler, *Die Alexandrinischen Chirurgen* (Wiesbaden 1968).

14. Particularly in the Roman period, the metropoleis Antinoopolis, Hermoupolis, and Oxyrhynchus have contributed a large portion of papyri with medical content, including, for example, over half of the texts of Hippocrates listed above, n. 11. For another text, perhaps from Hermoupolis, see below, pp. 39–47.

For scholars and professors of the Museum in Alexandria known to have lived in Oxyrhynchus, see E. G. Turner, 'Scribes and scholars of Oxyrhynchus', *Akten des VIII. internationalen Kongresses für Papyrologie* (Vienna 1955) 141–46.

15. For examples of medical questions, see Marganne, *op. cit.* (n. 5) nos. 23, 87, 111, 123, 147, and perhaps 26. For the genre, see J. Kollesch, *Untersuchungen*

or ostraka, or biographical literature about the Father of Medicine, could find readers among an even wider public of laymen with general valetudinarian and medical interests.

## I. Corpus Hippocraticum: *Epistulae* IV, V, XI[16]

*P. Berol.* 21137v + 6934v                          Arsinoite nome?

7.5 × 12.2 cm, 13 × 17.5 cm          Late 2nd or early 3rd c. A.D.[17]

*P. Berol.* 21137 has suffered severe damage. Nevertheless, it can be shown to belong to the roll whose verso, *P. Berol.* 6934,[18] was published in 1905 in volume III of the *Berliner Klassikertexte: Griechische Papyri medizinischen und naturwissenschaftlichen Inhalts*, edited by K. Kalbfleisch. This additional fragment, housed in the Ägyptisches Museum of West Berlin, supplies the column which directly precedes the published text, thus showing that the papyrus roll once contained at least *Epistulae* IV, V, and XI. Further, *P. Berol.* 21137 is stored with a group of papyri said to come from the Fayum, perhaps supplying a provenience for the entire roll. The

*zu den pseudogalenischen Definitiones medicae* (Berlin 1973) 35–46; and G. Zalateo, 'Papiri di argomento medico redatti in forma di domanda e risposto', *Aegyptus* 44 (1964) 52–57.

16. An earlier draft of this section was read by Dr J. Rubin and Professor W. D. Smith; I am indebted to both of them for useful suggestions.

17. In *ed. prin.* K. Kalbfleisch assigned the text on verso to the 3rd c., because the traces of cursive writing on recto had been dated by W. Schubart to the 2nd c., *BKT* III, p. 5. I would see the text of the *Epistulae* as written on verso in the earlier decades of the 3rd c., or even in the last decades of the 2nd c. The letters are individually formed, rounded, medium-sized, and somewhat flattened to give horizontal extension. While generally bilinear, *beta* always projects above the line, as does *iota* on occasion. A photo of what is now col. II is reproduced in *BKT* III as plate 2. The hand resembles that in plates 17 and 63 in E. G. Turner, *Greek Manuscripts of the Ancient World* (Princeton 1971): 17 = *P. Oxy.* x 1231, Pack² 1445, papyrus of Sappho, assigned to the 2nd c.; 63 = *Bibliotheca Bod. pap.* 2, Gospel according to St John, assigned to the earlier 3rd c. *Iota* adscript is employed throughout and a high dot to end a clause in col. II, line 17.

18. *P. Berol.* 6934v = Pack² 542 = Marganne no. 2. My attention was first drawn to the papyrus in the Ägyptisches Museum, West Berlin, by Professor H. Maehler, who had identified the fragment as Hippocratic and whose preliminary transcript I employed in the preparation of my own. I thank him and Dr W. Brashear for permission to publish the text. I inspected both columns of the roll in summer 1983, thanks to a faculty fellowship from Fordham University. Since that time I have relied on excellent photographs: that of inv. 6934v provided by Dr G. Poethke, and that of inv. 21137v provided by Professor Maehler.

mention of χέρσος, 'waste land', in the fragmentary accounts on recto of *P. Berol.* 21137 does not contradict this impression, in that distinctions among categories of land, especially one bringing exemption from taxes on land, would be of particular interest in an agricultural district. This additional column was easily passed over by the editors of *P. Berol.* 6934, because of its poor state of preservation. Perhaps the roll was already damaged in antiquity, with an outer column suffering more severely than one more to the center. In the newly identified fragment, *P. Berol.* 21137, a small portion of the top margin is preserved at right, as is the intercolumnar space between columns I and II, usually about 2.5 cm. *Epistula* IV begins at the top and occupies the first nine lines of the 17-line column; *Epistula* V, beginning in line 10, occupies the rest of the column and continues in the first six lines of the second column. *Epistula* XI follows in lines 7–17 of the second column, and must have continued through the entire third column as well, since among the initial letters of column III there is no *ekthesis*, the sign that a new letter is beginning. Intercolumnar space between columns II and III is usually between 2.5 and 3 cm. Although fading of ink and abrasions to the surface of the papyrus in the first column preclude certainty of reading at many points, the version of *Epistula* IV which it presents has closest affinities with other copies known on papyrus and in a group of late manuscripts, in particular *Parisinus gr.* 3052 (φ). On the other hand, its text of *Epistula* V is similar to the longer of the two versions which appear together, one after another, in another papyrus (*P. Berol.* 7094v, see below). The longer version of *Epistula* V is also known from the older manuscript tradition, represented by the large compendia of Hippocratic material, *Marcianus gr.* 269 (M, 10th c.) and *Vaticanus gr.* 276 (V, late 12th c.); by a small collection of medical material, *Urbinus gr.* 64 (U, 12th c.); and by a manuscript with no medical texts, but among other items, a selection of letters, including those of Hippocrates, Themistocles, and Diogenes the Cynic, *Palatinus gr.* 398 (b, 10th c.).[19] In the judgement of

19. The traditional dating of M to the 11th c. has been correctly moved back into the 10th c. by J. Irigoin: see the report by J. Jouanna in *Hippocrate. La nature de l'homme* (*CMG* I 1,3, Berlin 1975) 63 n. 2, and also N. G. Wilson, *Scholars of Byzantium* (Baltimore 1983) 139 (for M) and 212 (for U). Otherwise dates have been taken from G. Putzger, *Hippocratis quae feruntur epistulae ad codicum fidem*

G. Putzger, who edited the *Epistulae* in 1914, the shortened versions
are derived from, and are inferior in the text they present to, the
versions of the *Epistulae* in these older manuscripts.[20] The presence
of both longer and shorter versions in the same papyrus supports
the notion that the shorter versions derive from the longer: see
especially two versions of *Epistula* IV in *P. Oxy.* IX 1184v, or two
versions of *Epistula* V in *P. Berol.* 7094v; and a shorter version of
*Epistula* IV, coupled with a longer version of *Epistulae* V and XI in
*P. Berol.* 21137v + 6934v.

Portions of three papyrus rolls carry selections of Hippocratic
*Epistulae*: *P. Oxy.* IX 1184v; dated to the first half of the first century
A.D.;[21] *P. Berol.* 7094v, dated to the second or third century;[22] and
its contemporary, *P. Berol.* 21137v–6934v. The three rolls share a
number of features. They are relatively early in date. They contain
a similar group of *Epistulae*, in spite of differences in text presented
for a particular letter, in that two contain at least one copy of
*Epistulae* III, IV, V, and the third, at least one copy of IV and V, and
in the fact that in two of them *Epistula* V is followed directly by
*Epistula* XI. All three are placed on the back side of a roll, previously
used either for a documentary text, or a metrological treatise,[23]
suggesting that these copies were privately made for their owners.
Although height of column varies from roll to roll, the format of
the letters also reflects a similar style of presentation, with
*paragraphoi* separating *Epistulae* and *ekthesis* of the name of each
addressee extending two or three spaces into the left margin in
imitation of an actual letter. These similarities may point to a
particular vogue which this selection of *Epistulae* from the *Corpus*
enjoyed, as readers were taking pleasure in the moral principle
exemplified by the refusal of Hippocrates to treat Persians who are
enemies of the Greeks, in spite of the fact that the Great King is
offering wealth, honors, and position at court.[24]

*recensitae* (Wurzen 1914) v–vi. For contents of *Palatinus gr.* 398 (b), see
H. Stevenson, *Codices manuscripti Palatini Graeci Bibliothecae Vat.* (Rome 1885)
254–57. Cf. n. 27 below.

20. G. Putzger, *op. cit.* (n. 19) iv.    21. Pack² 540 = Marganne no. 135.
22. Pack² 541 = Marganne no. 1.    23. Pack² 2327.

24. See, for example, Galen's obvious appreciation of the ethical code which
leads Hippocrates to ignore Artaxerxes and to serve the sick who need his skill,
especially the poor in Kranon, Thasos, and other communities in the Greek
world, in *Quod optimus medicus* 3 (*Scripta Minora* II (Berlin 1891), 5.6–12 Müller).
See below pp. 34–35 and n. 28.

| | *P. Oxy.* 1184v ($p^1$) | *P. Berol.* 7094v ($p^2$) | *P. Berol.* 21137v+ 693v ($p^3$) |
|---|---|---|---|
| *Epistula* iii: King Artaxerxes is writing to Hystanes: offer gold to Hippocrates and send him to court. | Shortened version of ms. trad.; closing lines added in margin | Version of ms. trad. | (Papyrus not preserved before *Ep.* iv.) |
| *Epistula* iv: Hystanes is writing to Hippocrates, notifying him of the King's offer. | 1. Truncated version of older mss. ($p^{1-1}$) 2. Shorter version, similar to *P. Berol.* 7094 ($p^2$) and *P. Berol.* 21137 ($p^3$) ($p^{1-2}$). Unique editorial comment: 'This noble fellow preserved the reputation of his art and his love for the Greeks by refusing the offer and writing as follows.' | Shorter version, similar to *P. Oxy.* 1184 ($p^{1-2}$), *P. Berol.* 21137 ($p^3$), and some Paris *recc.* | Shorter version, similar to *P. Oxy.* 1184 ($p^{1-2}$), *P. Berol.* 7094 ($p^2$), and some Paris *recc.*, espec. φ. |
| *Epistula* v: Hippocrates is writing to Hystanes, refusing the King's offer of wealth and adding that he will not cure men who are enemies of the Greeks. | Abridgement of longer version of older mss., truncated at beginning so as to resemble *P. Berol.* 7094 ($p^{2-1}$) and some Paris *recc.* | 1. Longer version, similar to *P. Berol.* 21137+ 6934 ($p^3$), and older mss.; occupies 12 lines in pap. ($p^{2-1}$) 2. Unique 9-line version ($p^{2-2}$), apparently truncated at beginning as in $p^1$ and some Paris *recc.* | Longer version, similar to *P. Berol.* 7094 ($p^{2-1}$), and older mss. |
| *Epistula ad Gorgiam*: Hippocrates is writing about his refusal of the King's offer. | Unique. The *Ep. ad Gorg.* resembles *Ep.* vi of older mss. in that both report Hipp.'s refusal. | — | — |
| *Epistula* xi: Hippocrates is writing to the Council and People of Abdera, agreeing to come and cure Demokritos; he declines in advance any offer of salary and alludes to the exchange of letters with Artaxerxes. | (Papyrus not preserved after *Ep. ad Gorg.*) | Small portion preserved, but text seems to follow that of older mss. | Small portion preserved, but text seems to follow that of older mss. |

Five Paris manuscripts of the fifteenth century, known both to Littré and Putzger,[25] also place *Epistula* xi directly after *Epistula* v: *Parisinus gr.* 2652 (o), 2755 (σ), 3047 (τ), 3050 (υ), Suppl. 205 (ψ). And they omit the intervening letters known to the tradition of earlier Byzantine manuscripts of the *Corpus*.[26] Further, the shorter version for *Epistula* iv which the papyri offer is essentially the same abridged version as found in these Paris *recentiores*, as well as in another Paris manuscript of the sixteenth century, *Parisinus gr.* 3052 (φ), containing *Epistulae* iii–x. No other treatises from the *Corpus*, nor other medical material, appear in these Paris *recentiores*; rather their contents exhibit an epistolographic miscellany.[27] In some fashion these are descendants of the popular collections of letters of antiquity, known primarily from the papyrus copies circulating in Egypt nearly a millennium and a half earlier.

The textual tradition of the *Epistulae* preserved on papyrus is fluid in the early Roman empire, as the comparison of contents in the three papyrus rolls reveals (see Table).

The exchange of letters between the King, Hystanes, and Hippocrates, *Epistulae* iii–v, were well known wherever there was interest in trying to fashion a biography of the ideal physician that Hippocrates had come to represent. This correspondence is noted, for example, in section 8 of the *bios* derived from Soranus which accompanies the Byzantine compendia of the *Corpus*: 'He loved Greece so much, moreover, that when his reputation became

25. E. Littré, *Oeuvres complètes d'Hippocrate* ix (Paris 1861) 309–10 and 318 n. 3, where read 'ἱππ.... ἔρρωσο, p. 324, l. 21, om. οστυψ', and G. Putzger, *op. cit.* (n. 19) iv: '*epistulas 6–10 non exhibet*'.
26. H. Diels, 'Handschriften der antiken Ärzte i', *Abhand. der könig. Preuss. Akad. der Wissenschaften* (Berlin 1905) 36–38, lists a number of other late manuscripts which also lack letters 6–10.
27. According to H. Omont, *Inventaire sommaire des manuscrits grecs de la Bibliothèque Nationale* iii (Paris 1888): pp. 35–36, 2755 (σ) contains on fos. 154–200 letters of Euripides, Hippocrates, Heraclitus; p. 99, 3047 (τ), fos. 1–23, letters of Eur., Hipp., Diogenes the Cynic; p. 100, 3050 (υ), fos. 107–27, letters of Hipp., Diog. the Cynic; p. 231, Suppl. 205 (ψ), fos. 31–58, letters of Eur., Hipp., Herakl., Diog. the Cynic; p. 100, 3052 (φ), however, seems to share a different set of letters with τ and υ, and another set with σ. By contrast, 2652 (o), H. Omont, iii 19, is a Christian collection, assembled recently, in that it includes letters of Cardinal Bessarion.
According to H. Stevenson, *op. cit.* (n. 19) 254–57, the older ms. from the epistolographic tradition, *Pal. gr.* 398 (b), contains not only a full set of the letters of Hipp., but also those of Themistokles, followed by those of Diog. the Cynic.

known among the Persians and when, as a result, Artaxerxes with all manner of gifts pleaded with him through the agency of Hystanes, his ruler in the area of the Hellespont, to come to him, Hippocrates refused. His refusal came from his holiness, his lack of concern for money, and his love of his homeland. All this is abundantly clear in the letter he sent to him.'[28] The letter to Gorgias, unique to *P. Oxy.* ix 1184, is presumably addressed to the sophist from Leontinoi, who resided at Athens in the closing decades of the fifth century. He likewise appears in the biographic tradition of the *bios* derived from Soranus as Hippocrates' teacher.[29] The appearance of Gorgias within the Hippocratic orb satisfies more than one of the forces which activate the biographic mentality in antiquity: in this case, the desire to associate Hippocrates with his famous contemporary may coincide with detection of sophistic or Gorgianic influence within the *Corpus*, as well as with the appearance of Gorgias, albeit said to be a man of Larissa and husband of a patient, in *Epidemics* v 11 (v 210.12 Littré).[30]

The popularity of these *Epistulae* and their circulation among a wide audience contributes to fluidity not only in choice of letters which make up a collection, but also in the text of individual

28. τοσοῦτον δὲ φιλέλλην ὑπῆρξεν, ὥστε τῆς δόξης αὐτοῦ μέχρι Περσῶν διαπύστου γενομένης καὶ διὰ τοῦτο καὶ τοῦ ᾿Αρταξέρξου διὰ ῾Υστάνους τοῦ ῾Ελλησποντίων ὑπάρχου ἐπὶ μεγάλαις δωρεαῖς δεομένου πρὸς αὐτὸν ἐλθεῖν, διὰ τὸ σεμνὸν καὶ ἀφιλάργυρον καὶ φιλοίκειον ἀρνήσασθαι, ὡς καὶ τοῦτο διὰ τῆς πρὸς αὐτὸν ἐπιστολῆς δηλοῦται (*CMG* iv 176.18–23 Ilberg).

As J. Rubin has pointed out to me, the Suda quotes letter 3 and Stobaeus refers to Hippocrates' refusal, the subject of letter 5, in addition to the use of letters 3–5 by the *bios*, although there is no evidence that any of the three knew letters 1–2 or 6–9. By late antiquity this selection of letters influences the biographical tradition. For a thorough study of the history of this narrative about Hippocrates and Artaxerxes from its Hellenistic origin through the empire and into the early Islamic period, see J. Rubin, *Biographical Fiction in the Lives of Hippocrates* (U. of Penn. diss. 1983), chh. 4 and 7. I am grateful to her for sharing her work with me in advance of publication.

29. *CMG* iv, 175.8 Ilberg.

30. See M. R. Lefkowitz, *Lives of the Greek Poets* (London 1981) 64–65 and 125, for the inclusion of famous contemporaries in the *bioi* of poets; see also 131–32, where she cites examples to show that 'studied with' often means 'shared concepts with'. The μαθητὴς δὲ γέγονεν of the *bios* (*CMG* iv 175.7 Ilberg) is one of the usual expressions for such a relationship. Gorgian influence has been detected in *Ancient Medicine* of the *Corpus* in modern times: e.g. A. Lami, 'Un'eco di Gorgia in *Antica medicina*', *Critica Storica* 14 (1977) 567–74. For a poet's works as the source of biography, see Lefkowitz, viii.

letters. While the copy of the letters preserved on *P. Berol.*
21137v + 6934v lies closer to the late epistolographic tradition in
the text it presents for *Epistula* IV and its omission of *Epistulae* VI–X,
it is closer to the tradition of the letters in manuscripts of the *Corpus*
in its text for *Epistulae* V and XI.

Verso

Col. I

       [Υστανη]ς Ε[λλη]σͅποντου υπαρ-       *Epistula* IV
       [χος Ιππο]κρͅατει ιητρωι
       [Ασκλ]ηπ[ια]δων οντι ᾳ[πο-]
4      [γονωι]      χαιρειͅν
       [ην επ]εμψε [β]ασιλευς μεγας
       ]η. επ[ισ]τολην [σ]οͅ[υ] χ[ρ]η-
       [3ων π]επομφα σοͅι ινᾳ [την]
8      [σην] ᾳποφ[ασ]ιͅν κᾳ[τα τα]χοͅς
       π]εμψω      ερρ[ωσ]οͅ

       [Ιπποκ]ρͅατͅη[ς ιητρος Υστανει Ε]λ-      *Epistula* V
       [λησπ]οͅνͅτͅ[ου υπαρχωι χαιρειν]
12     [ην επ]ιͅσͅτοͅ[λην επεμψας φα-]
       [μενο]ς πͅ[αρα βασιλεως αφ-]
       (lines 14–17 totally lost)

Col. II

       [τηι εις βιον] ουσιηι [αρκε]ο[υ]
       [σηι χρεομα]ι Περσεων δ[ε]
       ολβ[ου ου μοι] θεμις επαυ-
4      ρεσθ[αι ου]δε βαρβαρους αν-
       δρας ν[ου]σων παυειν εχθ[ρ]ους  ιＩγ̄..( )
       υπαρχοντας Ελληνων [ερρ]ωσο

       Ιπποκρα[τη]ς Αβδηρειτω[ν] β[ουληι]      *Epistula* XI
8      και δημωι      χαι[ρ]ειν
       ο πολιτης υμων Αμελησαγ[ορ]ης
       ηκεν εις Κω και ετυχεν τ[οτ]ε
       ουσα της ραβδου η αναληψ[ι]ς
12     εν εκεινηι τηι ημερηι κ[αι]
       ετησιος ως ιστε πανηγυρ[ις]
       η[μ]ειν και πομπη ην [πολυ-]
       τελεα εις κυπαρισσον η[ν]
16     εθος αναγειν τοις τωι θεω[ι]
       προσηκουσι· επει δε σπου[δα-]

Col. III

Traces of initial letters, with uniform left margin, appear along the right edge of the papyrus: opposite line 5 in col. II, α[ ; line 6, ε[ ; line 8, θ[ ; line 12, ου[ ; line 13, ϙ[ ; line 15, μ[ ; line 17, κ[ .

## *Epistula* IV

The text of *P. Berol.* 21137v is compared with the shorter version of *Ep.* IV in *P. Oxy.* IX 1184 margin (p¹⁻²); *P. Berol.* 7094v (p²); codd. φ and R ( = '*codd. Parisini recentiores a Littraeo litteris* οστυχψω *insigniti omnes vel plerique*', as given by Putzger). For fuller collation of *Ep.* IV, see G. Putzger, *Hippocratis quae feruntur epistulae ad codicum fidem recensitae* (Wurzen 1914) 2–3.

Lines **1–4.** ['Υστάνη]ς Ἑ[λλη]σπόντου ὕπαρ/[χος Ἱππο]κράτει ἰητρῷ· / ['Ασκλ]ηπ[ια]δῶν ὄντι ἀ[πο/γόνωι] [ ] χαίρειν: the address is variously given.

p¹⁻²: lacks its own address and may be meant to share that of the longer version (identical headings for *Ep.* v precede in both p²⁻¹ and p²⁻²): Ὑ[σ]τάνης Ἱπποκράτει ἰητρῶι 〚ἀπὸ δὲ〛 'Κώωι' 'Ασκλη/πι〚ου〛 'αδέω[ν]' 〚γεγονότος`ι〛 '[ὄ]ντι ἐγγόνωι' χαίριν καὶ ὑγιαίνιν in p¹⁻¹.

p²: Ὑστάνης ['Ιπποκράτ]ει ἰητρῷ / 'Ασκληπ[ια]δ[ῶν ὄ]ντι ἀπογ[όν]ῳ / χαίρειν.

R: Ὑστάνης Ἱπποκράτει (-η οσψ) 'Ασκληπιαδῶν ὄντι ἀπογώνῳ (-νων ου) χαίρειν.

φ: Ὑστάνης Ἱπποκράτει ἰητρῷ Κώῳ 'Ασκληπιάδων ὄντι ἀπογόνῳ χαίρειν.

**5.** [ἔπ]εμψε [β]ασιλεύς: so also p². P¹⁻², φ: ἔπεμψεν βασ.; R (οστυψ) ἔπεμψεν ὁ βασ.

**6.** ]η. : ]ης is a possible reading. The space available, however, is too small to accommodate 'Αρταξέρξ]ης, although Ξέρξ]ης is of proper length. The allusion to the Hippocrates/Artaxerxes story in Stobaeus shows the substitution of 'Xerxes' for 'Artaxerxes' (*Eclogae* XIII, περὶ παρρησίας 51, O. Hense, *Ioannis Stobaei Anthologium* III (Berlin 1894) 464). Although it is possible that the error is characteristic of one branch of the epistolographic tradition, appearing in the papyrus and also known to Stobaeus, it seems more likely that this is an independent corruption, due in the papyrus to an erroneous attempt to supply the name of the Great

King, but in Stobaeus to carelessness with a name in the anecdotal transmission. I owe the reference to Stobaeus to J. Rubin.

[σ]ọ[ῦ]: so also p¹⁻¹, p¹⁻², φ; p² in lacuna. But Ionic σέο in R (οστυψ).

**7–9.** [π]έπομφά σọι ἵνα [τὴν] / [σὴν] ἀπόφ[ασ]ιν κα[τὰ τά]χọς / [ π]έμψω. ἔρρ[ωσ]ọ. There is space for two or three letters before π]έμψω, perhaps [ἀποπ]έμψω.

p¹⁻²: πέ/πομφά σοι / ἵνα κατὰ τά/χος ἐς βασι/λέα πέμ/ψωι. Om. ἔρρωσο.

p²: ἔ[πε]μ/[ψ]ά̣ σοι· γρ[άψο]ν [ο]ῦν πρὸς ταῦτα / ἵνạ κατ[ὰ τά]χ[ο]ṣ πρὸς βασι[λέ]α / πέμψω. ἔρρωσο.

R: ἔπεμψά σοι· γράψον οὖν πρὸς ταύτην (αὐτὴν υ) κατὰ τάχος, ἵνα πέμψω. ἔρρωσο. (οστυψ)

φ: πέπομφά σοι· γράψον οὖν πρὸς ταῦτα ἵνα κατὰ τάχος τὴν σὴν ἀπόφασιν πέμψω. Om. ἔρρωσο.

*Epistula* v

The text of *P. Berol.* 21137v is compared with the first version of *Ep.* v in *P. Berol.* 7094v (p²⁻¹) and *codd.*, as given by Putzger.

Line **10.** *Paragraphoi* separate letters in col. II, and also in p¹ and p²; hence a *paragraphos* has been restored above line 10. A *paragraphos* may also have stood above line 1 in this column, or alternatively at the close of the preceding column.

**10–11.** ['Ιπποκ]ρά̣τη[ς ἰητρὸς 'Υστάνει 'Ε]λ/[λησπ]ọ́ντ[ου ὑπάρχωι χαίρειν]: the address is variously given. Before 'Ιπποκ., φ adds ἀντίγραφος ἱπποκράτους πρὸς ὑστάνην. 'Ιητρός is omitted in p²⁻¹, V. Some members of R read ὑπάρχῳ 'Ελλ. (τυψ) and omit χαίρειν (τψ).

**12.** [ἣν ἐπ]ιṣτọ[λὴν ἔπεμψας]: this opening clause for *Ep.* v is unique to *P. Berol.* 21137v, but seems to have been modeled upon the opening of *Ep.* iv.

V and descendants read πρὸς τὴν ἣν ἔπεμψας ἐπιστολήν.
P²⁻¹ and *codd.* of older ms. trad.: πρὸς τὴν ἐπιστ. ἣν ἔπεμψας.
By contrast, p¹, p²⁻², and R omit πρὸς...ἀφῖχθαι (οστυψ), beginning the letter with πέμπε.

**14–17.** Assuming that the text lost at the bottom of col. I continues in its close resemblance to that in p²⁻¹ and in the *codd.*

of older ms. trad., the amount of text lost might have been distributed in the following manner:

15    ἴχθαι πέμπε βασιλεῖ ἂ
ἐγὼ γράφω ὡς τάχος διότι
καὶ προσφορῆι καὶ ἐσθῆ-
τι καὶ οἰκήσει καὶ πάσηι

Col. II

The text, as it appears in col. II (*P. Berol.* 6934v), was known to Putzger who both compares it with *codd.* and gives full collation of mss., *op. cit.* (n. 19) 3 and 6.

**5.** The purpose of the note in the right margin is unclear.

*Epistula* XI

Line **17.** Punctuation apparently only here, with a high dot to end a clause, although the state of preservation in col. I may preclude the possibility of seeing such marks.

II. Galen: *De placitis Hippocratis et Platonis* I[31]

| | |
|---|---|
| *P. Mon. Gr.* inv. 329 + *P. Berol.* 21141 | Hermoupolis?[32] |
| 3 × 4 cm, 5.6 × 8.3 cm | Early 3rd c. A.D. |

*P. Berol.* 21141 joins directly to the lower portion of the leaf from a papyrus codex of Galen's *De placitis Hippocratis et Platonis* I which is housed in the Staatsbibliothek in Munich as inventory number 329.[33] The two pieces may have been separated in antiquity, since the damage which has caused considerable fading of ink in the final five lines of the verso in the papyrus from Munich does not afflict the papyrus from Berlin, in which the ink remains uniformly dark and clear. The discovery of the new fragment in the collection of

31. An earlier draft of this section was read by Professor P. De Lacy and Dr V. Nutton to whom I am indebted for useful suggestions and corrections.

32. *P. Berol.* 21141 is stored with a number of other papyri said, in the inventories of the Ägyptisches Museum in West Berlin, to come from Hermoupolis.

33. *Editio princeps*: D. Manetti, 'Un nuovo papiro di Galeno', *Ricerche di filologia classica* I: *Studi di letteratura greca* (1981) 115–23, including a photo of the portions in Munich before restoration. Dr Manetti has been most gracious in sharing with me her information about the fragment in Munich. The Berlin fragment, inv. 21141, adds seven to ten letters to recto lines 17–20 before the lacuna at right, and approximately the same number to verso lines 16–20 before the lacuna at left. See Plate V.

the Ägyptisches Museum in West Berlin further defines the original shape of both folio and codex, and clarifies the position of the codex in the transmission of Galen's works.[34] The codex is dated by its hand to the first half of the third century A.D. at the latest,[35] and hence it is considerably earlier than the other papyrus evidence for works of Galen, which are dated by style of writing to the sixth century: from Antinoopolis come portions of *De compositione medicamentorum*;[36] from Hermoupolis, prolegomena to Galen's *De sectis ad tirones*,[37] displaying affinities with other fifth- and sixth-century neoplatonic commentaries on Porphyry's *Isagoge*. In addition, I have recently identified a small section from the beginning of *De naturalibus facultatibus* i in another Berlin papyrus.[38]

A *terminus post quem* for the date of the papyrus codex of *De placitis*

34. The fragment in Berlin was first brought to my attention by Professor H. Maehler. I am grateful to him and to Dr William Brashear for permission to publish the text, as well as for putting it at my disposal during a visit to Berlin in summer 1983.
For the fragment in Munich, I rely on a series of excellent photographs, one set of which was enlarged four times, and all of which were taken after the work of restoration, mentioned in *ed. prin.*, p. 116 n. 5, had been completed. In addition to cleaning, frag. A has been properly set above frag. B; unplaced frag. C has been detached from frag. A. The photographs of both are reproduced here through the kind permission of the Ägyptisches Museum in West Berlin and the Staatsbibliothek in Munich.
I have had no better success than the editor of *ed. prin.* in placing frag. C, and, as a consequence, have little confidence either in readings which I have thought possible in the fragment, or in those offered in the *ed. prin.* For the sake of completeness, I repeat the transcript of frag. C given in the *ed. prin.*, p. 116 n. 5: recto 1 ]ε.ε[ ; 2 ]ημ[ ; 3 ]ν.[ ; verso 1 ]..[ ; 2 ]α[ .
35. The first editor compares the hand to, in particular, *P. Oxy.* iii 412, pl. 5, containing the conclusion of Book xviii of the *Kestoi* of Julius Africanus on a matter of Homeric criticism; this latter example is probably to be dated after A.D. 221, the point at which Africanus completed his chronological writings and turned to the subsequent *Kestoi*, but before 275/6 and the reign of Tacitus, who figures in the imperial date on the verso. I would add as well, *ZPE* 51 (1983) 76–79 and pl. 1c, a commentary on Plato's *Alcibiades*, dated to the end of the 2nd c. or beginning of the 3rd c. A.D.
36. *P. Ant.* iii 186 = Marganne no. 69.
37. *P. Berol.* 11739 A–B, 6th c. papyrus codex from Hermoupolis = Pack² 456 = Marganne no. 72.
38. *P. Berol.* 21178, written in an irregular hand of the later 4th c. and housed with other papyri whose origin is the Fayum; the Greek text compares favorably with that in the edition by G. Helmreich (*Scripta Minora* iii (Berlin 1893) 102.1–5). I am preparing this text for publication.

is the composition of the work itself: in *De libris propriis* Galen says that the first six books of *De placitis* were written during his first sojourn in Rome, A.D. 162–166, at the request of Flavius Boethus, who took them with him when he went out as governor to Syria Palaestina; the last three books were begun only during Galen's second sojourn in the capital, after A.D. 169, and were completed by the return of Marcus Aurelius from his wars with the Germans late in A.D. 176. Internal evidence, however, largely in the form of references to works which Galen apparently composed later than this schema permits, suggests that revisions were made in *De placitis* after A.D. 176.[39] The letter forms in which the present text is written suggest a *terminus ante quem* of no later than the middle of the third century: the letters are for the most part individually formed, with occasional ligature after *tau*, *alpha*, and *epsilon*. The hand is practiced, yet casual; *alpha* and *mu*, for example, are written with a single flourish of the pen. The forms are broad and flat, yet they observe bilinearity in most instances. Neither punctuation nor *iota* adscript appears in the text as preserved. The orthography is of the highest standards.

The newly identified fragment from Berlin shows that line 20 on both recto and verso is the final line of the folio, after which follows a lower margin of at least 2.4 cm. The amount of text intervening between the conclusion of recto and the beginning of the text on verso can easily be accommodated in 24 lines, each containing between 28 and 33 letters; these 24 lines would have stood on the verso-folio above the now visible 20 lines. Although no longer preserved in its entirety, Book 1 of *De placitis* may have been longer than the other books in this work, perhaps as long as 101 pages in the Müller edition.[40] The 44 lines projected here for the verso-folio occupy 33 lines in the Müller edition, or two pages, suggesting that Book I might have occupied about 50 pages in the papyrus codex, if these projections are valid throughout. The entire text of *De placitis* measured according to pages in the Müller

39. See P. De Lacy, in his edition of *Galeni de Plac. Hipp. et Plat.* 1–v, *CMG* v 4, 1,2 (Berlin 1978) 46–48, with references to earlier literature, esp. J. Ilberg, 'Über die Schriftstellerei des Klaudios Galenos', *RhM* 44 (1889) 207–39. Also useful is L. G. Ballester, *Galeno* (Madrid 1972) 43–44 and 264–69.

40. P. De Lacy, *CMG* v 4, 1,2 (Berlin 1978) 13 and 32, discussing the text of *De placitis* by I. Müller, *Claudii Galeni de placitis Hipp. et Plat. Libri Novem* (Leipzig 1874).

edition would extend over some 760 pages and hence might have occupied about 380 pages in a codex of the proportions envisaged here on the basis of a single preserved folio. Such a codex approaches in configuration the size and shape projected for another third-century codex, that of Xenophon's *Cyropaedia*, number 281 in Turner's classification, and an aberrant of Turner's sub-class 2 in Group 8: its height is calculated as less than twice its breadth (13.5 × 23 cm), with perhaps 32–35 lines per page, and, if containing the entire *Cyropaedia*, perhaps about 300 pages.[41] The original editor of the Munich fragment of *De placitis* projected for the folia of that codex a written surface of about 9/9.5 × 18 cm, suggesting affinities with those codices whose breadth was half, or approximately half, the height – again Turner's Group 8. A lower margin of 2.4 cm re-enforces the impression that this codex was once relatively tall, but not broad, and generally somewhat short in height among the early codices in Turner's Group 8 and its sub-classes of aberrants.

Traces of a *kollesis* can occasionally be seen in the Munich fragment: on the recto at a distance of 0.8 to 1 cm from the left margin, visible especially in lines 5 and 13–16; on the verso at a distance of 0.6 to 0.8 cm from the right margin, visible especially in lines 5 and 12–15. The *kollesis* has become unglued toward the lower margin of the recto, and a strip of papyrus, about 0.5 cm in width and containing the first three (or two) letters of recto lines 17–20, has been totally lost.[42]

The passage which appears on the papyrus folio is part of Galen's description of arteries to the lower parts of the body and the legs, an anatomical digression designed to cap his refutation of Praxagoras' notion that arteries, as they divide and become smaller, constrict so as to become nerves. The text of Galen's *De placitis* I has come down to us in a single lacunose manuscript from the fifteenth century, purchased by the British physician John Caius on the Continent and brought by him to England, where

41. E. G. Turner, *The Typology of the Early Codex* (Philadelphia 1977) 21, 83, and 115, on number 281 = Pack² 1547. For discussions of Group 8 and its aberrants, see p. 24; for their application to *P. Mon. Gr.* 329, see D. Manetti, *op. cit.* (n. 33) 120–21.

42. The first editor argued for an *eisthesis* at recto, lines 17–20 (*op. cit.* (n. 33) 116 and 121–22), but the division of words across lines then becomes non-syllabic for both lines 16–17 and 19–20, and hence unlikely, however motivated.

it served him in the preparation of his edition of the Greek text with Latin translation, published in Basel in 1544.[43] The manuscript is now housed in the library of Gonville and Caius College, Cambridge (47/24 = C). C is generally inferior to the thirteenth-century H (Hamilton 270), when the two can be compared in Books ii–ix, though at times C preserves better readings; a number of errors in C are mechanical and others are due to unsuccessful attempts at editorial revision.[44]

A comparison of the readings from the papyrus codex with those of C shows a not dissimilar text in circulation, although about 1200 years intervene between their copying. In particular, the papyrus preserves a better reading at verso line 20 with [νῦν δ' ἀρκεῖ] καὶ τὰ λελεγμένα, rather than C's νυνὶ δὲ ἀρκεῖ τὰ λεγόμενα. Not only is the phrase in the papyrus the more striking one, but it resembles Galenic usage elsewhere: e.g. νῦν δ' ἀρκεῖ τὰ λελεγμένα παρα-δείγματος ἕνεκα, *De methodo medendi* x 9 (= x 705.7–8 Kühn) and νῦν δὲ ἀρκεῖ καὶ ταῦτα αὖθις ἐνδείξειν, *De respirationis usu* 4 (= iv 501.9–10 Kühn).[45] Admittedly, Galen does exhibit a marked preference for εἰρημένα over λελεγμένα in *De placitis*, both when he is quoting other authors and when he is directing a reader through his narrative by means of references to previous discussion. Nonetheless, there is τὸ νυνί μοι λελεγμένον twice in ii 5.90–91 in the system of internal references,[46] and τὰ λελεγμένα in viii 6.36.3,[47] introductory to a quotation from the Hippocratic *Aphorisms*. The thirteenth-century manuscript H reads the inferior λεγόμενον at ii 5.91.5, demonstrating that the present participle has replaced the perfect elsewhere in the tradition of the treatise. The other differences between the papyrus and C are neither numerous nor important: a possible variant at verso line 14; an

---

43. J. Caius, *De libris suis* (London, 1570) 76, as reprinted in *The Works of John Caius* (Cambridge 1912), and cf. V. Nutton, *Medical History* 24 (1980) 100.

44. For evaluation of the manuscripts of the *De placitis*, see P. De Lacy, *CMG* v 4, 1,2 (Berlin 1978) 12–21 and 24–35.

45. See also the recurring νῦν δ' ἀρκεῖ τό γε τοσοῦτον and its variations: *De semine* ii 5, iv 633.15–16 Kühn; *De probis pravisque alimentorum succis* 4, vi 766.14 Kühn and 7, vi 790.5–6 Kühn; *De differentiis febrium* i 2, vii 278.9 Kühn; *De marcore* 9, vii 700.9 Kühn; *De crisibus* i 7, ix 579.13–14 Kühn; *De methodo medendi* xi 20, x 802.11–12 Kühn; *De simplicium medicamentorum temperamentis ac facultatibus* iv 19, xi 687.10 Kühn and x 38, xii 243.12 Kühn.

46. *CMG* v 4, 1,2, vol. i, p. 146.8 and 16 (with λελεγ. μοι) De Lacy.

47. i 702.1 Müller = v 696.14–15 Kühn.

inferior reading at recto line 9; an omission which could be restored by an observant editor at recto line 20.

Galen complains that readers can buy from booksellers on the *vicus Sandalarius* at Rome a copy of one of his treatises variously mutilated by omissions, additions, and alterations, as well as treatises falsely attributed to him, a situation arising from the fact that many of his writings were produced at the behest of friends and not originally intended for formal publication.[48] At the death of such a friend, Galen explains, what had been a private copy might be taken by others in the deceased's company and subsequently enter circulation in a transformed state due to editorial activity of the later owner. The desire to authenticate his own treatises among those in circulation under his name motivated his *De libris propriis*. The papyrus codex of *De placitis* from Egypt, circulating already in the first half of the third century A.D., does not, however, exemplify the process Galen envisages, even though the recipient of Books I–VI, Flavius Boethus, died in his province of Syria Palaestina – unless manuscript C of the fifteenth century, the only other copy in Greek of portions of *De placitis* I now known, also derives from the same altered source, an unlikely possibility.[49] The essential closeness of the text contained on one folio from Book I in the papyrus codex with the text in manuscript C seems to offer instead a degree of correction to what may be another example of Galen's propensity to exaggerate in matters of personal involvement.[50] This early papyrus codex of *De placitis* also counters,

---

48. Introduction, *De libris propriis*: II 91–93 Müller = XIX 8–11 Kühn.

49. Some have argued that *Introductio sive medicus* (Εἰσαγωγή, above pp. 25–30) is a treatise which exemplifies Galen's experience among the booksellers in which he finds a work falsely attributed to him. J. Kollesch, *Untersuchungen zu den pseudogalenischen Definitiones medicae* (Berlin 1973) 33–34, re-examines the matter and prefers the explanation of H. Diels, that the treatise is more likely to have joined the Galenic Corpus after Galen's lifetime, as medical students depended upon it together with other treatises written by Galen himself.

50. V. Nutton, in his edition of *De praecognitione* ( = *CMG* v 8,1, Berlin 1979) 48–51, suggests that a copy of *De praecognitione* survived the fire in the Temple of Peace in A.D. 192, but that Galen himself was unaware of it and could find no trace of such a copy. Hence, Galen does not mention *De praecog.* in *De libris propriis*, because he despaired of its survival and saw no point in including a treatise which, as far as he knew, had already been lost. Galen's exaggerations in matters of personal importance are noted by Nutton: see, e.g., p. 146, and also 'Galen and medical autobiography', *Proceedings of the Cambridge Philological Society* n.s. 18 (1972) 50–62.

to some extent, the impression given by the text preserved in the sixth-century papyrus codex of Galen's *De compositione medicamentorum*,[51] where divergencies from the Kühn edition are more extensive. Yet these differences are to be attributed to the nature of that work itself, whereby the textual integrity of a series of prescriptions, of the kind that comprise *De compositione*, is more subject to changes, such as substitution among ingredients and interpolation of new prescriptions, because it is a living text and continually in use, ameliorated to suit present practice. By contrast, a serious work of medical philosophy and philosophical medicine, such as *De placitis*, is less subject to such changes.[52]

In any case, by virtue of its date, the papyrus codex of *De placitis* also provides some degree of independent corroboration for Galen's claim that in his lifetime, or shortly thereafter, he was known in the provinces. He boasts that he corresponded with farflung provincials and healed them at long distance by letter; his assertion implies wide circulation of his works.[53] The copy of his *De placitis*, circulating in Egypt, far from Rome, in the first half of the third century, lends support to that claim.

The following restorations of the two folia are offered by way of example. They differ on occasion from the arrangement in the

51. But see also the cautions of U. Fleischer regarding conclusions drawn on the basis of the text in the edition by Kühn, in his review of *The Antinoopolis Papyri* III in *Gnomon* 41 (1969) 640. The sixteen-syllable-to-a-line edition of Galen, posited by Schöne and perhaps exemplified by *P. Ant.* III 186 = Marganne no. 69 (so Fleischer), is not apparent in the codex of the *De placitis*.

52. So also D. Manetti, *op. cit.* (n. 33) 123. Revision of classical texts which remain in use continues: e.g. N. G. Wilson, *Scholars of Byzantium* (Baltimore 1983) 232, notes the corrections of Aratus by Maximus Planudes.

53. *De locis affectis* IV 2, VIII 224.7ff. Kühn. For the localities involved, see V. Nutton, 'Galen in the Eyes of his Contemporaries', *Bulletin of the History of Medicine* 58 (1984) 315–24 n. 6; I am grateful to Dr Nutton for sharing his work with me in advance of publication. Medical consultation by correspondence over some distance is perhaps exemplified by the letter of Chairas to Dionysios ἰατρός (A.D. 50, *P. Mert.* I 12). Galen's claims to importance within his lifetime have been seen as lacking objective confirmation outside Galen's own writings: for arguments and references to earlier literature, see J. Scarborough, 'The Galenic Question', *Sudhoffs Archiv* 65 (1981) 1–31; for counter-arguments, especially in regard to Galen's impact on fellow Greeks, see V. Nutton, 'Galen in the Eyes of his Contemporaries' (*art. cit.* above). Galen's early fame is also as a philosopher, although this aspect of his work has often been neglected because his position as doctor became dominant in the medical schools: M. Frede, 'On Galen's Epistemology', in V. Nutton, *Galen: Problems and Prospects* (London 1981) 65–86.

ed. prin.; the number of letters suggested here per line varies between 28 and 33 on recto, and between 29 and 34 on verso.

Recto                                                    Plate Va

De plac. 1 7.44–47 (CMG v, 4, 1,2, p. 88 De Lacy)
[μ]ειзο[νες πολλω της προειρημενης]
[α]λλαι δ[ε δυο κατ επιγαστριον τε και τας]
ψοας κα[θ εκαστον σπονδυλον εν зευ-
4      γος αχρι [του πλατεος οστου και μεν γε και]
εις τας μ[ητρας τε και ορχεις εντευθεν]
κ[ατ]ερχον[ται και τις αзυγης εις μεσεν-]
[τερι]ọṿ αλλα [και εις αυτον εισω τον νωτι-
8      [αιο]ṿ απο της μ[εγαλης αρτηριας καθ]
[ολη]ν την ραχιν εμ[φυονται τινες αρτη-]
[ρια]ι μικραι δυο καθ [εκαστον σπονδυλον]
[επ]ẹιδạṿ δε κατα τ̣[ο ιερον οστουν γενηται]
12     [σ]χ[ι]зετα[ι] τουντευ[θεν ηδη μεγαλα με-]
ρη [κ]ạι κατερχ[ε]ται τ[ις εις εκατερον]
σκελος εṿ τη παροδ[ω τοις καθ ιερον ο-]
[σ]τουν αποβλαστημạ[τα πεμψασα κυστει
16     [τε] κạị της μητρας [τοις κατω και ξυνελον-]
[τι φ]αναι τοις γεννητικ[οις απασι μορι-]
[οις] ουδεν γαρ ετι δεομαι λε[γειν ουδ εν-]
[ταυ]θα τον τροπον της διανọ[μης απο του-]
20     [τω]ṿ των αρτηριων επι τα σκ[ελη φερομενων]

Verso                                                    Plate Vb

De plac. 1 7.52–55 (CMG v 4, 1,2, p. 90 De Lacy)
[πνευμονα τοις зωοις απασιν] οις π̣[νευμων]
[εστιν οις δ ουκ εστιν εις ε]τερον [τι μορ-]
[ιον αναλογον υπαρχον πν]ευμο[νι καθαπερ]
4      [τοις ιχθυσιν εις τα βραγ]χια ταυτην [την]
[αρτηριαν εικασειεν αν τις] τω του πρε[μνου]
[κατωθεν εν αυτη τη γη] ε[μ]περι[εχ]ọμ[ενω]
[μερει του φυτου και δη κ]αι κα[τασχι]зε[σ-]
8      [θαι ταυτην μεν ως α]ṿ εις ριзας τι[νας]
[τας κατα τον πνευμο]να πεφυκυιας [αρ-]
[τηριας την μεγαλην] δε την εις ολον [το]
[σωμα νενεμημεν]ην οιονπερ κλα[δο]υς
12     [απομεριзειν εαυτ]ης απασα[ς] τας κατα το
[зωον αρτηριας] ολιγ[ο]ν εμπροσθεν ει-
[πον ουτως γαρ ηγο]υμαι και τον ιπποκρατ[ην]
[προσεικασαντα ρ]ιзωσιν αρτηριων αποφ[αι-]
16     [νεσθαι την καρ]διạṿ ωσπερ αμελει των φ[λε-]

[βων το ηπαρ ει]ρησεται δε μοι περι της ε̣[ικο-]
[νος επι πλεον] εν τοις εξης επειδα̣ν υπ[ερ]
[ηπατος τε] και φλεβων ο λογο̣[ς] περα̣ι[νηται]
[νυν δ αρκει] και τα λελεγμενα προ[ς ενδει-]

Recto

Line **9.** ἐμ[φύονται: ἐκφύονται C. Compare the similar examples of carelessness by a copier in C, corrected by editorial revision: Caius' correction of C's περαίνεται, verso line 19, and Einarson's correction of C's βρόγχια, verso line 4. For readings of C and the text of *De placitis* with which the papyrus has been compared, see the edition by P. De Lacy, *Galeni de Plac. Hipp. et Plat.* i–v, *CMG* v 4, 1,2 (Berlin 1978) 88–90.

**17.** The left edge of the *epsilon* in γεννητικοῖς appears on *P. Mon. Gr.* inv. 329 and the right edge of the horizontals in *P. Berol.* 21141.

**20.** τῶν ἀρτηρίων ἐπί: τῶν ἀρτ. τῶν ἐπί C, rightly. Compare the successful marginal additions in C by C² of περί, verso line 17, and εἰς, verso line 2.

Verso

Line **2.** [οἷς δ' οὐκ]: οἷς δὲ οὐκ C. Considerations of space favor elision here, as below in line 20.

**14.** [ἡγο]ῦμαι: οἴμαι C. Considerations of space and meticulous orthography elsewhere seem to favor the interpretation of ]υμαι as [ἡγο]ῦμαι, rather than as ]ῦμαι, a vulgar spelling of οἶμαι. In the *De placitis*, Galen employs οἶμαι, both parenthetically and as main verb, far more frequently than ἡγοῦμαι. Yet the latter appears at least four times in *De placitis* i–v, *CMG* v 4, 1,2: ii 5.24.5, iii 4.15.6, v 1.10.2, v 6.13.3, all principal verbs as here. (The occurrence at iii 8.33.2 is within a quotation from Plato.) The interchange of οι and υ, is admittedly '...the most frequent interchange in the [documentary] papyri next to the interchanges of ει with ι and of αι with ε': F. Gignac, *A Grammar of the Greek Papyri of the Roman and Byzantine Periods* i (Milan 1976) 197–99.

**16.** There remain in *P. Berol.* 21141 only small traces of the bottoms of about seven letters, but those traces are compatible with καρ]δ̣ι̣α̣ν̣ ω̣σ̣π.

**20.** [νῦν δ' ἀρκεῖ] καὶ τὰ λελεγμένα πρό]ς ἔνδει-/ξιν: νυνὶ δὲ ἀρκεῖ τὰ λεγόμενα πρὸς ἔνδειξιν C. Considerations of space favor νῦν δ' ἀρκ. in lacuna. The reading of the papyrus with καὶ τὰ λελεγμένα is superior to that preserved in C: above pp. 43–44.

47

# Istruzioni dietetiche e farmacologiche

ISABELLA ANDORLINI

*P. Lit. Lond.* 170\* è un frammento dello stesso rotolo da cui proviene *P. Mich.* inv. 1469, recentemente edito da L. C. Youtie–H. C. Youtie, *A Medical Papyrus*, in *Scritti in onore di O. Montevecchi* (Bologna 1981) 431–36 (tav. a p. 436). Il pregevole manufatto può esser stato scritto alla fine del II o agli inizî del III sec. d.C. La scrittura diritta mostra caratteristiche grafiche riscontrabili in esemplari di "stile severo",[1] temperate da un andamento morbido che attenua la rigidità nell'esecuzione delle lettere e tende a ridimensionare il contrasto tra lettere larghe e strette, dando l'impressione di una certa uniformità di modulo. Si inserisce dunque sulla linea grafica che dalle scritture dei *P. Oxy.* x 1234 (II[p] ex.), Pl. IV (anche in Schubart, *Gr. Pal.*, Abb. 84), *P. Oxy.* IX 1174 (II[p] ex., in E. G. Turner, *Greek Manuscripts of the Ancient World* (Princeton 1971) fig. 34) conduce ad esempi dell'inizio del III[p], quali *P. Oxy.* VII 1012 (*post* 205[p]) e 1016 (*post* 235[p], cfr. *ZPE* 21 (1976) 14).[2]

I due frammenti, di Londra e di Michigan, presentano formato e stato di conservazione analoghi, tanto da apparire quasi sovrapponibili: il papiro Michigan conserva la parte superiore di una colonna, quello di Londra la parte inferiore; quasi certamente si

---

\* Ho potuto controllare il papiro, conservato alla British Library (inv. 2559), sulla fotografia gentilmente concessa per studio all'Istituto Papirologico "G. Vitelli". Ringrazio il Dr T. S. Pattie e la British Library per il permesso di riedizione del testo. *P. Lit. Lond.* 170 è stato acquistato nel 1924. Corrisponde a Pack[2] 2404 ed è incluso in M.-H. Marganne, *Inventaire analytique des papyrus grecs de médecine* (Genève 1981) no. 106.

1. Come suggeriscono i paralleli citati nell'edizione di *P. Mich.* inv. 1469, *loc. cit.* 431. Peculiari la forma di ω, di ε e c a schiena appiattita, la larghezza del μ che conserva il disegno elementare dei tratti mediani; rompono il bilinearismo τ, ρ, υ, ε, φ: la parte terminale delle aste di tali lettere (come pure talvolta di π ed η) ha una leggera tendenza a curvare a destra.

2. Qualche affinità si può riscontrare anche con la scrittura di *P. Oxy.* XIII 1611 (III[p] in.) di cui ho visto una fotografia.

tratta di due colonne diverse del rotolo, in quanto la colonna ricostituita dai due frammenti sovrapposti risulterebbe troppo alta.

Nel papiro di Londra non restano segni di punteggiatura (come invece accade nel papiro Michigan); si osserva una *diple obelismene* (tra i rr. 15–16) che evidenzia l'inizio di un paragrafo esemplificativo, in cui si applica ad un caso specifico la normativa descritta poco sopra.[3] Lo *iota* muto ascritto (r. 19; 24) non è costante (vedi ιδιωτη r. 15).

I due testi si soccorrono a vicenda per l'interpretazione complessiva dell'argomento oggetto di trattazione. Nel papiro Michigan sono esposte norme dietetiche differenziate a seconda della costituzione dei pazienti e volte ad indicare il regime cui deve attenersi chi soffre di costipazione intestinale (rr. 11–12 τῆς [κάτω κοι]/λίας ἐπὶ πλέον ἐκλυθ[είσης); nel papiro di Londra è illustrato un trattamento terapeutico a base di farmaci, e per di più di rimedi composti (rr. 12; 15): si può intuire che il *kataplasma* è la forma medicamentosa di base dalla quale si possono ottenere varianti anche complesse. In entrambi i testi l'esposizione procede per casistiche alternative (*P. Mich.* inv. 1469.5 τοῖς μὲ[ν; 9 τοῖς [δ']) o successive (*P. Mich.* inv. 1469.15 συμβ[α]ί[ν]ει γά[ρ; *P. Lit. Lond.* 170.15–16 ὅ]/ταν μὲν οὔ[ν). Il fatto che nei due papiri ritorni la menzione degli occhi, forse come parte offesa, fa convergere la nostra attenzione su questo tema: in *P. Mich.* inv. 1469.13ss. si accenna al danno che i disturbi interni possono provocare agli occhi, mentre di una terapia a base di cataplasmi – forse da applicarsi sugli occhi – potrebbe trattarsi in *P. Lit. Lond.* 170.10 e ss.[4] Il trattato da cui sono stralciati i frammenti che possediamo sembra affrontare in modo complesso la terapia dei casi pratici, associando norme dietetiche a prescri-

3. Dobbiamo sospettare che si tratti dello stesso segno anche in *P. Mich.* inv. 1469.15–16? Con συμβαίνει γάρ (r. 15) si procede infatti ad una casistica diversa e specifica. Non è raro incontrare nella stessa trattazione segni di *paragraphos* e di *diple obelismene* intese a segnalare fasi di passaggio, oppure nuclei nello sviluppo del discorso: vedi *P. Oxy.* XIII 1611 (trattato letterario, III[p] in.) e in generale Turner, *Greek Manuscripts*, introd. 14s.

4. Da *P. Mich.* inv. 1469.13–15 si desume che del rischio che la costipazione offenda gli occhi si è già detto; da quel che segue però pare che l'autore si accinga a trattare più esaurientemente l'argomento, e questo fa pensare che il frammento di Londra possa venir dopo quello di Michigan.

zioni farmacologiche, come accade in ogni composizione pratica seria. Possiamo farci un'idea dei temi che rientrano in questo contesto leggendo il cap. 9 del Περὶ ὄψιος ippocratico,[5] oppure scorrendo i commentarî di Galeno *In Hipp. vel Polybi De salubri victus ratione* (xv 174ss. Kühn), oppure *In Hipp. De victu acutorum* (xv 418ss.). Merita riportare un passo di Oribasio in cui si avverte che, in caso di oftalmia causata da eccesso di umori, è bene prima di tutto liberare il ventre e poi applicare i farmaci adatti a disperdere umori e secrezioni (*Syn.* viii 40.8 = *CMG* vi 3, p. 263, 7ss. Raeder): πάχους δ' ὄντος τοῦ τὴν ὀφθαλμίαν ποιοῦντος, θεραπεύειν πρὸ πάντων μὲν τὴν κοιλίαν εὔλυτον ποιοῦντα, τὰς ὑπαλείψεις δὲ φαρμάκοις μήτε ἐμπλάσσουσι μήτε παχύνουσι τὰ ὑγρά, ἀλλὰ διαχέειν τε καὶ ὑγραίνειν καὶ ἐκκρίνειν δυναμένοις.[6]

Il testo di *P. Lit. Lond.* 170 contiene nozioni di un certo interesse: menziona rimedi che si ottengono combinando prodotti con proprietà diverse (si tratta cioè di σύνθετα, *scil.* φάρμακα), di facile preparazione anche per un profano (ἰδιώτης r. 15): segno che la materia trattata si propone anche ad un pubblico di non iniziati.[7] Il rimedio di cui si dà la composizione appartiene alla categoria di quelli complessi:[8] al tuorlo d'uovo va mescolato un quantitativo di un preparato già pronto, cosiddetto τὸ 'Ανδρώνειον φάρμακον. La citazione di un farmaco rinomato del medico Androne, già

---

5. Nel caso di oftalmie accompagnate da dolori è prevista innanzi tutto la κάθαρσις, cui giova un regime dietetico adeguato: Hipp. *Vid. ac.* ix 1–3 (in *Hippocrate*, tome xiii, par R. Joly (Paris 1978)) 'Οφθαλμίης τῆς ἐπετείου καὶ ἐπιδημίου συμφέρει κάθαρσις κεφαλῆς καὶ τῆς κάτω κοιλίης. (...) ἐπειδὰν ἥ τε ὀδύνη παύσηται καὶ διαχωρισθῇ μετὰ τὴν ἐσάλειψιν τοῦ φαρμάκου, τότε συμφέρει καταπλάσσειν τῶν καταπλασμάτων ὅ τι ἄν σοι δοκῇ συμφέρειν.

6. Vedi anche Aët. vii 46 (*CMG* viii 2, p. 300, 26s. Olivieri: il paragrafo è intitolato Περὶ ὀφθαλμῶν) χρῆσθαι δὲ καὶ ὑδροποσίᾳ καὶ διαίτῃ μέσῃ. E ancora Alessandro di Tralle (ii 59–62 Puschmann) descrive il regime dietetico da osservare in caso di affezioni agli occhi particolarmente fastidiose.

7. Agli ἰδιῶται sono destinate tra l'altro le opere di carattere dietetico, quasi dei manuali divulgativi accessibili anche al grosso pubblico: Ps. Hipp. *Vict.* 1 Τοὺς ἰδιώτας ὧδε χρὴ διατᾶσθαι (cfr. il commento di Galeno, xv 175–77 Kühn) ed in generale J. Jouanna, 'Le problème de l'unité du traité du régime dans les maladies aiguës', in *Actes du colloque hippocratique de Mons, 22–26 septembre 1975*, ed. R. Joly (Mons 1977) 297 e nota 23.

8. La nozione dei σύνθετα φάρμακα rientra nelle teorie dei medici empirici, cfr. K. Deichgräber, *Die Empirikerschule*, Fr. 106. Una traccia della polemica anti-empirica di Erasistrato, su questo punto, resta in Gal. *De sect.* v 16–17 (= iii, p. 9, 16–17 Helmreich).

ricordato da Erasistrato (Gal. xii 905 = Deichgräber, *Die Empiri-kerschule*, Fr. 65), utilizzato da Eraclide di Taranto e ampiamente menzionato da Galeno,[9] può aiutarci a collocare culturalmente e cronologicamente la materia medica conservata nei nostri papiri.

P. *Lit. Lond.* 170
Recto

```
                    . . .
                ].[
    [    ].τω..[
    [...]υς οτευ.[
    [...]δυνος α[
5   α[ἱ] φλεγμον[αὶ
    καὶ τὰ ἄλγη ..[
    πολὺ παύεται κ[
    τὴν εἰρημέν[ην θεραπεί-
    αν πρὸς δ[..]ομ[
10  τῶν ὀφθαλμῶν [κατ]απ[λάσ-
    ματι χρῆσθαι κα[.].ουτ[
    συντίθεται δὲ πλείω π[
    καταπλασμάτων· η[
    ται δὲ αὐτ[ῶ]ν τὰ χαρίε[ντα
15  καὶ ἰδιώτη εὐσύνθετα[· ὅ-
    ταν μὲν οὖ[ν ὁ ὁ]φ[θαλμὸς ἐπώ-
    δυνος ἦ μ[    ].[
    καταπλάσμασ[ι
    ᾠὸν ὀπτήσαντ[ες τὸ πυρ-
20  ρὸν αὐτοῦ τρείβ[ειν λεῖον,
    μιγνύειν δὲ τού[τῳ τοῦ 'Αν-
    δρωνείου τοῦ πρ[ὸς τὰ ῥεύ-
    ματα φαρμάκο[υ τὸ τρίτον
    μέρος, τοῦ ᾠο[ῦ δὲ
```

3 ὅτε ὑσ[τερον?  4 [ἀνώ]δυνος *ed. princ.*: possibile anche [κίν]δυνος *e.g.* P. *Mich.* inv. 1469, 13  7–8 κ[ατὰ τὴν αὐ]/τήν?  9 αντιος α[.]ομ[ *ed. princ.*: /αν πρὸς δ[ὲ τ]ὸ μ[ ?  10 [τε κ]αὶ *ed. princ.*  13–14 ϡη[τεῖ]/ται? 15 εὐσυνθέτω[ς *ed. princ.*  16–17 περιώ]/δυνος *ed. princ.*  17–19 μ[ιγν]ύ[ειν δεῖ τοῖς]/ καταπλάσμασ[ι τοῦτο· τὸ]/ ᾠὸν ὀπτήσαντ[ες?  19 ωιον pap. 20 *l.* τρίβειν  24 ωιο[ pap.

9. Il medicamento di Androne è quindi presente nella letteratura medica posteriore, greca e latina. Eraclide utilizzò le ricette di Androne nell'opera Πρὸς 'Αντιοχίδα, cfr. Gal. *Comp. sec. loc.* vi 8 (xii 983s. Kühn = Deichgräber, Fr. 205). Vedi *R-E* i.2 (1894) s.v. Andron 16 (M. Wellmann) e, per le citazioni in Galeno (desunte da Andromaco e da Asclepiade), cfr. C. Fabricius, *Galens Exzerpte aus älteren Pharmakologen* (Berlin/New York 1972) 27 nota 31; 121 ("Ars medica ii 2").

Rigo **6.** Preferirei leggere in questo punto ἀλγήμᾳ[τα ὡς ἐπὶ τὸ] o sim.; tuttavia prima della lacuna potrebbe esserci spazio per tre lettere (cioè αλγη[.]..[ pap.), ma non abbastanza per il primo *alpha* di ᾳνᾳ[ *ed. princ.* Per intendere la frase si può provare [ἐ]κλ[ύεται, ma la lettura ᾳ[ resta senz'altro più plausibile. La soluzione meglio compatibile con le tracce in fine rigo (in accordo col testo di *P. Mich.* inv. 1469) mi pare τὰ ἄλγη κᾳ[τω κοιλίας].

**9.** La lettura αγτιος *ed. princ.* porta con sé la difficoltà di collegare col resto della frase una forma nom., ad es. ἐναντίος, ὑπεναντίος o sim. Concettualmente l'aggettivo ἐναντίος può collocarsi nell'ambito del principio *contraria contrariis*, cui obbediscono la dietetica e la farmacologia: cfr. Deichgräber, *op. cit.* 69ss. Una lettura alternativa: πρὸς δ[ὲ τ]ὸ μ[ . Poteva seguire un vocabolo indicante la διάθεσις degli occhi, come il nome di un'affezione piuttosto comune curabile con un *kataplasma*. Un termine specifico quale μ[υοκέφαλον risultrebbe inadeguato al contesto; forse non abbastanza indicativa una locuzione relativa alla parte dell'occhio da curare, ad es. πρὸς δ[ὲ τ]ὸ μ[όριον πέριξ] (cfr. Gal. xii 711, 24 Kühn), oppure πρὸς δ[ὲ τ]ὸ μ[όνον ἄνω?] (cfr. Aët. vii 24 καὶ τὸ ἄνω μόνον βλέφαρον καταπλαττέσθω). Una frase del tipo πρὸς δ[ὲ τ]ὸ μ[ὴ παύσασθαι/(*scil.* τὰ ἄλγη) τῶν ὀφθαλμῶν non si regge grammaticalmente, tanto da indurci a provare l'integrazione ὀφθαλμ[ι]ῶν. Senz'altro migliore πρὸς δ[ὲ τ]ὸ μ[έγα ῥεῦμα] che ricorda le indicazioni terapeutiche frequenti in Galeno e altrove, cfr. Gal. *Comp. sec. loc.* iv 7 (xii 742s. Kühn) *passim*: πρὸς μεγίστας ἐπιφοράς, πρὸς ῥεῦμα πολὺ καὶ περιωδυνίας.

**11.** Fa difficoltà l'integrazione in fine rigo, dal momento che prima di συντίθεται δέ (r. 12) dobbiamo ammettere una pausa. Non saprei pensare ad altro che a κα[ὶ] τουτ[ (sembra di scorgere in margine alla lacuna anche la traccia finale dell'asta del primo τ): forse κα[ὶ] τούτ[οις, *scil.* ὀφθαλμοῖς? Ricorrere al *kataplasma*, magari già impiegato in precedenza per malanni dell'apparato digerente (rr. 5–6), va bene anche per le infiammazioni agli occhi. Se invece ammettiamo che la lacuna possa essere colmata da una sola lettera (lo scriba ha già occupato più spazio del consueto scrivendo κα[ pap.), risulterebbe più appropriata la formula κα[ὶ] οὔτ[ως], intesa ad introdurre la successiva descrizione dell'impiego del farmaco, ovvero la χρῆσις.

**12–13.** τ[ερὶ] (opp. τ[ρὸς])/ καταπλασμάτων? L'espressione

53

non si collega però né con ciò che precede, né con ciò che segue. Preferirei senz'altro γ[ε τῶν]/ καταπλασμάτων, se non fosse troppo lungo per la lacuna.

**13–14.** ȝη[τεῖ]/ται? Forse resta appena una traccia della parte superiore di una lettera prima di *heta*; ῥη[θήσε]/ται è troppo lungo per lo spazio. Questo il senso del discorso: "fra i cataplasmi si richiedono (?) quelli gradevoli e di facile composizione anche per un profano". – χαρίε[ντα: la lettura del χ, compromessa da un foro del papiro proprio in questo punto, sembra però inevitabile per la ricostruzione della parola. Il termine χαρίεν per qualificare un tipo di medicina è insolito, ma non sarà difficile sentirlo come la logica antitesi di ἀχάριστος: per il senso vedi in *BASP* 18 (1981) 6ss. Rimedio "gradito e utile" al tempo stesso, inteso a venire incontro alle esigenze del paziente, che nel nostro caso si identifica con l'ἰδιώτης (r. 15). Pur nei termini sintetici della trattazione pratica, riusciamo a cogliere il riflesso della persuasione della medicina ippocratica dell' ὠφελεῖν ἢ μὴ βλάπτειν (Hipp. *Epid.* I 11.11 Jones). Per intendere il concetto e per ulteriori spunti, vedi Ippocrate, *Epidemie* VI, a cura di D. Manetti e A. Roselli (Firenze 1982) 87. Con questo stesso significato credo debba essere inteso il vocabolo nella formula χαρίεν δὲ καὶ πρός, in *P. Hibeh* II 191.6 e 8, dove il termine è usato parallelamente a σπουδαῖον, *scil.* φάρμακον.

**15–18.** Il passo si presta perlomeno ad una duplice interpretazione. (1) La terapia consiglia di applicare, nel caso di manifestazioni dolorose, cataplasmi a base di tuorlo d'uovo: ὅταν μὲν οὔ[ν ὁ ὀ]φ[θαλμὸς ἐπώ]/δυνος ᾖ, μ[ιγν]ύ[ειν δεῖ τοῖς]/ καταπλάσμασ[ι τοῦτο· τὸ]/ κτλ. (né si può escludere ἡ κε]φ[αλὴ ἐπώ]/δυνος; περιώδυνος sembra invece troppo lungo). Questa ipotesi è confortata da una prescrizione di Eraclide di Taranto riportata da Galeno (XII 743, 2ss. Kühn) Καταπλάσματα ὀφθαλμιώντων πρὸς περιωδυνίας καὶ μεγίστας ἐπιφοράς, οἷς ἐχρήσατο Ἡρακλείδης ὁ Ταραντῖνος; la ricetta si conclude con ὠοῦ ὀπτοῦ τὴν λέκιθον τρίψας...χρῶ. (2) Se utilizziamo puntualmente il passo di Ippocrate sopra citato (*Vid. ac.* IX, ed. R. Joly), dobbiamo pensare che ai cataplasmi si ricorra quando è cessato il dolore (cioè ἀνώ]/δυνος), oppure che si preferisca un rimedio a base di tuorlo d'uovo e di "pillola" di Androne: μ[ὴ δεῖ χ]ρ[ῆσθαι τοῖς]/ καταπλάσμασ[ι, ἀλλὰ τὸ]/ ὠόν κτλ.

**18.** Per la forma del *kataplasma*, cfr. D. Goltz, "Studien zur altorient. und griech. Heilkunde", in *AGM* 16 (Wiesbaden 1974) 213s. Il *kataplasma* agisce contro ogni tipo di infiammazione: Diosc. *Simpl.* 1 30 (III, p. 162 Wellmann) πρὸς δὲ τὰς φλεγμονὰς τῶν ὀφθαλμῶν καταπλάσματα ἁρμόζει; Orib. *Ad Eunap.* IV 15. 4 (*CMG* VI 3, p. 445, 14–15 Raeder) μεγάλης δ᾽ οὔσης τῆς ἐπιφορᾶς μετὰ περιωδυνίας, κατάπλασσε οὕτως; Aët. VII 98 (*CMG* VIII 2, p. 342 Olivieri) καταπλάσματα ὀφθαλμῶν.

**19–20.** L'impiego del tuorlo d'uovo (che è sempre chiamato λέκιθος), per la preparazione dei cataplasmi antinfiammatorî, è ampiamente documentato: Diosc. *Mat. med.* II 50 (I, p. 136, 14ss. Wellmann) ὡὸν τὸ ἁπαλὸν πολυτροφώτερον τοῦ ῥοφητοῦ, καὶ τοῦ ἁπαλοῦ τὸ σκληρόν. ἡ δὲ λέκιθος αὐτοῦ ἑφθὴ χρησίμη πρὸς ὀφθαλμῶν περιωδυνίας σὺν κρόκῳ καὶ ῥοδίνῳ. Gal. *Simpl. medic.* XI 31 (XII 352.3ss. Kühn) ἔστι δὲ καὶ ἡ λέκιθος τῶν ὡῶν ὁμοίας φύρεως (= potenzialità essiccante), καὶ διὰ τοῦτο μίγνυται κηρωταῖς ἀδήκτοις ἑψηθέντων ἢ ὀπτηθέντων τῶν ὡῶν...μίγνυται δὲ καὶ καταπλάσμασι ἀφλεγμάντοις. L'uso di τὸ πυρρόν per indicare il rosso dell'uovo è piuttosto raro: rientra in farmaci emollienti in Hipp. *Mul.* II 171 (= VIII, p. 352, 11 Littré) ὡοῦ τὸ πυρρόν; in un collirio cosiddetto πηλάριον, in Aët. VII 103 (*CMG* VIII 2, p. 360, 19 Olivieri) κατουλοῖ μάλιστα τῷ πυρρῷ μιγνύμενον; in un rimedio oftalmico esterno troviamo πυρρῶν ὡῶν ἑπτὰ ἑκζεστῶν, in Alex. Trall. II 7. – τρείβ[ειν: per la compiutezza dell'operazione è di solito richiesto l'aggettivo λεῖος (ad es. *P. Oxy.* 1088.28–29), oppure λείως, καλῶς.

**21–23.** τοῦ Ἀν]/δρωνείου...φαρμάκο[υ: questo medicamento aveva la forma farmacologica del *trochiscos* ed eccelleva per potenzialità astringenti, cfr. Gal. *Comp. sec. loc.* VI 1 (XII 904.2–3 Kühn) καὶ αὐτὸ τὸ Ἀνδρώνειον ἐν τῷ στύφειν ἔχει τὸ κῦρος τῆς θεραπείας. In questo caso andrà a comporre un rimedio esterno, come è previsto anche dalla distinzione che leggiamo in Oribasio, *Coll. med.* X 24.1 Τροχίσκων εἴδη εἰσὶ τρία· οἱ μὲν γάρ εἰσι πινόμενοι, οἱ δ᾽ ἐνιέμενοι, οἱ δὲ καταχριόμενοι. E la "pillola" di Androne rientrava in questa categoria, cfr. Orib. *ibid.* 24.10 οἱ δὲ κατάχριστοι τροχίσκοι δυνάμεως μέν εἰσι παραπλησίας τοῖς ἐνιεμένοις· οἱ μὲν γὰρ στύφουσιν, ὡς ὁ Ἄνδρωνος καὶ ὁ Πολυείδου.

**22–23.** πρ[ὸς τὰ ῥεύ]/ματα. Per i suoi effetti astringenti la "pillola" risulterebbe adatta "contro le secrezioni (oftalmiche?)";

tuttavia il confronto con Gal. XII 984.3–5 Kühn τῇ 'Ανδρωνείῳ δυνάμει, ἣν ἐν τοῖς τραυματικοῖς ἐκθήσομαι, rende possibile anche τραύ]/ματα (οἰδήματα?).

**24.** μέρος: cfr. *P. Hibeh* II 192.11 e 16; *P. Berl. Möller* 13.8 (= Marganne, *Inventaire*, no. 71); il sistema di indicare in "parti" proporzionali i quantitativi di prodotto richiesto, è adottato, ad esempio, da Eraclide di Taranto, cfr. Deichgräber, *Die Empirikerschule*, Fr. 208.

# Six ἐντεύξεις de Mouchis

## JEAN SCHERER

Dans le lot des papyrus de Mouchis acquis par l'Institut de Papyrologie de la Sorbonne[1] figurent six fragments qui ont cette caractéristique commune d'être, *grosso modo*, des moitiés d' ἐντεύξεις. Alors que l'ἔντευξις complète a normalement une largeur d'environ 33 cm, la largeur de nos fragments varie entre 15,5 et 17 cm;[2] manifestement ces ἐντεύξεις faisaient partie d'une liasse que l'artisan, qui fabriqua le cartonnage, coupa par le milieu dans le sens de la hauteur. Seul le texte V est une moitié droite; les cinq autres sont des moitiés gauches. On peut croire que les moitiés manquantes ont servi pour un autre cartonnage.[3]

C'est dans l'espoir que celles-ci seront un jour retrouvées que nous publions ces fragments. Ce sont proprement des textes "en attente": ils attendent leur complément et avec lui leur véritable interprétation. Dans leur état actuel, le commentaire est malaisé et il serait hasardeux de vouloir présenter avec précision les affaires en question.

Les apostilles sont écrites en toutes lettres, sans abréviations. Aucune ne se lit en entier. Mais les éléments conservés dans les textes I, II, III, V et VI permettent de reconstituer la formule: Δημητρίωι· μάλιστα μὲν (I et VI) διάλυσον αὐτούς (II)· εἰ δὲ μή, ἀπόστειλον αὐτοὺς (V, ἀπόστειλον πρὸς ἡμᾶς III) ὅπως (III) ἐπὶ τοῦ καθήκοντος κριτηρίου (VI) διακριθῶσιν (II, V).

---

1. Voir *P. Turner* 16 et les *P. Sorbonne* inv. 2410 et 2414 publiés dans *Mém. Inst. fr. Arch. or.* 104 (1980: *Livre du Centenaire*) 307–10.

2. Ces moitiés ne sont donc pas strictement égales et le nombre des lettres n'est pas exactement le même dans la partie conservée et dans la partie manquante. Nous indiquons quel est, selon nous, le nombre approximatif des lettres manquantes, compte tenu de la largeur du fragment conservé et aussi de la marge (plus ou moins importante, variant de 0,7 cm à 3 cm) ménagée à gauche, en début de lignes, par le scribe.

3. Sur la dispersion des documents dans des cartonnages, ou des momies, différents, cf. O. Guéraud, Ἐντεύξεις, p. x, et l'introduction de *P. Sorbonne* 46.

L'apostille de IV fait exception: elle demande à l'épistate un *rapport* (διασάφησον) sur l'affaire.

La date figure seulement sur V qui conserve la partie droite du document; son déchiffrement est incertain; si la lecture (ἔτους) α était exacte, l'ἔντευξις serait de 221 av. J.-C. Comme toutes ces plaintes demandent l'intervention du stratège Diophanès, elles se placent dans la période 224/3–219/18 (*Prosop. Ptol.* I et VIII no. 247).

Le verso de II présente, au coin inférieur gauche, une courte notice du type ὁ δεῖνα πρὸς τὸν δεῖνα, sans date et sans résumé de l'affaire introduit par περί. Il en est peut-être de même au verso de I. Au verso de I, II, III et IV, bien détachée à droite (c'est-à-dire au milieu de l'ἔντευξις complète) et en grandes lettres, l'adresse de l'épistate: ΔΗΜΗΤΡΙΩΙ.

## I. Différend au sujet d'un gymnase

*P. Sorbonne* inv. 2401

16,5 × 11 cm; marge de 1,7 cm

Le plaignant est un Macédonien, Peukestès, qui apparemment jouit d'un σταθμός (l. 6). Sa plainte est dirigée contre deux Egyptiens et concerne un gymnase qu'il a construit (ἔκτισα, 3), peut-être après avoir élevé un mur qui partageait en deux son σταθμός (ἥμισυ διοικοδομήσας, 3). Complète, cette ἔντευξις apporterait sans doute un élément nouveau et intéressant sur le problème encore obscur de la création des gymnases à l'époque ptolémaïque et de la part qu'y prenait l'initiative privée; cf. les remarques d'O. Guéraud à propos de *P. Ent.* 8.

Βασιλεῖ Πτολεμαίωι χαίρειν Πευκέστης δ . [   ±26   ἀδικοῦμαι ὑπὸ
αρσοντωυτος καὶ 'Εφιμήνιος. 'Υπάρχοντος γάρ μοι[   ±38
ἥμισυ διοικοδομήσας ἔκτισα γυμνάσιον· ἐν δὲ τ . [   ±38
. . καὶ καταγεινομένου ἔτι πλεῖον καταγνόντες[   ±38
5 νι εγτων ἐν τῶι γυμ[ν]ασ[ί]ωι . υ . σο[ . . . ] . [ . ]ιβ . . [   ±40
σταθμὸν εἰσπορεύεσθαι φάμενος . . . . κέναι αυ . [   Δέομαι οὖν σου,
                              βασιλεῦ, προστάξαι Διοφάνηι τῶι
στρατηγῶι γράψαι Δημητρίωι τῶι ἐπιστάτ[ηι   ±36
τοὺς προγεγραμμένους ἀποστεῖλαι ἐπὶ Διο[φάνην   ±26   Τούτων
γὰρ γενομένων, διὰ σέ, βασιλεῦ, τοῦ δικαίου τ[εύξομαι.

10 (2ᵉ main) Δημητρίωι· μάλιστα [μὲν διάλυσον αὐτούς· εἰ δὲ μή,
ἀπόστειλον ὅπως ἐπὶ τοῦ καθήκοντος
κριτηρίο]υ διακριθῶσιν.

Verso
Traces d'écriture?          ΔΗΜΗΤΡΙΩΙ

Ligne **2.** Nous ne savons comment analyser le premier nom propre. Pour Ἐφιμῆνις, cf. J. Vergote, *Les noms propres du P. Bruxelles Inv. E. 7616 (Pap. Lugd.-Bat.* VII 1954) 8, no. 22.

**4.** Au début de la ligne, on est tenté de lire spontanément δε, mais la lecture est douteuse; le *ductus* serait anormal aussi bien pour le *delta* que pour l'*epsilon*.

**6.** Seules les lettres κεναι sont certaines; ρ κεναι est probable. Ni εἰρηκέναι ni πεπρακέναι ne nous paraissent cadrer clairement avec les traces d'écriture.

**11.** Après διακριθῶσιν des traces noirâtres qui sont peut-être les vestiges de la date.


## II. Plainte d'une femme contre son mari

*P. Sorbonne* inv. 2402
17 × 10,5 cm; marge de 1,8 cm

Une femme, Thauès, porte plainte contre son mari, Horos; il l'a chassée (ἐγβαλών, l. 2) et a commis quelque autre méfait concernant des vêtements (ἱματισμόν, 3). Dans sa requête elle demande l'intervention de l'"épistate Glaukos". Cependant l'apostille est adressée, comme d'habitude, à Démétrios; cf. aussi l'adresse du verso.

Le texte est d'une belle écriture, large et régulière (sauf à la dernière ligne) avec des "blancs" de ponctuation (après χαίρειν et avant δέομαι).

Βασιλεῖ Πτολεμαίωι χαίρειν Θαυῆς Φαυῆτος ἐγ Μο[ύχεως   ±19
                            ἀδικοῦμαι ὑπὸ
Ὥρου τοῦ Φάβιτος τοῦ ἀνδρός μου. Ἐγβαλὼν γάρ με ἐ[κ   ±35
ἱματισμὸν παραδεδωκυίας τέ μου αὐτὸν . [   ±36
αὐτὸν ἐξαιρεῖται. Δέομαι οὖν σου, βασιλεῦ, ε[ἴ σοι δοκεῖ, προστάξαι
                          Διοφάνει τῶι στρατηγῶι
5 γράψαι Γλαύκωι τῶι ἐπιστάτηι ἀποστε[ῖλαι   ±32

αὐτὸν ἐπὶ Διοφάνην, ὅπως τὰ δίκαιά μοι π[οιῆι καὶ διὰ σέ, βασιλεῦ,
τὸν πάντων κοινὸν
εὐεργέτην [τῆς παρὰ σοῦ] βοηθείας τύχω.
(2ᵉ main) Δημητρί[ωι· μάλιστα] μὲν διάλυσον αὐτούς·[
ὅπως ἐπὶ .[..]..[.....]ηρίου δι̣α̣κριθῶσιν.

Verso
Θαυῆς π[ρὸς]                                       ΔΗΜΗΤΡΙΩΙ
Ὧρον

**Lignes 3–4.** Etant donné l'importance des lacunes, il est peut-être imprudent de rapprocher les mots ἱματισμὸν...ἐξαιρεῖται.

**4–5.** Si la lacune de la ligne 4 peut être facilement suppléée *exempli gratia*, on voit mal ce qu'on pourrait suppléer à la ligne 5. Notre moitié de texte semble apporter la formule attendue ἀποστεῖλαι αὐτὸν ἐπὶ Διοφάνην. Faut-il supposer une variante dans le formulaire ou un biffage important dans la lacune?

**5.** Glaukos n'est pas épistate mais phylacite : φυλακίτης κώμης Μούχεως, cf. l'article des *Mém. Inst. fr. Arch. or.* (cité ci-dessus, n. 1) 310.

**9.** ἐπὶ τοῦ καθήκοντος κριτηρίου est un peu trop long pour la lacune.

## III. Vol d'objets

*P. Sorbonne* inv. 2405
17 × 20,7 cm; marge de 2,5 cm

L'origine de l'affaire n'apparaît pas clairement. A la suite, semble-t-il, du décès de Stratonikè (l. 4), la plaignante, dont le nom n'est pas conservé, eut à subir les mépris (καταφρονήσας, 7) et les procédés malhonnêtes d'un certain Démétrios qui, amenant son frère avec lui (παραλαβὼν αὐτοῦ τὸν ἀδελφόν), emporta chez lui (ἀπηνέγκατο πρὸς ἑαυ[τόν, 8–9) plusieurs objets appartenant à la plaignante et dont la liste est donnée, avec indication de leur valeur, en appendice de l'ἔντευξις (17–19).

Βασιλεῖ Πτολεμαίωι χαίρειν[   ±27
τῆς Πολέμωνος μερίδος. Ἀδι[κοῦμαι ὑπὸ  ±18
Ἀλκιμάχου τῶν ἐκ τῆς αὐτῆς κ[ώμης  ±23
Στρατονίκης τελευτησάσ[ης  ±28
5 ἀνέπεισέν με τοῦ γ (ἔτους) επ...[  ±27

αὐτοὺς ἐπὶ τοῦ τάφου, ἐμοῦ δ[ὲ   ± 28
Δημήτριος καταφρονήσας . [   ± 28
παραλαβὼν αὐτοῦ τὸν ἀδελφὸν[   ± 28
  . αι καὶ ἀπηνέγκατο πρὸς ἑαυ[τὸν   ± 25
10 Δέομαι οὖν σου, βασιλεῦ, μὴ περ[ιιδεῖν με   ± 19
ἀδικ]ουμένην ἀλλὰ προστάξα[ι Διοφάνει τῶι στρατηγῶι γράψαι
Δη]μητρίωι τῶι ἐπιστάτηι ἀπ[οστεῖλαι αὐτὸν ἐπὶ Διοφάνην καὶ
ἐὰν ἦι ἃ λέγω] ἀληθῆ, ἐπανα[γκάσαι αὐτὸν ἀποδοῦναί μοι ταῦτα ἢ
τ[ὴν] ὑπογεγ[ρα]μμένην τιμήν. [   ± 10   Τούτου γὰρ γενομένου,
15 ἔσομαι ἐπὶ σὲ καταφυγοῦσα, βασιλ[εῦ, τὸν πάντων εὐεργέτην τοῦ
δικαίου
τετευχυῖα.
Ἔστιν δὲ τὸ καθ᾽ ἕν· χιτὼν ἄνθινος[   ὠτίων
χρυσῶν ζεύγη δύο ἄξια (δρ.) κδ γρύ[τη
ἀλάβαστροι δ (δρ.) η καὶ ἑτέραν γρύτ[ην
20 (2ᵉ main) Δημητρίωι· μάλιστ[α μὲν διάλυσον αὐτούς· εἰ δὲ μή, ἀπόστειλον πρὸς ἡμᾶς ὅπως [ἐπὶ τοῦ καθήκοντος κριτηρίου διακριθῶσιν.

Verso

ΔΗΜΗΤΡΙΩΙ

Ligne 5. ἀνέπεισέν με: même emploi de ce verbe pour une tentative d'escroquerie dans *P. Ent.* 49.4. – τοῦ γ (ἔτους): 220–19.

13–14. Si les restitutions et la lecture sont exactes, la plaignante demande soit qu'on lui rende ces objets, soit qu'on lui en paye la valeur: cf. *P. Ent.* 30. Cependant, ligne 14, les lettres sont gravement mutilées et effacées. La lecture τιμήν est loin d'être assurée.

17–19. Tout est "féminin" dans cette "liste détaillée": la tunique bariolée, les deux paires de boucles d'oreilles, les vases à parfum et aussi les deux "coffrets"; cf. le *Thesaurus* s.v. γρύτη: Σαπφὼ δὲ γρυτὴν καλεῖ τὴν μύρων καὶ γυναικείων τινῶν θήκην.

19. καὶ ἑτέραν γρύτ[ην: le passage à l'accusatif est une erreur du scribe, à moins qu'il ne soit justifié grammaticalement par la suite du texte dans la lacune.

## IV. Dommages causés à un κλῆρος

*P. Sorbonne* inv. 2406

17,5 × 10,7 cm; marge de 0,7 cm

Nikandros, un Grec d'Ainos, cavalier de la 3e hipparchie, dépose une plainte contre deux Egyptiens: au moment de l'irrigation des terres (ποτίζοντες, l. 3), ils s'y sont pris de telle sorte qu'une digue toute neuve de son κλῆρος a été emportée par les eaux (ἐξεκλύσθη χῶμα καινόν, 4) créant ainsi un dommage que le plaignant a fait constater ([ἐ]πέδειξα τὸ βλάβος, 5), – l'épistate Démétrios intervenant en quelque manière dans ce constat.

Βασιλεῖ Πτολεμαίωι χαίρειν Νίκανδρος Αἴνιος, τῆς τρίτης ἱππ[αρ-
                        χίας ±39
χου τοῦ Πάιτος καὶ Πνεφερῶτος τοῦ Πετεύριος τῶν ἐκ Μου[χέως ±41
ρα τοῦ κλήρου μου καὶ ποτίζοντες κατέλιπον τὸν κλῆρον. [ ±45
τὸν ἐμὸν καὶ 'διὰ ταύτην τὴν αἰτίαν' ἐξεκλύσθη χῶμα 'μου' καινὸν εἰς
                      ὃ ἀνηλῳκένα[ι ±44
5 Δημητρίου τοῦ ἐπιστάτου [ἐ]πέδειξα τὸ βλάβος....[ ±25 Δέομαι
                      οὖν σου, βασιλεῦ,
εἴ σοι δοκεῖ, προστάξαι Διοφάνει τῶι στρατηγῶι γράψαι Δ[ημητρίωι
                καὶ, ἐὰν ἦι ἃ λέγω ἀλη-
θῆ, ἐπαναγκάσαι αὐτοὺς τό τε βλάβος μοι ἀποτεῖσαι .[ ±45
ἀποσταλῆναι αὐτοὺς ἐπὶ Διοφάνην ὅπως ἐπ' αὐτοῦ μοι [τὰ δίκαια ποι-
ῶσιν περὶ ὧν διὰ τῆς ἐντεύ-
ξεως ἐπικαλῶ αὐτοῖς. Τούτου γὰρ γενομένου, ἔσομαι δι[ὰ σέ, βασιλεῦ,
                τοῦ δικαίου τετευχώς.
10 (2ᵉ main) Δημητρίωι· ἐπισκεψάμενος διασάφη[σον ἡμῖν περὶ τούτων.

Verso

ΔΗΜΗΤΡΙΩΙ

Ligne 1. Αἴνιος: cet ethnique a été lu, dubitativement, dans *P. Teb.* III 815 fr. 2, recto 9. Fr. Uebel (*Die Kleruchen Ägyptens unter den ersten sechs Ptolemäern* (Berlin 1968)) a proposé (p. 62, no. 101) de le retrouver dans *P. Ent.* 45.2 Ἀπολλώνιος [Α]ἴνιος, et de corriger (p. 63, no. 108) Αἰνιάς en Αἴνιος dans *P. Petr.* III 55 (b).30, en identifiant ce personnage avec celui de *P. Teb.* 815. – Sur les relations d'Ainos avec l'Egypte sous les règnes d'Evergète et de Philopator, cf. R. S. Bagnall, *The Administration of the Ptolemaic Possessions outside Egypt* (Leyden 1976) 159–63, et L. Robert, *BCH* 106 (1982) 328.

**4–5.** Le participe à suppléer devant Δημητρίου peut être [παρόντος] ("en présence de Démétrios"), mais ce peut être aussi bien un mot qui mette sérieusement en cause l'épistate; cf. ci-dessous n. 10.

**6.** Restitution *exempli gratia*, un peu courte pour la lacune: lire [ἐὰν ἦι τὰ διὰ τῆς ἐντεύξεως ἀλη]θῆ?

**8.** Cf. *P. Ent.* 41.6 περὶ ὧν ἐπικαλῶ αὐτῶι διὰ τῆς ἐντεύξεως.

**10.** [περὶ τούτων] ou [περὶ ὧν γράφει], *P. Ent.*, p. lx. L'apostille ne comporte pas la formule de tentative de conciliation mais demande une *enquête* et un *rapport* au stratège. Cette formule se rencontre, dit O. Guéraud (*P. Ent.*, p. lxiv), "dans les cas où des fonctionnaires, parfois l'épistate lui-même, sont mis en cause par le plaignant". Or, dans notre papyrus, l'épistate est intervenu, en quelque manière, dans le constat des dommages (l. 5). Cf. aussi H. J. Wolff, *Das Justizwesen der Ptolemäer* (Munich 1970) 147.

## V. Prêt d'argent et violences

*P. Sorbonne* inv. 2407            Plate VI
17 × 9,4 cm

La plainte formulée par une femme de Mouchis à l'encontre du "Macédonien" [An]tilochos porte principalement sur un prêt d'argent qui a fait l'objet d'un contrat (ll. 4 et 11), et aussi sur des violences (ἐξέβαλέν με, 5, βιαίου ἀνθρώπου, 7), et, semble-t-il, le vol d'un manteau.

Le papyrus est de qualité médiocre; l'écriture, tracée avec un calame épais, est irrégulière et sans grâce et, en plusieurs endroits, résiste au déchiffrement.

Βασιλεῖ Πτολεμαίωι χαίρειν    ± 12    ].ινεβαχις καλεῖται τῶν κα-
                                         τοικουσῶν ἐν Μούχει
τῆς Πολέμωνος μερίδος. Ἀδικοῦμαι ὑπὸ Ἀν]τιλόχου τοῦ Ἀντιγόνου
                                          Μακέδον[ο]ς. Δανεισα-
           ±35      ]τόκ[ου ὡς] ἐγ δύο δραχμῶν
                             τῆς μνᾶς τὸν μῆνα ἔ-
καστον      ±29      συ]νγρα[φὴ]ν τὴν παρὰ Καλλι-
                             φῶντι του δ. (ἔτους) α μη
5           ±35      ].....ν ὃ ἦν ἄξιον (δρ.) κ
                             ἐξέβαλέν με καὶ οἷός ἐστιν
          ±35      ]έδωκα τὰς Σ (δρ.) . . ᾳ τὸν
                             σταθμὸν τοῦτον. Δέο-

μαι οὖν σου, βασιλεῦ, μὴ περιιδεῖν με ἀδικουμ]ένην ὑπὸ βιαίου ἀνθρώπου
καὶ ἀποστερουμένην
±22         ἀλλὰ προστάξαι] Διοφάνει τῶι στρατηγῶι
γράψαι Δημητρίωι
τῶι ἐπιστάτηι ἀποστεῖλαι αὐτὸν ἐπὶ Διοφάνη]ν ὅπως ἐπισκέψηται καί,
ἐὰν ἦι ἃ γράφω ἀληθῆ,
10 ἐπαναγκάσαι τὸν ἐγκαλούμενον ἀποδοῦν]αί μοι τὸ ἱμάτιον καὶ συν-
ταγῆναι αὐτῶι μήπω
±32         συν]γραφὴ τοῦ δανείου ἐκ τῶν ὑπαρχόν-
των αὐτοῦ
±14       Τούτου γὰρ γενομένου, βασ]ιλεῦ, ἔσομαι τῆς παρὰ σοῦ
βοηθείας τετευχυῖα.
Εὐτύχει.
(2ᵉ main)Δημητρίωι· μάλιστα μὲν διάλυσον αὐ]τούς· εἰ δὲ μή, ἀπόστειλον
αὐτού[ς]
15        ὅπως ἐπὶ τοῦ καθήκοντος κριτηρίο]υ διακριθῶσιν [] (Ἔτους)
α Ἀπελλ[α]ίου ...χ.ν̅

Ligne 2. Sans doute δανεισά[σης γάρ μου ou δανεισα[μένου γὰρ
αὐτοῦ. Il semble, en effet, que la plaignante soit la créancière
puisque, ligne 11, le texte suggère qu'elle réclame, conformément
au "contrat de prêt", le remboursement de sa créance "sur les
biens" du défendeur. Cependant, cette interprétation serait sujette
à caution si, ligne 6, il fallait restituer ἀπ]έδωκα, ce qui ferait dire
à la plaignante: "j'ai restitué les 200 drachmes".

3. Papyrus mutilé, lettres effacées ou mal tracées, le déchiffrement de cette ligne est malaisé. La lecture τῆς μνᾶς nous a paru
plus probable que τὴν μνᾶν.

4. La fin de la ligne nous reste obscure. Si (ἔτους) α est correct,
il s'agit de l'an 221 av. J.-C.

5. Cet objet d'une valeur de 20 drachmes pourrait être le
ἱμάτιον dont il est question ligne 10; mais il nous a semblé
impossible de faire cadrer la lecture ἱμάτιον avec les lettres
conservées: ιạ(ou λ)ημ..ν.

14. L'apostille comportait, à la fin, une double date; le déchiffrement est incertain: Apellaios correspondant à Pachôn?
Du quantième du mois égyptien, il ne subsiste que le trait horizontal qui le surmontait.

VI. Plainte: non-observation d'un contrat

*P. Sorbonne* inv. 2408

15,5 × 12 cm, marge de 1,7 cm

L'objet de la plainte n'apparaît pas clairement. Un contrat a
été conclu en l'an 25 d'Evergète pour une durée d'un an (l. 4)
concernant peut-être la location d'un σταθμός (lire [μισθωσάμε]νος,
3 et ἐνοίκ[ιον, 4?), qui en dépit de multiples réclamations n'a pas
été restitué ([ἀπῃτη]μένος ὑπ' ἐμοῦ πλειονάκι οὐκ ἀποδίδω[σι],
5). Le plaignant réclame en outre le remboursement du prix de
certains objets, soit douze drachmes (7 et 9).

Βασιλεῖ Πτολεμαί[ωι χαί]ρειν Σωσίπολι[ς    ±24        Ἀδικοῦμαι
ὑπὸ Πυθέο[υ .].. ρινα[. . .]ης τῶν μ...κ[    ±34
νος γὰρ παρ' ἐμοῦ τὸν ὑπάρχοντά μοι στα[θμόν    ±30
κε (ἔτους) κατὰ συγγραφὴν εἰς ἐνιαυτὸν ἐνοικ[    ±28        ἀπῃτη-
5  μένος ὑπ' ἐμοῦ πλειονάκι οὐκ ἀποδίδω[σι    ±34
γου........λκωμενος κατακέχρητ[αι    ±34
ἃ ἦν ἄξια (δρ.) ιβ. Δέομαι οὖν σου, βασιλεῦ, π[ροστάξαι Διοφάνει
                                τῶι στρατηγῶι γράψαι
[Δ]ημητρίωι τῶι ἐπιστάτηι ἐὰμ μὲν ἔτι[    ±34
τιμὴν τῶν προγεγραμμέν[ω]ν· εἰ δὲ μή, ἀ[ποστεῖλαι αὐτὸν ἐπὶ
                                Διοφάνην ὅπως ἐπα-
10  ναγκάσῃ αὐτὸν τὰ δίκαιά μου ποιῆσαι. Τ[ούτου γὰρ γενομένου,
                                ἔσομαι διὰ σέ, βασιλεῦ, τοῦ
δικαίου τετευχώς.
(2ᵉ main) Δημητρίωι· μάλιστα μὲν διά[λυσον αὐτούς· εἰ δὲ μή,
                                ἀπόστειλον ὅπως
ἐπὶ τοῦ καθήκοντος κριτηρίου [διακριθῶσιν.

Ligne 4. ἐνοικ[ : en suppléant ici une forme de ἐνοίκιον, *loyer*,
on donnerait un peu de vraisemblance à une conjecture [μισθω-
σάμε]νος, lignes 2-3 – An 25 d'Evergète: 223/2.

5. [ἀπῃτη]μένος (ou ἀπαιτούμενος) ὑπ' ἐμοῦ οὐκ ἀποδίδωσιν,
la formule est banale dans les *Enteuxeis*: cf. *P. Ent.* 35.3; 40.3; 42.3;
46.4.

8-9. La conditionnelle ἐὰν μὲν...reste sans apodose. Pour le
mouvement de la phrase, cf. *P. Ent.* 21.7: ἐὰν μὲν ἔτι καὶ ν[ῦν]
ὑπομένωσιν [ἡ]μῖν ἀποδοῦναι τὸ ταφικόν· εἰ δὲ μὴ ἀποστεῖλαι
αὐτὰς ἐπ[ὶ] Διοφάνην ὅπως ἐπαναγ[κασ]θῶσι ἀποδοῦναι ἡμῖν.
Sur cette forme d'aposiopèse par omission d'une apodose telle que

καλῶς ἔχει, cf. R. Kühner, B. Gerth, *Grammatik* II.2³ (Hannover 1890–94) 484–85; F. W. Blass, A. Debrunner, R. W. Funk, *A Greek Grammar of the New Testament* (Chicago 1961) 482, et E. Mayser, *Grammatik* II.3 (Berlin–Leipzig 1934) 8 n. 3. Dans notre ἔντευξις le sens est sans doute: "si mon adversaire est disposé aujourd'hui à me rembourser le prix des objets ci-dessus désignés, c'est bien, restons-en là; sinon, que l'épistate l'envoie devant Diogénès, pour que celui-ci le contraigne à remplir ses obligations envers moi".

# Receipts for wool and a woollen garment, 215–213 B.C.*

## P. J. SIJPESTEIJN

The three texts published here belong to a lot of papyri recovered from one and the same piece of mummy-cartonnage. It was acquired by the Papyrussammlung of the ÖNB in 1979. Among these papyri one is datable by eponymous priests to 222 B.C. Palaeography forbids us to see in the regnal years 8 and 9 those of Ptolemy III Euergetes. The dates in question, then, are year 8 (215/14 B.C.) and 9 (214/13 B.C.) of Ptolemy IV Philopator (cf., e.g., *P. Sorb.* 1 43 = pl. 19, and above pp. 57–58).

The central figure in these three texts is a certain Onnophris, agent of the hitherto unknown topogrammateus Choapis. In text I he acknowledges, together with a certain Sarapion, agent of a Metrodoros, having received from two shepherds of the village of Mouchis in the Arsinoite nome one and two talents of wool respectively. The same Onnophris appears in II as the person through whom the same Sarapion has received one talent of wool from a shepherd of the same village of Mouchis. In III, Onnophris acknowledges that he has received from a certain Semtheus who acts for a shepherd of Mouchis one συρία.[1]

* I wish to thank Frau Dr H. Loebenstein, Direktor of the Papyrussammlung of the ÖNB, for the permission kindly given to publish these texts. Dr H. Harrauer drew my attention to these texts. With him and with Dr W. Clarysse I discussed these texts thoroughly. They both are here thanked again. Dr R. W. Daniel corrected my English for which I thank him.

1. Metrodoros' title is not given, but he probably was not a topogrammateus. In II Sarapion acknowledges receipt through Onnophris. It is likely, then, that Sarapion is more important and the agent of an official higher than the topogrammateus Choapis. It may be for this reason that Sarapion is mentioned before Onnophris in I.

I assume that the Sarapion mentioned in II is the same person as the one mentioned in I. I assume that the Onnophris mentioned in III is the same person as the Onnophris mentioned in I and II, although in III he is not styled ὁ παρὰ Χοάπιος. All three texts originate from the same piece of mummy-cartonnage and in all of them it is a question of the shepherds of the village of Mouchis, and of wool or a woollen garment.

In the first two texts the shepherds have already received from the bank the price for the wool which they now deliver. The price is not stated.

The production and sale of raw wool does not seem to have been subject to a royal monopoly.[2] Texts I and II by themselves shed no further light on the matter; they simply state that the shepherds have handed over a certain quantity of wool for which they had received a price beforehand. There is nothing in either the status of the persons who acknowledge receipt of the wool[3] nor in the fact that the price paid for the wool is not mentioned to indicate that we are dealing necessarily with a monopoly. On the other hand, in III the same Onnophris is concerned with the receipt of one συρία. We know that the production of συρίαι was governed by a royal monopoly (cf. *P. Sorb.* 1 21), and that the king bought the συρίαι at a set price (cf. *P. Hib.* 1 51).[4] This fact could induce us to see in Onnophris an official connected with the collection of wool and woollen garments in connection with a royal monopoly.

From I, 6 and II, 3 it appears that the shepherds of Mouchis acted corporately at this time.

I

*P. Vindob.* G. 40589                                                    Mouchis
13.5 × 9.5 cm                                                  24 May 213 B.C.
                                                                    Plate VII

Light brown papyrus. All original edges visible. At the top and the left side *ca* 1 cm has been left free; at the bottom 0.5 cm. The back is blank. The writing is along the fibres.

("Ετους) θ Φαρμοῦθι ιβ̄. ὁμολογεῖ Σαραπίων ὁ παρὰ
Μητροδώρου καὶ 'Οννῶφρις ὁ παρὰ Χοάπεω[ς]
τοῦ τοπογρ(αμματέως) παραδεδωκέναι Πομβῶν
Φανήσιος καὶ Παλοῦς Φανήσιος
εἰς τὰ ἔρια, ὧν τὴν τιμὴν ἔχου-
σιν οἱ ἐγ Μούχεως ποιμένες
[ἀ]πὸ τραπέζης, Πομβῶς μὲν

5

2. Cf. C. Préaux, *L'économie royale des Lagides* (Brussels 1939) 95ff. and 106ff.
3. Although the topogrammateus is connected also with the collection of the revenues. Cf. C. Préaux, *op. cit.* (n. 2) 447ff.
4. This fact may be the reason why in text III there is no question of a price. Cf. C. Préaux, *op. cit.* (n. 2) 106f.

ἐρίας τάλαντον ἕν (γίνεται) (τάλαντον) α
καὶ Παλοῦς Φανήσιος τάλαντα
10   δύο (γίνεται) (τάλαντα) β, (γίνεται) (τάλαντα) γ.
(2nd hand) ὁμολογεῖ Σαραπίων ὁ παρὰ Μητροδώρου
[παραδεδόσθαι δι᾽ ἐμοῦ παρὰ τῶ]ν
προγεγρ(αμμένων) ἐγ Μούχεως ποιμένων
[ἐ]ρίων τάλαντα τρία, (γίνεται) (τάλαντα) γ.
15 (3rd hand) ὁμολογεῖ ᾽Οννῶφρις ὁ παρὰ Χοάπιος
παραδεδόσθαι δι᾽ ἐμοῦ παρὰ τῶν
[π]ρογεγραμμένων ἐρίων τάλαντα τρία,
(γίνεται) (τάλαντα) γ.

Year 9, Pharmouthi 12. Sarapion agent of Metrodoros and Onnophris agent of Choapis the topogrammateus acknowledge that Pombos son of Phanesis and Palous son of Phanesis have delivered toward the (total amount of) wool, for which the shepherds of Mouchis have received the price from the bank, Pombos one talent (tal. 1) and Palous son of Phanesis two talents (tal. 2), total 3 tal. (2nd hand) Sarapion agent of Metrodoros acknowledges that through me three talents of wool, total 3 tal., have been received from the abovementioned shepherds of Mouchis. (3rd hand) Onnophris agent of Choapis acknowledges that through me three talents of wool, total 3 tal., have been received from the abovementioned.

Line 1. The persons mentioned in this and the following texts are not yet listed in the *Prosopographia Ptolemaica*. For the singular verb where we expect the plural, cf. E. Mayser, *Grammatik* II.3 (Berlin–Leipzig 1934) 32.

3. Πομβῶν: cf. line 7. This name is new. The proper names Παμβῶς and Πομβᾶς are known.

3–4. Pombos and Palous may be brothers. However, the fact that the same father's name is mentioned with each of them and the wording in lines 7–10 do not compel such a supposition.

4. Read Παλοῦν or assume Παλοῦς to be an indeclinable form.

6. ἐγ Μούχεως: Here and elsewhere the scribe writes the common ἐγ instead of ἐκ: cf. E. Mayser and H. Schmoll, *Grammatik* I.1² (Berlin 1970) 156; F. T. Gignac, *A Grammar of the Greek Papyri of the Roman and Byzantine Periods* I (Milan 1976) 174.

For Mouchis see A. Calderini and S. Daris, *Dizionario dei nomi geografici e topografici dell'Egitto greco-romano* III (Milan 1982) 301f.

8. ἐρίας: either the scribe made a mistake and wrote an *iota* instead of an *epsilon*, intending ἐρέας (cf. Mayser–Schmoll, *Grammatik* I.1² 45), or he originally wanted the accusative plural (ἔρια)

69

and thoughtlessly added a *sigma* when he discovered that a genitive was needed. I do not exclude the possibility that the scribe intended to write (and indeed wrote?) the genitive plural one way or another (ἐρ⟨ί⟩ων, ἐρίῳ⟨ν⟩, ἐρίων). Cf. Gignac, *Grammar* I, 252f.

11–12. Cf. 15–16. ὁμολογεῖ...δι' ἐμοῦ: an understandable confusion of objective and subjective formulas.

17. Comparing line 13 we could assume that ἐγ Μούχεως ποιμένων was mistakenly left out after προγεγραμμένων, but the repetition of these words is not needed for clarity.

## II

P. Vindob. G. 40590                                          Mouchis
12 × 9.7 cm                                             214/13 B.C.

Light brown papyrus. Original edges partly preserved. Between lines 7 and 8 a space of 2 cm. At the top 1 cm has been left free; at the left side 1.5 cm; at the bottom 0.5 cm. Two horizontal folds are still visible. The back is blank. The writing is along the fibres.

(Ἔτους) θ . [            ] . ὁ[μ]ο̣λ̣ο̣γεῖ Σαραπίω[ν]
παραδεδωκέναι Κωλύλων
τῶν ἐγ Μούχεως ποιμένων,
ὧν τὴν τιμὴν ἔχει
5     ἀπὸ τραπέζης, διὰ 'Οννώ-
φριος τοῦ παρὰ Χοάπιος ἐρε̣ίω(ν)
τάλαντον ἕν, (γίνεται) (τάλαντον) α.

(2nd hand)[Σ]αραπίων ὁμολογεῖ̣ παρειληφέναι με διὰ 'Ο̣ν̣νώφριο[ς]
10    τοῦ παρὰ Χοάπιος τὸ τάλαντο̣[ν]
[ἓν] ἐρίων, (γίνεται) (τάλαντον) α.

6 ἐρίων

Year 9 – – –. Sarapion acknowledges that Kolylos one of the shepherds of Mouchis has delivered through Onnophris agent of Choapis one talent of wool, total 1 tal., of which he has received the price from the bank. (2nd hand) Sarapion acknowledges that I have received through Onnophris agent of Choapis the one talent of wool, total 1 tal.

Line 2. Κωλύλων: an alternative reading is Κω- or Κάλυλιν. Both names are new, but cf. the variants of the name Κελῶλ. The end of the name could also be read as -ην.

**8–9.** ὁμολογεῖ παρειληφέναι με: the same confusion as noticed in text I, 11–12 and 15–16. Cf. also text III, 4–5.

**11.** [ἐν]: an alternative supplement is [τῶν]. Cf., however, text III, 5–6.

### III

P. *Vindob.* G. 40591                            Mouchis

14.4 × 8.9 cm           15 November–14 December 215 B.C.

Light brown papyrus. Original edges on all sides. Between lines 3 and 4 a space of 1 cm. At the top 4 cm have been left free; at the bottom 6 cm; at the left side 1 cm. Two horizontal and one vertical folds are still visible. The back is blank. The writing is along the fibres.

(Ἔτους) η Φαῶφι [.]. Σεμθεὺς τῶν παρὰ
Στοτοήτιος υἱοῦ Τασώτιος
ποιμένος ἐγ Μούχεως συρίαν μίαν, (γίνεται) α.

(2nd hand) ὁμολογεῖ Ὀννῶφρις παρα-
5       δεδόσθαι δι' ἐμοῦ τὴν
συρίαν μίαν, (γίνεται) α.

Year 8 Phaophi [.]. Semtheus agent of Stotoëtis son of Tasotis(?), shepherd of Mouchis, (I have delivered) one Syrian garment, total 1. (2nd hand) Onnophris acknowledges that through me one Syrian garment, total 1, has been delivered.

**Line 1.** Semtheus is the agent of the shepherd Stotoëtis. The absence of a verbal form is noteworthy.

**2.** υἱοῦ Τασώτιος: instead of the usual τοῦ we read υἱοῦ. This may be explained by the fact that Tasotis is not the father but the mother of Stotoëtis.

The proper name Τασῶτις is unknown. Since the proper name Σῶτις is known we have here a normal formation with Τα. An alternative reading is Τασήτιος. The name Τασῆτις is equally unknown, but cf. Πασῆτις.

# Frammenti di documenti agoranomici tolemaici della British Library

GABRIELLA MESSERI

Procedendo nel progetto di rendere noto il testo di quei pochi documenti tolemaici recanti nomi di agoranomi e conosciuti soltanto per brevi descrizioni, pubblico qui il *P. Lond.* III 888a (descr. a p. xliii);[1] ad esso faccio seguire l'edizione di altri due frammenti della stessa collezione (*P. Lond.* III 615 e 686d) da me riconosciuti quali resti di documenti agoranomici durante la classificazione di fotografie di papiri della British Library destinate a far parte dell'archivio fotografico dell'Istituto Papirologico "G. Vitelli". Oltre che doveroso, mi è gradito ringraziare il Sig. T. S. Pattie non solo per l'autorizzazione a pubblicare questi papiri, ma anche per la gentilezza e la pazienza con cui ha ispezionato per me gli originali controllando le mie trascrizioni.

## I. Ricevuta

*P. Lond.* III 888a (p. xliii)   Krokodilopolis (Pathyrites)
5,7 × 31 cm                     6 gennaio 107$^a$

Questa ricevuta attesta che Panebkhounis di Totoes ha restituito otto talenti di bronzo a Phmois di Phentenmoutis. Del documento sopravvive la parte centrale per tutta la sua altezza compresi gli ampi margini superiore e inferiore; la scrittura segue le fibre del recto, mentre sul verso, capovolta rispetto al testo dell'atto, si legge la annotazione del contenuto; le porzioni di testo perdute a sinistra e a destra di ciascun rigo sono trascurabili e ripristinabili con sicurezza.

---

1. Il *P. Amh.* II 166, riunito al *P. Grenf.* I 19, è stato da me edito in *ZPE* 47 (1982) 275–80; l'edizione di *P. Cairo* 10357 è comparsa negli *Studi Biscardi* v (Milano 1984) 522–25. Dunque dei documenti agoranomici utilizzati sulla sola base della loro descrizione al momento della compilazione della mia "Lista degli agoranomi di età tolemaica" (in *Papyrologica Florentina* VII (Firenze 1980) 185–271), rimangono inediti i *P. Cairo* 10352 e 10389.

L'edizione della ricevuta consente, fra l'altro, di rettificare la descrizione nota quanto alla località di stesura: nell'ufficio agoranomico di Krokodilopolis e non di Pathyris fu steso il documento; se ne può essere sicuri dato che è di mano di Paniskos il cui nome è seguito dalla precisazione "agoranomo della toparchia meridionale del Pathyrites"; altrimenti il prescritto avrebbe recitato semplicemente "in Pathyris, davanti ad Hermias delegato di Paniskos agoranomo". Oltre a ciò la conoscenza del testo della ricevuta si rivela fruttuosa sotto vari aspetti: prima di tutto constatiamo che essa proviene dall' archivio di Peteharsemtheus, in secondo luogo fornisce una ulteriore attestazione di Sosos, il predecessore di Paniskos, e di Hermias che lo rappresentava a Pathyris; infine ci informa di un contingente di fanteria, dislocato da Pathyris a Krokodilopolis, appartenente alle truppe comandate da Antaios, un ufficiale ignoto alla documentazione papirologica di età tolemaica.

Recto

```
       Ἔτ]ους ι Χοίαχ κ̅ ἐν Κ[ροκοδίλων
       πόλ]ει ἐπὶ Πανίσκου ἀγορ[ανόμου
       τῆς] ἄνω τοπαρχίας τοῦ Π[αθυρίτου
       κα]τέβαλεν Πανε[β]χοῦ[νις
 5     Τοτ]οέους πέρσης τῆς ἐ[πιγονῆς
       τῶν] ἐκ Παθύρεως Φμό[ιτι
       Φεν]τεμμούτιος τῶν ἐκ [τῆς
       αὐτ]ῆς Παθύρεως φερομέ[νων
       ἐν τ]ῆι 'Ανταίου πεζῶν[ χαλκοῦ
10     τάλ]αντα ὀκτὼ τὰ δανεισ[θέντα
       αὐτ]ῶι κατὰ συγγραφ[ὴν] τὴ[ν τεθεῖ-
       σα]ν ἐν τῆι προειρημ[ένηι
       Παθύ]ρει τοῦ θ (ἔτους) Μεχεὶρ ⌐.[ ἐφ'
       Ἑρμί]ου τοῦ παρὰ Σώσου ἀγορ[ανόμου
15     καὶ π]αρὼν ἐπὶ τοῦ ἀρχείου [ὁ Φμόις
       ἀν]ωμολογήσατο ἀπέχειν [τὰ
       χαλ]κοῦ (τάλαντα) η κ[αὶ μηδ]ὲν ἐ[γκαλεῖν
       αὐτῶ]ι περὶ μηδενὸς τῶν[ κατὰ
       τὴν τ]οῦ δανείου συγγραφὴ[ν τὴν δη-
20     λουμέν]η[ν π]άντων παρευρ[έσει
       ἧιτι]νιοῦν
              Πανίσκος κ[εχρη(μάτικα)] (ἔτους) ι Χ[οίαχ κ̅
```

*Frammenti di documenti agoranomici tolemaici*

Verso
ἔτους ι Χοίαϰ [κ̄
κατέβαλεν Πα[νεβχοῦνις
Φμόιτι χα(λκοῦ) (τάλαντα) [ η

Rigo **1.** Il nome della località di redazione del contratto è caduto in lacuna; sulla linea di frattura permane una esigua traccia dell'asta verticale di κ, qui, forse, più corta che non altrove in questa scrittura. La informazione fornita a p. xliii del vol. III dei *P. Lond.* e che si rivela ora errata: cioè che l'atto fosse stato scritto a Pathyris, si basava, probabilmente, più che sulla presenza dell'agoranomo Paniskos, sulla frequente menzione di questa città nel corpo del contratto (cf. rr. 6, 8, 13) (così è anche in Messeri, "Lista degli agoranomi", 220).

Ma oltre al fatto che la traccia di lettera alla fine di r. 1 non può adattarsi a π e che la lacuna sarebbe comunque troppo grande per il solo Παθύρει, ci sono motivi di ordine diplomatico basati sulla formulazione del prescritto dell'atto cui abbiamo già accennato nella introduzione, che si oppongono recisamente all'ipotesi che il documento potesse esser stato confezionato a Pathyris; senza contare che sia Panebkhounis sia Phmois sono militari τῶν ἐκ Παθύρεως, il che vuol dire quanto meno che al momento di questa definizione non si era a Pathyris (cf. anche *P. Grenf.* II 24. 5 e 8 e, per il caso opposto, *P. Grenf.* II 31.5). Dunque con questa ricevuta, scritta a Krokodilopolis, viene estinto un debito risultante da un contratto di mutuo, redatto a Pathyris, che sarà stato esibito da una delle parti affinché l'agoranomo ne traesse gli estremi (che sono, per questo motivo, così precisi). Un caso analogo presenta *P. Grenf.* II 31 con cui un *misthophoros hippeus* di Krokodilopolis estingue a Pathyris un debito risultante da un contratto redatto a Krokodilopolis. Era, questa, una prerogativa riservata ai soli militari in considerazione della loro mobilità?

**2.** Le date estreme della conduzione degli uffici agoranomici di Krokodilopolis e Pathyris da parte dell'agoranomo Paniskos sono il 28.5.108ª (*P. Adler Gr.* 5) e il 20.11.98ª (*P. Baden* II 10, cf. *BL* VI 7): v. Messeri, "Lista degli agoranomi", 220ss.

**4.** La grafia Πανεβχοῦνις, per quanto meno frequente rispetto a Πανοβχοῦνις, sembra preferibile in questo caso poiché al di sopra della linea di frattura rimane traccia di una lettera alta sul rigo, come è appunto ε in questa scrittura (cf. *P. Lips.* 7, scritto da

75

Paniskos!). Panebkhounis, figlio di Totoes, è il padre di quel Peteharsemtheus che conservò il grosso archivio di famiglia il cui insieme di documenti, greci e demotici, è stato organizzato e studiato da Pestman; *P. Lond.* III 888a si pone, cronologicamente, dopo il no. 24 di quella classificazione (v. P. W. Pestman, *P. Lugd.-Bat.* XIV, pp. 47–105). Il contratto di mutuo citato nella ricevuta (rr. 11–14) non risulta conservato.

**6–9.** *l.* Φεν]τευμούτιος; per la struttura dei due nomi si veda Th. Hopfner, "Theophore Personennamen", *Archivum Orientale Pragense* 15 (1944) 34 par. 36, 37 par. 44. Di Phmois, figlio di Phentenmoutis, non c'è traccia nei documenti dell'archivio di Peteharsemtheus, ma è noto altrimenti: possediamo il contratto in demotico con cui, nel 111ª, acquistò del terreno (*P. Strassb. dem.* 7; *PP* II 3997 e Add., IV 10796; P. W. Pestman, *Aegyptus* 43 (1963) 36 no. 34); grazie a ciò conosciamo l'intero suo nome, Leon alias Phmois, e quello di suo padre, Leon alias Phentenmout. I soli nomi egiziani sono riportati nella attestazione della banca di Krokodilopolis circa il pagamento della tassa sulle compravendite (*SB* I 5116). La posizione che Phmois occupava nel 111ª nei ranghi dell'esercito è così indicata in *P. Strassb. dem.* 7: "uomo che riceve vestiario e nutrimento...iscritto fra gli uomini di Horos figlio di P;'-nfr-htp" (v. *PP* II 3997 e Add., II 1857 e Add.); la località in cui era stanziato, allora, il contingente di cui faceva parte Phmois, non pare nota (così J. K. Winnicki, *Ptolemäerarmee in Thebais* (Warszawa 1978) 72). *P. Lond.* III 888a ci informa che qualche anno più tardi Phmois era ancora in servizio attivo e faceva parte "dei fanti immatricolati nella divisione comandata da Antaios, trasferiti da Pathyris stessa". Rispetto alla situazione documentata dal *P. Strassb. dem.* 7 è probabile che Phmois non abbia cambiato funzioni o corpo di appartenenza, ma soltanto località di operazioni; per quanto riguarda gli ufficiali eponimi, Horos figlio di P;'-nfr-htp e Antaios, è possibile che non si siano avvicendati nello stesso grado militare, ma che siano ufficiali comandanti di diverso livello gerarchico o a capo di settori territoriali di diversa estensione. Maggiore precisione non è possibile dato che l'uno e l'altro sono attestati soltanto nei due papiri considerati; di un certo peso potrebbe rivelarsi la considerazione che l'uno è, molto probabilmente, di nazionalità egiziana, l'altro ha un nome greco ed è identificabile anche senza la specificazione del patronimico (per il conto in cui vanno tenuti questi elementi, v. W. Peremans, *Ancient Society* 3 (1972) 67–76).

ἐν τ]ῆι, sarà sottinteso ἡγεμονίαι; una ἡγεμονία poteva avere dimensioni assai diverse a seconda delle circostanze (v. P. W. Pestman, *P. Lugd.-Bat.* xxii 34–37), quella di Lochos, per esempio, arrivò ad estendersi a quasi tutta la Tebaide (le attestazioni vanno dal 124ª al 113ª).

Sulla presenza di unità dell'esercito nel Pathyrites, si veda P. W. Pestman, *P. Lugd.-Bat.* xiv, pp. 49–51; J. K. Winnicki, *Eos* 60 (1972) 343–53; idem, *Ptolemäerarmee in Thebais* e *Proceedings of XVIth Int. Congr. of Pap.* (Chico 1981) 547–52.

**13.** Forse κ̄[ (T. S. Pattie).

**14.** Le date estreme dell'attività di Sosos sono il 27.6.111ª (*BGU* iii 994) e il 24.10.108ª (*P. Grenf.* i 28, *BL* iii 70) (v. Messeri, "Lista degli agoranomi", 218ss.); la nuova attestazione (febbr./mar. 108ª) si pone fra *P. Grenf.* i 26 (30.11.109ª) e *P. Lond.* iii 881 (p. 11) (10.3.108ª).

## II. Mutuo

*P. Lond.* iii 686d (p. xxv)                                    Pathyris
9,3 × 14,3 cm                                                  114–97ª

Il testo del frammento, mutilo in alto e a destra, conserva gli ultimi righi di un contratto di mutuo e la sottoscrizione agoranomica. Il contratto fu scritto lungo le fibre del recto di un foglio di papiro percorso, a una distanza di circa cm 6 dal bordo sinistro, da una *kollesis* verticale fin troppo evidente e mal fatta; né questo è l'unico segno di trascuratezza e di noncuranza nella scelta del foglio destinato ad accogliere il testo dell'atto.[2] Si tratta dell'ennesimo documento agoranomico di breve estensione scritto su fogli scadenti o su pezzi di risulta.[3] Il verso è bianco.

Dai righi superstiti, appartenenti al formulario notarile in uso, ricaviamo due informazioni: e cioè che si trattò, con ogni probabilità, di un mutuo e non di un prestito di generi, poiché l' ἑκαστ[

2. La *kollesis* è molto stretta (non misurando più di 5 mm) e i fogli che unisce sono spessi e di colore diverso (il destro più chiaro del sinistro); queste informazioni devo alla cortesia del Dr T. S. Pattie.

3. Sulla diplomatica dei documenti agoranomici brevi, si veda P. W. Pestman, *P. Lugd.-Bat.* xix 6, Introduzione.

di r. 1, nella posizione in cui si trova, è fortemente indiziato di essere ciò che resta dell'espressione καὶ τοῦ ὑπερπεσόντος χρόνου τόκους διδράχμους τῆς μνᾶς τὸν μῆνα ἕκαστον (cf. *P. Grenf.* II 18.16–18; 21.15–18); in secondo luogo possiamo esser certi che uno solo fu il debitore (r. 2: ἐκ τοῦ δεδανεισμένου; r. 3: αὐτῷ) così come, quasi sicuramente, una sola persona figurava in veste di creditore poiché alla fine di r. 1 non c'è spazio per più di un nome proprio.

La presenza della firma dell'agoranomo è l'unico elemento di una certa importanza in quanto ci permette di stabilire la provenienza del papiro e i limiti cronologici entro cui deve porsi, allo stato attuale della documentazione, la stesura dell'atto. Infatti l'Ammonios che scrisse il nostro contratto di mutuo, operò nell'ufficio agoranomico di Pathyris almeno dal 114ᵃ (*P. Strassb.* II 84) al 97ᵃ (*P. Lond.* III 1208), qualificandosi alternativamente nel prescritto degli atti o come delegato degli agoranomi di Krokodilopolis, Heliodoros, Sosos, Paniskos, o come agoranomo titolare (cf. i *P. Strassb.* II 84, *P. Cornell* 4, *M. Chrest.* 233, *P. Lond.* II 218, *P. Lond.* III 1208 e Messeri, "Lista degli agoranomi", 259–60). Tuttavia è difficile sostenere che il prescritto degli atti rifletta fedelmente la struttura della agoranomia nel Pathyrites; è possibile invece che l'uso da parte di Ammonios dell'espressione ἐπ' Ἀμμωνίου ἀγορανόμου si giustifichi con la semplice rispondenza ad una realtà di fatto, poiché gli Οἱ παρὰ τοῦ Δεῖνος ἀγορανόμου di Pathyris non dovevano distinguersi se non formalmente dagli ἀγορανόμοι τῆς ἄνω τοπαρχίας τοῦ Παθυρίτου che redigevano gli atti a Krokodilopolis. Tornando al nostro frammento, la sottoscrizione ci autorizzerebbe con una buona dose di probabilità a supporre un prescritto del tipo ἐπ' Ἀμμωνίου ἀγορανόμου come nei documenti sopra citati, ma non ce ne può dare la sicurezza (cf. *P. Lond.* III 1204 e, per Hermias, i *P. Adler Gr.* 9 e 18). I documenti scritti a Pathyris da Ammonios e giunti fino a noi sono in numero di venti: si tratta per la massima parte di contratti di compravendita; abbiamo un solo contratto di mutuo (*P. Grenf.* II 21) ed un solo contratto di prestito di grano (*P. Lond.* II 218), entrambi completi; un frammento dell'inizio di un contratto di mutuo è attribuito ad Ammonios in via congetturale (*P. Cairo Goodsp.* 8, *BL* I 172). Ammonios, comunque, non è per noi soltanto quel tal agoranomo redattore di certi documenti, poiché le nostre informazioni su di lui, come sugli altri agoranomi responsabili dell'ufficio di Pathyris, sono insolitamente ampie: si deve allo studio parallelo intrapreso da Pestman, dei documenti greci e demotici che da Pathyris ci sono giunti in gran numero se di Ammonios conosciamo la data di nascita, il nome egiziano, i membri della sua famiglia e le relazioni di parentela che lo legavano con gli altri agoranomi di Pathyris (si veda per tutto ciò P. W. Pestman, "L'agoranomie: un avant-poste de l'administration grecque enlevé par les Egyptiens?" in *Das Ptolemäische Ägypten* (*Akten des Intern. Symposions 27.–29. Sept. 1976 in Berlin*) 203–210).

$$
\begin{aligned}
&\cdot \quad \cdot \quad \cdot \quad \cdot \quad \quad \cdot \quad \cdot \\
&\text{ἕκαστ[ον ἡ δὲ πρᾶξις ἔστω} \ldots \ldots \\
&\text{ἐκ τοῦ δεδανει[σμένο]υ [καὶ ἐκ τῶν} \\
&\text{ὑπαρχόντων αὐτῷ πάν[των} \\
&\text{καθάπερ ἐγ δίκης} \\
&\qquad\qquad\text{Ἀμμώ(νιος) κεχ[ρη(μάτικα)}
\end{aligned}
$$

5

## III. Divisione di beni

*P. Lond.* III 615 (p. xx)            Tebaide
7,3 × 14,1 cm            128[a]

Il frammento reca sul verso un testo mutilo a destra e a sinistra; si conservano il margine superiore, in parte (0,7 cm), e quello inferiore (3,2 cm); girato il foglio, la stessa mano ha scritto, in breve nota, il contenuto dell'atto. Si tratta della copia di un atto stilato nella forma della ὁμολογία oggettiva da un agoranomo; per questo suo carattere di documento agoranomico ho già avuto occasione di occuparmene nella "Lista degli agoranomi", 250–51 n. 119. Dell'originario documento rimangono, purtroppo in cattive condizioni di conservazione, la data, il prescritto, la presentazione delle parti, l'inizio della enunciazione degli immobili soggetti a transazione e qualche resto della griglia formulare sulla quale l'atto fu impiantato. La copia occupò più colonne – forse due a giudicare dalla posizione in cui si trova, sul retro, la nota di contenuto e considerando che molti dati non saranno stati trascritti (età, connotati delle persone). Gli elementi di maggiore interesse, cioè la località di redazione dell'atto e il nome dell'agoranomo, ci sono negati dalla quasi totale illeggibilità del r. 2 e dalla lacuna alla fine del r. 3. Ciò nonostante ritengo opportuno pubblicare il testo di questo frammento nella speranza che un domani possa ricevere apporti chiarificatori da altri documenti. In realtà fin da ora *P. Lond.* III 615 presenta connessioni col gruppo dei *P. Lond.* II 219–28, estratti dal cartonnage di una cassa di mummia che il Rev. Greville J. Chester aveva acquistato il 14.5.1892 e con i frammenti, ugualmente provenienti da cartonnage, di cui parla U. Wilcken nella introduzione a *P. Würz.* 7. Informazioni di carattere generale su i due gruppi di papiri sono fornite da Kenyon in *P. Lond.* II, p. 1, e da Wilcken nella citata introduzione. Il nostro frammento giunse per altra via a far parte della collezione londinese: si trovava nel lotto di papiri che Grenfell acquistò il 9.11.1895 (Pap. 605–50). Ma in effetti la sua appartenenza a questo gruppo deve essere stata abbastanza accidentale poiché la gran parte dei documenti proviene dal Pathyrites; essi furono, con poche eccezioni (Pap. 610, 615, 641–45, 648), immediatamente pubblicati dallo stesso Grenfell (cf. *P. Grenf.* 1 10–46, 48, 50).

La omogeneità di provenienza di tanti documenti del gruppo è all'origine dell'ipotesi che anche il nostro frammento potesse essere stato scritto a Pathyris (v. *P. Lond.* III, p. xx); invece l'unica cosa certa è che proviene da una località, purtroppo neppure questa volta precisabile, della Tebaide come i *P. Lond.* II 219–28 e i *P. Würzb.*, con i quali concorda anche nella data (alcuni di quei testi portano date comprese fra il 178ª e il 118ª).

Ma l'elemento che accomuna decisamente *P. Lond.* III 615 a quei papiri, in particolare ad alcuni (*P. Lond.* II 219b, verso e 220, *P. Würz.* 7 i), è la menzione di un contingente militare di stanza ad Itos/Iton, cui appartiene uno dei contraenti (τῶν ἐξ Ἴτου στρατιωτῶν). L'antica Itos, o Iton, si trovava sul sito della moderna Edfa (v. S. Sauneron, *BIFAO* 62 (1964) 42–50; Z. Borkowski, *Une description topographique des immeubles à Panopolis*, (Warszawa 1975) 53, col. VII 5) ed era compresa nei confini amministrativi del Panopolites; da lì partiva la strada per la Grande Oasi, ed era quindi un punto strategico che richiedeva la presenza continua di soldati (v. J. K. Winnicki, *Ptolemäerarmee in Thebais*, 34–37), come sappiamo appunto dai papiri sopra citati, i quali ci informano anche del fatto che ad Itos/Iton c'era un ufficio agoranomico (*P. Lond.* II 219b, verso 1); ciò costituisce un particolare interessante poiché, riproducendo la situazione di Pathyris e Krokodilopolis, dimostra come la presenza dell'agoranomo sia da attendersi là dove si individuano stanziamenti di soldati e delle loro famiglie. Tuttavia il nostro documento non fu scritto ἐν Ἴτῳ come assicurano, da una parte, l'ampio spazio occupato dalla indicazione della località (rr. 2–3) e, dall'altra, la specificazione τῶν ἐξ Ἴτου στρατιωτῶν che sarebbe stata omessa o diversamente espressa. A meno di non riuscire a leggere qualcosa nel r. 2, nessuna ipotesi è lecita circa la località di redazione dell'atto, poiché non sappiamo niente di questo contingente di soldati: ignoriamo dove potevano essere (o erano di norma) dislocati e per quanto tempo.

L'atto, della cui copia resta il nostro frammento, doveva essere una divisione di beni fra congiunti. In questo senso orientano la forma della ὁμολογία oggettiva, la redazione agoranomica, la clausola di apertura che ricaviamo dalla nota scritta sul retro, il verbo διαιρέω al r. 16 e, infine, la possibilità che fra le parti interessate vi fossero rapporti di parentela.

Verso

```
        Ἀντίγραφον (ἔτους) μβ Με[
        ε̅.[  ]ε...............[
       .[  ]η τῆς Θηβαΐδος ἐπὶ Σ[
          ἀ]γορανόμου ὁμολο[γία
5         ]η Διδύμου τοῦ Μέν[ωνος
     τοῦ .]ρμαιεως τῶν ἐξ Ἴτ[ου
     στρα]τιωτῶν καὶ Κ....[
          ]ς τῆς Μέν[ω]νος τοῦ .[
          ]μετὰ κυρίου τοῦ ἑαυτῆ[ς ἀ-
10    δελ]φοῦ Διδύμου τοῦ καὶ Π[
     καὶ].. ν.. τῆς Νικάνορο[ς τοῦ
          ].ς μετὰ κυρίου τοῦ ἑαυτ[ῆς ἀ-
     δελφ]οῦ ...κέους τοῦ Νικά[νορος
          ]..ου τῆς {ε} ἐπιγον[ῆς καθ᾽
15       ἣν ὁμο]λογοῦσι Δίδυμ[ος καὶ
          ]θ.γατρα διειρ[ῆσθαι
     τὴν ὑπ]άρχουσαν αὐτοῖς .[
          ].ω ἀδελφῷ ..ο..[
          ]φρουρίου ἐν τοῖ[ς πρὸς
20   ἀπηλ]ιώτην μέρεσι τοῦ φ[
```

Recto

ὁμολογία ἦν [ἑκό]ντες
καὶ συνχωρήσα[ντες ἔθεντο
πρὸς ἑαυτοὺς . [
· · · · [
· · · · [

Rigo 1. A sinistra di α, proprio sul filo della frattura, rimangono due tracce di inchiostro puntiformi, al di sopra e al di sotto di α, come se ci fosse stata una parentesi tonda.
In fine: Με[χείρ o Με[σορή.

**2.** La scrittura di questo rigo è talmente svanita da parer cancellata (il numero dei punti che nella trascrizione segnalano tracce di lettere è approssimativo); impossibile dunque, almeno sulla base della fotografia, recuperare il nome della località di redazione dell'atto (v. Introd.).

**4.** Sulla base della notazione scritta sul recto possiamo essere certi che l'atto, concluso il prescritto, si apriva con la formula ὁμολογία ἦν ἑκόντες καὶ συγχωρήσαντες ἔθεντο πρὸς ἑαυτοὺς Δίδυμος κτλ. (cf. *P. Cairo Goodsp.* 6, *P. Grenf.* II 25, *P. Lond.* VII 2191; R. Taubenschlag, *The Law of Greco-Roman Egypt in the Light of the Papyri*[2] (Warszawa 1955) 312); ma nel copiarlo si è operata una drastica semplificazione poiché alla fine del r. 4, dopo ὁμολο[γία, non doveva esserci altro mentre il r. 5 doveva cominciare con una specificazione di ὁμολογία per poi continuare subito con la elencazione delle parti (a sinistra e a destra di ogni rigo sono andate perdute pochissime lettere: 3–4 a sinistra e 2–4 a destra; cf. rr. 6–7, 9–10).

**5.** La integrazione Μέν[ωνος in fine rigo mi sembra molto plausibile poiché questo tipo di atti si conclude di norma fra parenti stretti (cf. *P. Cairo Goodsp.* 6, *BGU* 241, *P. Grenf.* II 25, *P. Lond.* III 880, VII 2191); se è così le prime due persone enunciate nell'atto sono fratello e sorella; più difficile a determinarsi il vincolo di parentela che lega ai primi due personaggi l'altra donna che prende parte al contratto (r. 11): probabilmente è nipote di Didymos in quanto figlia (cf. r. 16 e nota) di sua sorella.

**6.** Probabilmente del nome del nonno di Didymos manca qui soltanto la lettera iniziale, quella di cui rimane una traccia alla fine di r. 9; con qualche riserva, dovuta soprattutto alla incerta lettura di ρ, si potrebbe pensare ad Ἀρμάϊς (la traccia di r. 9 non è incompatibile con α), per la cui flessione si veda E. Mayser, *Grammatik* 1.2 (Berlin–Leipzig 1934) 21.

τῶν ἐξ Ἴτου στρατιωτῶν, v. Introd.

**15–16.** Dovevano essere qui citate le due donne coinvolte nella divisione; lo spazio potrebbe ammettere la ripetizione dei nomi propri, ma le tracce all'inizio del r. 16 non coincidono con quelle del nome che doveva essere scritto al principio di r. 11. Altrettanto valida è l'ipotesi di una concisa enunciazione dei reciproci rapporti di parentela (e.g. Δίδυμος καὶ ἡ ἀδ(ελφὴ) καὶ ἡ ταύτ(ης) θυγάτηρ), ma fa difficoltà il dover supporre nella possibile lettura θυγατρα un errore prodottosi copiando un θυγάτηρ che, nell'originale, dobbiamo presupporre scritto correttamente. Diversamente, nella terza ipotesi che alle due donne si facesse riferimento in maniera molto generica (e.g. Δίδυμος καὶ αἱ ἀλ(λαι)), a completamento del r. 16 si dovrebbe pensare ad una clausola intesa a richiamare le caratteristiche della divisione.

**16–17.** Fra i due righi non c'è spazio per inserire πρὸς ἑαυτούς.

**17.** Nell'interlineo, sopra ]αρχουσαν si legge ]αρχον; evidentemente si è pensato ad una frazione del terrenno in oggetto.

**18–20.** In questi righi si dava la posizione del terreno (rr. 18–19, e.g., πρὸς περίστασιν τοῦ φρουρίου); l'ultima parola della colonna doveva essere il nome di un ἐποίκιον.

# Publius Petronius, Augustan prefect of Egypt*

ROGER S. BAGNALL

We do not know the prefects of Egypt under Augustus very well. Ann Hanson has recently shown, on the basis of a newly-published Michigan papyrus, that the Ostorius Scapula who served as governor in the first decade of our era was not the Q. Ostorius Scapula who was praetorian prefect a few years before, but Publius.[1] Our fasti of prefects of Egypt have more holes than doughnut from 21 B.C. to A.D. 10,[2] and the density of documentation for those who are known is mistlike.[3] A papyrus in the Library of Congress, published below, allows us now to see that the praenomen of Petronius, the third prefect, was also Publius, rather than (as is usually thought) Gaius.[4] Reflection suggests that we ought to have known this even without the papyrus.

## I. The papyrus

The Lessing J. Rosenwald Collection of the Library of Congress (Washington, D.C.) contains a fragmentary Greek papyrus, given to Mr Rosenwald by Harold J. Maker, its first known owner. The papyrus is broken at the right and bottom. At the left, the original margin is preserved except for the upper left corner and a rectangle to the left of lines 5–6. At the top, the surviving text suggests that there has been lost space for a few lines preceding line 1.

* I am deeply indebted to Alan Cameron and Klaas Worp for advice and references.

1. 'P. Ostorius Scapula: Augustan Prefect of Egypt', *ZPE* 47 (1982) 243–53, using her 'Two Copies of a Petition to the Prefect', *ibid.* 233–43.

2. See G. Bastianini, *ZPE* 17 (1975) 268–69.

3. Augustus' 43 years are 13.4% of the 321 years covered in the standard lists; but they occupy only 5% of the space in Reinmuth's list.

4. I am grateful to Svato Schutzner (Library of Congress, Special Materials Cataloging Division) for first bringing this piece to my attention, and to Kathleen T. Hunt (Librarian for the Rosenwald Collection, Rare Book and Special Collections Division) for permission to publish it here.

```
      [τὸ ἀν(τίγραφον) ὑπό]κειται.  Φα῾ῶ῾(φι) [
        (2nd hand) Πόπλιος Πετρώγ[ιος
                λέγει·    [
4               τοῖς ἀπὸ τῶν ἐπᾳν[ω χρόνων
                γεωργοῖς ἐνεκλη[
                [ἐ]πισκευῆς βαιᾶ[ς
                ἀπαρενοχλήτω[ν              τῆς πέμ-]
8               πτης καὶ εἰκάδος [
                γενεθλίου ἡμέρᾳ[ς
                .....[
```

Line 1. This line is written in a somewhat faster hand than the remainder of the text. The remains of the month name seem to me sufficient to exclude Phamenoth and Pharmouthi. The line, and what preceded it, are evidently parts of a normal formula of transmittal for an edict from a higher official or any other document: Preisigke, *WB* II 662, lists many examples.

2–3. The formula giving the prefect's name plus λέγει is normal in prefects' edicts. The earliest examples I know of come from L. Aemilius Rectus in *P. Lond.* VI 1912 and *W. Chr.* 439 (A.D. 41 and 42). There are no earlier edicts in which the relevant place is preserved. The addition of the phrase ἔπαρχος Αἰγύπτου to the prefect's name is not found in any edict prior to that quoted in *P. Oxy.* II 237 viii.27–43 (M. Mettius Rufus, A.D. 89). (For a list of documents emanating from or concerning prefects see P. Bureth, *RIDA* 46 (1968) 246–62; an annotated list of the 59 extant prefectural edicts, followed by a commentary, is given by R. Katzoff, *ANRW* XIII (Berlin–New York 1980) 809ff.) The losses at right in later lines seem sufficient to indicate that something more than the last three letters of Petronius is needed in the restoration in line 1. It is hard to see what it can be except Petronius' cognomen, which we do not know: cf. section III below.

4. The phrase οἱ ἐπάνω χρόνοι is amply documented in *WB* II 531. What in earlier times are referred to is not clear, but it is very possible that a modifier after χρόνων, in the dative with γεωργοῖς, provided something like 'to the cultivators [burdened? who abandoned their property? etc.] in former times...'

5. ενεκλη[ seems likely to be a form of ἐνεκλήθην, the aorist passive of ἐγκαλέω, to complain. If so, it is not at once apparent how this finite form is to be related to the preceding construction.

**7.** 'Undisturbed' may likely refer to some privilege, property, or status; it is used in *BGU* IV 1140.24 to refer to being thus undisturbed by previous prefects.

**8–9.** See section II, immediately below.

## II. The date

The tone of even the remains of this edict can leave little doubt that the issuer was the prefect. But which one? There are several Petronii among the prefects, but of almost all we know the praenomen, and they are not in any case Publii. One Petronius Quadratus was prefect later, in the second century,[5] but one would hardly be comfortable with such a late date for the hand of this papyrus. It seems much earlier, in fact. The only other candidate is Augustus' prefect, and the hand can quite comfortably be assigned to the later first century B.C. It is less cursive than *P. Ryl.* II 73 (pl. 3; also in O. Montevecchi, *La papirologia*, Tav. 29), but more connected than *P. Oxy.* XII 1453 (pl. 2), of 33–30 and 30–29 B.C., respectively.

The third prefect of Egypt under Augustus, to whom palaeography and elimination of other possibilities point, is almost always listed as C. Petronius.[6] The praenomen rests on Dio (LIV 5.4), who has nearly universally been preferred to the testimony of the elder Pliny (*Nat. Hist.* VI 181), who refers to this Petronius as Publius. Given Pliny's testimony, I have no hesitation in assigning the papyrus to the Augustan prefect. There are interesting consequences for the man and his family connections; these are explored in section III below.

With an Augustan date in mind – Petronius' known dates are 25 or 24 to 21 B.C. – let us turn to lines 8–9. Line 8 might most conservatively be read as πτης και ει⟦δ⟧αδος [ . A line has been drawn through the *delta*. Now neither ειδαδος nor ειαδος makes any sense. But if we see the vertical cancelling line as an attempt to convert the *delta* into a *kappa*, we get the text given above, εἰκάδος. We thus have a reference to a twenty-fifth day of a month. Can we tell which?

5. Bastianini, *op. cit.* (n. 2) 284.
6. A noteworthy exception: R. Syme, *The Roman Revolution* (Oxford 1938) 338 n. 4, refers to him as P. Petronius without discussion and citing Dio.

Line 9 refers to γενεθλίου ἡμέρα[ς, a birthday. Whose birthday can be meant in such an edict? Surely the emperor's. Augustus was born on 23 September, which in normal years fell on Thoth 26; in a leap year, however, it would fall on Thoth 25. Since the date of the covering letter falls in Phaophi, the next month after Thoth, the attractiveness of taking the 25th as Thoth 25 is increased. The covering letter may be only a few days or a week after the date referred to. As it happens, Petronius' prefecture did include a leap year, namely 22/21. I surmise, therefore, that the date referred to is 23 September 22 B.C.

At this date (or at any time under Petronius, for that matter), this fragment becomes the earliest preserved edict of a prefect of Egypt by some five and a half decades, the next being that of C. Avillius Flaccus in *W. Chr.* 13 (A.D. 34/5). Bureth's list does not even give an allusion to an edict of a prefect before C. Turranius, some 15 years after Petronius. Nor have any come to light since Bureth wrote, so far as I know (see the list of Augustan papyri in C. Balconi, *Aegyptus* 56 (1976) 218; a check of more recent editions did not turn up anything pertinent).

### III. Petronius and his family

First, the praenomen. The passages of Dio and of Pliny mentioned above are the only evidence hitherto; all other sources simply call the man 'Petronius'. The major reference works[7] have accepted Dio's testimony explicitly in preference to that of Pliny, though without arguing the point. In their wake, most other modern scholars have taken the point as settled, giving no indication that a controversy could exist.[8] Why Pliny – a first-century equestrian himself – should have known less in such a matter than Dio, in the third century, is unclear.

An interesting parallel is provided by the case of T. Petronius, a Neronian courtier mentioned by Pliny in *Nat. Hist.* xxxvii 20. What is surely the same person is mentioned by Tacitus in one

7. Stein, *R-E* 19 (1937) 1197–99, Petronius 21: 'bei Plin. n.h. vi 181 steht *P. Petronio*, was auf falscher Überlieferung beruhen dürfte'. Similarly *PIR* iii P 196.
8. E.g. S. Jameson, 'Chronology of the Campaigns of Aelius Gallus and C. Petronius', *JRS* 58 (1968) 71–84.

place (*Ann.* xvi 18) as C. Petronius. The analysis by K. F. C. Rose[9] has shown that Pliny is almost certainly correct and the Tacitean mss. incorrect. Interestingly, Rose cites a contrary argument by G. Bagnani, who argued against Pliny's trustworthiness here on the grounds that he had made a similar error in the case of the Augustan prefect! The discovery that Pliny was correct in the case of the prefect must surely strengthen the case in favor of his correctness in the case of the other Petronius.[10] (This latter is identified by Rose with the author of the *Satyricon*.)

About Petronius' own career, we know nothing else.[11] Jameson has argued[12] that he was active in Egypt already in the fall of 25, and that his last attested date is probably in 21. On the other hand, his successor (P. Rubrius Barbarus) is not attested in office until 13/12, leaving open the possibility that one, two, or even more prefects held office in the interim. And Petronius' own term may have extended longer than we know.

About his family, more has been thought to be known or surmised. *PIR* iii P 236 provides a stemma for the supposed C. Petronius, in which he is the ancestor of a line of C. and M. Petronii Umbrini. This connection now evaporates, and we must look for what other family members, if any, can be found. As it happens, *PIR* also provides a stemma of Publii Petronii (under P 198), which is given in Figure 1.

A bit more flesh may be put on this skeleton. The *triumvir monetalis* has been assigned by K. Pink to 19 b.c.[13] As this position was a classic point of entry into the senatorial career by a young

9. *The Date and Author of the Satyricon* (*Mnemosyne* Suppl. 16, Leiden 1971) 47–48. There is also a scholiast to Juvenal who refers to a Pontia, daughter of P. Petronius; it looks as if the scholiast (fourth century) has confused P. Petronius *suff.* 19 (who will be discussed below) with C. Petronius Pontius Nigrinus *cos. ord.* 37.

10. Jameson, *op. cit.* (n. 8), though tacitly rejecting Pliny's praenomen for Petronius, concedes in the matter of Petronius' status while campaigning that Pliny 'should have known his equestrian order'.

11. In P. A. Brunt, 'The Administrators of Roman Egypt', *JRS* 65 (1975) 124–47, he is (p. 142) among those (in the majority) about the remainder of whose career nothing is known.

12. *Op. cit.* (n. 8) 76.

13. *The Triumviri Monetales and the Structure of the Coinage of the Roman Republic* (*Num. Stud.* 7, New York 1952) 47.

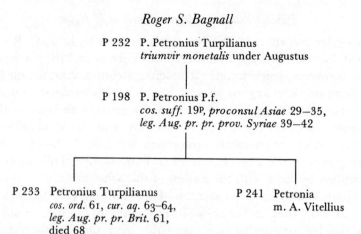

P 232  P. Petronius Turpilianus
*triumvir monetalis* under Augustus

P 198  P. Petronius P.f.
*cos. suff.* 19P, *proconsul Asiae* 29–35,
*leg. Aug. pr. pr. prov. Syriae* 39–42

P 233  Petronius Turpilianus
*cos. ord.* 61, *cur. aq.* 63–64,
*leg. Aug. pr. pr. Brit.* 61,
died 68

P 241  Petronia
m. A. Vitellius

Fig. 1. *A stemma of Publii Petronii*

man of equestrian family,[14] we may suppose that P. Petronius Turpilianus was born in the late 40s B.C. We have no further evidence on his career, which presumably did not reach the consulate. His presumed son, whose cognomen is not known, was suffect consul in 19, thus born presumably in the late 20s B.C. He had a distinguished career and was saved from an order of Caligula to commit suicide only by the death of the latter.[15] He was close to Claudius, but at the latter's accession he must have been in his early sixties: there is some reason (see below) to think that he had died by 46/7.[16]

Another Petronius, a C., was suffect in 25. It has been suggested that he was the younger brother of Publius, the suffect of 19.[17] This cannot be demonstrated, but the evidence to be discussed later about property in Egypt provides some basis for accepting the suggestion.

The presumed son and daughter of the suffect of 19 were intimately involved in court politics at the highest level. The suffect had married a Plautia, daughter of A. Plautius and a

14. Cf. e.g. A. Stein, *Der römische Ritterstand* (*Münch. Beitr.* 10, Munich 1927) 298–99, with the case of C. Rubellius Blandus, son of an equestrian, himself a mint magistrate, and father of a suffect consul.

15. Cf. P. Franke, 'Publius Petronius und C. Aelius Seianus', *ArchAnz* 83 (1968) 474–82.

16. On the relationship with Claudius, see R. Syme, *Tacitus* I (Oxford 1958) 331 with n. 8.

17. R. Hanslik, *R-E* 19 (1937) 1199 Petronius 22.

Vitellia, and his daughter was married to the future emperor Aulus Vitellius. We find no further trace of this family of Petronii after the events of A.D. 68.[18]

The sequence of Petronii described above makes sense, therefore, both in terms of chronology and in terms of career pattern. P. Petronius Turpilianus, born in the late 40s B.C., reached the first stage of a senatorial career. His son, born in the late 20s B.C., became suffect and held two governorships. The younger brother, if such he was, also became suffect. In the next generation, born perhaps around A.D. 20, came an ordinary consul and connections to the highest circles. The prefect of Egypt is a logical ancestor for this line, the family's last equestrian and one who held an office at the pinnacle of that order, born perhaps in the 70s B.C. and at maturity in the late 20s when he was prefect. The Ostorii Scapulae provide a parallel,[19] and they are only one instance among many.

With this picture in mind, we turn to the problem of the Petronian estate in Egypt. Two published papyri of the reign of Claudius (*BGU* II 650 = *W. Chr.* 365, of 46/7; *SB* VI 9224 ii 24, of 50/51) refer to a Πετρωνιανὴ οὐσία. In *BGU* II 650 it is specified that this property belongs to the emperor.[20] There is evidence of its continued existence under Nero, but not later.[21] The published papyri refer to Herakleia and Philadelphia in the Arsinoite nome, indicating (as is normal) that the *ousia* consisted of parcels at a number of locations.[22] It has generally been believed that the Petronius after whom the estate is named is the prefect, but the evidence is essentially the absence of other good candidates, and Parássoglou has recently expressed some lack of conviction.[23]

18. For the family connections see Syme, *Tacitus*, 386 with n. 5.

19. Cf. Hanson, *op. cit.* (n. 1) 240, with bibliography, above all referring to Stein, *op. cit.* (n. 14).

20. It is often claimed in reference works that *P. Giss.* 101.6 also refers to a Petronian estate. But G. M. Parássoglou, *Imperial Estates in Roman Egypt* (*Am. Stud. Pap.* 18, Amsterdam 1978) 16 n. 6, has pointed out that this mention is partially restored, does not fit the context in the papyrus, and is too late (third century) to be credible. (It should be noted that Parássoglou, by a slip, refers to the papyrus both here and on his p. 81 as '*P. Hamb.*' 101.)

21. The evidence under Nero comes from an unpublished papyrus described in a catalogue issued by H. P. Kraus, *Greek Papyri (& Greek Ostraca)* (New York n.d.) no. 9.

22. Cf. Parássoglou, *op. cit.* (n. 20) 69–83, Appendix II, for a survey of estates which shows this point clearly.

23. Parássoglou, *op. cit.* (n. 20) 16.

The picture is complicated by the mention in *P. Ryl.* II 127.4–5 (29ᴾ) of an ἐποίκιον Ποπλίου καὶ Γαίου Πετρωνίων in the northwest part of the Themistes division of the Arsinoite. This has normally been taken as evidence for ownership of an estate by the two *suffecti*, but Parássoglou has again expressed some doubts: 'I am not convinced that the Gaius and Poplius Petronii, owners of a farmstead in Euhemeria in 29, are in any way connected with Gaius Petronius, a personal friend of Augustus and prefect in 24–21 B.C. I suspect that the Petronii brothers are veterans who had settled in the Arsinoite after their discharge, as so many of their comrades did throughout the Roman occupation.'[24]

We may, to be sure, allow that the identity of the Petronii here is incapable of definitive proof with the present evidence. But it seems perverse to give the balance of probabilities as Parássoglou does. If, as does seem likely, the *suffecti* are brothers, the elder was presumably Publius. Their names in the Rylands papyrus would thus be in the correct order; the date coincides with the known time of activity of the brothers; and we know from the existence of the imperial Petronian estate that at some time there had been property in the Arsinoite belonging to Petronii or a Petronius (for the emperors did not have estates named after former retired legionaries). The most likely course of events, surely, is that the prefect acquired property in Egypt, passed it on to his son and he to his sons; on the death of Publius (not long after his last appearance in 42, perhaps), the property was bequeathed to his friend the emperor Claudius. Gaius, who does not appear after his suffectship, had perhaps died before holding another major office, in any case before his older brother.[25]

24. *Ibid.* He adds in a note, 'For the prefect, see *PIR*¹ P 196 with stemma (many Gaii, no Poplii [*sic*]); cf. *PIR*¹ P 198 (many Poplii, no Gaii).' He shows no awareness of the hypothetical character of these stemmata, nor of the articles in *R-E*; and his remarks seem to suggest a belief that *all* males in a line would have the same praenomen, which he himself contradicts by calling the Petronii 'brothers'.

25. A. Lippold, *Kleine Pauly* IV, 672 no. 2, suggests that P. Petronius P.f. was the grandson of the prefect, following Hanslik's remarks in *R-E*; but both of them were supposing that the prefect was a Gaius. If that were so, it would be somewhat curious if the older brother were the Publius, given the tendency to give at least the first son the same praenomen as the father; cf. B. Doer, *Die römische Namengebung* (Stuttgart 1937/New York 1975) 99, 120ff. But this is a tendency, not a rule.

Though there are gaps in our knowledge, a clearer picture of this branch of the Petronii emerges, with the transition from equestrian to senatorial status under Augustus and an increasingly close relationship to the imperial family and its inner circle. The death of their close connection Vitellius will have brought this rise to an end. What remains unclear is the connection of the Publii Petronii to the other Petronii of the time – the line of Umbrini, the C. Petronius Pontius Nigrinus (*cos.* 37) mentioned above, and T. Petronius Niger (*suff.* 62), the author of the *Satyricon*.

# Affitto di un uliveto

## MANFREDO MANFREDI

ῥοδέας κάλυκας, θαῦμα ἰδέσθαι
alla memoria di H. C. Youtie

*PSI* inv. Cap. 371                                                  Arsinoites
11,2 × 14,8 cm                                                      141ᵖ (?)

Il papiro fa parte di un gruppo donato nel 1970 all'Istituto Papirologico "G. Vitelli" di Firenze dalla Signorina Paola Capovilla, in esecuzione delle volontà del fratello, Professore Giovanni Capovilla, deceduto il 1° gennaio di quello stesso anno.[1] Proviene da un antico acquisto sul mercato antiquario.

Il documento in esso contenuto è un contratto d'affitto, nella forma ipomnematica consueta, di una parte di un uliveto, con ogni probabilità situato nei dintorni di Kerkesoucha della Herakleidou meris nel nomos Arsinoites. I contraenti portano nomi che compaiono anche nell'archivio di Petaus,[2] e non si può escludere che di fatto appartenessero a una precedente generazione della stessa cerchia.

Il maggior interesse di questo testo è costituito dalla lista degli *exaireta*, che completano il *phoros* pattuito, com'era consuetudine specialmente per questo tipo di coltivazioni.

Oltre agli elenchi offerti da J. Herrmann, *Studien zur Bodenpacht im Recht der graeco-aegyptischen Papyri* (München 1958) 247–88, con l'aggiornamento di J. D. Thomas, *JJP* 15 (1965) 129 n. 1, di grande utilità è l'indice della documentazione analoga reperibile in D. Hennig, *Untersuchungen zur Bodenpacht im ptolemäisch-römischen Ägypten* (Diss. München 1967); vedi anche O. Montevecchi, *La papirologia* (Torino 1973) 214ss.

---

1. Altri pezzi appartenenti alla stessa raccolta sono stati editi in *Trenta testi greci da papiri letterari e documentari* (Firenze 1983): vedi la Premessa di M. Manfredi a p. vii.

2. Vedi *Das Archiv des Petaus* (*Papyrologica Coloniensia* iv, Köln & Opladen 1969).

Manfredo Manfredi

Per la scrittura si può confrontare e.g. *P. Merton* II 68 (5.7.137ᵖ), o il papiro del Museo del Cairo SR 3049/36 (1.8.144ᵖ), in *ZPE* 50 (1983) tav. III.

Ζωΐδι τῇ καὶ Θεναπύγχι ἀπάροτει μετ̣[ὰ κυρίου
   τοῦ ἀνδρὸς Ἡρακλ̣ε̣ί̣του Θέῳ[νος
Παρὰ Ἥρωνος Δείου τοῦ Ἀνεικήτου ἀ[πὸ ἀμφόδου
Λυκίων Πέρσου τῆς ἐπιγονῆς. Βούλ[ομαι μισθώσασ-
5  θαι παρὰ σοῦ εἰς ἔτη τέσσαρα ἀπὸ τοῦ ἐ̣[νεστῶτος?
  πέμπτου ἔτους Ἀντωνίνου κ(αί)σαρ[ος τοῦ κυρίου     141/142ᵖ
  τὸ ὑ̣πάρχον σοὶ περὶ κώμην Κερκ[εσοῦχα …
  τον μέρος ἐλαιωνοπαραδείσου ἀρου[ρῶν …
  ἢ ὅσω[ν] ἐὰν ὦσι, φόρου κατ' ἔτος ἀργ[(υρίου) (δραχμὰς) ..
10  ἑξήκοντα κ(αὶ) ἐξαιρέτων ἐπὶ τὴν [τετραετίαν
  κατ' ἔτος φοίνεικος ξηροῦ πατητοῦ ἀ[ρτάβ..
  κ(αὶ) ἐπὶ τὴν ὅλην τετραετίαν φοίν[ε]ικ[ας ..
  ἐνκάρπους δύο ἐπ' ἐγλογῇ κ(αὶ) κατ' ἔτο[ς
   ]ων γόμον ἕνα κ(αὶ) σπυρίδα λευκο[φύλλων ἀρτα-
15  βιαίαν μίαν κ(αὶ) συκαμείνων κάνειστ[ρ..
    ]. κ(αὶ) ῥόδων κάλυκας πεντακο[σίας, τὰ δ' ἐκφό-
  ρια ἀποδώσω] μέτρῳ θησαυροῦ τῆς κώμ[ης
    ]ντα ἐπὶ τρίτῳ μέρει ἐμοὶ τῷ [μεμισ-
θωμένῳ    ].ε̣.[   ]. ἐγβησομένῳ[ν καρ-
20  πῶν    ].τ̣ατ̣.[   ]των μισθού[ντων?
  καὶ ἐπιτελέσω τὰ το]ῦ ἐδάφους χωματ[ικὰ] ἔ[ργα
  πάντα καὶ τοὺς ποτισμ]οὺς βοτανισμοὺς τ̣.ιμ[
    ] κα[τω]χείας κατασπασ[μοὺς
    ]τῶ[ν   ]ινων φυτῶν π[
    ]ξ[        ]α[
25    ]οσ[      ].. [
    ].οι.[

Sul *verso*, contro le fibre, in senso opposto alla scrittura del *recto*:

χι]ρόκραφον Δίου τὸ Ἐπαγάθωι [  .

1 ȝωΐδι    3 *l.* Δίου τοῦ Ἀνικήτου    10 εξαιρεσων a.c.    11 *l.* φοίνικος πατηθου a.c.?    12 *l.* φοίνικας τρτραετιαν a.c.    15 *l.* συκαμίνων *verso*, *l.* χειρόγραφον

A Zois, detta anche Thenapynchis, di padre ignoto, avente come tutore il marito Herakleitos figlio di Theon,

da parte di Heron figlio di Dios, figlio di Aniketos, del quartiere dei Lici, persiano dell'epigone. Intendo prendere in affitto da te, per anni quattro a partire dal corrente (?) anno quinto di Antonino cesare signore,

96

la ⟨...⟩ parte di uliveto di ⟨...⟩ arure, o quante esse siano, che tu possiedi presso il villaggio di Kerkesoucha, per un canone annuo di dracme d'argento ⟨...⟩sessanta e per questi extra: per il ⟨quadriennio⟩ annualmente artabe ⟨...⟩ di datteri secchi zuccherini, e per l'intero quadriennio due ⟨...⟩ palme fruttifere a scelta, e ogni anno un carico di ⟨legna da ardere ?⟩ e un cesto da una artaba fatto di foglie bianche e ⟨...⟩ paniere/i di more di gelso e cinquecento bocci di rosa. Verserò tali extra con la misura del granaio del villaggio, ⟨......⟩ per la terza parte a me fittavolo ⟨...⟩ dei (frutti) che risulteranno ⟨...⟩ degli affittanti (?) e compirò tutte le operazioni di sistemazione dei canali del terreno e ⟨...⟩ le irrigazioni e falciature, ⟨...⟩ le operazioni di fecondazione delle palme e di bacchiatura ⟨...⟩ delle piante (di ulivo?)...

Atto di Dios per Epagathos...

Rigo 1. Come si è accennato nell'Introduzione, molti nomi dei contraenti compaiono poi anche nell'archivio di Petaus. Ad es., per Ζωΐς, vedi *P. Petaus* 126.78; per Θεναπύγχις, *P. Petaus* 55.23, 66.23, 71.11 (tutti intorno al 185ᵖ), ecc.

*l.* ἀπάτορι, e cfr. H. C. Youtie, "'Απάτορες: Law vs. Custom in Roman Egypt", in *Le monde grec. Hommages à Claire Préaux* (Bruxelles 1975) 723–40 (= *Scriptiunculae posteriores* I (Bonn 1981) 17–34).

3. Spesso il formulario prevede ἀναγραφομένου ἐπ' ἀμφόδου, che potrebbe essere ammissibile soltanto presupponendo abbreviazioni molto stringate.

3–4. L'ἄμφοδον Λυκίων della metropoli dell'Arsinoites è noto da varî documenti risalenti per lo più al sec. IIᵖ; rare le testimonianze posteriori che giungono peraltro fino al 543ᵖ (A. Calderini e S. Daris, *Dizionario dei nomi geografici* III.3 (1982) 208).

5. Meno probabile τοῦ ε[ἰσιόντος, benché, com'è noto, contratti concernenti uliveti e relativi raccolti potessero venir stipulati verso la fine dell'anno egiziano, in previsione del raccolto delle olive che avveniva nei primi mesi dell'anno successivo; cfr. *P. Soterichos* 4.10 e *P. Mich.* IX 561, dove si rinvia anche alle osservazioni di J. Herrmann e di N. Hohlwein.

7. Per la localizzazione di Kerkesoucha cfr. *P. Petaus*, Introd., pp. 25–27. In fine rigo un numero ordinale frazionario le cui lettere finali sono da riconoscere nel τον di r. 8.

**8.** ἐλαιωνοπαράδεισος: non frequente ricorre questo termine che, forse preferito nell'Arsinoites, indica probabilmente un *hortus conclusus* piantato ad ulivi.

**9.** Se si tiene conto delle dimensioni medie di un uliveto e dei canoni noti per quest'epoca, ammontanti a somme mediamente assai più elevate (cfr. ad es. le 160 dracme d'argento di *BGU* II 603.16–17, del 168ᵖ), è probabile che, anche nel nostro caso, la cifra complessiva del φόρος debba essere analogamente reintegrata nel testo con ἑκατόν. Tuttavia, essendo ignota l'effettiva estensione dell'uliveto, non è opportuno scrivere come certa tale integrazione a fine rigo.

**10ss.** Per tutti gli ἐξαίρετα cfr. *P. Flor.* III 369.12ss.

**11.** Sul φοῖνιξ πατητός, oltre a N. Hohlwein, *Et. Pap.* 5 (1939) 18ss., vedi anche le note a *P. Vindob. Boswinkel* 8.15 (332ᵖ), *BGU* XI 2105.4 (114ᵖ), *P. Mich.* XII 657.7–8 (II/IIIᵖ).

**13–14.** ξύλων καθάρσεως γόμον?, cfr. *P. Flor.* III 369.17.

**14.** Se la lettura di *P. Oxy.* XIV 1631.25 (280ᵖ) ci avrebbe indotti a pensare che in λευκο[ dovesse riconoscersi un tipo di derrata agricola da presentare nella σπυρίς, come i [σικύ]δια λευκοπε[ίο]να μεγάλα τέσσαρα, sia la collocazione fraseologica del vocabolo, sia l'analogia con *P. Soterichos* 4.17–18 (Thead. 87ᵖ) fanno ritenere che si tratti piuttosto di un qualificativo della σπυρίς, che costituisce essa stessa l'ἐξαίρετον (cfr. *P. Panop.* 10, 10 e la nota con i rimandi a *P. Flor.* III 369.14 e a *PSI* I 33.17 (= *P. Phil.* 12)).

**15.** Non si può escludere una forma di κανίσκιον, benché il ϗ sia di improbabile lettura. Per esso vedi comunque *SB* VI 9509.2–3 e la nota di S. Daris in *Aegyptus* 38 (1958) 53 (*P. Oslo* III 159.10 e *PSI* XIV 1419.5).

**16.** Una lettera privata (*P. Oxy.* XLVI 3313, IIᵖ) evidenzia i modi di utilizzazione e la richiesta di mercato per i fiori, tra i quali vengono in prima linea le rose (r. 8). Per la coltivazione delle rose in Egitto, a partire dall'epoca tolemaica, cfr. *P. Cair. Zen.* II 59269.6; IV 59735.5; 59736.23; *O. Tait* 1991 (IIᵖ).

κάλυξ sembra non attestato nei papiri documentarî. Nella letteratura, in connessione con le rose, ricorre, poeticamente, nell'*hymn. Cer.* 427, in un epigramma di Stratone (*Anth. Pal.* XII 8.5), in un testo epigrafico funerario dall'Egitto (*SB* V 7541.10) e tecnicamente nell'*Hist. Pl.* di Teofrasto (IV 10.3). Per la coltivazione ottimale e per sistemi di conservazione dei bocci di rose, vedi il capitolo dei *Geoponica* 11.18.

**17.** Per il μέτρον θησαυροῦ τῆς κώμης, cfr. D. Hennig, *Untersuchungen*, 14. Il papiro comprova l'esistenza di un θησαυρός a Kerkesoucha (cfr., tra gli altri, A. Calderini, ΘΕΣΑΥΡΟΙ (Milano 1924) 31 e 114).

**19.** Cfr. *P. Mich.* xi 609, 12–13 (Tebt., 244ᵖ) ἐφ᾽ ἡμισίᾳ τῶν ἐκβησομένων καρπῶν e J. Herrmann, *Studien zur Bodenpacht*, 206.

**23.** Per κατωχεία in luogo del semplice ὀχεία, vedi *P. Soterichos* 4.27.

Il κατασπασμός, o bacchiatura delle olive (e dei datteri), ricorre in contesti affini, come quelli di *P. Ryl.* iv 600.16 o di *P. Mich.* vii 488.9 (lettera privata).

**24.** Probabilmente il testo citava qui la cura degli ulivi garantita contrattualmente dal fittavolo ( ]τῶ[ν ἐλα]ινῶν φυτῶν). Cfr. il papiro del Cairo SR 3049/37, n. 4, r. 14, edito da Sayed Omar, *ZPE* 50 (1983) 82.

L'annotazione sul *verso* riprende in apparenza soltanto il nome del proponente l'affitto noto dal contesto, mentre fa la sua comparsa un Ἐπάγαθος. Questo, oltre ad essere attestato come nome di schiavi, è il nome di un collaboratore di L. Bellenus Gemellus (in varî papiri Fayum, intorno al 100ᵖ), di un banchiere in *P. Brem.* 46.1 (?, 110ᵖ) e 47.1 (?, 118ᵖ), e infine di un personaggio in connessione con Kerkesoucha in *PSI* vii 810.13, datato congetturalmente al III/IVᵖ, ma forse più antico.

# A ration-warrant for an
## *adiutor memoriae*

JOHN R. REA

ROBERT P. SALOMONS   KLAAS A. WORP

Bodleian Library, Oxford

Ms. gr. class. c 126 (P)

19 × 25.5 cm (h.)

Caesarea (in Palestine?),

but found somewhere in Egypt

6 December 293

Plate VIII

Light brown papyrus, practically complete (except for a rectangle 8.5 × 2.5 cm (h.) lost at the top right) but internally damaged by worm holes. The left margin measures 2–3.5 cm, the upper *ca* 1.5 cm, the right 3.5–8 cm, the lower *ca* 3.5 cm. The ink has faded in places. The text is in a Latin cursive, with a Greek subscription by a second hand. The back is blank. There is a sheet-join (*kollesis*) running vertically *ca* 2.5 cm from the right edge. It overlaps right upon left, which indicates that the piece of papyrus was turned upside down after it was cut from the roll. None of the writing reaches so far to the right as to touch the join. In its present worn state it is easy to see that the top sheet had no vertical fibres for a width of *ca* 1.5–2 cm along the join; see E. G. Turner, *Recto and Verso* (*Pap. Brux.* 16) 20, and *P. Oxy.* LI, p. 61, for this method of reducing the bulk of sheet-joins.

>    *Aureli[u]s* . [6–8?] (vac.?) *mag(istris) s* . [
>                (vac.)                   *salutem.*
>    *annonas* . . . *as* . . *capitum trium Alogio*
>    *adiutori memoriae apud Caesariam*
> 5  *quousque bonam ualetudinem perceperit*
>    *et proficiscenti per* . . *em in sacrum*
>    *comitatum d(omini) n(ostri) Maximiani*
>    *nobilissimi C[a]esaris usque*
>    *ex die* [. . . .]*um iduum Dece[m]brium*
> 10 *in diem q[u]o ad comitatum*
>    *uenerit.*         (vac.)
>                       (vac.)
> *dat(a) uiii idus Dec(embres)*
>          *d(ominis) n(ostris) Diocletiano Aug(usto)* `u´ *et*
>                *Maximiano Aug(usto) iiii co(n)s(ulibus).*
>          (vac.)

## J. R. Rea, R. P. Salomons, K. A. Worp

(2nd hand)'Αλόγιος βοηθὸς τῆς μνήμης
τοῦ Αὐτοκράτορος.

1 *maggs* . [    4 *l. Caesaream*    7 *d̄*(?)*n̄*    12 *dat·* (or *dat'*), *dec·*    13 *d̄d̄nn̄*,
*aug·, augiiiicǫs*

Aurelius... to the *magistri s*..., greeting. Give(?)...rations of three units
to Alogius, *adiutor memoriae*, in Caesarea, until he recovers his good health,
and as he makes his journey...to the divine *comitatus* of our master
Maximianus, the most noble Caesar, from the ...th day before the ides
of December to the day on which he reaches the *comitatus*.

Given the eighth day before the ides of December, in the consulate of
our masters Diocletian Augustus for the fifth time and Maximian
Augustus for the fourth time.

(2nd hand) Alogius, assistant of the Memory of the Emperor.

Line **1**. *Aureli*[*u*]*s.* [6–8?] (vac.?). For the probable shape of
-[*u*]*s*, with a small raised 'u' , cf. *idus*, 12. The trace of the first
letter of the *nomen* is a speck at the top level of the average letter.
A darker blob at the base-line seems not to be ink. The surface
before *magg* seems to be well enough preserved for a distance of
*ca* 1.5 cm to have shown remains of letters if they had been there.
Consequently there is room only for a short *nomen* of 6–8 letters and
it is improbable that a title was given, cf. below, Commentary.

*magg s.* [ . There is no sign of abbreviation in *magg* apart from
a slight lengthening of the final horizontal. The traces on the edge
are a speck at the height of the tops of average letters and an arc
at the lower left. These would suit a round-backed 't', which
occurs here frequently (e.g. *salutem*, 2). See below, Commentary,
for the suggested supplement *st*[*ationum*.

**3**. *annonas ...as.. capitum trium*. Cf. *CPL* 267 (= *SPP* xiv no.
xiii) .5 *annonas quaternas kapitum quatuor*, 'four rations of four units'.
The recipients are four *protectores*, i.e. imperial bodyguards, or at
least persons ranked as such. At first sight the phrase might seem
to mean 'four rations for four persons', i.e. one ration each, but
when we take into consideration the practice of giving superior
officers and officials their salaries in multiples of *annonae* (see
A. H. M. Jones, *LRE* ii 643–44, cf. i 396–98), we begin to wonder
whether these distinguished officers were not getting quadruple
rations, and the question is further complicated by the development
of *caput* and cognates to mean 'fodder ration', see Jones, *locc. citt.*;

*TLL* s.vv. *capitum, capitus, caput* v (col. 427). Certainly *CPL* 267 bears a remarkable resemblance to *C. Theod.* 8.1.10: *actuariis...pseudocomitatensium...quaternas annonas et quaternum capitum ex horreorum conditis praecepimus ⟨dari?⟩* (there is a lacuna in the text). The reading of *CPL* 267 is confirmed by the plate in *SPP* xiv Taf. XIII. We need to compare also *P. Oxy.* 1 43 *recto* iv 8–10 ἐλάβομεν παρὰ σοῦ εἰς διάδοσιν τῶν στρατιωτῶν κάπιτα ἁπλᾶ ἑκατὸν πεντήκοντα ἓξ ἡμερ(ῶν) γ, 'we received from you for distribution to the soldiers 156 simple *capita* for 3 days'. The receipt is issued by an *optio*, a *tesserarius*, and one other (his name is lost and the word for his rank is damaged), to an ἐπιμελητὴς ἀχύρου, so it is fairly clear from this document of 295 that κάπιτον/*caput* at that date already had the sense of 'animal fodder', cf. Amm. Marc. 22.4.9 *uicenas...annonas totidemque pabula iumentorum, quae uulgo dictitant capita.* So possibly 'four rations each, of four *capita*' means four times the daily ration of a private soldier for human consumption, plus four times the daily ration of fodder for one horse. It seems quite probable that part of these could be commuted into money, although evidence for this is lacking till a later date: see A. H. M. Jones, *LRE* II 629–30.

In spite of the odd grammatical formulation with *capitum* in the genitive, this looks like the most probable interpretation, and it is likely that the present text had a similar phrase. However, the patch of damage should also have contained a main verb, unless it was entirely omitted. *CPL* 267 has *annonas quaternas kapitum quatuor...preuere* (= *praebere*) *curate*. Here there is obviously no room for periphrasis, so we expect an imperative or jussive subjunctive meaning 'deliver', preferably in the plural. Since the remains are intractable on this hypothesis, we have reluctantly accepted that, after ..*as*, *da̧* might be possible, on the supposition that the document would be presented to only one *magister* at a time. It is not a persuasive reading, but the remains are very much damaged. *CPL* 267 suggests that in ..*as* we should look for an adjunct to *annonaş*, e.g. *ternas, trinas, singulas, simplas.* None of these convincingly fits the traces. All are too long. Before *as* there is a short upright, seemingly free at the top, which in this hand suits only 'i' or 'u'. It is joined from the left near the foot by a descending oblique stroke, which favours 'u', since ligatures forward to 'i' join it at the top. Before the possible 'u' is the foot of a rather thick upright which descends below the base-line, though only for a short distance. This is joined or approached from the left not far above the base-line by a rising stroke. Possibilities might be *b*, *d*, *q*, *ci*, *ei*, *ti*. Probably no letters are missing between *annonaṣ* and these traces. In point of sense *dụas* might be tolerable, but none of the other 'd's is formed in a precisely similar way. Moreover we expect rather *binas*. -*tịụas* recalls *statiuas*, 'lodgings', but there is certainly no room for that.

For the name Alogius cf. H. Solin, *Die griechischen Personennamen in Rom* II, 707; *P. Vindob. Salomons* 19.5 (late Byzantine period).

4. *adiutọrị memoriae*, cf. 14 βοηθὸс τῆс μνήμηс τοῦ Αὐτο-κράτοροс. This post is attested here for the first time, but it is not surprising to find an *adiutor* in a palatine department, see e.g. *ILS* III.1, pp. 414–15 (Index s.v.). On the department of the *magister memoriae*, for which there is not very much evidence, although it must have been important because of its proximity to the emperor, see *R-E* xv 655–57, s.v. *memoria* (Fluss), IIA 897–98, s.v. *scrinium* (Seeck); F. G. B. Millar, *The Emperor in the Roman World* (New York/London 1967) 265–66; A. H. M. Jones, *LRE* I, 367–68. This passage confirms that Galerius had his own *memoria* department right from the beginning of his reign: see further below, p. 110, and cf. Jones, *op. cit.* 50–51. In the fourth century the *memoriales* became very influential: see Ch. Vogler, *Constance II et l'administration impériale*, 173.

Antiquarians may like to recall that the ancient title of King's, now Queen's, Remembrancer still exists in the English legal profession, although the duties are now ceremonial.

*Caesariam* = *Caesaream*. On the phonetic change of 'e' to 'i' in hiatus, see J. N. Adams, *The Vulgar Latin of the Letters of Claudius Terentianus*, 18. On the likely location of Caesarea, see below, Commentary, pp. 110–11. For literature on Caesarea in Palestine, see *Talanta* 12–13 (1980) 38–39 n. 31.

5. *quoụsque...perceperit*. The meaning is obviously best expressed in English by 'until he recovers his good health', but Lewis and Short, *Latin Dictionary*, and P. W. Glare, *Oxford Latin Dictionary*, do not record the extension of the meaning of *quousque* from 'so long as' to 'until at length', which is needed here; nor do they record 'get back' rather than 'get' for *percipere*. Perhaps this verb is used because of its association with the perception of feelings (*uoluptates*,

*dolores, luctus, gaudia* – Lewis and Short s.v., B, cf. *Oxford Latin Dictionary* s.v. 6), which might be applicable to states of health too, i.e. 'until he feels good health' is equivalent to 'until he feels well'.

**6.** *et* co-ordinates the subordinate clause *quousque...perceperit* and the participle *proficiscenti*, which therefore means 'as he makes his journey' rather than 'as he sets out'. This is confirmed by the indefinite term for the validity of the warrant – *in diem q[u]ọ ad comitatum uenerit* (10–11).

*per. .em.* The first trace is probably a short length of a vertical, slightly sloping to the right, but could be part of a rounded letter; the second is a rounded foot. Letters with risers are excluded in both places, and the second letter has no descender either. For the first the possibilities seem to be *a, g, i, n, o?, p?* (generally too broad, too straightbacked), *t, u*; for the second only *a, i?* (generally too straight), *o*, and *t* seem possible. No sense has so far emerged from these possibilities, unless *per item* could represent *per idem* (cf. M. Jeanneret, *Rev. phil.*[2] 41 (1917) 9: *eatem = eandem*) and mean 'at the same rate'.

Two other desperate solutions have been thought of. One is to take it that the rounded lower half of 'e' is also doing duty for 'u' and read *per nạuẹm*, 'by ship', cf. *Dig.* 35.1.122.1...*quas (merces) Brentesio empturus esset et per nauem Beryto inuecturus*. If true, this would reinforce the identification of Caesarea with Caesarea Maritima in Palestine, but it introduces an exceptional winter voyage and an exceptional ligature of *ue* not supported by *quousque* (5) and *usque* (8). The other is to read the final *m*, which is undamaged and at first seems a clear reading by comparison with several other idiosyncratic final 'm's in the document, as *ṛ*, i.e. *per iṭeṛ*, 'by road', cf. *Dig.* 9.3.1.1 *publice enim utile est sine metu et periculo per itinera commeari*; 22.5.3.6 *testes non temere euocandi sunt per longum iter*. These passages are hardly compelling, but perhaps this could be taken as a reference to the public post, which was bound to follow the official routes, cf. *C. Theod.* 8.5.25 ...*si quis...ab itinere recto deuerterit...*, *poena in eum conpetens proferatur* (A.D. 365). Palaeographical support for *ṛ* can be found in *P. Lat. Strassb.* 1.18, 19 (plates in *Archiv* 3 (1904–6) opp. p. 338; R. Seider, *Paläographie d. lat. Papyri* 1, no. 51, Taf. XXVII), where the small hand of the subscription has the final 'r' of *semper* (18) in a very similar form; *gaudear* (19) is not unlike. The date of that papyrus is *ca* 317–24, see *P. Ryl.* IV, p. 104; T. D. Barnes, *The New Empire of Diocletian and Constantine*, 153.

None of these suggestions is more than a possibility.

**6–7.** *sacrum comitatum.* On the early tetrarchic *comitatus*, see A. H. M. Jones, *LRE* I, 49–55, cf. 366–73, chiefly on the later stages. For a brief summary of its origin and development, see Millar, *Emperor in the Roman World*, 42–43, with ch. 3 (Entourage, Assistants and Advisers, 59–131) for a detailed account.

**7.** *Maximiani*: i.e. C. Galerius Valerius Maximianus, known usually as Galerius, see Barnes, *New Empire*, 4, 37–38, 61–64.

**8.** *nobilissimi C[a]esaris.* See H. G. Pflaum, in *Recherches sur les structures sociales dans l'antiquité classique*, ed. C. Nicolet, 160–61.

**9.** [. . . .]*um.* One of the ordinal numbers between *octauum* and *tertium* must be supplied, i.e. 6–11 December. A date earlier than the day of issue, 6 December, is excluded, because 5 December in the Roman calendar is the Nones; 12 December is *pridie idus*. The day of issue, [*octau*]*um* (see line 12), seems also the most likely here; the day after, [*septim*]*um* looks too long for the gap. It seems unlikely that there would be an interval of two or more days between the issue of the warrant and the beginning of the entitlement, because that might leave an opening for the abuse of the warrant.

For the accusative after *ex die*, cf. *P. Grenf.* II 110 (= *RMR* 86 = *ChLA* III 205) .3, *ex ḍ[i]e septimum.* Our document seems to confirm that it was not uncommon to omit *ante diem* (cf. 12 below and *BGU* II 696 *passim*, where, however, the days are given in figures), but to let the ordinal stand in the accusative as if *ante diem* was there, cf. *CPR* v 13.8 n.

*iduụm Dece[m]brium.* Here *idum* (*sic*) would be the easiest reading; perhaps read *idu⟨u⟩m*, but *Dece[m]brium* is clear enough and suggests that *iduụm* was just written rapidly and carelessly, cf. *P. Ryl.* IV 609 (= *ChLA* IV 246) .7 *ex die iduum* [. . . . .]. *m.* Below in 12 we have the conventional *uiii idus.*

**14–15.** This Greek subscription could well be by Alogius himself, see *C. Theod.* 8.6.1, where veterans presenting imperial letters authorizing travel are supposed to append their own subscription, *sua subscribtione subiecta.* However, in *SPP* XIV Taf. XIII (= *CPL* 267) the names of the four *protectores* seem to be in the same Latin hand as the text, certainly not in four different hands. The Greek subscription there, though damaged, does not seem to mention names.

## Commentary

This papyrus, which has already been illustrated and described,[1] takes a unique position among papyri hitherto published and thus seems worthy to be published in the present volume celebrating the centenary of papyrology as a discipline.

It is a warrant, dated 6 December 293, for the issue of rations to an *adiutor memoriae*, that is, a subordinate of a *magister memoriae*. The rations were to be issued to him at a place called Caesarea for as long as it took him to recover from an illness and for the duration of his subsequent journey to rejoin the retinue of Galerius. The mere fact of its survival without special indication of its provenance is enough to show that the papyrus was found in Egypt. Dr Barker-Benfield informs us that it is one of a number of papyri presented to the Bodleian Library by Mrs A. S. Hunt in 1934, and we can be sure that A. S. Hunt would have taken special care to record a non-Egyptian provenance. We can deduce that the warrant was kept till the nominee rejoined Galerius in Egypt and was discarded there after its usefulness had expired. It therefore brings strong support to the recent demonstration that Galerius went to Egypt near the end of 293 to put down a revolt in the Thebaid.[2] Most earlier accounts[3] placed him on the Danube frontier. A. H. M. Jones, though not anticipating Barnes, was sceptical.[4]

Barnes concluded that the passages of Lactantius, Praxagoras, and Aurelius Victor which say that Galerius had responsibility for the Danube frontier refer to no date earlier than 299.[5] This seems convincing; it would be very hard to take their flat statements to

1. *Manuscripts at Oxford: An Exhibition in Memory of R. W. Hunt*, ed. A. C. de la Mare and B. C. Barker-Benfield (Bodleian Library, Oxford 1980) p. 2 fig. 3, p. 8 no. 1.20. We are grateful to the Keeper of Western Manuscripts in the Bodleian Library for permission to publish it here, and to Dr Bruce Barker-Benfield for his help and advice on various questions.

2. See T. D. Barnes, 'Imperial Campaigns A.D. 285–311', *Phoenix* 30 (1976) 180–82, 187; *idem*, *New Empire*, 62.

3. For example *CAH* XII 334; A. Mócsy, *Pannonia and Upper Moesia*, 272.

4. *LRE* I 39.　　　　　　　5. *Phoenix* 30 (1976) 187.

refer to a few months in 293 or to that short period in combination with the long one from 299 or 300 to 311. Nevertheless, Barnes also concluded from the evidence of the movements of Diocletian in the first half of 293 that it was somewhere near the Danube, perhaps at Sirmium, Diocletian's chief residence at that time, that Galerius was invested as Caesar. Moreover the troops who were still with Galerius in Egypt in 295, as evidenced by *P. Oxy.* I 43, were detached from legions normally serving in Moesia, viz. *IV Flavia*, *VII Claudia*, and *XI Claudia*.[6] A detachment of *V Macedonica*, from the same area, was in Egypt during the reign of Diocletian and Maximian, quite possibly at the same time.[7] Therefore, although we have nothing to show exactly how long Galerius may have remained on the Danube frontier, we have indications that at least part of his army was mustered there and probably accompanied him from Moesia to Egypt.

In passing we may note that *O. Mich.* 441, dated at Karanis on 28 May 293 by regnal years 9 (Diocletian), 8 (Maximian) and 1 (Constantius and Galerius), is another strong argument in favour of Barnes,[8] in accepting that the investiture of Galerius took place on 1 March (*Paneg. Lat.* 8(5).3.1; Lactantius, *Mort. Persec.* 35.4) and not on 21 May (*Chr. Min.* 1.229). Seven days are not enough for news to have got to Karanis, even from Nicomedia, where the Paschal Chronicle places the investiture.

The date of 6 December, provided by line 12 of our papyrus, is of importance for the chronology of the imperial movements. While Galerius and the *comitatus* were in Caesarea, sufficient care could be taken of Alogius by the army's medical department.[9] But the moment Galerius was about to leave for Egypt it became necessary to make special arrangements for Alogius, who was forced by his illness to remain behind. One of these arrangements was that from a day in December which was probably the 6th again (see line 9n.), rations had to be supplied to him by others, viz. the *magistri s.*[ mentioned in line 1, obviously for the reason that the Caesar and his *comitatus* had left Caesarea at that date and

6. Cf. B. Filow, *Die Legionen der Provinz Moesia* (*Klio Beiheft* VI, 1906) 86.

7. See *P. Oxy.* XLI 2950 introd.; A. K. Bowman, *BASP* 15 (1978) 27 n. 11.

8. *New Empire*, 62 n. 73.

9. Cf. A. von Domaszewski–B. Dobson, *Rangordnung des römischen Heeres* (1981) 45 and xv; R. W. Davies, *Epigr. Stud.* 8 (1969) 83ff. and 9 (1972) 1ff.

thus were no longer able to take care of Alogius. Not long afterwards Galerius will have reached Egypt. This chronology is perfectly in accord with the conclusions reached by Barnes.

A fragmentary Latin papyrus which mentions *equites promoti* of the tetrarchs seems to give us a date of 26 December (line 3) 293 (line 6), see *P. Grenf.* II 110 = *ChLA* III 205 = *RMR* 86. This does not make it perfectly clear that the expedition headed by Galerius was in Egypt by this date, but in combination with the other evidence it certainly suggests so.[10] If our Caesarea is the city in Palestine (see below for discussion), we may adduce *P. Ryl.* IV 630–38.388–486 (pp. 143–45; cf. L. Casson, *Travel in the Ancient World*, 192–93) to show that a party of travellers went from there to Pelusium in Egypt in six days, 30 July–4 August, *ca* 317–23.

Whether or not this warrant should be described as a *diploma* is a question which we must leave unanswered for the moment.[11] This warrant authorizes the supply of rations only, saying nothing about lodging or the use of the animals or the vehicles of the public post, unless *per . em* in line 6 can be interpreted in that sense: see note. The closest parallel text authorizes rations and lodging, *annonas...cum solitis statibis.*[12] Nevertheless, the most likely places to supply rations were the *mansiones* of the public post, at least according to the view of D. Van Berchem.[13]

The chief objection to describing this document as a *diploma* is the expectation raised by the sources that a *diploma* should be issued by an emperor himself or in his name by a provincial governor. In this text, although the *comitatus* of Galerius is mentioned in the body of the warrant, the person who issues it is an Aurelius with a *cognomen* of not more than about eight letters, the restricted space suggesting that no title was stated. Pflaum thought that an emperor's name should stand at the head of a *diploma.*[14] The inscription published by Mitchell makes it clear that in the reign

10. See Barnes, *New Empire*, 62 n. 74.

11. See S. Mitchell, *JRS* 66 (1976) 125–27, for a recent summary of what is known and concluded about the *diploma* system.

12. Wilcken, *Archiv* I (1901) 373 n. 1; *l. statiuis*. See *CPL* 267 = *SPP* XIV no. XIII 5–6.

13. *L'Annone militaire*, 181–87; cf. H.-G. Pflaum, 'Essai sur le cursus publicus', *Mémoires présentés par divers savants a l'Académie des inscriptions et belles-lettres* 14.1 (1940) 358 n. 1.

14. Pflaum, *op. cit.* (n. 13) 313.

of Tiberius there were circumstances in which a *diploma* was not required for the requisition of animals and vehicles, . . . *militantibus, et iis qui diplomum habebunt, et iis qui ex ali⟨i⟩s prouinciis militantes commeabunt* (lines 16–17).[15]

The involvement here of the department of the imperial *memoria* recalls the inscription of a freedman with the title of *of⟨f⟩iciali ueteri a memoria et a diplomatibus* (*ILS* 1 1678), from which it has been concluded that the issuance of *diplomata* was entrusted to this very department.[16] If that is true, an *adiutor memoriae* might be in a particularly strong position to acquire a *diploma* and this document might be one. However, in the closest parallel, *CPL* 267 = *SPP* xiv no. xiii (p. 4), the issuing authority is a *trib(unus) quintanor(um)*, i.e. a tribune of the *legio V Macedonica*.[17]

Whether or not the document is a proper *diploma*, in the circumstances the issuing authority is likely to be a palatine official, very possibly from the *memoria* department, perhaps the *magister* himself, or perhaps a subordinate with the title of *a diplomatibus*. If, as it appears, no title was given here, this may suggest that the authority was very highly placed, so that his name was well known.

In passing we may note that the papyrus now gives certain proof that right from the beginning of his reign Galerius had his own department of the *memoria*, as argued by A. H. M. Jones.[18]

An ἀντιγραφεὺς τῆς μνήμης called Sicorius Probus, who was sent as ambassador to the Persians several years later, is usually taken to be Galerius' *magister memoriae*.[19] Even if this is correct, he need not be supposed to have held the office in 293.

The warrant, having the formal features of a letter, was addressed to *magistri s.* [ , an unknown title. Who are these persons? It is clear from the text that it was to them that Alogius had to apply for rations on his way to and in Egypt. These rations used to be supplied to holders of *diplomata* in so-called *mansiones* or *stationes*. These were more or less well-equipped inns or hostels

15. *Op. cit.* (n. 11) 107; cf. 126, where Mitchell concludes that the regulations had been tightened up by the reign of Domitian.

16. See Pflaum, *op. cit.* (n. 13) 315; cf. E. J. Holmberg, *Zur Geschichte des Cursus Publicus* (diss. Uppsala 1933) 58.

17. Cf. *R-E* xii 1581–82 (W. Kubitschek).

18. *LRE* 1 50–51.

19. Jones, *loc. cit.* (n. 18), *PLRE* 1 740; for the disputed date, see T. D. Barnes, *op. cit.* (n. 2) 186.

along the routes at intervals of 25–35 miles, i.e. the length of an average day's travel.[20] In view of these data it is very attractive to fill the gap in line 1 with *st*[*ationum*. The trouble is, however, that *magistri stationum* are nowhere attested. According to *C. Theod.* 8.5.35 the manager of a *mansio* is called *praepositus* or *manceps*, but not *magister*.[21]

The parallel, *CPL* 267 = *SPP* xiv no. xiii, unfortunately dating from a much later period, *ca* A.D. 400 to judge from the hand, is addressed *prepositis horiorum et susceptoribus d*[*e*]*botis singuloru*[*m*] *lo*[*co*]*r*(*um*) – read *praepositis horreorum*, and *deuotis* if the reading is correct, but the plate suggests *ẹṭ ḍịaḍotis*, i.e. *diadota* (cf. *C. Theod.* 7.4.28), is a Latin version of the Greek διαδότης, cf. e.g. *P. Beatty Panop.* 1.276–331n. (pp. 123–25). If *magistri st*[*ationum* is correct, this looks like an attempt to find a broad term to cover the various types of heads of post stations, cf. *C. Theod.* 8.5.35 ...*si quis eorum, qui praepositi uocantur aut mancipes, publico denique cursui nomine aliquo praesunt...modum patiatur excedi, seuerissime...compescetur: aut militans exauctoritatem subibit aut decurio uel manceps relegatione annua plectetur.* Three types emerge, municipal liturgists (*decuriones*, e.g. *susceptores, diadotae*), contractors (*mancipes*), and military officers (*militantes*, i.e. *stationarii*, cf. *C. Theod.* 8.5.1).[22]

We must still try to determine which Caesarea is meant in line 4, since seventeen places of this name are listed in *R-E* iii 1288–95. In the interval between 1 March and 6 December 293 we have no clue where Galerius was (see above), so we are reduced to assuming that his track lay between Sirmium and Egypt, not necessarily directly. In ancient times navigation was difficult between October and May. We cannot say positively that Galerius and his army would not have gone by sea, because a revolt is the sort of emergency which might have enforced a sea voyage in the winter season,[23] but the probability is that they travelled overland. By such a route the only Caesarea that it would be nonsensical to avoid is Caesarea in Palestine. This was an important place and is by far the most likely candidate for our text. If we trace the route

---

20. Cf. L. Casson, *Travel in the Ancient World*, 184, 201; Pflaum, *op. cit.* (n. 13) 343.
21. Cf. *R-E* xiv 1242, s.v. *mansio* (Kubitschek).
22. On all this, see Pflaum, *op. cit.* (n. 13) 355–56.
23. Casson, *Travel*, 151.

further away from Egypt, it seems likely that the army came out of Europe across the Bosporus and traversed Asia Minor. If so, there were at least three Caesareas in Asia Minor which might have been visited: a small town in Bithynia near Prusa, the more important Mazaca Caesarea in Cappadocia, and Caesarea Anazarbus in Cilicia. To judge from the map in K. Miller, *Itineraria Romana* (1916) 628 fig. 202, none of these is on the shortest route (Nicomedia–Nicaea–Ancyra–Tyana–Tarsus) or on any likely detour, but none can be absolutely excluded. Winter weather and other factors outside our knowledge or judgement may have affected the line of the journey. All we can say is that the only very likely candidate is Caesarea in Palestine, and that several others are possible but not favoured by any special indications. Caesarea Panias in Phoenicia, due east of Tyre and east of the Jordan, is by no means on a likely route, see K. Miller, *Itineraria*, 807 fig. 260.

We may support this view of the route by reference to the *Itinerarium Antonini*, which probably traces a journey of Caracalla between Rome and Upper Egypt in A.D. 214/15.[24] This took him through Sirmium, Nicomedia, Antioch, and Alexandria (*Itin. Ant.* 124.2–5), and the intermediate stages (131.4–154.5) include no Caesarea but the one in Palestine (150.1).

An estimate of the palaeographical importance of the document will have to await analysis by the experts, but it is clear that its chief interest lies in the presumption that it was written by a clerk in the palatine civil service of Galerius, a clerk who may have come from any part of the Roman Empire and who was in contact with the highest political circles. It is not, to our eyes, strikingly different from papyri without such a pedigree. Perhaps we should bear in mind the possibility, not necessarily a strong one, that it is a copy of the original document made in Egypt.

The rapid script is far from calligraphic. The slope varies from one passage to another, so that the writing is sometimes backhand, sometimes sloping forward, and sometimes upright. The beginnings of lines tend to creep inwards with each successive line, so that the margin widens rapidly. The letters are, with few exceptions, in the developed forms of the new Roman cursive. Some specimens of 'l' have an oblique descending to the right which

24. Cf. Millar, *Emperor in the Roman World*, 44.

recalls the old Roman cursive, but in ligature (*salutem* 2, *Alogio* 3) it has the later form. A few instances of 'r' in two well-separated strokes (*Aureli*[*u*]*s* 1, *sacrum* 6) have an older look, but most are clearly linked in the later style. A few instances of 's' too, notably *salutem* (2), have the older form. The only marked idiosyncrasy is the exaggerated shape of final 'm', which forms a long zig-zag descending stepwise towards the right.

Papyri of similar date in new cursive which may be compared are *ChLA* III 205 (m. 1), *P. Oxy.* XLI 2953 (pl. 1), *PSI* I 111 (plate in G. Cencetti, 'Note paleografiche sulla scrittura dei papiri latini dal I al III secolo d.C.', *Memorie dell'Accademia delle Scienze dell'Istituto di Bologna, Classe sci. mor.*, Ser. 5 (1950) pl. 5). A convenient short account of the new Roman cursive is given in B. Bischoff, *Paläographie des römischen Altertums und des abendländischen Mittelalters* (Berlin 1979) 80–86; cf. S. Hornshöj-Möller, 'Die Beziehung zwischen der älteren und der jüngeren römischen Kursivschrift', *Aegyptus* 60 (1980) 161–224. A short historical account of the controversy in the palaeographical literature over the origins of the new Roman cursive is given in A. K. Bowman and J. D. Thomas, *Vindolanda: The Latin Writing-Tablets*, 53–59; there is a useful comparison of the basic alphabets of the two types on p. 54.

# The earliest occurrence
# of the *exactor civitatis* in Egypt
# (*P. Giss.* inv. 126 recto)

## J. DAVID THOMAS

The verso of *P. Giss.* inv. 126 was published by E. Kornemann as
long ago as 1912 as *P. Giss.* 103. In his introductory remarks the
editor commented, 'Die Vorderseite des Papyrus enthält Quit-
tungsabschriften, die dem Gelasios, dem στρατηγὸς ἤτοι ἐξάκτωρ
'Οάσεως Μεγάλης...eingereicht und ins Jahr 309 zu setzen sind.
Ich behalte sie einer späteren Publikation vor.' This later publication never materialised and the recto of the papyrus has
remained unpublished until now. In 1937, in the first edition of
his *Cities of the Eastern Roman Provinces*, A. H. M. Jones pointed out
that *P. Giss.* 103 recto was the first attestation of the office of *exactor
civitatis* in Egypt. For this reason alone the text would be worth
publishing. In addition to its information on the exactor there
are a number of interesting features which it presents, despite
its fragmentary condition, as will be clear from the edition of
the papyrus which forms the subject of this paper. Professor
H. G. Gundel provided me with a photograph of the papyrus and
encouraged me to publish it.[1] I owe a considerable debt of
gratitude to Professor Dieter Hagedorn and Frau Bärbel Kramer,
who took the trouble to visit Giessen especially to examine the
papyrus in order to check my readings and answer queries.

The papyrus as it survives measures 8 × 26 cm, i.e. it is a long,
narrow strip. It is obvious that after the recto had been used the
papyrus was cut down to take the letter on the verso published
as *P. Giss.* 103. What survives of the recto is badly rubbed in places
and contains a number of holes, in particular in lines 1–12. The
text is naturally incomplete at left and right, and we can see from
the consular dates to be supplied in lines 10–11, 22–23, and 26–27,
that the loss is quite considerable. Furthermore, although there
is a margin of 1.2 cm at the top and 2 cm at the foot, which shows

1. I am also grateful to Professor C. A. Nelson and Professor G. Wagner for
enabling me to publish this text.

that the papyrus is complete at top and bottom, it is quite certain that the document in lines 1–14 did not begin in line 1 and that the document in lines 32–38 did not end in line 38; additionally, therefore, at least one column of writing has been lost at both left and right. In the transcript which follows, the words supplied in each line have been evened out at left and right for convenience. It should, however, be pointed out that the loss at the left will in fact have been much less than the loss at the right, since we can see that in lines 15 and 32 only the nomen of the strategos/exactor is missing at the left.

Essentially the points made in the introduction to *P. Giss.* 103 concerning the text on the recto are correct: the papyrus does indeed contain a series of receipts addressed to the strategos/exactor of the Great Oasis,[2] and its date was there correctly given as A.D. 309 (see lines 10–11 and 26–27). The month is lost. As remarked above, A. H. M. Jones regarded this as the earliest attestation of an exactor in Egypt, a view accepted by me in an article on the exactor published in 1959 and by Lallemand in her book published in 1964.[3] It is also the first firm date for an exactor recorded in the recently published list of exactors in *P. Amst.* I, pp. 168–71.[4] Vandersleyen suggested in his book on the prefects which appeared in 1962 that *P. Cairo* cat. 10466, where an exactor is mentioned, was 'antérieur à septembre 308' because of the reference in this same text to Valerius Victorianus, supposedly prefect of Egypt at a date prior to September 308.[5] However, we now know that the prefect in office during this period was Valerius Victorius, whereas Valerius Victorianus was praeses of the Thebaid

---

2. The statement in *P. Giss.* 103 introd. is inaccurate only in stating that the word Μεγάλης followed Ὀάσεως, when in fact the papyrus breaks off after Ὀάσεως. However, there is no doubt that the Oasis in question is the Great Oasis, see below, end of the Introduction.

3. J. D. Thomas, *Chr. d'Eg.* 34 (1959) 124 (cf. also A. H. M. Jones, *Cities of the Eastern Roman Provinces*² (1971) 337 and 490 n. 52); J. Lallemand, *L'administration civile de l'Egypte* (1964) 118.

4. It is true that the editors regard the three occurrences of an exactor or former exactor in *P. Landlisten* as falling in the period 307/8–316/25, but *P. Giss.* 103 recto remains the first exactor for whom an exact date is given.

5. C. Vandersleyen, *Chronologie des préfets d'Egypte* (*Coll. Latomus* 55, 1962) 107 n. 1.

in about 323.[6] This reference to an exactor, therefore, belongs *ca* 323 and *P. Giss.* inv. 126 = 103 recto remains the earliest occurrence of the *exactor civitatis* in Egypt.[7] It should be noted that Gelasios in our document is not called simply exactor but στρατηγὸς ἤτοι ἐξάκτωρ.[8]

It is clear that the recto contains the remains of three documents, lines 1–14, 15–31, and 32–38, and that all three were receipts (hereafter designated A, B, C). Receipt B and Receipt C were addressed to the strategos/exactor; presumably Receipt A was similarly addressed. After the transcript and notes I attempt a reconstruction of one of these receipts. It seems reasonably certain that all three were acknowledgements by military officers that they had been paid cash by the public bankers of Hibis, according to the warrant of the strategos or his deputy (see line 19n.) and the orders of the procurator or acting-procurator of the Lower Thebaid (see line 21n.). The receipts were issued in four copies and are dated and signed. Since all three of the extant documents are in the same hand, the Giessen papyrus must have contained a series of copies of original receipts.

Apart from its evidence concerning the exactor, the most important feature of the papyrus is the fact that the officer responsible for Receipt C (and probably the one responsible for Receipt B: see line 16n.) was from the *ala I Abasgorum* (line 33).[9] To the best of my knowledge this is the first papyrological attestation of this *ala*, which is known from the *Notitia* to have been stationed in the Great Oasis. If the name of this *ala* is to be read

6. See J. R. Rea's note to *P. Oxy.* xxxiii 2674.3; cf. also D. Hagedorn, *Proc. XIIth International Congress of Papyrology* (*Amer. Stud. in Papyrology* vii 1970) 210, and *ZPE* 10 (1973) 127 (no. 27.1n.).

7. It is perhaps worth remarking that the only certain occurrence of the word ἐξάκτωρ in our text is in line 32, and in this receipt the date is lost. Conversely where the date is certain, in Receipt B, the addition of ἤτοι ἐξάκτορι to the title of the strategos is probable but not wholly free from doubt: see the note to line 15.

8. In a paper to the XVIIth International Congress of Papyrology at Naples in 1983 I discussed some of the implications of the title στρατηγὸς ἤτοι ἐξάκτωρ. I hope at a later date to return to this point and to the whole question of the strategos/exactor in the fourth century, on which much new evidence has accumulated.

9. I owe the reading of the name of the *ala* in line 33 to Professor G. Wagner.

in line 16, the unit was already stationed in the Great Oasis at the date of our text.[10]

Receipt B was issued by an ὀπινιάτωρ (line 16). This official occurs several times in *P. Beatty Panop.* 2 and is discussed by Skeat in his note to line 41. According to the Legal Codes it denotes a soldier acting as *exactor militaris annonae* (see *TLL* s.v. *opinator*), a description which suits the official's activities in *P. Beatty Panop.* 2 well enough and would no doubt do to describe his function in the present papyrus (see below). In *P. Beatty Panop.* 2 ὀπινιάτωρ is used of a decurion, a cavalryman, a centurion, a *signifer*, an *imaginifer*, and an ordinary soldier; our text adds a *kataphraktarios* to this list. Skeat commented on the form, which in Latin is *opinator* but in *P. Beatty Panop.* 2 always ὀπινιάτωρ. This led him to suggest that in *P. Oxy.* XVII 2114.10 (A.D. 316) Hunt's ὀπιν{ν}ατόρων might conceal a misreading of ὀπινιατόρων. I have examined the papyrus in the Ashmolean Library and should be strongly inclined to read ὀπιγγιατόρων (*sic*). Skeat regarded this as the only other certain occurrence of the word in papyri, though pointing out that it should perhaps be read in *P. Erlang.* 105.46 (early 4th c.). It has subsequently appeared in *P. Oxy.* XLII 3029.4 (Valerian), where however only ὀπιν[ survives. Skeat had overlooked *P. Oxy.* XII 1419 (A.D. 265), not surprisingly, since Grenfell and Hunt considered the ὀπεινάτορι ἀπαι(τητῇ) τι(μῆς) πυροῦ occurring there to be a tax-collector whose name was Opinator; the word is therefore only indexed as a proper name. Piganiol, however, argued that it should be understood as the title of a military tax officer, and this is the view taken in *TLL*.[11] In the context this must surely be right and provides one instance of the title in Greek in the form ὀπινάτωρ, as in Latin. Both forms seem linguistically defensible: *opinator* would be derived from *opinor* (so *TLL*), and *opiniator* from *opinio*. For *opinio* used in a military context see *P. Flor.* II 278 v 4 and 8; the editor takes it as a proper name ('Ὀπινίων), but Daris is certainly right to reject this in his re-edition of the text.[12]

---

10. For the equivalence of the Hibite nome and the Great Oasis see H. Gauthier, *Les nomes d'Egypte* (*Mém. Inst. Eg.* 55, 1935) 130, and A. Calderini, *Dizionario*, s.v. Ἱβίτης. The reference in the *Notitia* is *Not. dign. orient.* 41 and 55.

11. A. Piganiol, *REG* 59/60 (1946/47) p. xiii; *TLL*, s.v. *opinator: vix nomen proprium ut edd. putant.*

12. S. Daris, *Documenti per la storia dell'esercito Romano in Egitto* (1964) no. 64; see the note *ad loc.*

The purpose for which the *opiniator* has been paid the money in the receipts in our papyrus is lost in all three examples. All we know is that the payments were for a purpose which involved the mention of a consular date (lines 4–6 and 22–23). This is somewhat unusual, but occurs, for example, in *P. Cair. Isid.* 41.18–22, and in several places in *P. Beatty Panop.* 2. In his note to 2.41 Skeat describes the *opiniator* as 'a soldier of any rank detailed to collect amounts of cash for the issue of pay and donatives'. No doubt his function in our papyrus falls into the same category. We may compare in particular *P. Beatty Panop.* 2.36–42, an instruction to the strategos to pay *opiniatores* for the *stipendium* of cavalry for 1 January, followed by the consular date for A.D. 300.

The title used of the public bankers also merits a brief comment. It is δημοσίων χρημάτων τραπεзῖται, followed by the name of the city (lines 3, 37–38), not δημόσιοι τραπεзῖται. The latter was the regular title during most of the Roman period, but it is quite certain that by the date of our papyrus the title had been changed to the longer expression δημοσίων χρημάτων τραπεзῖται. There are numerous fourth-century examples, e.g. *P. Oxy.* XII 1430, *P. Cair. Isid.* 54, *CPR* V 6, *P. Mich.* XV 720. The suggested reading which I earlier put forward in line 16 of *P. Oxy.* XLIV 3194 (A.D. 323), τῷ δημ(οσίῳ) τρα(πεзίτῃ), must therefore be wrong (cf. the comment in the note on the state of the papyrus at that point), and we should read an abbreviated form of the longer title, e.g. δη(μοσίων) χρη(μάτων) τρα(πεз- ).

One final point of interest concerns the organisation of the Thebaid at the time of this papyrus. Gelasios is addressed as strategos/exactor Ὀάσεως. In view of the reference in line 38 to Ἰβιτῶν πόλις ( = Hibis), there can be no doubt that the Oasis in question was the Great Oasis. Ὀάσεως would almost certainly have been further qualified in the lost part of the papyrus, either by adding Μεγάλης or Θηβαΐδος.[13] At the time of our text the Thebaid was divided into two subdivisions, the Upper and the Lower Thebaid, each under a procurator: see T. C. Skeat, *P. Beatty Panop.*, pp. xv–xx. On geographical grounds one might have expected the Great Oasis to belong to the Upper Thebaid. This is what is implied by the evidence of *P. Beatty Panop.* 2, which apparently gives us a complete list of the nomes comprising the

13. Either word is possible, see Calderini, *Dizionario*, s.v. Ὄασις Μεγάλη.

## J. David Thomas

Lower Thebaid in A.D. 300 and does not mention the Great Oasis
(see *P. Beatty Panop.*, *loc. cit.*). This would also agree with the
evidence of Georgius Cyprius, who places the Great Oasis in the
Upper Thebaid.[14] However, *P. Beatty Panop.* 2 provides no more
than an argument from silence, and we must set against Georgius
Cyprius the evidence of Hierocles, who includes the Great Oasis
in the Thebaid ἔγγιστα; this must mean the Lower Thebaid (so
Gauthier and Jones, *locc. citt.*). Line 21 of our text thus becomes
important for this question. After Θηβαίδος Hagedorn was unable
to read the traces as part of the title of the procurator of the Upper
Thebaid but believed them consistent with the reading κατωτ, i.e.
with the title of the *Lower* Thebaid. We can hardly doubt that the
procurator who was giving orders to be followed by the strateg-
os/exactor of the Great Oasis was the procurator in charge of the
division of the Thebaid to which this nome belonged. From this
it seems to follow that at the date of our papyrus the Great Oasis
was administratively part of the Lower Thebaid.

*P. Giss.* inv. 126 recto               Hibis

8 × 26 cm                        A.D. 309

```
      ἀκολούθως τοῖς κ]ελευσθεῖσι ὑ[πὸ    ±6      ]...κα.[
                     ]αρχος Πασι[      ±9      ] traces [
      δημοσίων χρη]μάτων τραπ[εζῖται    ±5      ] traces [
             ] δεσπότου ἡ[μῶν    ±8      ]ανο[
  5    δεσπ]οτῶν ἡμῶν [      ±11      ]υπα[
             ]ανοῦ Σεβαστο[ῦ    ±10     ].μο.[
      ἐν ν]ούμμοις τάλ[αντα    ±7      ]διε.[
             ] ἐξεδόμην τε[τρασσήν, τρ]ισσὴ[ν μὲν ἐπ' ὀνόματός σου τοῦ
                                                    στρατηγοῦ
      μοναχὴν δὲ ἐπ' ὀ]νόματος τῶν προ[κειμένων] τραπ[εζιτῶν
 10          ]. ὑπατείας τῶν δ[εσποτῶν] ἡμῶ[ν Οὐαλερίου Λικιννιανοῦ
                                                    Λικιννίου
      Σεβαστοῦ καὶ Φλαο]υίου Οὐαλερίου Κων[σταντίνο]υ υἱ[οῦ 'Αγούστων
             ]μενος ἠρίθ[μη]μαι [   ±5    ]ε..β.[
             ]νας καὶ ἐξεδόμην τὴ[ν] ἀποχ[ὴν ὡς πρόκειται
             ]      vacat        [
 15    Γ]ελασίῳ στρατηγῷ traces [
      ὁ]πινιάτωρ Ἴλ[η]ς (πρώτης) Ἀ[βάσγων (?)
             ] ἐν τῷ Ἰβίτῃ νομῷ χαίρειν. μετεβ[άλοντό μοι
      καὶ Πτο]λεμαῖος ὁ καὶ Τιμ[    ±7    ]οντε[
      ἐξ ἐπ]ιστάλματός σου τοῦ σ[τρατηγο]ῦ δ[
```

14. See Gauthier, *op. cit.* (n. 10) 129–33, and Jones, *op. cit.* (n. 3) 550 (note
to Table xlvi).

20                          ] traces                   [

                        ] τὴν ἐπιτροπὴν Θηβαΐδ[ο]ς traces [

               ὑπατείας τῶν δε]σποτῶν ἡμῶν Οὐαλερ[ί]ου Λικινν[ιανοῦ

                                     Λικιννίου Σεβαστοῦ καὶ

Φλαουίου Οὐαλερίου Κωνστα]ντίνου υἱοῦ 'Αγούστων . . . δαδ[

                  ] τάλ(αντα) ξς (δηνάρια) Ε καὶ τὴν ἀποχὴν

                                 τα[ύτην ἐξεδόμην

25                      σο]ῦ τοῦ στρατηγοῦ μοναχὴν δὲ ἐπ' [ὀνόματος

                   ] . νομον καὶ ἐπερωτηθεὶς ὡμολό[γησα.

                          ὑπατείας τῶν δεσποτῶν ἡμῶν

         Οὐαλερίου Λικιννι]ανοῦ Λικιννίου Σεβαστοῦ καὶ [Φλαουίου

                             Οὐαλερίου Κωνσταντίνου

υἱοῦ 'Αγούστων           ]ος Πυλάδης καταφρακτάριος ὁ[πινιάτωρ

                      ]ιμενα τοῦ ἀργυρίου ἐν νούμμ[οις

30                     καὶ ἐ]περωτηθεὶς ὡμολόγησα. ἔγραψ[α ὑπὲρ αὐτοῦ

                         ]        vacat        [

                Γελ]ασίωι στρατηγῷ ἤτοι ἐξάκτορι 'Οάσ[εως

                  ] . . ν εἴλης (πρώτης) 'Αβάσγων ὑπὸ Αὔλου . [

                  ] χαίρειν. μετεβάλο[ν]τό μοι ἐξ ἐπι[στάλματος

35                  -γ]ένους ἄρξαντος διαδεχομένου τ[ὴν

                   κ]υρίου μου διαδεχομένου τὴν . [

                   ]ν ὁ καὶ 'Ωριγένης καὶ Πτολεμαῖος [

             τραπε]ζεῖται τῆς 'Ιβιτῶν πόλεως ὑπὲρ [

11, 23, 28 *l.* Αὐγούστων      11 φλαο]υῖου      16 ἵλης α/      17 ἴβιτη      24 ταλ ✳

33 α/      38 *l.* τραπε]ζῖται

[In the notes which follow quotations in German are from the report on the papyrus sent to me by Professor Hagedorn.]

Line **1.** Above the line a trace of ink can be seen, possibly part of a column number.

] . . . κα . [ . 'Der 2. Buchst. Epsilon oder Sigma, der letzte Sigma oder Ny, auch Gamma.' If this receipt follows the pattern of the other two, one would expect the previous column to have recorded the authorisation of the strategos and the words here to be stating that he was acting on the orders of the procurator or acting-procurator (see line 21n.). However, what remains at this point cannot be part of the procurator's title. Could it be part of his name?

**2.** ]αρχος. Compare line 18; this suggests that we have here the name of one of the bankers and that the name was Ptolemaios also called Timarchos. If this is correct the letters following must be part of a patronymic. There is no patronymic in line 18 nor line 37. In the other two receipts the names must have been in the reverse order if the same names occurred in all three.

## J. David Thomas

**3.** δημοσίων χρη]μάτων τραπ[εζῖται. On the form of title see the introductory remarks. In line 38 the title is completed by the words τῆς Ἰβιτῶν πόλεως. Hagedorn comments on the present line, 'Am Ende Ἰβι]τῶν nicht unmöglich, aber unsicher.'

**4–6.** There can be little doubt that we have here two consular dates. Note in particular the use of δεσπότης and not κύριος; δεσπότης is never found in regnal dates at this period but is becoming increasingly common in consular dates, see D. Hagedorn and K. A. Worp, *ZPE* 39 (1980) 165–77, esp. 168–69. This being so, it is very tempting to insert in lines 5–6 the consular date for 308, which would fit very well in the form ὑπατείας τῶν δεσπ]οτῶν ἡμῶν [Διοκλητιανοῦ το]ῦ πα[τρὸς τῶν βασιλέων τὸ ι/ καὶ Γαλερίου Μαξιμι]ανοῦ Σεβαστο[ῦ τὸ 3/ (for this form see R. S. Bagnall and K. A. Worp, *Chronological Systems of Byzantine Egypt* [1978] 105–6). For line 4 it is almost equally tempting to read the consular date for the preceding year 307, since towards the end of that year only one consul is mentioned and the date takes the form ὑπατείας τοῦ δεσπότου ἡμῶν Μαξιμίνου Καίσαρος (Bagnall–Worp, *Chronological Systems*, 105). If this is correct, however, the scribe must have written Μαξιμιανοῦ where he intended Μαξιμίνου (for this same error see J. D. Thomas, *ZPE* 6 (1970) 181–82, and H. C. Youtie, *ZPE* 22 (1976) 46 n. 13).

**7.** ἐν ν]ούμμοις. It is curious that almost all examples of this phrase are in documents from the Great Oasis, e.g. *P. Grenf.* II 75.6–7, *SB* I 5679.9. The plate suggests that it might well also be read in *PUG* I 21.6–7 (ἐν] νού|μοις (*sic*)), and it could easily be restored in *PUG* I 20.5 after ἀρ[γυρίου.

]διε.[ . This is baffling; we expect a number.

**8–9.** Restored by comparison with lines 24–25. It is theoretically possible to suppose that of the four copies, two went to the strategos, one to the bankers and one to some other official. However, there is not really room for all this, and Hagedorn comments that δ]ισσή[ν is less good as a reading than τρ]ισσή[ν, since one ought to be able to see something of the *delta*. On the other hand he reports that *tau* in τραπ[εζιτῶν is very difficult and looks more like *gamma*.

**10.** The stroke visible at the start of the line may be the end of a flourish on *alpha*; read ἐπερωτηθεὶς ὡμολόγησ]α?

**10–11.** For the date in this form see Bagnall–Worp, *Chronological Systems*, 106.

**12.** Presumably προκεί]μενος at the start. At the end 'Beta scheint mir ganz sicher. Etwa ] ἐν Ἰβι[τῶν?'

**15.** After στρατηγῷ '[ἤ]τοι ἐ[ξ]άκτορ[ι ist vertretbar'.

**16.** ὁ]πινιάτωρ. On this official see the Introduction.

ἴλ[η]ς (πρώτης) Ἀ[βάσγων (?). After ιλ the reading is doubtful in the extreme (Hagedorn). For this *ala* see the Introduction.

**17.** The reference here is to the nome in which the *ala* is stationed. On the equivalence of the Hibite nome and the Great Oasis see the Introduction.

**18.** On the name see the note to line 2. Ptolemaios must be one of the two public bankers of the nome; cf. lines 3 and 37–38.

]οντε[ . One expects a title describing a magistracy held by the bankers. ἄρχ]οντε[ς is not attractive but I can suggest no alternative.

**19.** A common phrase in comparable contexts. We may confidently supply it in *P. Oxy.* xiv 1718.3–4, reading ἠρίθμημαι παρὰ σοῦ ἐ[ξ ἐπιστάλματος τοῦ στρατηγοῦ] Αὐρηλίου Ζηναγένους.

Hagedorn reports that a *delta* just before the papyrus breaks off is almost certain (for the omission of ἤτοι ἐξάκτωρ in the title of the strategos within a receipt cf. line 25). Comparison with lines 34–35 suggests that in both places we have a reference to a warrant issued by the strategos through a deputy, restoring here δ[ιά and in line 35 διαδεχομένου τ[ὴν στρατηγίαν.

**20.** 'Am Anfang wurden wir ] ̣εν[ lesen, statt Ny eventuell auch ϙϙ. Mehr ist nicht zu erkennen.' If the suggestion made in the previous note is correct, we might have here διαδεχο]μέν[ου.

**21.** This line, taken in conjunction with line 36 (and perhaps line 1), suggests that we have a reference to orders of an acting-procurator of one of the divisions of the Thebaid. I know of no parallel for such an acting-procurator in the fourth century, but the idea in itself is reasonable enough, and the epistrategos, who was in many ways the predecessor of such procurators, was often replaced by an acting-epistrategos (see nos. 25–26, 66, 73, 75 in J. D. Thomas, *The Epistrategos in Ptolemaic and Roman Egypt. Part 2: The Roman Epistrategos (Pap. Colon.* vi, 1982) 186–91). For the reading after Θηβαΐδ[ο]ς, see the Introduction.

**23.** . . .δαδ[. 'Der 1. Buchst. könnte sein Lambda, Alpha, kaum Chi; der 2. viell. Ypsilon, der 3. viell. Lambda.' I cannot offer any suggestions for a possible reading.

**24.** ] τάλ(αντα) ςϛ (δηνάρια) Ε. No doubt this was preceded by a statement of the amount in words. At the end of the line a restoration such as that in line 8 would seem probable.

**26.** ]. νομον. Final *nu* is oddly made and might be read σι; neither reading suggests any obvious restoration.

**27–28.** The supplement is on the long side, since we must allow room for the month and day to have been recorded.

**28.** On the *kataphraktarios* see *CPR* v 13.14–15n. *Omicron* could also be the start of ὁ [προκείμενος.

**29.** ]ιμενα. Presumably προκε]ίμενα, with reference to the sums recorded in line 24. *P. Oxy.* 1 84.22–24 is somewhat similar.

**30.** It is odd to find the 'illiteracy' statement beginning with ἔγραψα and not with the name of the person writing on behalf of the illiterate.

**32.** The reference is to the Great Oasis, see the Introduction.

**33.** ]. . ν. Seemingly this officer was not designated *opiniator*.

᾽Αβάσγων. Instead of *gamma* it would be much easier to read *tau*; but this cannot be right. For this *ala* see the Introduction.

ὑπὸ Αὔλου. Hagedorn reports the reading as certain. This is most unexpected; in such expressions ὑπό is always followed by an accusative and the scribe must surely have intended an accusative here.

**35.** See the notes to lines 19 and 20.

**36.** The letter before the break is most like *sigma*, but this would appear to give no sense (we do not expect τὴν σ[τρατηγίαν at this point). Comparison with line 21 (where see note) suggests that the reference here is to an acting-procurator, in which case the reading should be τὴν ἐ[πιτροπήν.

**37.** Πτολεμαῖος[ . No doubt the Ptolemaios also called Timarchos who appears in line 18 and perhaps line 2. After this will have come the titles of the bankers ending in δημοσίων χρημάτων τραπε]ζεῖται τῆς Ἰβιτῶν πόλεως.

## THE FORMULAIC PATTERN OF THE RECEIPTS

In order to indicate the way in which I should like to understand these receipts I append a conjectural reconstruction of Receipt B (lines 15–31). It must be stressed that this reconstruction depends heavily on Receipts A and C having followed the same pattern as Receipt B. This assumption may not be correct, but in favour of it is the fact that in several places phrases which survive occur at more or less the exact point in the text at which they would be expected if all the receipts were restored in the same way: cf., e.g., lines 7–12 with 24–8, lines 15–17 with 32–34, and lines 19–21 with 34–36.

Note that in Receipts A and C items (v) and (vi) of the following list precede item (iv). In Receipt A items (i) to (v) are lost, and items (vii) to (xiii) are lost in Receipt C.

(i) Addressee: (Aurelios?) Gelasios, strategos/exactor of the Great Oasis.

(ii) Description of the person issuing the receipt: Aurelios(?) Pylades, *kataphraktarios, opiniator* of the *ala I Abasgorum*, under the command of Aulus ——, stationed in the Hibite nome.

(iii) χαίρειν. μετεβάλοντό μοι.

(iv) Names of the public bankers with their titles: ]n also called Horigenes and Ptolemaios also called Timarchos...bankers of the public funds of the city of the Hibites.

(v) Authorisation I: 'As a result of a warrant issued by you the strategos through ]genes, former magistrate, acting-strategos'.

(vi) Authorisation II: 'In accordance with the orders of my lord the acting-procurator of the Lower Thebaid'.

(vii) Purpose of the payment (including the date A.D. 309).

(viii) Amount of payment: 66 talents 5000 denarii.

(ix) Statement that the receipt has been issued in four copies, three addressed to the strategos and one to the aforesaid bankers.

(x) καὶ ἐπερωτηθεὶς ὡμολόγησα.

(xi) Date: A.D. 309 (including month and day, here lost).

(xii) Signature of (Aurelios) Pylades, *kataphraktarios*, stating that he has had paid to him (in the city of the Hibites?) the aforesaid sum in cash and has issued the receipt as aforesaid and in answer to the formal question has given his assent.

(xiii) Illiteracy statement.

# Sulla datazione di *P. Wash. Univ.* 4: un epistratego in più, un prefetto d'Egitto in meno

GUIDO BASTIANINI

La datazione proposta dall'editore per *P. Wash. Univ.* 4[1] è basata sui seguenti elementi:

(1) al r. 7 è citato un "corrente" 7° anno;

(2) essendo la scrittura databile tra la fine del II e l'inizio del III secolo, la scelta è ristretta tra il 7° anno di Settimio Severo (198/99$^p$) e il 7° di Severo Alessandro (227/28$^p$);

(3) poiché al r. 6 si legge ὑπὸ τοῦ λαμπροτάτου ἡγεμόνος Κα. [ ,[2] essendo nel 7° anno di Settimio Severo attestato in carica Aemilius Saturninus,[3] non resta che supporre per *P. Wash. Univ.* 4 una data al 7° anno di Severo Alessandro (227/28$^p$), anno per il quale non era noto finora il nome del prefetto in carica. Questo nome risulterebbe ora, almeno in piccola parte, da *P. Wash. Univ.* 4: Ca$_*$[ .

Malgrado l'ineccepibile consequenzialità del ragionamento, nell'enunciazione dei dati esiste tuttavia un punto debole che, unito a una nuova lettura/congettura, determinerebbe una datazione piuttosto al 198/99$^p$.

1. Il testo, gravemente lacunoso (soprattutto sulla sinistra), è articolato in tre sezioni (rr. 1–7; rr. 8–13; rr. 14–15) chiaramente separate da uno spazio bianco; le sezioni sembrano riguardare ognuna un magistrato (di Ossirinco?) che nello svolgimento della sua ἀρχή si è reso in qualche modo debitore (?). Un piccolo miglioramento di lettura: al r. 15 vedrei, dalla foto (pl. 5): (γίνονται) (δραχμαὶ) ᾿Βψ⟦οεΓχγ⟧π [ (sembra trattarsi cioè di un arrotondamento per eccesso, della cifra, alla decina: 2775 dr. 3 ob. 3 ch. → 2780 dr.). Una congettura: la sezione seconda (rr. 8–13) non credo debba necessariamente considerarsi redatta in un 8° anno per il fatto che al r. 13 si legge ἀπὸ τοῦ ἑξῆς θ (ἔτους): anzi, dato che la sezione prima (rr. 1–7) è chiaramente da riferire a un "corrente" anno 7°, e considerando che, se la sezione seconda fosse davvero relativa a un 8° anno, ci si aspetterebbe piuttosto, al r. 13, ἀπὸ τοῦ εἰσιόντος θ (ἔτους), io penso che anche la sezione seconda possa essere stata redatta in un 7° anno.

2. Come osserva giustamente l'editore, non può trattarsi del prefetto Calvisius Statianus, perché questi fu in carica negli anni dal 10° al 15° di Marco Aurelio.

3. Cfr. in *ZPE* 17 (1975) 304.

127

Il punto debole è costituito dal fatto che non necessariamente le lettere Κα. [ (r. 6) devono essere considerate come l'inizio del nome prefettizio: non si contano i casi in cui, nei documenti, si dice per es. τὰ κελευσθέντα ὑπὸ τοῦ λαμπροτάτου ἡγεμόνος senza che sia specificato il nome proprio (per es., *BGU* I 139.6–8, 202ᵖ). Cade quindi la necessità di escludere il 7° anno di Settimio Severo (198/99ᵖ): l'ἡγεμών citato al r. 6 potrebbe essere benissimo Aemilius Saturninus.[4]

La nuova lettura interessa l'inizio del r. 12, dove, invece che ]νκησου, io vedrei piuttosto (cfr. pl. 5) ]νκεσσου, e sarei incline a riconoscervi il nome proprio Κο]νκέσσου, cioè l'epistratego dei Sette Nòmi Calpurnius Concessus,[5] attestato in carica dal 4° al 6° anno di Settimio Severo.[6] Il contesto purtroppo è così disperato che non si può stabilire se qui Calpurnius Concessus sia citato come ancora o non più in servizio:[7] certo è che il suo nome ci riporterebbe comunque al regno di Settimio Severo, per cui il 7° anno del r. 7 è il 198/99ᵖ, e resterebbe così definitivamente escluso il nome del "nuovo prefetto" (Ca*[ ) di Severo Alessandro.[8]

Un ulteriore elemento, meglio congruente forse alla datazione più alta (che mi è stato fatto notare da J. D. Thomas),[9] potrebbe essere individuato ai rr. 5 e 11, dove sono menzionati οἱ ἀπὸ τῆς πόλεως: per quanto rimanga incerto chi esattamente si intenda indicare con questa espressione, sta di fatto che οἱ ἀπὸ τῆς πόλεως

---

4. Le lettere κα.[ sarebbero quindi l'inizio di una parola per ora non precisabile (dalla foto non distinguo bene le tracce dell'ultima lettera prima della frattura), non l'inizio del nome proprio del prefetto.

5. Nell'eccellente lavoro di J. D. Thomas sull'epistratego nel periodo romano, si possono trovare gli elementi per giustificare la presenza dell'epistratego in un testo relativo (come sembra) alle ἀρχαί municipali: cfr. J. D. Thomas, *The Epistrategos in Ptolemaic and Roman Egypt*. Part 2: *The Roman Epistrategos* (Opladen 1982) 94–102.

6. Cfr. Thomas, *Roman Epistrategos*, 110 no. 58: 13.8.196ᵖ–26.8.198ᵖ.

7. Per il 7° anno di Settimio Severo (198/99ᵖ) non è noto il nome dell'epistratego dei Sette Nòmi: il primo epistratego noto dopo Concessus è Arrius Victor, la cui prima attestazione è del 5.11.199ᵖ (8° anno): cfr. Thomas, *Roman Epistrategos*, 110 no. 59.

8. In teoria si potrebbe sempre argomentare che, se Calpurnius Concessus è citato al r. 12 come ex-epistratego, nulla vieterebbe allora di considerare il "corrente" 7° anno del r. 7 come un anno del regno di Severo Alessandro (227/28ᵖ). Il contesto tuttavia, per quel poco che ne rimane, sembra non congruente a questa ipotesi, che comporterebbe la menzione di Calpurnius Concessus in relazione a un fatto posteriore di 30 anni.

9. Lettera del 2.10.1981.

ricorrono per ora soltanto (mi sembra) in un altro testo, *P. Ryl.* II 77.33 (192$^{\text{p}}$),[10] anteriore all'istituzione delle βουλαί nelle metropoli egiziane (200$^{\text{p}}$); e in effetti sembra strano che, se *P. Wash. Univ.* 4 fosse del regno di Severo Alessandro, non ci sia menzione appunto della βουλή. Tuttavia, la lacunosità del testo non consente affermazioni troppo decise su questo punto.

10. A. K. Bowman, *The Town Councils of Roman Egypt* (*American Studies in Papyrology* 11, 1970) 18 n. 46 (riprendendo una conclusione di P. Jouguet, in *REG* 30 (1917) 294–328), interpreta l'espressione οἱ ἀπὸ τῆς πόλεως in *P. Ryl.* II 77.33 come riferita genericamente al "pubblico" presente alla seduta: ma qui in *P. Wash. Univ.* 4 sembra che l'espressione indichi qualcosa di più giuridicamente definito (anche se purtroppo le condizioni del testo non consentono di andare agevolmente più avanti nell'interpretazione).

# Aigialos (αἰγιαλός), la "terre riveraine" en Egypte, d'après la documentation papyrologique

## DANIELLE BONNEAU

Αἰγιαλός, "terre riveraine", est un substantif grec classique qui, en Egypte, a eu une vie constante dans la documentation papyrologique depuis le IIIe siècle avant notre ère[1] jusqu'à l'époque byzantine.[2] D'autres mots apparentés ont été aussi utilisés dans la vallée du Nil: l'adjectif αἰγιαλῖτις qualifiant la terre apparemment définitivement dégagée des eaux,[3] l'adjectif αἰγιαλοφόρητος, "terre emportée par le lac",[4] et le nom composé αἰγιαλοφύλαξ, "gardien de la terre riveraine", titre d'un fonctionnaire qui, à la tête de l'ensemble du nome Arsinoïte, a de grandes responsabilités dans l'irrigation du Fayoum.[5] Nous ne nous occuperons ici que des mots qui concernent la terre elle-même, d'une part pour rappeler à quelle réalité géographique ils répondent en Egypte, et d'autre part pour réunir les renseignements sur son statut juridique et fiscal en relation avec l'administration de l'irrigation.

## I. Réalités géographiques

### (a) Nature de la "terre riveraine"

Au sens général, l'aigialos est une terre éventuellement recouverte d'eau, en bordure de mer ou de fleuve, un rivage plus ou moins étendu[6] selon les circonstances. Aussi aigialos désigne-t-il tantôt une

---

1. Première attestation: P. Cairo Zen. 59119.6, 24 janvier 256 av. n.è.

2. Dernière attestation: probablement SB 9402.10, VIe–VIIe s.

3. Les attestations de terre αἰγιαλῖτις s'insèrent dans une fourchette chronologique allant du 22 avril 152 (SB 11116) à 212 (P. Lond. 350.6).

4. P. Teb. 701 (a).12, ca 131 av. n.è.

5. Un développement sur l'aigialophylax prend place dans Le régime administratif des eaux en Egypte d'après la documentation papyrologique, en préparation. Actuellement, voir P. J. Sijpesteijn, P. Wisconsin p. 114.

6. Voir la définition donnée par E. Spohr en 1913: agri litorales dicuntur qui aqua sive Nili, sive lacus seu fossae detecti, revelati sunt (P. Iand. p. 85). La suite de la présente étude montrera que, pour l'Égypte, il y a des réserves à faire sur: sive Nili, seu fossae.

étendue d'eau, tantôt un sol dégagé des eaux qui l'avaient envahi temporairement. C'est en cela qu'il se distingue de ἀκτή, "bord de mer" ou "bord de rivière", qui est moins plat et suggère une dénivellation plus accentuée entre l'eau et la terre qui la borde.[7] Dans ce sens large et fluctuant, on trouve αἰγιαλός en plusieurs régions d'Egypte: un *Megas Aigialos* est connu en bordure de la Mer Rouge[8] par un texte littéraire; nous n'avons aucune occurrence papyrologique pour le Delta; pour la vallée du Nil proprement dite un seul témoignage de *megas aigialos* de l'époque byzantine nous est parvenu,[9] non localisé. D'autre part, un acte de partage entre deux frères aux environs du monastère d'Ama Tapollôs dans le nome Panopolite, révèle, par la précision apportée à décrire les constructions qui existent sur la propriété partagée,[10] la valeur de l'exactitude dans la description de la terre; on y mentionne "une île qui est à cet endroit" et "les rives" ou plus précisément les "terres riveraines qui s'y adjoignent avec la grâce de Dieu". L'emploi jusqu'ici unique de ce mot pour les bords du Nil paraît être dû à une particularité de langage de la famille qui fait le partage. Car les autres attestations du mot αἰγιαλός qui s'échelonnent sur un millénaire sont toutes du Fayoum. L'emploi du mot semble bien relever d'une terminologie régionale.

Pour l'équivalent démotique, une supposition est possible: *kl sj*,[11] mais dans le nome Arsinoïte, *ḥ n y* correspond mieux aux réalités marécageuses de l'*aigialos*.[12] Le copte ⲕⲣⲟ "rivage, limite (d'une mer, d'un fleuve)" rend le grec *aigialos*.[13] Sous différentes formes de ce mot copte, nous avons des attestations de "terre riveraine" en divers points de la vallée: en Haute-Egypte à Pathyris, une terre dite ⲡⲕⲣⲱ se trouve à l'ouest du Nil[14] dans

---

7. Un passage de Pausanias (II 34.9) où les deux mots se rencontrent en même temps, montre bien qu'il ne s'agit pas de la même réalité géographique.

8. A. Calderini, *Dizionario* IV (1981) 251, renvoie, sans complément, au vol. I p. 35 (1915).

9. *Stud. Pal.* III 410, VIe s.

10. *P. Cairo Masp.* 67313.45, VIe–VIIe s. Pour le vocabulaire des constructions dans ce document, voir G. Husson, *Oikia*, s.v. πύργος, μονή, αὐθεντική.

11. *P. Ox. Griffith* 1.5, 2.6, 12.5; IIe s. av. n.è.: "la riva del lago".

12. Voir *P. Vindob. D. gr.* 6933.11 (E. A. E. Reymond, "Dimê and its Papyri", dans *Bull. of John Rylands Library* 52 (1969–70) 222).

13. W. E. Crum, *A Coptic Dictionary* (Oxford 1939) 115 a.

14. *P. Strassb.* 89.9, en 99 av. n.è.

la bande formée d'anciens atterrissements du Nil (*tainia*).[15] On rencontre aussi пекрєω comme nom de terrains dans le nome Hermopolite.[16] Peut-être avons-nous une preuve de la permanence de ce mot à l'époque arabe, pour le nome Arsinoïte.[17] Un autre toponyme пкро ѝтоот correspondant au grec ἐποικίον Βουνῶν, présente пкро comme une terre émergée.[18] Cet aspect de ce qu'est пкро concorde avec les données des documents papyrologiques qui permettent de préciser la nature géographique de l'*aigialos*. Mais pour ce faire, nous sommes amenés, faute d'autres matériaux, à ne pouvoir étudier l'*aigialos* que dans le nome Arsinoïte.

### (b) Localisation de l'aigialos dans le Fayoum

Il y avait deux zones de terres riveraines, l'une au bord méridional du Lac Moeris et l'autre dans l'actuelle dépression d'El Gharaq, dans la partie sud-ouest. L'*aigialos* des bords du Lac Moeris (Birket Karoun) se divise lui-même en deux zones, séparées par de petites éminences de 16m d'altitude, au milieu de la rive sud du lac. Les témoignages relativement abondants permettent de voir quels villages se trouvaient à proximité de ces rivages à l'époque gréco-romaine. A l'est et au sud-est, l'*aigialos* s'étendait jusqu'au territoire des villages de Soknopaiou Nèsos,[19] de Karanis,[20] de Niloupolis[21] et probablement de Théogenes Philopatôr.[22] L'expression αἰγιαλῖτις γῆ est employée pour cette seule région. Au sud-ouest de ce même lac, l'*aigialos* avançait au sud de la limite actuelle des eaux de plusieurs kilomètres. Certains papyrus[23]

---

15. *P. Lips.* 2.7, en 99 av. n.è. Voir Pestman, "Les archives privées de Pathyris", dans *P. Lugd.-Bat.* XIII p. 82 n. 236.

16. *P. Flor.* 383.13, en 232 de n.è. Voir M. Drew-Bear, *Le nome Hermopolite*, p. 206 (ces terrains seraient dans la circonscription de Pesla Anô, p. 200; corriger l'erreur de numéro 383 et non 384).

17. *P. Lond.* 1763 (v p. 221).7: пекро. Une autre équivalence copte (ммоопє, "place de l'eau", Crum, *op. cit.* (n. 13) 153b) montre le flottement terminologique de ces mots.

18. Crum, *op. cit.* (n. 13) 115a. On ne sait rien de la réalité géographique traduite par Βουνῶν, dont on a peu d'exemples.

19. Une quinzaine de papyrus concernent Soknopaiou Nèsos en relation avec l'*aigialos*.

20. Par ex. *P. Cairo Goodsp.* 22, en 158/9. Ajouter probablement *P. Cairo Zen.* 59119; 59748.

21. *P. Lond.* 194.29.

22. *Stud. Pal.* XXII 88.7, IIIe s. de n.è.

23. *P. Iand.* 30.16, en 105 ou 106. Cf. encore *P. Iand.* 27.12, en 100/1.

montrent que les habitants de Théadelphia et Euhéméria avaient à faire avec les terres de l'*aigialos*. L'agglomération de Bérénikis Aigialou emprunte son nom au rivage au bord duquel elle se trouvait.[24]

Au sud du nome, la dépression d'El Gharaq contenait, dans sa partie nord-ouest, à l'époque romaine, un lac résiduel, de nature analogue au Lac Moeris dont les bords étaient également appelés *aigialos*.[25] Une dizaine de documents suggèrent que cette "terre riveraine" n'était pas loin des villages suivants: Magdôla,[26] Bérénikis Thesmophorou, Narmouthis,[27] Kerkèsis[28] et Oxyrhyncha.[29] C'est l'*aigialos* du district Polémon[30] et il figure sur certaines cartes modernes.[31] Les papyrus nous apportent à son sujet deux précisions: par l'une nous savons qu'il était non loin du temple de Hérôn à Magdôla[32] sur les terres duquel il se répandait;[33] par l'autre, il semble qu'il était bordé par le désert; d'où l'expression ἐρήμου αἰγιαλοῦ, connue pour ce seul endroit.[34]

24. Les nombreux papyrus où figure le nom de ce village ne nous renseignent pas sur l'histoire de sa formation; son nom est d'époque ptolémaïque; sa vie agricole paraît correspondre à des terres depuis longtemps dégagées des eaux du lac; son existence doit être bien antérieure à la domination grecque.

25. Les papyrus qui concernent cet *aigialos* d'El Gharaq sont: *P. Teb.* 826.21, en 172 av. n.è.; *P. Teb.* 79.66, 74–75, après 148 av. n.è.; *P. Teb.* 82.38, en 115 av. n.è.; *P. Teb.* 83.51 à 56, fin IIe s. av. n.è.; *SB* 7259.13, 15 mars 94 av. n.è.; *P. Teb.* 308 (= *W. Chrest.* 319).5, en 174 de n.è.; *BGU* 1035 (= *W. Chrest.* 23).4, 1ère moitié du Ve s. Probablement: *P. Teb.* 998.5, début IIe s. av. n.è.; *PSI* 901.7 et 17, en 46 n.è.; *P. Oxy.* 918 xi 14, IIe s.; *SB* 9402.10, VIe–VIIe s. Dans *P. Petaus* 25.22, le mot lu ἐγιαλοῦ a été utilisé par erreur pour une terre au voisinage de Ptolémaïs Hormou, pour laquelle nous n'avons aucun témoignage de "terre riveraine".

26. *P. Teb.* 82.38.

27. *PSI* 901.7 et 17.

28. *BGU* 1035.4, *SB* 9402.10.

29. *BGU* 1035.

30. *P. Berol.* 21877.6, en 152/3 (C. A. Nelson, "Report from Supervisors of Fishing", dans *Museum Philologum Londiniense* 2 (1977) 233–43).

31. Voir par ex. O. Toussoun, *Mémoires sur l'histoire du Nil* 3 (1925) pl. 17 représentant la carte des canaux du Fayoum d'après des renseignements de l'année 1091 de n.è. Voir sur ce petit lac d'El Gharaq: E. Bernand, *IG Fayoum* 3, p. 29 n. 3 et 30 n. 1; D. Bonneau, *Le Fisc et le Nil*, 181 n. 4.

32. *SB* 7259.13. Voir W. Rübsam, *Götter und Kulte in Faijum* (Bonn 1974) 121.

33. Voir *IG Fayoum* no. 152 (*SB* 7259) commentaire pp. 48–49. Tandis que κατακλύζειν indique un débordement accidentel, προσκλύζειν signifie que les eaux gagnent de proche en proche en dépassant les limites habituelles (même sens du préfixe προσ- dans πρόσβασις; cf. Bonneau, *op. cit.* (n. 31) 40 n. 165).

34. *P. Teb.* 308.4–5; voir le commentaire de Grenfell–Hunt en 1907 *ad loc.*

### (c) L'étendue de l'aigialos

Les variations de l'état des bords de ces lacs (Moeris ou El Gharaq)
sont grandes à l'époque gréco-romaine; mais elles vont dans le sens
d'un assèchement progressif connu par les études géographiques
concernant tout le Fayoum. Nos papyrus illustrent ce processus en
nous montrant l'*aigialos* tantôt comme une étendue d'eau, tantôt
comme une terre ("riveraine"). Nous avons rencontré ce même
double sens (terre et eau) pour le mot *drymos*;[35] celui-ci évolue du
"fourré aquatique" à la terre cultivée, mais paraît d'une nature
différente: tandis que le *drymos* est un marais formé d'eaux
d'infiltration qui se situe entre les canaux et la bordure désertique
sur le pourtour de la cuvette du Fayoum, l'*aigialos* est exclusivement
le marécage des bords d'un lac d'où proviennent les eaux qui le
recouvrent d'une pellicule plus ou moins profonde,[36] où sans doute
est possible la pousse des papyrus.[37] La pêche y est réglementée;
les eaux territoriales affectées à tel ou tel village y sont délimitées
par des marques matérialisées par des pieux.[38] Deux papyrus
reflètent l'existence de ces réglementations, à l'occasion de disputes
qui naissent du franchissement illicite de ces limites; l'un concerne
un conflit entre les pêcheurs de Thrasô et le village de Sentrepai,[39]
localités sises au sud-ouest du Lac Moeris. L'autre document est
un serment de pêcheurs jurant de ne pas prendre les poissons sacrés
(oxyrhynque et lépidote); rédigé par le "scribe des pêcheurs de
l'*aigialos* de Bérénikis Thesmophorou",[40] il concerne l'*aigialos* d'El
Gharaq, pour lequel des querelles éclatent encore au Ve siècle
entre habitants de différents villages des environs (Kerkèsis,
Oxyrhyncha).[41] Seuls les habitants d'Oxyrhyncha y sont dits
"(pêcheurs) de l'*aigialos*". Ce village était probablement à l'ouest
de la dépression d'El Gharaq, non loin de l'endroit où l'*aigialos*

---

35. D. Bonneau, "Le *drymos*, marais du Fayoum", dans *L'Egyptologie* en 1979,
pp. 189–90. Les deux mots se trouvent dans un même document: *P. Teb.* 308;
voir Nelson, *op. cit.* (n. 30) n. 6 et 9.
36. Ἐφ' ὕδωρ: *Stud. Pal.* I 32.11.
37. *P. Teb.* 308.
38. *P. Flor.* 275.19: καμακια; voir n. *ad* l. 11.
39. *P. Flor.* 275, lettre de Héroninos à Alypios, *ca* 260.
40. *PSI* 901.7 et 17. Voir H. Henne, "La police de la pêche dans l'Egypte
gréco-romaine dans ses rapports avec la religion", *Aegyptus* 31 (1951) 184–9.
41. *BGU* 1035.

était en bordure du désert, ce qui expliquerait qu'il ressentît lui-même les effets de l'assèchement progressif de cette zone, comme en témoigne un "jardin-désert", παράδεισος ἔρημος où des palmiers portent des fruits en 159 av. n.è.[42] Le processus de dessèchement s'est assurément fait en dents de scie, comme nous le montrent nos documents papyrologiques.

Lorsque l'*aigialos* s'assèche, le retrait de l'eau peut être préjudiciable aux habitants des villages que le bord de cette sorte de lac alimente. Quelques années avant notre ère, du côté de Soknopaiou Nèsos, les prêtres du temple du dieu Crocodile, signalent, dans une plainte adressée au préfet d'Egypte, que l'*aigialos* par lequel ils ont l'eau s'est retiré, et que les villageois se sont enfuis; eux-mêmes, qui sont restés à cause des nécessités du culte impérial entre autres obligations religieuses, n'ont plus de ressources; le document, quoique lacuneux, permet de comprendre qu'ils ont enregistré des variations dans les avancées et les retraits de l'eau de l'ordre de deux cents mètres (4 schoinioi).[43]

Dans des cas moins dramatiques, le sol découvert par les eaux, après qu'on en ait ôté la végétation sauvage,[44] peut procurer quelque rapport agricole. Son état humide en fait un lieu de pâturage[45] où paît le bétail à partir du moment où les eaux de la crue ne font plus sentir leurs effets en bordure du Lac Moeris, c'est-à-dire en octobre. La terre devient alors un éventuel sujet de dispute: les gens de Théogenis Philopatôr s'en saisissent au détriment des percepteurs de Soknopaiou Nèsos.[46] La "terre riveraine découverte", ἀποκαλυφὴ αἰγιαλός,[47] devient l'objet de contrats de location. L'un d'eux,[48] décrivant les limites d'une "terre riveraine découverte" d'une superficie de 1,65 ha près de Soknopaiou Nèsos, résume en quelques mots le processus de

42. *P. Moen.* inv. 16.10–12 (P. J. Sijpesteijn, "Ptolemaic Property-Return", *Chr. d' Eg.* 106 (1978) 307–12; voir commentaire *ad loc.*), 13 août 159 av. n.è.

43. *CPR* VII 1.9, entre 7 et 4 av. n.è.

44. Βοτανισμός sur le "terre riveraine" sur 4,13 ha: *P. Cairo Zen.* 59119.6, 24 janvier 256 av. n.è.

45. *BGU* 35.7, 8 octobre 222 de n.è.: plainte au stratège: "A partir du 1er octobre, ma vache paissait sur l'*aigialos*; mon bouvier en se réveillant tôt le matin l'a trouvée tuée par je ne sais qui...".

46. *P. Lond.* 924 ( = *W. Chrest.* 355), en 187/8. Voir Hobson, "Apias", *Aegyptus* 62 (1982) 86.

47. *BGU* 640.7, 16 janvier d'une année inconnue du Ier s. de n.è. *CPR* 32.7.

48. *CPR* 32, en 218 de n.è.

dessèchement dans cette région; il précise ainsi la nature des terrains qui entourent le lopin loué: au sud, la terre χερσός, déjà desséchée, et entrée dans la catégorie fiscale reconnue "sèche";[49] à l'est et à l'ouest, les sols plats désignés par le terme ἐδάφη.

Ἔδαφος, quand il s'agit d'une terre considérée du point de vue de l'irrigation, est le sol aplani, la terre qui, selon les géographes, après avoir été submergée, a subi le planage. En Egypte, l'irrigation par submersion à l'aide de bassins, n'exige pas ce procédé; à plus forte raison, l'eau du lac en se retirant, laisse un sol égalisé, bien "plané".[50] Au nord du terrain loué dont il est question ici, se trouve la "terre riveraine sous l'eau". Ce contrat de location rend bien compte du mouvement général du retrait des eaux qui, à cet endroit, se produit en effet du sud au nord. Il arrive que la "terre riveraine" cultivée soit saturée d'humidité et que, à la suite d'une inondation accidentelle, elle devienne "saline"; un tel cas nous est connu pour les alentours du lac d'El Gharaq au début du IIe siècle avant notre ère.[51] Une avancée des eaux peut entraîner l'anéantissement du sol cultivable, qui est alors αἰγιαλοφόρητος.[52] Malgré ces alternatives de retrait des eaux ou de bienfaits dus à l'inondation,[53] l'assèchement poursuit son cours globalement au long des siècles. L'exploitation de ces terres gagnées sur des rives marécageuses en vient à avoir besoin d'être soutenue par le creusement de canaux en vue de l'irrigation (ποτισμός), et non pas de drainage dont nous n'avons pas de témoignage. C'est d'abord aux alentours de l'*aigialos* d'El Gharaq que des canaux neufs sont construits dans ce but en 172 avant notre ère.[54] Pour ce qui est des bords du Lac Moeris nous en avons des preuves indirectes: au IIIe siècle de notre ère, le canal (*diôryx*) qui borde la "terre

49. Terre constamment sèche...qui n'entrait pas dans les rôles d'impôts. Voir *P. Col.* VII 172, introd. Voir aussi Bonneau, *op. cit.* (n. 31) 78.

50. Αἰγιαλοῦ ἐδάφη: *P. Iand.* 30.16; *SB* 8976.13; *P. Lond.* 350; *P. Ryl.* 171.

51. *P. Teb.* 998.5: superficie "saline" de 2,75 ha. Voir Bonneau, *op. cit.* (n. 31) 67, n. 284 et 327.

52. *P. Teb.* 701 (a).12, *ca* 131 av. n.è.

53. Le cas du contrat de location *BGU* 831 (26 janvier–24 février 201) pour *ca* 5 ha de "terre sèche riveraine", χέρσος αἰγιαλοῦ, ne peut s'expliquer que par ces variations et sa position entre le désert (au nord) et le canal (au sud, probablement celui qui s'infléchit vers Soknopaiou Nèsos), du moins pour une partie de la superficie louée. Voir *P. Teb.* II pp. 377–78 s.v. Herakleia.

54. *P. Teb.* 826.24.

riveraine sèche" à l'est du lac, non loin de Soknopaiou Nèsos,[55] doit exister depuis fort longtemps. Au sud-ouest du même lac, l'*aigialos* qui fait partie des terres gérées par Héroninos, intendant d'Alypios dans la seconde moitié du IIIe siècle de notre ère, est en partie en marécage et lieu de pêche,[56] en partie asséché et cultivé en blé.[57] Le réseau hydraulique allait jusqu'à l'*aigialos*, puisqu'une lettre d'Héroninos mentionne une "digue vers la terre riveraine".[58]

## II. Statut juridique et fiscal de l'*aigialos*

La nature géographique de l'*aigialos* fait que, comme le *drymos*,[59] cette sorte de sol, alternativement terre et eau, appartient au Souverain d'Egypte. Lorsqu'elle est en eau, les revenus sont ceux de la "chasse-pêche" dont nous avons évoqué les activités ci-dessus. Nous n'avons qu'un papyrus comme témoin précis de ce stade de la fiscalité sur l'*aigialos*:[60] en 152/3, les ἐπιτηρηταὶ θήρας ἰχθύας ὑδάτων αἰγιαλοῦ Πολέμωνος μέριδος ont perçu des droits de pêche sur les concessionnaires de l'année et ils en font rapport aux conservateurs de comptes publics; ce document se place donc entre les exploitants de l'*aigialos* en question, en l'occurrence celui d'El Gharaq, et la comptabilité des revenus de l'Etat. Cette situation fiscale est liée à l'état hydrologique de l'*aigialos* qui est variable, sinon chaque année, du moins par périodes; l'opportunité d'avoir nommé des "épitérètes de la chasse-pêche des eaux de l'*aigialos* du district Polémon" peut s'expliquer par une succession de crues abondantes de 137 à 150[61] qui ont ré-alimenté en eau la dépression d'El Gharaq pourtant en voie d'assèchement, comme l'attestent des papyrus du IIe siècle avant notre ère. Ce document montre bien, quand il est replacé dans le contexte de géographie historique,

55. *BGU* 831. Voir ci-dessus, n. 53.

56. *P. Flor.* 275.

57. *P. Flor.* 150.5; 11 juillet 266: Héroninos s'occupe de faire le dépiquage des moissons, récoltées sur la "terre riveraine", que les rats sont en train de manger aux environs d'Euhéméria.

58. χ]ώματος εἰς τὸν αἰγιαλόν, *P. Flor.* 275.15–16.

59. D. Bonneau, "Loi et coutume: un exemple, les marais du Fayoum appelés drymoi", *JESHO* 26 (1983) 1–13.

60. *P. Berol.* 21877 (voir ci-dessus n. 30).

61. Bonneau, *op. cit.* (n. 31) 244–47.

la souplesse administrative d'un système fiscal obligé de tenir le plus grand compte des variations du fleuve ainsi que des conséquences de celles-ci, et de "coller au terrain" pour ainsi dire.[62] De ce point de vue, la fiscalité concernant l'*aigialos* lorsqu'il est en eau, paraît plus étroitement institutionnalisée que celle du *drymos*, qui, elle, est comprise de façon plus générale dans le titre des "épitérètes des autres revenus des eaux c'est-à-dire ceux qui adviennent par accident",[63] ἐπιτηρηταί... τῆς ἄλλης ὑδατικῆς προσόδου ἢ καὶ ὑποπίπτει.

Lorsque les eaux se retirent et que l'*aigialos* devient "terre riveraine", elle est "royale", et ce terme est toujours employé à l'époque romaine,[64] bien que le Souverain soit alors l'empereur. Elle est, à l'époque ptolémaïque, concédée parfois à des clérouques, comme nous le savons par des exemples du IIe siècle avant notre ère à Magdôla.[65] Elle est aussi affectée au revenu du temple du "dieu du village" pour 10 aroures (2,75 ha) dans ce même Magdôla.[66] A l'époque romaine, la terre αἰγιαλῖτις se trouve dans les terres domaniales: *ousia* Antonianè,[67] Camelianè,[68] Doryphorianè,[69] Germanicianè,[70] Lourianè,[71] Mecenianè,[72] Senecianè,[73] Severianè.[74] Les témoignages que nous avons à leur

---

62. Cette interprétation diverge ici de celle de Nelson, *op. cit.* (n. 30) 242, commentaire *ad* ll. 4–6.

63. *P. Oslo* III 91, en 149; *P. Leit.* 14 (= *SB* 10206). 9–10, en 148.

64. *P. Ryl.* 171.13, en 56/7 à Heraklia; *SB* 8976.12–13, 28 novembre 105, à Soknopaiou Nèsos; *BGU* 234.9 et 13 (*BL* I 28–29), 28 juillet 142, à Karanis; *P. Oxy.* 918 xi 14 (voir introd. p. 272), IIe s. Nome Ars.: *Stud. Pal.* XXII 174.6, en 218 à Soknopaiou Nèsos (voir G. Poethke, *Epimerismos* 22).

65. *P. Teb.* 83.51–56, fin IIe s. av. n.è.; *P. Teb.* 79.65.

66. *P. Teb.* 82.38.

67. *P. Mich.* 224.6023. Pour la suite des présentes remarques sur la fiscalité de la "terre riveraine", j'ai calculé les surfaces imposées en prenant pour base de calcul le *naubion* à 100 drachmes/aroure (taux de la terre catoecique, S. L. Wallace, *Taxation in Roman Egypt*, 60), bien que nous ignorions le taux appliqué en réalité. Pour *P. Mich.* 224.6023: *ca* 3 m².

68. *P. Mich.* 224.4249: 23 m²; 4941: *ca* 14 m²; *P. Mich.* 357B3: 14 m².

69. *P. Mich.* 224.4213: *ca* 12 m²; 5914: 9 m².

70. *SB* 11116.9, 22 avril 152, à Karanis.

71. *P. Mich.* 224.5569: 16 m²; 5579: 11 m²; *P. Mich.* 357A3: 14 m².

72. *P. Mich.* 224.3685: *ca* 7 m²; 5431: 8 m²; 6016: *ca* 14 m²; 6184: *ca* 5 m²; 6200: *ca* 5 m²; *P. Mich.* 357B27: *ca* 6 m².

73. *P. Mich.* 224.4111: *ca* 5 m²; 4200: *ca* 4 m²; 4223: *ca* 20 m²; 4228: *ca* 14 m²; *P. Mich.* 225.3287: *ca* 2 m².

74. *P. Mich.* 224.4009: 24 m²; 5909: 10 m².

sujet concernent tous Karanis[75] et ses environs, à savoir Patsontis et Psenarpsenêsis.[76]

Le fait que la terre y ait été à l'origine *aigialos* explique sans doute en grande partie son statut. Le terme αἰγιαλῖτις, qui n'apparaît que dans les documents papyrologiques officiels, reflète une situation particulière gardant le souvenir d'un état ancien, antérieur à la domination romaine et même grecque. La "terre riveraine" encore susceptible d'être en eau (*aigialos*), fait partie des terres difficiles à cultiver qui sont assignées aux villages.[77] Elle est cependant, sous l'angle des travaux agricoles, cultivée selon la coutume.[78] Aussi longtemps que l'*aigialos* est en eau, il est mesuré en schoinioi,[79] mais une fois "découverte", la "terre riveraine" est mesurée en aroures.[80] Elle reçoit, comme les autres terres cultivables, un prêt de semence.[81] Les surfaces assignées sont parfois grandes, par exemple 93 aroures ( = 25,6 ha) à Soknopaiou Nèsos, quand il s'agit de tout un groupe de cultivateurs.[82] Elle est l'objet d'inspection de contrôle (*épiskepsis*) effectué par le cadastre,[83] qui, au IIe siècle de notre ère, après l'avoir trouvée sous l'eau, constate qu'elle est en partie en pâturage plus d'une dizaine d'années plus tard;[84] il y a alors une "nouvelle mensuration (*anametresis*)".[85] Des fragments de cadastre de la "terre riveraine" assignée (*épibolè*) aux cultivateurs de Soknopaiou Nèsos,[86] nous restent; les fluctuations de l'état de cette terre indiquent à elles seules que l'*épibolè* n'était pas permanente.[87] Quand cette terre est louée par contrat, on y trouve la clause courante prévoyant une

75. Voir H. Geremek, *Karanis* (Wrocław 1969) 86.

76. Patsontis: *ousia* Antonianè. Psenarpsenèsis: *ousia* Camelianè et Mecenianè (*P. Mich.* 224.3685, 6184). Sur ces lieux, voir Geremek, *op. cit.* (n.75) 22–24. Sur ces domaines, voir G. M. Parássoglou, *The Imperial Estates in Roman Egypt*, 47.

77. *P. Gen.* 16 ( = *W. Chrest.* 354). *P. Cattaoui* II (*SB* 4284). Voir Rostowzev, *Kolonat*, 116–78.

78. *P. Gen.* 16.21.

79. *CPR* VII 1.9 sq.; *P. Flor.* 275.21.

80. *P. Gen.* 16.13–14.

81. *P. Cairo Good.* 22.3, en 158/9.

82. *CPR* I 33.4. Voir Rostowzev, *Kolonat*, 170.

83. *P. Teb.* 83.52, 54, 56, fin IIe s. av. n.è.

84. *P. Oxy.* 918 xi 14; une IIème année du IIe s.

85. *Ibid.* Voir Bonneau, *op. cit.* (n. 31) 203: "...mensuration reprenant tout à zéro".

86. *P. Princ.* 172.4, 5, 6, 7, 15, 19, 20, IIe s.: αἰγιαλῖτις.

87. Cf. Wallace, *op. cit.* (n. 67) 21.

diminution du loyer (et des impôts) "dans le cas où (la terre) serait non-inondée ou bien sous l'eau".[88] Cette même clause se retrouve dans les contrats du début du IIIe siècle de notre ère pour la terre dite "riveraine sèche", χέρσος αἰγιαλός[89] aux environs de Soknopaiou Nèsos. Près d'Euhéméria, à l'autre bout du Lac Moeris, une location est faite pour 5 ans, ce qui prouve la confiance des cultivateurs sur son état d'assèchement.[90] La demande de location de "terre riveraine découverte" est adressée au basilico-grammate au Ier siècle de notre ère,[91] et il en est toujours responsable au IIe siècle;[92] il agit ici en gérant des biens "royaux", à mon avis, car dans la terminologie des catégories juridiques de la terre, la "terre riveraine" reste distincte de la terre "publique" (*demosia gê*).[93]

C'est dans le domaine de la fiscalité que la "terre riveraine" paraît être dans une situation différente de la terre cultivable normale. Les conditions du loyer sont fort libres, et le loyer peu élévé: $2\frac{1}{3}$ artabes à l'aroure[94] ou $2\frac{1}{2}$.[95] Celui-ci semble être l'objet d'un forfait dans un document de nature imprécise, où il est question de ἀποτάκτου αἰγιαλοῦ.[96] Mais si ingrate que cette terre soit à cultiver, elle est le sujet de disputes. Quand les querelles qui surgissent entre les cultivateurs auxquels elle est assignée et les accapareurs deviennent violentes, la situation relève de l'ordre public et elles sont signalées au stratège du district concerné[97] et, à l'époque byzantine, au comte.[98] Naturellement, un des motifs de conflit peut être la question des limites, ce qui nécessite l'inter-vention de l'*horiodiktès*, expert pour classer les terres dans telle ou

---

88. *BGU* 640.12–14, Ier s. de n.è. (13,75 ha). Cf. encore *CPR* I 239.10–11, 31 janvier 212; *BGU* 831; *SB* 8976.16: la clause est ici pour ainsi dire renforcée par l'addition suivante: "Si (la terre) est visible, le loyer sera comme il est dit ci-dessus".

89. *BGU* 831.5, 8, 11, 26 janvier–24 février 201 de n.è. (voir sur ce document Grenfell–Hunt, *P. Teb.* II p. 377 s.v. Herakleia); *CPR* I 239.6; *P. Lond.* 350.6.

90. *P. Iand.* 30.

91. *BGU* 640; *P. Lond.* 350; *CPR* I 239.

92. *P. Iand.* 30.

93. *BGU* 659 ii 7, 21 mai 229.

94. *CPR* 32, en 218.

95. *CPR* I 33, en 215.

96. *PSI* 1043.12 et 18, 29 mai 103.

97. *P. Iand.* 27.12, en 100/1. Le mot αἰγιαλός n'apparaît pas, mais ἀπο-καλυφείσας la désigne sûrement.

98. *BGU* 1035.4; première moitié du Ve s.

telle catégorie fiscale;[99] comme nous le voyons dans la plainte de deux habitants de Soknopaiou Nèsos, la décision de l'*horiodiktès* est contestée au sujet de la terre αἰγιαλῖτις qu'ils cultivent depuis 25 ans[100] et sur laquelle ils paient les impôts. La confusion est grande au début du IIIe siècle dans cette partie du nord-ouest du Fayoum; plusieurs pétitions sont adressées au centurion;[101] les cultivateurs, invités par le préfet à rentrer dans leur village,[102] obtempèrent, mais ne savent pas dans quel statut fiscal se trouve la terre riveraine qu'ils cultivent et n'y comprennent plus rien.

En effet, au moment où la "terre riveraine" est en eau (statut géographique initial), elle se trouve sous le statut des pêcheries. Au moment où elle est en pâturage (stade géographique inter-médiaire), elle est l'objet de διαγραφή, enregistrement (plus ou moins occasionnel) dont s'occupent les épitérètes.[103] Au moment enfin où elle est devenue "terre découverte par les eaux" (stade final), elle est imposée en tant que terre cultivable. Mais le stade intermédiaire, les allées et venues de l'eau, variables au cours d'un même siècle, est fiscalement très compliqué. Il semble qu'il y ait des arrangements possibles; ce serait alors que les cultivateurs font une "convention parallèle", παραγραφή, qui serait un accom-modement fiscal entre divers groupes de villageois.[104] Une fois la terre riveraine devenue cultivable, elle sert, semble-t-il, de base de calcul à toutes les taxes habituellement assises sur la terre.[105] Mais à ce dernier stade, restent des particularités propres telles que l'extrême morcellement fiscal que révèle l'imputation des parcelles de terre αἰγιαλῖτις dans le "journal de banque" de Karanis.[106] Les superficies suggérées par le calcul des impositions établies sur cette catégorie de terre sont minuscules: de *ca* 2 m$^2$ à 25 m$^2$. Cette constatation rejoint celle qui a été faite sur le peu d'étendue des terres possédées par les habitants de Karanis, pris individuellement,

---

99. Voir *SB* 10556.17 et le commentaire *ad loc.* (W. Van Rengen, *Chr. d'Eg.* 86 (1968) 335). Cf. *P. Col.* vii 172, introd.

100. *Stud. Pal.* xxii 49.14, en 201 (2½ ha).

101. Julius Claudianus: *Stud. Pal.* xxii 49; *P. Gen.* 16.

102. Cf. N. Lewis, *BASP* 7 (1970) 111–12.

103. Cf. Nelson, *op. cit.* (n. 30) 238.

104. *P. Lond.* 924 (entre Bacchias et Soknopaiou Nèsos à propos de pâturage).

105. Cf. V. B. Schuman, "P. Mich. iv: A Commentary", dans *Arch. f. Pap.* 29 (1983) 57.

106. Voir ci-dessus n. 33.

et la dispersion de la propriété foncière sur le territoire de ce village.[107]

Notre documentation, à peu près tarie à la fin du IIIe siècle, ne nous permet pas de dire comment s'est résolue la situation compliquée de la "terre riveraine": poursuite de l'assèchement? certainement. Désintérêt pour une fiscalité trop fine et finalement peu rentable? peut-être. En tout cas, la réforme de Dioclétien a éliminé toutes ces complications autour des années 300.

Il nous reste à faire quelques remarques conclusives:

(1) Les particularités géographiques de l'évolution de l'histoire du sol en Egypte ont engendré des situations complexes du point de vue administratif et fiscal.

(2) Elles sont antérieures à l'organisation étatique grecque puis romaine et, dans ces régions du Fayoum, elles rejoignent d'autres permanences connues (celle de la langue égyptienne, des cultes, tel celui du Nil à Niloupolis).

(3) L'emploi du mot αἰγιαλός paraît spécifique pour désigner initialement les rivages des lacs du Fayoum (Moeris, El Gharaq). Il est, à mes yeux, le reflet du souvenir de leur origine géologique marine[108] connue par les habitants de la vallée du Nil.[109]

107. Voir Geremek, *op. cit.* (n. 75) 57.
108. Voir P. Chantraine, *Dictionnaire étymologique*, s.v. αἰγιαλός.
109. Hérodote II 4, *in fine*. Cf. A. B. Lloyd, *Herodotus. Book II: Commentary 1–98* (1976) 35–37.

# Le epigrafi di Terenouthis e la peste[1]

## GERARDO CASANOVA

Il villaggio di Terenouthis, situato nel Delta del Nilo, nel nomo Prosopite, a nord-ovest del Cairo, ai margini del deserto libico, vicino alla valle Nitria,[2] non ha dato papiri,[3] forse in ragione del clima della zona. La sua necropoli (Kôm Abu Billu), invece, è stata prodiga di stele ed iscrizioni funerarie, portate alla luce da campagne di scavo o acquisite attraverso il commercio internazionale ed ora appartenenti a svariate collezioni di tutto il mondo, dal Cairo ad Ann Arbor.

Le epigrafi che ci interessano particolarmente, in quanto testimonianza abbastanza certa di epidemie letali, sono di epoca romana, alcune di un ventesimo anno, altre fra un dodicesimo e un quattordicesimo.[4]

1. Per una prima presentazione generale dell'argomento, vd. G. Casanova, "La peste nella documentazione greca d'Egitto", in Atti del XVII Congresso Internazionale di Papirologia (Napoli 1984) III, 949–56; cf. inoltre Aegyptus 64 (1984) 163–201.

2. Cf. e.g. W. Berg, Historische Karte des alten Ägypten (Sankt Augustin 1973) tav. IV D 7.

3. Il villaggio e persone di questo villaggio compaiono in P. Bas. 18 (primo periodo romano), P. Gen. 29, P. Lond. III 1132 b, BGU II 453 = M. Chr. 144, BGU II 648 = W. Chr. 360 (tutti del II sec. d.C.) e P. Lond. II 231 = W. Chr. 322 (IV sec. d.C.); nessun papiro è stato però ivi rinvenuto; solo BGU II 648 sembra provenire dal nomo Prosopite stesso. La grafia Τερενοῦθις compare in P. Lond. II 231; negli altri papiri troviamo Θερενοῦθις.

4. Sulle iscrizioni di Terenouthis, in particolare su quelle qui esaminate, vd. Zaki Aly, "Some Funerary Stelae from Kom Abou Bellou", BSAA 38 (1949) 55–88, e "More Funerary Stelae from Kom Abou Bellou", BSAA 40 (1953) 101–50; J. Schwartz, "Les stèles de Terenouthis et la mort d'Alexandre Sévère", Chr. d'Eg. 30 (1955) 124–26; P. M. Fraser, JEA 38 (1952) 120, 41 (1955) 131 e 42 (1956) 106; J. F. Gilliam, "The Death of Alexander Severus and the Stelae from Terenouthis", Chr. d'Eg. 31 (1956) 149–51; F. A. Hooper, "Data from Kom Abou Billou...", Chr. d'Eg. 31 (1956) 332–40; P. M. Fraser, JEA 43 (1957) 106; F. A. Hooper, Funerary Stelae from Kom Abou Billu (Ann Arbor 1961) (= "Hooper"); A. Calderini, Aegyptus 41 (1961) 255; P. M. Fraser, JEA 48 (1962) 143–44, e Cl. Rev. 12 (1962) 321–22; J. Schwartz, Rev. Phil. 36 (1962)

Quelle del ventesimo anno sono dieci, di cui sette dello stesso giorno (11 Hathyr = 7 novembre) e riguardano: una un gruppo familiare costituito da due donne, dalla figlia diciannovenne (della prima delle due?) e dal figlio di un anno (di questa?);[5] altre due, probabilmente, due giovani padri e le loro due piccole figlie;[6] la quarta solo un uomo;[7] la quinta due uomini, una donna e un bambino;[8] la sesta due donne e una bambina;[9] la settima una donna.[10] In totale per quel giorno sono documentati, quindi, ben 17 decessi, di persone di ambo i sessi, ma con prevalenza femminile, e in maggioranza di adulti (12 fra uomini e donne). Le altre tre iscrizioni, datate col ventesimo anno, ma senza indicazione del mese e del giorno, riguardano una donna,[11] un padre e una figlia (la lettura dell'anno non è peraltro sicura) e infine un giovinetto.[12]

324–25; J. Bingen, *Chr. d'Eg.* 37 (1962) 213–14; J. e L. Robert, *REG* 75 (1962) 215–16; H. Petersen, "The Earliest Christian Inscriptions of Egypt", *Class. Phil.* 59 (1964) 154–74; J. e L. Robert, *REG* 78 (1965) 183–85; K. Parlasca, "Zur Stellung der Terenuthis Stelen. Eine Gruppe römischer Grabreliefs aus Ägypten in Berlin", *MDAIK* 26 (1970) 173–98; G. Wagner, "Inscriptions grecques d'Egypte", *BIFAO* 72 (1972) 139–67 (139–49); S. A. A. El-Nassery e G. Wagner, "Nouvelles stèles de Kom Abu Bellou", *BIFAO* 78 (1978) 231–58. I riferimenti successivi nel testo e nelle note vanno intesi per queste pubblicazioni.

5. *BSAA* 40 (1953) n. 16b = *SEG* XIV 868 nota = *SB* VIII 9996 nota; cf. Parlasca, *MDAIK* 26 (1970) 178 nota 37.

6. *BSAA* 38 (1949) n. 13 = *SEG* XX 555 = *SB* VIII 10162, la prima; l'altra è Liebieghaus inv. M 149: vd. Parlasca, *MDAIK* 26 (1970) 179 e nota 53.

7. *SB* I 695 = *SEG* XX 556 = *SB* VIII 10162.

8. *BSAA* 40 (1953) n. 16c[1] = *SEG* XX 553 = *SB* VIII 10162 = Hooper n. 136. La composizione della famiglia è stabilita in base alla raffigurazione, dato che il testo epigrafico non è completo; però non sempre le raffigurazioni sono sicure, cf. Bingen, *Chr. d'Eg.* 37 (1962) 213.

9. *BSAA* 40 (1953) n. 16c[2] = *SEG* XX 554 = *SB* VIII 10162 = Hooper n. 171.

10. *SEG* XX 557 = *SB* VIII 10162 = Hooper n. 73; il sesso è definito in base alla raffigurazione, perchè del nome restano solo due lettere. In effetti la datazione completa di questa epigrafe è frutto di integrazione (Bingen): il $\overline{\kappa}$ potrebbe pur sempre essere l'età, così come interpretato da Hooper ed anche da Petersen, *Class. Phil.* 59 (1964) 167 e nota 163 (che, comunque, non riferisce l'integrazione di Bingen). Nessuna lettura del testo è riferita in *Koptische Kunst – Christentum am Nil* (Ausstellung, Essen 1963) 216 n. 34.

11. *SEG* XX 558 = *SB* VIII 10162 = Hooper n. 90. Per il nome della donna, non molto frequente, cf. F. Preisigke, *Namenbuch*, e D. Foraboschi, *Onomasticon alterum papyrologicum* s.vv. Τβελλῆς, Τιβέλλα, Τιβελλῆς; vd. anche Ταβελλι( ), Ταβέλλις e Ταβελλῆς; Fraser, *JEA* 48 (1962) *loc. cit.*, accenta Τιβέλλης, da intendere come il femminile di Βελλῆς.

12. *BIFAO* 78 (1978) n. 49 = *SEG* XXVIII 1531 e *BIFAO* 78 (1978) n. 13 = *SEG* XXVIII 1503. Un anno ventesimo appare ancora in un'altra iscrizione, ma si tratta del 32 a.c., in quanto l'indicazione è L κ τοῦ ξ, *SB* III 6119; cf.

Ora, sull'anno a cui attribuire queste epigrafi le opinioni sono diverse: ad es. Z. Aly, che si basa sullo stile delle acconciature dei capelli, preferisce per le stele da lui studiate il II sec. d.C.; Schwartz pensa al 211; Hooper, che colloca le iscrizioni da lui pubblicate fra l'ultimo quarto del III sec. e la metà del IV sec. d.C., sulla base delle monete ritrovate nella necropoli, le attribuisce a Diocleziano o Costantino (303/4 oppure 325/6); Bingen ritiene che non si possa decidere in base alla scrittura o allo stile dei rilievi e che sia necessario un particolareggiato riesame numismatico ed archeologico delle tombe; Petersen, su base stilistico-iconografica, giunge invece alla conclusione che la gran parte delle epigrafi di Terenouthis è cristiana e ritiene l'insieme delle stele un lotto pressochè omogeneo cronologicamente, collocandole nel periodo fra Costantino I e Costanzo II;[13] Parlasca, sempre con motivazioni di carattere stilistico, non condivide queste affermazioni[14] e, datando il complesso delle iscrizioni di Terenouthis fra l'epoca tolemaica e il IV sec. d.C., in particolare per le iscrizioni Hooper nn. 90, 136 e 171 dapprima propone la possibilità che siano del ventesimo anno di Settimio Severo e Caracalla, oppure anche del II sec.,[15] mentre poi data la sola n. 171 con l'11/10 a.C.;[16] inoltre ritiene non posteriore al I sec. d.C. Hooper n. 73.[17]

Petersen, *Class. Phil.* 59 (1964) 173 nota 113, Parlasca, *MDAIK* 26 (1970) 174 nota 5 e 182, El-Nassery and Wagner, *BIFAO* 78 (1978) 237.

13. Riguardo all'articolo di Petersen è bene fare alcune precisazioni: nell'indicare alla nota 117 le iscrizioni del ventesimo anno tralascia Hooper n. 90 e *BSAA* 40 (1953) n. 16b; alla nota 120, riguardante quelle del quattordicesimo anno, omette Aly, *BSAA* 38 (1949) n. 8; ritiene inoltre, in base ad una argomentazione, a mio parere, alquanto macchinosa, che Hooper n. 171 riguardi decessi avvenuti almeno a 4 anni di distanza fra i primi due ed il terzo (p. 159); riguardo infine a Hooper n. 136 cade in contraddizione nella stessa pagina 163, dove prima afferma che il numero che appare nell'epigrafe si riferisce agli anni di vita e non alla data (vd. nota 111 e così pure 159 e nota 59, 167 e nota 163), mentre poco dopo attribuisce la stessa epigrafe al ventesimo anno di regno (vd. nota 117): di fatto nell'iscrizione c'è una sola cifra finale, ma l'età doveva essere prima di questa e dopo l'ultimo nome.

14. Per altra bibliografia, riguardante in particolare la datazione, cf. *MDAIK* 26 (1970) 187–88; ultimamente, per un'ampia datazione, fra il II sec. a.C. e il IV sec. d.C., è anche J. Kubińska, "Une pierre funéraire de Terenouthis...", *Eos* 68 (1980) 150.

15. Vd. *MDAIK* 26 (1970) 182; per il II sec. si tratterebbe, ovviamente, o di Traiano o di Adriano o di Antonino Pio o di Marco Aurelio.

16. Vd. *ibid.* 183.

17. Vd. *ibid.* 180; cf. sopra, nota 10. A p. 183 e nota 80, Parlasca riferisce di un'altra iscrizione (*Coptic Stone Sculpture: The Early Christian and Late Classical*

A mio parere non è possibile disgiungere fra loro le iscrizioni datate con lo stesso giorno e lo stesso anno: scarsissime sarebbero le probabilità che si riferissero ad anni di diversi imperatori. Ammesso ciò, credo che pensare ad una pestilenza come causa dei decessi sia un'ipotesi assai fondata.[18] Il fatto che di fronte ad un'iscrizione che testimonia due o più persone defunte non si possa essere del tutto certi dell' effettiva contemporaneità della loro morte, non solo quando non appare nessuna data, ma anche quando ne appare una,[19] non inficia questa ipotesi, data la pluralità di testimonianze riguardanti quel giorno: supponendo anche che le morti a cui si riferisce una stessa iscrizione siano avvenute in tempi diversi, resterebbe pur sempre da chiarire perchè tutte quelle iscrizioni vennero così datate (ci sarebbe da pensare che in quel giorno avvennero per lo meno gli ultimi decessi).

Sulla base di queste considerazioni, data l'ambiguità e la relativa opinabilità degli elementi forniti dalle analisi stilistiche delle epigrafi di Terenouthis, osservato che, se non è certo asseribile un'epoca tarda per tutte le iscrizioni della necropoli di Kôm Abu Billu, ciò parrebbe comunque valido per una gran parte di esse (tant'è vero che anche l'ultimo lotto di iscrizioni pubblicato sembra nella sua quasi totalità "to belong to the IIIrd and perhaps even early IVth centuries A.D."[20]), escluderei comunque che le iscrizioni del ventesimo anno siano del 303/4 o del 325/6. Infatti in quegli anni non è documentata, per lo meno in Egitto, nessuna pestilenza. Una, invece, dovette manifestarsi verso la fine del regno di Massimino Daia, così come tramandato da Eusebio per la parte orientale dell'impero (e quindi anche per l'Egitto): "Durante l'inverno le piogge abituali e gli acquazzoni non caddero sulla terra nella misura usata. Si fece sentire una carestia inattesa e a

*Art of Egypt* (Ausstellungskat., A. Emmerich Gallery, New York 1962) Abb. 10) che ricorda due bambini morti anch'essi un 11 di Hathyr, ma di un anno sconosciuto, e che egli colloca nel primo periodo imperiale. Ci sono ancora due altre iscrizioni dell'11 di Hathyr, ma l'una è di un undicesimo anno (*SB* III 6125, cf. più avanti, nota 37) e l'altra di un quarto (o quinto, cf. più avanti, nota 43).

18. Cf. Z. Aly, *op. cit.* (nota 4), *ad loc.*; Schwartz, *Chr. d'Eg.* 30 (1955) 124–26; Hooper, *Funerary Stelae*, 28; Bingen, *loc. cit.*, che ipotizza anche guerra o incidente collettivo non meglio precisato.

19. Cf. Hooper, *Funerary Stelae*, 28–29; Z. Aly, *BSAA* 40 (1953) 125–26; cf. sopra, nota 1.

20. *BIFAO* 78 (1978) 235.

questa si aggiunse la peste…"[21] L'inverno a cui il passo si riferisce è quello successivo alla morte di Galerio,[22] ossia quello del 311/12. Ora, le nostre iscrizioni potrebbero far riferimento al ventesimo anno di Galerio, ossia proprio al 311/12: la data sarebbe quindi 7 novembre 311 d.C.[23] Essa può sembrare un po' in anticipo rispetto alla successione data da Eusebio, ma da una parte si tratterebbe di alcuni mesi, dall'altra la peste non fu di per sè originata dalla carestia e quindi necessariamente posteriore ad essa in tutte le regioni orientali, nè si può parlare per l'Egitto di carestia per scarsità di piogge invernali.

Ancora nella prima metà del IV secolo gli altri imperatori che fanno registrare un ventesimo anno di regno sono Costantino II e Costanzo II, ma neanche quelle date (335/6 e 343/4) coincidono per l'Egitto con anni funestati dalla peste: a quanto mi risulta, una nuova manifestazione epidemica si verificò nel 346, secondo quanto narrano le biografie del monaco Pacomio e forse testimonia *P. Lond.* III 982, che però è privo di esplicite indicazioni cronologiche.[24]

Volendo, invece, andare indietro nella datazione, seguendo le ipotesi di Parlasca, si hanno due altre possibilità tra le sette date comprese fra la conquista romana e la fine del III sec. d.C., ossia il 179/80 e forse il 116/17, per le quali possediamo testimonianze papiracee.[25]

Tre epigrafi del quattordicesimo anno, sulla base dell'iconografia dei motivi scultorei e di (presunte) concordanze cronologico-storiche, furono attribuite da Schwartz al 234/5, ultimo anno del regno di Alessandro Severo, e collegate ad un'iscrizione del I anno,

21. *Hist. Eccl.* IX 8.1ss. (trad. in *Storia ecclesiastica e I martiri della Palestina*, testo greco con trad. e note di Mons. G. Del Ton (Roma 1964) 698ss.); cf. sopra, nota 1.

22. Avvenuta, forse per cancro, nel maggio del 311 d.C.: cf. e.g. Zosimo (ediz. Belles Lettres) I, 198; Eusebio, *Hist. Eccl.* (Del Ton) 686.

23. Vd. R. S. Bagnall–K. Worp, *Chronological Systems of Byzantine Egypt* (*St. Amstel.* VIII, Zutphen 1978) 71: le datazioni di Galerio continuano ancora per qualche anno dopo la sua morte; cf. ivi anche pp. 2, 4 e 38; cf. J. Lafaurie, "Remarques sur les dates de quelques inscriptions du début du IV$^e$ siècle", in *CRAI* 1965, p. 199.

24. Cf. e.g. *Sancti Pachomii vitae graecae*, edid. H. Bollandiani (*Subsidia Hagiographica* 19, Bruxelles 1932) *Vita Prima*, capp. 114ss.; vd. sopra, nota 1.

25. Cf. nota 1. Le altre date corrispondenti ad un ventesimo anno di regno sono: 11/10 a.C., 33/4 d.C., 135/136 d.C., 156/157 d.C., 211/212 d.C.

che egli interpretava come 235 (ossia all'inizio del regno di Massimino Trace), per cui la sequenza dei giorni dei decessi sarebbe: 5.12.234, 4 e 21.1.235, 20.2.235. Ma Fraser e Gilliam misero in questione la validità degli argomenti stilistici, poichè "all the stelae resemble one another in so far as all are of abominable workmanship, and all present the same or very similar scenes" (Fraser), oltre a negare la cronologia proposta da Schwartz, in quanto la data più probabile dell'assassinio di Alessandro Severo è il marzo e non il gennaio 235. In effetti è proprio marzo la data comunemente e fondatamente accettata dalla storiografia[26] e, pertanto, le tre iscrizioni del quattordicesimo anno vanno separate da quella del I. Possiamo, invece, unire a queste una nuova epigrafe che è di Hathyr del quattordicesimo anno[27] ed, anche se per queste quattro iscrizioni non c'è la coincidenza cronologica riscontrata nel precedente gruppo, il tempo è pur sempre abbastanza ristretto (4 mesi) e si può ritenere con Schwartz che i decessi ivi testimoniati siano conseguenza di un'epidemia che colpì, parimenti, adulti e bambini (mentre, come si è visto, nelle epigrafi del ventesimo anno erano in prevalenza adulti). In particolare, un' iscrizione riguarda una donna e un bambino, probabilmente madre e figlio;[28] un'altra, un bambino, del quale sono precisati addirittura il giorno e l'ora della nascita (e ciò può essere "explained quite satisfactorily on the grounds of horoscope", derivante da "the evil hour and day of his birth");[29] la terza un

26. Cf. e.g. *CAH* xii(1) 71.
27. L'iscrizione di Mecheir del primo anno è *BSAA* 40 (1953) n. 7 = *SEG* xiv 863 = *SB* viii 9996 e ricorda un bambino di "circa 8 anni"; quella del quattordicesimo è *BIFAO* 78 (1978) n. 34 (attribuita al III sec. d.C. o all'inizio del IV) = *SEG* xxviii 1520. Un'altra iscrizione del quattordicesimo anno è Hooper n. 118 (non ripubbl. in *SEG* xx), ma è del 2 di Thoth e riguarda un uomo anziano, per cui escluderei il collegamento con le altre quattro e la peste. Di un primo anno sono inoltre Hooper n. 113 = *SEG* xx 512 = *SB* viii 10162 (una giovane morta in Tybi), *BSAA* 38 (1949) n. 14 = *SEG* xx 513 = *SB* viii 10162 (un bambino morto in Mecheir); *BIFAO* 78 (1978) n. 7 = *SEG* xxviii 1497 (un giovane morto in Mesorè e sua sorellina); e Parlasca, *MDAIK* 26 (1970) n. 13 (un giovane? morto in Mecheir), ma non è un'ipotesi seria quella di ritenere che il primo anno sia sempre lo stesso.
28. *BSAA* 38 (1949) n. 1 = *SEG* xx 547 = *SB* viii 10162; così appare dalla raffigurazione.
29. *BSAA* 38 (1949) n. 2 = *SEG* xx 548 = *SB* viii 10162; vd. *BSAA* 38 (1949) 69–70 anche per il valore apotropaico del nome del bambino: Εὐδαίμων.

uomo e un bambino, probabilmente padre a figlio;[30] la quarta solo un uomo.[31]

In un dodicesimo anno e opera della stessa mano, del III sec. d.C. (o dell'inizio del IV), secondo quanto ritengono gli editori, troviamo tre epigrafi che commemorano complessivamente tre uomini e una bambina, morti nello spazio di tre mesi consecutivi: un uomo in Phaophi, un altro uomo in Hathyr, un terzo uomo con una bambina (probabilmente sua figlia) in Choiak.[32] A queste possiamo aggiungerne una quarta, relativa ad una quattordicenne, dal momento che è del mese immediatamente successivo, Tybi.[33]

Pertanto, poichè da una parte per la vicinanza cronologica delle morti possiamo pensare ad una pestilenza (come suggeriscono anche El-Nassery e Wagner) e dall'altra le prime tre stele del dodicesimo anno sono probabilmente della stessa mano della quarta del quattordicesimo, non è azzardato pensare che le stele di questi due anni siano in relazione alla stessa epidemia.

Questa potrebbe anche essere la causa dei decessi del tredicesimo anno che compaiono in altre iscrizioni: con maggiori probabilità in tre che riguardano tre uomini, morti nello spazio di un mese, fra giugno e luglio,[34] con minori probabilità per la ottantenne deceduta in febbraio.[35]

Se, pertanto, queste stele sono effettivamente del III sec. d.C., tali anni imperiali cadono in periodo di pestilenza solo per quanto riguarda il regno di Gallieno, e sono quindi il 264/5, il 265/6 e il 266/7: la loro testimonianza verrebbe, quindi, a confermare ulteriormente la larga diffusione in Egitto della peste del 250–70 (*ca*), alla quale troviamo riferimenti in vari papiri.[36]

Oltre a quelle di cui abbiamo fin qui detto, parecchie altre iscrizioni del villaggio recano gli stessi numeri di anni di regno, ma essi sono troppo bassi perchè si possa pensare che tutte le

---

30. *Ibid.* n. 8 = *SEG* xx 549 = *SB* viii 10162.   31. Vd. sopra, nota 27.

32. *BIFAO* 78 (1978) nn. 30, 31 e 53 = *SEG* xxviii 1516, 1517 e 1532.

33. *BSAA* 40 (1953) n. 6 = *SEG* xiv 862 = *SB* viii 9996. Vi sono ancora altre due iscrizioni datate col dodicesimo anno, ma la prima, riguardante un'anziana donna, è distaccata di vari mesi (Payni), mentre la seconda non riporta il mese del decesso dell'uomo commemorato: Hooper nn. 101 e 123 = *SEG* xx 542 e 541 = *SB* viii 10162.

34. Hooper nn. 34, 55 e 112 = *SEG* xx 544, 545 e 546 = *SB* viii 10162.

35. Hooper n. 129 = *SEG* xx 543 = *SB* viii 10162.

36. Vd. sopra, nota 1.

epigrafi datate allo stesso modo si riferiscano allo stesso imperatore; inoltre riguardano quasi sempre decessi singoli, che in taluni casi sono di persone molto anziane, e solo per alcune c'è una possibile vicinanza temporale; non ho, quindi, tenuto conto di esse ai fini della presente ricerca.[37] Altre sette iscrizioni che si riferiscono ad una sola persona ciascuna, datate quindicesimo, sedicesimo e diciassettesimo anno, non offrono elementi sufficienti per vederle legate fra loro nè a quelle del dodicesimo-quattordicesimo anno prima considerate.[38]

37. Per l'anno secondo troviamo: Hooper nn. 13, 36, 46 = *SEG* xx 516, 515, 514 = *SB* viii 10162; *BSAA* 40 (1953) n. 23 = *SEG* xiv 873 = *SB* viii 9996; *BIFAO* 72 (1972) n. 3; *SB* i 619; *MDAIK* 26 (1970) n. 13 (l'iscrizione riguarda due persone morte in anni successivi; cf. sopra, nota 27).
  Per l'anno terzo: Hooper nn. 33, 59 = *SEG* xx 518 = *SB* viii 10162; *SB* i 703; *SEG* i 557 = *SB* iii 6586; *BIFAO* 78 (1978) nn. 32, 45 = *SEG* xxviii 1518, 1528.
  Per l'anno quinto: Hooper n. 139 = *SEG* xx 521 = *SB* viii 10162 (che riguarda una coppia di coniugi; vd. più avanti, nota 43); *BIFAO* 78 (1978) n. 15 = *SEG* xxviii 1505; *BSAA* 40 (1953) n. 13 = *SEG* xiv 866 = *SB* viii 9996.
  Per l'anno sesto: Hooper nn. 58, 88, 89, 114, 156 = *SEG* xx 522, 524, 523, 560, 525 = *SB* viii 10162; *MDAIK* 26 (1970) n. 4; in *SEG* i 558 = *SB* iii 6587 la cifra va interpretata più probabilmente come l'età che non come la data.
  Per l'anno settimo: Hooper n. 172 = *SEG* xx 526 = *SB* viii 10162 e *MDAIK* 26 (1970) n. 10.
  Per l'anno ottavo: Hooper nn. 21, 188, 189 = *SEG* xx 527, 529, 530 = *SB* viii 10162; Hooper nn. 57 e 124 = *SEG* xx 589 e 528 = *SB* viii 10162 potrebbero sembrare contemporanee, in quanto entrambe datate 20 Hathyr, ma è più probabile che la cifra sia nella prima l'età della defunta, come anche mi sembra dalla raffigurazione; cf. anche Petersen, *Class. Phil.* 59 (1964) 163 nota 111 (anche per *BSAA* 38 (1949) n. 3 = *SEG* xx 531 = *SB* viii 10162, dove pure è meglio intendere (ἐτῶν) η'); *BIFAO* 78 (1978) nn. 6, 12 = *SEG* xxviii 1496, 1502.
  Per l'anno nono: Hooper nn. 10, 43, 44, 79, 92 = *SEG* xx 537, 536, 538, 535, 534 = *SB* viii 10162; *MDAIK* 26 (1970) n. 1 (che Parlasca colloca non oltre il I sec. d.C.: vd. *ibid.* 180, 181, 186 e 190) e n. 2.
  Per l'anno decimo: Hooper nn. 47, 108 = *SEG* xx 539, 540 = *SB* viii 10162; *MDAIK* 26 (1970) n. 14.
  Per l'anno undicesimo: *SB* i 697 (attribuita al I sec. d.C.); *SB* iii 6125 (cf. Petersen, *Class. Phil.* 59 (1964) nota 113 e Parlasca, *MDAIK* 26 (1970) 174 nota 5; sopra, nota 17).
  Per l'anno primo, vd. sopra, nota 27; per l'anno quarto, più avanti, nota 43.
  38. Per il quindicesimo anno: Hooper n. 120 = *SEG* xx 550 = *SB* viii 10162; *SEG* xxvi 1796 (attribuita al III sec. d.C.); *SB* iii 6121 (cf. Petersen, *Class. Phil.* 59 (1964) nota 113, e Parlasca, *MDAIK* 26 (1970) 174 nota 5); più probabilmente si tratta dell'età e non della data in *SEG* i 563 = *SB* iii 6592 (cf. Petersen nota 111); per *BIFAO* 78 (1978) n. 56 cf. più avanti, nota 43.
  Per il sedicesimo: *BSAA* 38 (1949) n. 19 = *SEG* xx 551 = *SB* viii 10162 (nulla si dice dell'anno sedicesimo e di questa iscrizione in Petersen 163); *BIFAO* 78 (1978) n. 44 = *SEG* xxviii 1527.

Ci sono infine altre epigrafi che testimoniano due o più persone defunte, spesso senza data (ma anche quando è espressa, esse appaiono isolate) e senza elementi utili per precisare la reale situazione riguardo alle cause e ai tempi dei decessi. Ad esempio una stele non datata che ricorda tre persone (madre, padre, figlio)[39] potè essere posta in occasione di una loro morte contemporanea avvenuta per epidemia (o per qualche altro tragico motivo), ma anche, come già si è osservato, solo dopo l'ultimo decesso, se le morti avvennero separatamente;[40] un'altra epigrafe, ritenuta da Schwartz del venticinquesimo anno di Commodo o Caracalla (184/5 o 216/17)[41] e testimoniante la morte di una donna diciassettenne e di suo figlio,[42] è, a mio modo di vedere, da non considerare fra i decessi per epidemie letali, perchè la mancanza di età per il bambino e la giovane età della madre fanno pensare piuttosto a una morte per parto.[43]

Per il diciassettesimo: Hooper n. 175 = *SEG* xx 552 = *SB* viii 10162; *BIFAO* 78 (1978) n. 3 = *SEG* xxviii 1493 (attribuita al I–II sec. d.C.).

39. *BSAA* 40 (1953) n. 16 a = *SEG* xiv 868 = *SB* viii 9996. Da notare una curiosa svista da parte del lapicida nell'indicare il figlio: tale indicazione è riferita ad Athàs di 45 anni e non al piccolo Ares di 7. L'ultimo nome, Τικονν[ας? ⟨*sic*⟩, che dovrebbe essere quello della madre, poichè il rilievo rappresenta un gruppo familiare, non compare nè nel *Namenbuch*, nè nell'*Onomasticon*.

40. Vd. sopra, p. 148.

41. *SEG* i 566 = *SB* iii 6585.

42. Mi pare questa l'interpretazione esatta dell'epigrafe, la cui lettura va pertanto modificata alla r. 1: (ἐτῶν) 13 e non (ἔτους) 13. Petersen annovera l'iscrizione fra quelle non datate: vd. *Class. Phil.* 59 (1964) 172 nota 111; Parlasca, *MDAIK* 26 (1970) 183, corregge la lettura dell'anno in 29 e la data quindi al 188/9 d.C. (effettivamente è scritto *ad loc.* IE (= 25) e IΘ (= 29), ma evidentemente si tratta di errori di stampa).

43. Le iscrizioni relative a più persone sono: Hooper nn. 66, 137, 138, 139 (vd. sopra, nota 37), 140, 166, 167, 169, 176 (cf. Fraser, *JEA* 48 (1962) 144) 190 = *SEG* xx 629–36 = *SB* viii 10162 (la 167 riguarda due morti, ma uno dei due decessi fu dovuto a suicidio: cf. Fraser, *loc. cit.*); *BIFAO* 72 (1972) n. 7, che sembra essere del II sec. d.C., cf. *ibid.* p. 147; *BIFAO* 78 (1978) nn. 4, 7, 54 = *SEG* xxviii 1494, 1497, 1533: la prima viene datata I sec. d.C. *ca*, la seconda e la terza sembrano del III o inizio del IV sec. d.C.; la rappresentazione figurata dell'ultima presenta una madre con quattro figli, ma l'iscrizione commemora la madre e un bambino morti in un quarto anno: poichè la data è scritta (ἔτους) δ̄ 'Επὶφ κ̄ 'Αθὺρ ῑα, nel commento si fa la supposizione che "celui ou celle qui est mort en Hathyr l'ait été l'an 5"; da parte mia penso che potrebbe anche trattarsi di una errata disposizione nella successione dei due mesi da parte del lapicida; riguardo al quarto anno si può aggiungere che sempre nel mese di Epeiph occorre il decesso di un uomo in *BIFAO* 78 (1978) n. 8 = *SEG* xxviii 1498, mentre alla prima parte dell'anno spettano Hooper n. 14 = *SEG* xx 519 = *SB* viii 10162 che ricorda il

Gerardo Casanova

decesso di una bambina e la frammentaria iscrizione Hooper n. 66 = *SEG* xx 629 = *SB* vⅢ 10162 relativa a una coppia di coniugi (la data di questa epigrafe non è certa e su *SEG* e *SB* l'abbreviazione L viene sciolta in (ἐτῶν): ora se questo scioglimento pare essere strutturalmente più adeguato, d'altra parte la raffigurazione sembra quella di una coppia di adulti; forse il δ non è tale, ma dalla fotografia non si vede assolutamente nulla del testo iscritto; Petersen, *Class. Phil.* 59 (1964) nota 113, considera δ come data) ed anche *BSAA* 38 (1949) n. 7 = *SEG* xx 520 = *SB* vⅢ 10162 riguardante una bambina. Osservando una certa vicinanza cronologica, il fatto che si tratta anche in alcuni casi di due decessi, che i morti sono di varia età, verrebbe la tentazione di pensare a una pestilenza, ma, come ho già detto, quando si tratta di anni di regno così bassi, è quanto mai azzardato ritenere che si tratti sempre dello stesso. Troviamo ancora: *SB* i 699, che è attribuita al I sec. d.C.; cf. Parlasca, *MDAIK* 26 (1970) 185; *ibid.* nn. 5 e 6; *Coptic Stone Sculpture*, Abb. 10, su cui vd. sopra, nota 17; Brooklyn Mus. Inv. 16.106, la cui ultima edizione, che riporta la precedente bibliografia, è K. Herbert, *Greek and Latin Inscriptions in the Brooklyn Museum* (New York 1972) n. 6 (nello stesso volume è ripubblicata anche un'altra epigrafe funeraria non datata di Terenouthis, al n. 29 = Inv. 16.90); essa, nei vari studi in cui è stata presentata, viene datata (con una certa varietà) fra il III e il II sec. a.C. ed è quindi la più antica iscrizione del villaggio; *BIFAO* 78 (1978) n. 56 = *SEG* xxvⅢ 1534 che commemora due bambini, ed è datata con un quindicesimo anno, attribuito al II sec. d.C.; due stele rese note da K. Wessel, *L'Art Copte* (Bruxelles 1964) 94–96, tavv. 75 e 74, collocate tra la fine del III e l'inizio del IV sec. d.C. (cf. anche G. De Francovich, *Riv. Ist. Arch. e St. Arte* n.s. 11/12 (1963) 89) e dichiarate provenienti da Terenouthis (e non Témouthis, come scritto effettivamente a p. 94 e nell'indice; cf. già A. Hermann, "Die Beter-Stelen von Terenouthis...", *Jahrb. Ant. Christ.* 6 (1963) 113 nota 9, riguardo alla precedente edizione tedesca); cf. inoltre Parlasca, *MDAIK* 26 (1970) 185; per la 74 è meglio vedere nella donna ivi raffigurata una nonna (come fa Parlasca) più che una madre (come Wessel), data l'età dei defunti: 56 anni la donna, 1 – 3 – 7 i bambini; per quanto riguarda la 75 il nome Kollouthion è sì assai raro (Wessel), ma bisogna considerare che è il diminutivo del ben diffuso Kollouthos; che poi esso "ne concerne que des Egyptiens" non è possibile affermarlo data l'epoca tarda, in quanto i nomi indigeni si erano sempre più diffusi anche fra la popolazione di origine "greca".

Possediamo inoltre parecchie stele con la sola raffigurazione di più persone, senza alcuna iscrizione; non è stata quindi possibile una loro utilizzazione in questo contesto.

# The papyri and the Greek language

FRANCIS T. GIGNAC

The papyri and ostraca from Roman and Byzantine Egypt, amounting to some 35,000 documents already edited, constitute the main body of evidence for non-literary Koine Greek. They reflect a living language in a time of transition from the morphologically complex language of the classical period to the predominantly analytical language spoken in Greece today. They reflect this Greek Koine spoken and written within the confines of Egypt, open to foreign influences and subject to dialectal variations. They allow us to trace the early steps of subsequent developments in the Greek language and to examine their causes, to establish the relationship of the common language of the Roman and early Byzantine world both to the classical dialects and to Medieval and Modern Greek, and to analyze the effect of bilingual interference in one branch of a language widely adopted by speakers of other tongues.

In phonology, the pronunciation of Greek in the Roman and Byzantine periods, in so far as it can be reconstructed from orthographic variations or misspellings in the papyri, is somewhat closer to that of Modern Greek than to that of Classical Greek. The classical long and short diphthongs in both -ι and -υ have all been reduced to simple vowels or, in the case of ηυ, αυ, and ευ, to a vowel plus a consonantal element. This is indicated by the normal omission of the -ι or -υ in long diphthongs and by the very frequent interchange of the symbols for the short diphthongs with those for simple vowels. Thus, ει interchanges with ι /i/, αι with ε /ε/, οι and υι with υ /y/, and ου with ω and ο /o/, while αυ and ευ are frequently written simply α or ε or conversely expanded to αου and εου or even to αυου and ευου.[1]

The simple vowels for the most part preserve their classical

1. Examples may be found in F. T. Gignac, *A Grammar of the Greek Papyri of the Roman and Byzantine Periods* I: *Phonology* (Milan 1976) 183–234.

pronunciation.[2] All quantitative distinction, however, has been lost. This in turn reflects a change in the nature of the accent from pitch to stress, which also accounts for the great confusion and frequent loss of vowels in unaccented syllables.[3]

The determination of the sound or sounds represented by the letter η, however, presents a particular type of problem. There is, on the one hand, a very frequent interchange of η with ι and ει, suggesting that η may already represent its Modern Greek sound /i/.[4] On the other hand, there is a frequent interchange of η with ε and αι throughout the Roman and Byzantine periods.[5] The problem presented by these data is how η can be confused at one and the same time with symbols representing two distinct phonemes, /i/ and /ε/.

A similar problem arises on examination of the evidence for the pronunciation of the consonants. There is some evidence already in papyri of the early Roman period that the classical voiced stops /b g d/, represented by β, γ, δ, have shifted to fricatives, as in Modern Greek.[6] On the other hand, there is abundant evidence throughout the Roman and Byzantine periods that these sounds remained voiced stops, for γ and δ interchange very frequently with κ and τ respectively, and β interchanges occasionally with π.[7] Similar evidence is found for the aspirated stops represented by χ, θ, φ, which also interchange frequently in some papyri with the symbols for their corresponding voiceless stops.[8]

Other anomalies in the phonology of the papyri also appear foreign to Greek. One is the frequent interchange of the symbols for the liquids, λ and ρ, which is attested elsewhere in Greek in specific phonetic conditions but nowhere as frequently or unconditionally as in the papyri from Egypt.[9] Another is the occasional interchange of the symbols for the sibilants, σ and ӡ, not only before voiced consonants as observed in Attic and Delphian inscriptions, but in other positions as well.[10] Another is the frequent interchange of α with ε or ο, mainly in unaccented syllables but occasionally in accented syllables as well.[11]

2. *Ibid.* 235–94.   3. *Ibid.* 295–327.
4. *Ibid.* 235–42.   5. *Ibid.* 242–49.
6. *Ibid.* 68–76.   7. *Ibid.* 76–86.
8. *Ibid.* 86–101.   9. *Ibid.* 102–7.
10. *Ibid.* 120–26.   11. *Ibid.* 278–89.

These anomalies cannot be explained from the viewpoint of historical Greek grammar alone. But an analysis of the Coptic phonemic system indicates that these anomalies are the result of bilingual interference. For there was no phonemic distinction between voiced and voiceless stops in any dialect of Coptic. Aspirated stops were phonemic only in the Bohairic dialect of the Delta, from which area relatively few papyri have come. There was no phonemic distinction between voiced and voiceless sibilants nor between liquids in at least the Fayumic dialect. The Coptic letter H represented at least two different sounds, and in no dialect of Coptic were there more than two phonemes corresponding to the three Greek phonemes represented by α, ε, and o.[12]

Bilingual interference also provides a more adequate explanation of phenomena attested elsewhere in Greek but much more in evidence in the papyri. The advanced itacism of the papyri may have been furthered by the existence of fewer phonemes in the Coptic vowel system than in the Greek. Indications of a strong stress accent may be attributed to the Coptic accent, in which stress was so strong that few vowel qualities were distinguished in unaccented syllables. The fricative quality of the bilabial consonant represented by β and of the velar consonant represented by γ postulated when they interchange with ου coincides with the qualities of the Coptic voiced bilabial fricative /β/ and the labiovelar fricative /w/. The frequent omission of symbols for the nasals, especially in internal position before a stop, may reflect the fact that the Coptic voiceless dental and velar stops had voiced allophones (therefore not phonemically distinct) following a nasal. Finally, the widespread loss of initial aspiration may be connected in Egypt with the similar phenomenon in Coptic in the early Byzantine period.

Bilingual interference is not common in morphology because the inflectional systems of Greek and Coptic are not at all parallel. What little evidence there is for interference consists mainly of the abandonment of such obligatory categories in Greek as noun cases; many nouns, and especially names of all declensional types, are used indeclinably. The most striking morphological phenomena

12. For Coptic phonology, see especially J. Vergote, *Grammaire copte* ia (Louvain 1973) 7–59.

157

in the papyri reflect the language in transition from Ancient to Modern Greek.

The dual has disappeared except occasionally in the genitive and dative of δύο and ἄμφω and sporadically in nouns. There is much analogical levelling within each declension and among the various declensional types. Nouns of the first declension in -ρᾰ tend to form their genitive singular in -ρης, e.g., ἀρούρης, leading to the extension of one or the other vowel throughout the paradigm in Modern Greek. These forms are less Ionicisms in the Koine than levelling of the inflectional system on the analogy of other nouns in -ᾰ whose stem ends in a consonant, as θάλασσα, θαλάσσης. Masculine nouns of the first declension in -ης and -ας sometimes replace the anomalous genitive -ου borrowed at an earlier stage of the language from the second declension by the stem vowel -η or -α. These genitives, which are regular in Modern Greek, are also ancient dialectal forms (Doric, Ionic), but the renaissance of these forms in Egypt several centuries later is more likely the result of analogical levelling. Certain types of masculine and neuter nouns of the second declension in -ιος, -ιον, including especially names and titles among the masculines and diminutives among the neuters, very frequently drop the -ι- from the nominative and accusative singular and apparently shift the accent to the ultima in the genitive and dative, as /'kyris, kyr'ju, kyr'jo, 'kyrin/, anticipating the Modern Greek declensional type for neuters, /pe'δi, pe'δju/. Also in the second declension, the so-called Attic declension, arising first among Ionic speakers through quantitative metathesis or contraction, is becoming extinct, with λαός and ναός being used in their common Greek dress. Only ἅλως is declined regularly according to the long vowel declension, as well as appearing in an *n*-stem by-form ἅλων, ἅλωνος. Similarly, contract nouns tend to fluctuate between open and contracted forms or to show heteroclitic forms of the consonantal third declension.[13]

Nouns of the third declension show considerable variation from classical Attic both in the endings and in the formation of the stem. Consonantal stem nouns frequently form their accusative singular in -ν on the analogy of vocalic stem nouns of all declensions. This in turn led to the back-formation of the Modern Greek nominative

13. Examples may be found in F. T. Gignac, *Grammar* II: *Morphology* (Milan 1981) 3–43.

in -α(ς), as θυγατέρα. The accusative plural of masculine and feminine nouns of the third declension -ας is sometimes given up in favor of the nominative -ες. This represents a middle stage in the process by which the nominative plural came to supplant the accusative, resulting in the adoption of the nominative–accusative -ες as the ending for the plural of all *a*-stem nouns in Modern Greek. Analogical levelling is also observed in the mixed dental and *i*-stem nouns, which tend to extend the dental stem throughout the paradigm, so that the accusative singular, for instance, is frequently χάριτα instead of χάριν.[14]

Adjectives are in general subject to the same influences as the nouns of the declensional types to which they belong. In addition, many adjectives of the first and second declensions that in Classical Greek are adjectives of only two terminations tend increasingly frequently to form a distinct feminine, as βεβαία and σπορίμη. This tendency has reached its completion in Modern Greek, where all adjectives are of three terminations. The comparison of adjectives shows a tendency towards regularization by extension of the -τερος, -τατος formations to adjectives that form the comparative on a different stem in Classical Greek, as ἀγαθώτατος. These same suffixes are also occasionally added pleonastically to the primary comparative formations in -ίων, as καλλιότερος and μειζότερος, heralding the loss of the primary suffix formation in Modern Greek, the normal comparative now being the periphrastic πιό καλός and ὁ πιό καλύτερος.[15]

Pronouns show many morphological developments that closely approach the Modern Greek forms, such as the expanded accusative singular in -ν(α) of the first and second personal pronouns, ἐμένα and ἐσένα, attested from the second century on, together with the emphatic ἐ- forms of the second personal pronoun, ἐσοῦ, etc. The partial replacement of the distinctive reflexives of the first and second persons by those of the third person, that is, ἑαυτούς for ἡμᾶς αὐτούς or ὑμᾶς αὐτούς, is already known in classical Attic.[16]

Anticipations of the Modern Greek forms are found in several numerals, as τριάντα, while many compound cardinal and ordinal numerals and fractions undergo phonetic and morphological alterations, sometimes consequent upon a transposition in word

14. *Ibid.* 43–91.              15. *Ibid.* 105–59.
16. *Ibid.* 161–82.

order, so that in the numerals above ten the larger number precedes, as δεκαδύο. This transposition of the common classical order seems connected with a transposition in the word order of the substantive, which itself now generally precedes the entire numeral.[17]

In conjugation, syllabic and temporal augment and reduplication are often omitted or misplaced, leading to the partial loss of augment and the complete loss of reduplication in Modern Greek.[18] Stem formation tends to be regularized by the occasional levelling of vocalic or consonantal variations. This occurs when a single stem vowel is extended throughout the paradigm, as is -ε- in some denominative -έω verbs, as ὀφειλέσω instead of ὀφειλήσω, on the model of original *s*-stems like τελέω, or when the *e*-grade of the present is extended to the second aorist passive, as ἐκλέπην instead of ἐκλάπην. Both of these phenomena are normal in Modern Greek. Similarly, velar stems that in classical Attic-Ionic, as opposed to West Greek, normally lose the velar in the formation of the sigmatic tenses, as ἁρπάзω and βαστάзω, now frequently have the velar in these tenses.

The tendency towards regularization has led further to the replacement of many contract futures by sigmatic ones, as καλέσω, τελέσω, and κομίσω, and to the elimination of some suppletive futures formed on different stems by the formation of new futures based on stems of other tenses within the paradigm, as the replacement of οἴσω as the future of φέρω by ἐνεγκῶ, developed from the aorist stem ἐνεγκ-. This same tendency has also led to the replacement of some ancient root aorists by new sigmatic ones, as ἔλειψα for ἔλιπον and ἦξα for ἤγαγον. The second aorist passive is generally preferred in the Roman period to the first aorist, but the Attic first aorist forms tend to recur during the Byzantine period.[19] Many Attic *futura medii*, as ἀκούσομαι, are formed actively in the papyri, as often in the New Testament and other Koine literature.[20]

Very much analogical levelling is found in the interchange of endings of the various tense systems of thematic verbs in the papyri. The endings of the first aorist encroach upon those of the second aorist; those of the present, imperfect, and second aorist upon those

17. *Ibid.* 183–211.  
18. *Ibid.* 223–54.  
19. *Ibid.* 255–319.  
20. *Ibid.* 321–27.

of the first aorist and perfect. The present, future, and aorist are sometimes confused, especially in the infinitive and imperative. In addition, the subjunctive is often confused with the indicative, the imperative with the infinitive, and less regular endings tend to give way in the individual moods to more regular ones.[21] There is some identification of contract verb classes,[22] while the transfer of athematic -μι verbs to the regular -ω conjugation is well advanced, so that present formations like ὀμνύω appear instead of ὄμνυμι, ἱστάνω instead of ἵστημι, and τιθῶ instead of τίθημι. These phenomena reflect an early stage in the process by which all -μι verbs except εἰμί lost their athematic inflection in the transition from Ancient to Modern Greek. Anticipations of the Modern Greek forms εἶμαι, etc., are already found.[23]

The morphological system of the Greek of the papyri is thus fundamentally that of classical Attic, but it incorporates some forms of other dialects and introduces very many analogical formations, which serve to level the greater irregularities of the classical system and to anticipate the more simplified forms of Modern Greek.

In syntax, the two effects of internal development of the Greek language and of bilingual interference are both very much in evidence. The following main features of syntax may be traced to the historical evolution of Greek apart from bilingual interference.

There are frequent inconcinnities in concord, especially in the use of participles, in which the accusative case predominates, as in the indeclinable Modern Greek usage.[24] Personal pronouns are often used redundantly,[25] and the frequent and indiscriminate use of the intensive αὐτός has led to extensions of usage in which αὐτός serves simply as the third personal pronoun in the nominative as well as in the oblique cases.[26] The reflexive pronoun is sometimes used for the third personal pronoun,[27] and even for the intensive αὐτός with the first or second person.[28] This suggests that a form

21. *Ibid.* 329–62.   22. *Ibid.* 363–73.   23. *Ibid.* 375–414.
24. E.g. *P. Oxy.* VII 1021.14–18 (A.D. 54); *P. Ryl.* II 113.9–12 (2nd c.).
25. E.g. *P. Mich.* III 216.3–4 and 217 = *SB* III 7249.13–14 (both A.D. 296).
26. E.g. *SB* IV 7352 = *P. Mich.* VIII 490.15–16 (2nd c.); *P. Oxy.* XIV 1671.7, 15 (3rd c.).
27. E.g. *P. Ryl.* II 161.31 (A.D. 71); *P. Oxy.* XVI 1880.11 (A.D. 427).
28. E.g. *P. Thead.* 19.6 (A.D. 316–20); *SB* III 7250 = *P. Mich.* III 218.6–8 (A.D. 296).

of αὐτός, even when used reflexively in the papyri, represents not the Attic contracted reflexive form αὑτοῦ, etc. (with rough breathing), but simply a form of the personal pronoun. The reciprocal ἀλλήλων, etc., is likewise sometimes replaced by the reflexive ἑαυτοῦ, etc., without distinction of person,[29] a usage found already in Classical Greek. The possessive pronominal adjectives of the first and second person are still used in the papyri but did not survive into Modern Greek; they were replaced by the simple genitive of the personal pronoun or by forms of δικός μου, perhaps a contamination of ἴδιος, often used to strengthen the possessive in the papyri, and εἰδικός. The demonstrative ὅδε rarely occurs as a substantive pronoun,[30] but it is frequent as an attributive, generally limited to recurring formulae.[31] The pronoun ἕτερος, which did not survive into Modern Greek, is still used frequently in its proper dual sense of 'the other', in which it is sometimes replaced by ἄλλος,[32] but it more commonly refers to 'another'.[33] The relative pronoun is often replaced by the definite article,[34] as in many Classical Greek dialects and still in some dialects of Modern Greek, although the normal relative is now the indeclinable ποú, apparently a simplification of the ancient adverb ὅπου.[35] The replacement of the indefinite pronoun τις by the numeral εἷς occasionally in papyri from the third century on[36] is common to the later Koine and has led to the adoption of the numeral as the ordinary indefinite pronoun in Modern Greek.

There is much irregularity in the use of the various cases. In particular, the genitive and the accusative are often used for the dative, especially when a personal pronoun is the indirect object,[37] which reflects the elimination of the dative in Modern Greek except in some few stereotyped expressions. Many of the syntactic

29. E.g. *P. Lips.* 26.5–6 (early 4th c.); *P. Cair. Isidor.* 91.6–7 (A.D. 309).
30. *BGU* I 195.17 (A.D. 161); *SB* I 6000 R. 1, etc. (6th c.).
31. E.g. *BGU* I 2 = *M. Chr.* 113.16–17 (A.D. 209); *Stud. Pal.* III 411.6 (7th c.).
32. E.g. *P. Merton* II 92.22 (A.D. 324); *P. Lips.* 40 iii.3 (late 4th/early 5th c.).
33. *SB* V 7568 = *P. Mich.* V 232.11 (A.D. 36); *P. Cair. Isidor.* 62.16–17 (A.D. 296).
34. E.g. *SB* VI 9017 (14).9 (1st/2nd c.); *P. Oxy.* XVI 1862.26–27, 43 (7th c.).
35. For highly doubtful examples of ποú in the papyri, see Gignac, *Grammar* II, 179 n. 6.
36. E.g. *P. Flor.* II 185.10–11 (A.D. 254); *PSI* I 98.4 (6th c.).
37. E.g. *P. Grenf.* II 41 = *M. Chr.* 183.20–22 (A.D. 46); *P. Oxy.* I 119.4 (2nd/3rd c.).

device functions of the individual cases have been taken over by prepositions. Thus, the partitive genitive is usually introduced by ἀπό or ἐκ,[38] the accusative of extent of time by ἐπί or εἰς,[39] and the dative of means or instrument is replaced by διά or μετά with the genitive.[40] These phenomena reflect a linguistic state in which Greek, like most of the other languages of modern Europe, has increasingly substituted analytical expressions for synthetic ones. Grammatical relations that were earlier expressed by word inflection are now expressed by adverbial particles used originally in parataxis to define the meaning of the case more precisely, thus centering the meaning in the superfluous preposition and depriving the case endings of much of their function and meaning.

The prepositions themselves are frequently confused in the papyri, with διά used for περί in the meaning 'about',[41] εἰς for ἐν,[42] etc. In Modern Greek, all true prepositions take the accusative case; thus the multiple case constructions that Attic had distinguished have been abandoned. The fine distinctions that Attic also made, e.g. among the prepositions with ablative force like παρά, ἀπό, ἐκ, and ὑπό, are lost and they become virtually interchangeable. This led to the phonologically strongest ἀπό finally supplanting all the others.

The syntax of the verb is intimately connected with its morphology. Confusion of endings led to confusion of tenses and moods. The tendency to replace the perfect by periphrastic formations, not only in the subjunctive and optative as in Classical Greek, but also occasionally in the indicative,[43] led eventually, aided by the gradual loss of distinction in meaning between aorist and perfect, to the elimination of the perfect as an inflectional system in Modern Greek except for the perfect participle passive used periphrastically with forms of εἰμί or ἔχω. The extension of aorist passive formations to deponent and other intransitive verbs without a true passive led to a blunted feeling for the force of the middle; the indirect middle, where the subject is not the immediate

---

38. E.g. *P. Lond.* II 196.29 (*ca* A.D. 138); *P. Oxy.* I 131.5 (7th c.).
39. E.g. *P. Oxy.* VI 911.10 (3rd c.); *P. Fay.* 117.28 (2nd c.).
40. E.g. *P. Mich.* VIII 492.22 (2nd c.); *P. Oxy.* XVI 1851.3 (6th/7th c.).
41. E.g. *P. Oxy.* XVI 1871.5–6 (5th c.) and 1862.41–42 (7th c.).
42. E.g. *P. Mich.* VIII 514.30 (3rd c.); *P. Oxy.* XVI 1842.7 (6th c.).
43. E.g. *P. Mich.* IX 524.6, 15–16 (A.D. 98); *P. Mich.* VIII 512.5 (early 3rd c.).

object of the verb, is often accompanied by a reflexive pronoun for clarity.[44] These phenomena led eventually to the elimination of the middle voice as a morphemic system in Modern Greek. The replacement of the optative by the subjunctive in purpose clauses in secondary as well as primary sequence, the restricted use of ὅπως, and the frequent use of ἵνα with the subjunctive in place of a complementary infinitive[45] led to the elimination of the infinitive in Modern Greek and its replacement by the subjunctive introduced by νά (from ἵνα). The most frequent conditional protasis in the papyri is ἐάν with the subjunctive, but there are irregularities: ἐάν is sometimes used with the indicative[46] and εἰ with the subjunctive.[47] Sentence structure in the papyri is more often co-ordinate than subordinate, and asyndetic parataxis is very common.[48]

The features that characterize Modern Greek and mark it off distinctly from Ancient Greek were thus already present in the language of the Roman and early Byzantine periods. There are other syntactical usages in the papyri, however, that do not fit in with the general evolution of the Greek language and have no obvious explanation in terms of historical Greek grammar. As in phonology, these phenomena have their simplest and most adequate explanation in terms of bilingual interference. One phenomenon is an error in gender in a Greek word under the influence of the corresponding Coptic word, e.g. τοῦ ἡμέρας;[49] the Coptic word for 'day' is masculine. Another is the use of a resumptive pronoun in the case required by the syntax of its own clause to refer back to a pendent nominative subject of the sentence;[50] this phenomenon is characteristic of colloquial language but also corresponds exactly to the normal Coptic word order. Another is the use of a resumptive personal pronoun after a relative, e.g. μηδενὸς ὧν ἔχομεν αὐτῶν φειδομένη.[51] This type of

44. E.g. *P. Oxy.* I 71 ii.9 (A.D. 303); *P. Grenf.* II 78.3 (A.D. 307).
45. E.g. *P. Mich.* III 216 = *SB* III 7248.7–8 (A.D. 296); *P. Oxy.* XVI 1847.5 (6th/7th c.).
46. E.g. *P. Teb.* II 333.13 (A.D. 216); *P. Oxy.* VII 1071.4–5 (5th c.).
47. E.g. *P. Ryl.* II 234.12 (2nd c.); *P. Oxy.* VI 904.4 (5th c.).
48. E.g. *P. Oxy.* I 113.6–7 (2nd c.); *P. Oxy.* VIII 1165.8–9 (6th c.).
49. *P. Oxy.* VI 893 = *M. Chr.* 99.7 (late 6th/7th c.).
50. E.g. *P. Lond.* II 235 = *P. Abinn.* 29.7–9 (*ca* A.D. 346); *P. Oxy.* XVI 1862.43–46 (7th c.).
51. *P. Oxy.* VII 1070.24–25 (3rd c.).

construction is regular in Coptic, in which, as in the Semitic languages, there are relative signs, not pronouns, that are indeclinable and require specification in gender and number by a pronoun/pronominal suffix, adverb, or substantive. This is a case of overdifferentiation of syntagmemes in Greek, in which the relative is itself a pronoun and adequately marked by gender, number, and case. Distribution in the papyri is often expressed by repeating the numeral, e.g. ἀνὰ ἓν ἕν,[52] or the substantive, e.g. κατὰ πρᾶγμα πρᾶγμα.[53] This is exactly paralleled in Coptic. Another is the occasional use of the particle ἰδού, familiar from biblical Greek, in the middle of a sentence for emphasis or even in a temporal sense;[54] this is paralleled by the use of a corresponding Coptic interjection.

Other syntactical anomalies in the papyri can also be explained in terms of bilingual interference, especially in the use of the article and in the function and pleonastic repetition of personal pronouns. These examples illustrate the rich possibilities a bilingual approach to Koine Greek offers, not only in Egypt, but wherever this common language of everyday commerce was adopted by speakers of other linguistic affinities.

52. *SB* v 7660.31 (*ca* A.D. 100).
53. *P. Lond.* v 1732.31: cf. *Berichtigungsliste* III 98 (A.D. 586?).
54. *BGU* III 948.4–6 (4th/5th c.).

# Zum Amt des διοικητής im römischen Aegypten*

### DIETER HAGEDORN

Eine vielfach beklagte Besonderheit der auf Papyrus erhaltenen historischen Quellen liegt darin, dass die Masse der Urkunden aus der χώρα, dem flachen Lande Ägyptens stammt, weil nur dort in der Wüste südlich von Kairo das absolut regenfreie Klima ein Überleben des unter dem Einfluss von Feuchtigkeit verwesenden Materials erlaubte. Dokumente hingegen aus dem Zentrum der Verwaltung, der Stadt Alexandria, sind überaus selten. Sie hatten normalerweise nur dann eine Chance zu überdauern, wenn sie schon in der Antike von Alexandria in die Gegend südlich des Deltas gelangten.

Dieser Umstand bringt es mit sich, dass wir über die Vielzahl der kleinen lokalen Beamten mit beschränkten Befugnissen häufig viel besser Bescheid wissen als über die höheren Chargen; das trifft für alle drei Epochen zu, mit denen der Papyrologe es zu tun hat, die ptolemäische, die römische und die byzantinische. So konnte den Tätigkeitsbereich von Steuerpraktoren, Sitologen und Dorfschreibern, um Beispiele zu nennen, die auch die römische Zeit betreffen, schon Oertel in seinem Buch über die Liturgie ziemlich präzise beschreiben;[1] seitdem ist noch viel Material hinzugekommen, das neues Licht auf diese niedrigen liturgischen Ämter wirft, deren Inhaber normalerweise der rein ägyptischen Bevölkerung hauptsächlich der Dörfer angehörten. Auch die Beamten der nächsthöheren Verwaltungsebene, des Gaues, also z.B. Strategen und βασιλικοὶ γραμματεῖς, die in der Regel der in den Gaumetropolen ansässigen gräzisierten oder gar auf lange Familientraditionen zurückblickenden griechischen Bevölkerungs-

* Überarbeitete und mit Anmerkungen versehene Fassung eines Vortrags, der im Sommer 1980 an der Universität Trier gehalten wurde. G. Alföldy (Heidelberg) und J. D. Thomas (Durham) verdanke ich wertvolle Hinweise.

1. F. Oertel, *Die Liturgie. Studien zur ptolemäischen und kaiserlichen Verwaltung Ägyptens* (Leipzig 1917) bes. 195ff., 250ff. und 157ff.

schicht entstammten, sind aus den Papyrusurkunden gut kennt-
lich und haben eine wissenschaftliche Behandlung erfahren.[2]
Schwieriger schon ist es, sich ein Bild vom Aufgabenkreis der
Epistrategen zu machen, jener Amtsträger also, in denen wir,
wenn wir in der Verwaltungshierarchie weiter aufwärts steigen,
erstmals römischen Rittern begegnen; die Epistrategen waren
Procuratoren mit spezieller Kompetenz für aus mehreren Gauen
bestehende administrative Einheiten, die Epistrategien. Original-
dokumente aus dem Büro eines Epistrategen gehören schon zu den
Seltenheitsfunden unter den Papyri, und wir wissen beispielsweise
bis heute immer noch nicht mit Sicherheit zu sagen, wie viele
Epistrategien es im römischen Ägypten gegeben hat, ob drei oder
vier, da uns klare Informationen über die Aufgliederung des Deltas
fehlen.[3]

Ganz besonders spärlich aber fliessen die Quellen für die
übrigen in Alexandria tätigen Procuratoren, das heisst die auf
zentraler Ebene für ganz Ägypten zuständige Beamtenschaft, wenn
man einmal absieht vom *praefectus Aegypti* selbst, dem Haupt der
Provinzialverwaltung; für seine Kompetenzen haben Historiker
und Juristen sich immer lebhaft interessiert, die Literatur zu
seinem Amt ist kaum überschaubar, und auch die Quellenlage ist
insgesamt doch recht befriedigend.[4] Von den ihm zur Seite
stehenden Procuratoren haben jedoch nur manche eine wissenschaftliche Behandlung erfahren; es ist dies einmal der ἐπίτροπος
τοῦ ἰδίου λόγου, dessen Amt schon in zwei umfänglicheren
Studien behandelt worden ist, von denen eine sogar der jüngeren

2. Zum Strategen s. z.B. Oertel, a.a.O. (Fussn. 1) 290ff.; F. Bilabel, Artikel
"Strategos", *R-E* IV.1 184–252; N. Hohlwein, *Le stratège du nome* ( = *Papyrologica
Bruxellensia* 9, Bruxelles 1969). Zum Basilikos Grammateus: E. Biedermann,
*Studien zur ägyptischen Verwaltungsgeschichte in ptolemäischer und römischer Zeit. Der
βασιλικὸς γραμματεύς* (Berlin 1913).

3. Zu dem Procuratorenamt des Epistrategen s. jetzt die umfassende Untersuchung von J. D. Thomas, *The Epistrategos in Ptolemaic and Roman Egypt*, Part 2:
*The Roman Epistrategos* ( = *Papyrologica Coloniensia* 6.2, Opladen 1982). Zur Frage
der Anzahl der Epistrategien s. dort S.29–39.

4. Ich nenne nur O. W. Reinmuth, *The Prefect of Egypt from Augustus to
Diocletian* ( = *Klio Beiheft* 34, Leipzig 1935); A. Stein, *Die Präfekten von Ägypten in
der römischen Kaiserzeit* (Bern 1950); M. Humbert, *La juridiction du préfet d'Egypte
d'Auguste à Dioclétien* (in: F. Burdeau u.a., *Aspects de l'empire romain*, Paris 1964)
95–147; P. A. Brunt, "The Administrators of Roman Egypt", *JRS* 65 (1975)
124–47; G. Bastianini, "Lista dei prefetti d'Egitto dal 30ª al 299ᵖ", *ZPE* 17
(1975) 263–328 mit "Aggiunte e correzioni" in *ZPE* 38 (1980) 75–89.

Zeit angehört.[5] Möglicherweise hat hier neben der Bedeutung des Amtes, auf das ich unten kurz zurückkommen werde, auch seine Neugier weckende Bezeichnung das Interesse der Forscher hervorgerufen. Ferner ist dem *procurator usiacus* innerhalb einer Untersuchung über die kaiserlichen Domänen in Ägypten jüngst ein Kapitel gewidmet worden,[6] und dem δικαιοδότης oder lateinisch *iuridicus* hat H. Kupiszewski besonders unter juristischen Gesichtspunkten eine Behandlung zuteil werden lassen.[7] Über ebenso wichtige Ämter wie das des διοικητής oder das des ἀρχιερεύς gibt es dagegen praktisch überhaupt keine Literatur,[8] ganz zu schweigen von niedriger stehenden Procuratoren, z.B. den *procuratores Neaspoleos, ad episcepsin, ad Mercurium Alexandriae* usw. Der Grund für diese Zurückhaltung seitens der Forscher liegt zweifellos in der anfangs erwähnten ungünstigen Quellenlage. Zu wenige konkrete Ergebnisse scheinen erreichbar.

Einen bescheidenen Beitrag zur Bewältigung noch ausstehender Aufgaben möchte ich im Folgenden zu leisten versuchen, indem ich drei mit dem Amt eines der ranghöchsten Procuratoren, dem des Dioiketen, zusammenhängende Fragen diskutiere. Zunächst will ich seinen Aufgabenkreis anhand einer Reihe von Urkunden skizzieren, in denen der Dioiket persönlich eine Rolle spielt. Danach will ich mich spezielleren Fragen zuwenden und zunächst nach dem Rang des Dioiketen innerhalb der alexandrinischen Verwaltungshierarchie fragen und zum Schluss die Zeitpunkte der Einführung und des Verschwindens des Amtes erörtern. Als Anhang gebe ich eine prosopographische Liste der bekannten Inhaber des Amtes und solcher Procuratoren, in denen man Dioiketen vermutet hat.

5. G. Plaumann, *Der Idioslogos. Untersuchungen zur Finanzverwaltung Ägyptens in hellenistischer und römischer Zeit* (*Abh. d. Preuss. Akad. d. Wiss., Phil.-hist. Kl.*, Jahrgang 1918, Heft 17, Berlin 1919); P. R. Swarney, *The Ptolemaic and Roman Idios Logos* ( = *American Studies in Papyrology* 8, Toronto 1970).

6. G. M. Parássoglou, *Imperial Estates in Roman Egypt* ( = *American Studies in Papyrology* 18, Amsterdam 1977), bes. 84–90.

7. H. Kupiszewski, "The Iuridicus Alexandreae", *JJP* 7–8 (1953–54) 187–204.

8. P. M. Meyer, "Διοίκησις und Ἴδιος Λόγος", in *Festschrift zu Otto Hirschfelds 60. Geburtstag* (Berlin 1903) 131–63, ist veraltet. Zum Archiereus vgl. jetzt immerhin die Skizze von M. Stead, "The High Priest of Alexandria and All Egypt", in *Proceedings of the XVIth International Congress of Papyrology* ( = *American Studies in Papyrology* 23, Chico 1981) 411–18; s. auch G. M. Parássoglou in *ZPE* 13 (1974) 21–37.

*Dieter Hagedorn*

## I. Aufgaben des Dioiketen

Der Wirkungskreis des Dioiketen ist bereits durch die Bezeichnung des Amtes deutlich gekennzeichnet: Der Dioiket ist der Leiter des Finanzressorts mit dem Namen διοίκησις, das uns in den Papyri auch in einer Fülle von Steuerlisten, Steuerquittungen und ähnlichen Texten entgegentritt. Wäre diese Definition nicht schon aus sich heraus einleuchtend, so würde es genügen, zum Beweis ihrer Richtigkeit auf eine Gruppe von Papyri zu verweisen, die ich noch verschiedentlich erwähnen werde. Es handelt sich dabei um noch unpublizierte[9] Kölner carbonisierte Papyri aus dem im Nildelta gelegenen Gau von Bubastos. Sie enthalten in ca. 55 Fragmenten in Abschrift die Korrespondenz, die um 223/4 n.Chr. der Dioiket Claudius Severianus mit dem Strategen des Bubastites geführt hat; es werden darin verschiedene an den Dioiketen adressierte Anträge von Einwohnern des Bubastites zitiert, die einzelne Objekte – Ländereien oder Gebäude – aus dem Besitz des Finanzressorts διοίκησις kaufen wollen. Die Anträge beginnen mit den Worten βούλομαι ὠνήσασθαι ἐκ τῶν εἰς πρᾶσιν προκειμένων τῆς διοικήσεως oder ähnlich, wobei für τῆς διοικήσεως auch eintreten kann τῆς σῆς ἐπιτροπῆς. Die διοίκησις ist also die ἐπιτροπή des Dioiketen, der Dioiket ist der Procurator der διοίκησις.

Die nächste Frage lautet nun logischerweise: Was ist denn die διοίκησις? In dem hier gesteckten Rahmen mag es genügen, unter Aussparung aller Detailfragen eine grobe Definition zu geben. Sie könnte lauten: In die Zuständigkeit der Dioikesis fiel die Bewirtschaftung der allgemeinen Staatsfinanzen der Provinz. Eine Eingrenzung erfährt die Zuständigkeit der Dioikesis durch die beiden daneben existierenden Finanzressorts, den ἴδιος λόγος und den οὐσιακὸς λόγος. Letzterem oblag die Verwaltung der grossen Landgüter, der οὐσίαι, die im Laufe des 1. Jhdts. n.Chr. durch verschiedene Erbgänge in den Privatbesitz der römischen Kaiser gekommen waren; als selbständiges Finanzressort ist der

---

9. Ein vorläufiger Bericht über diese Texte ist mein Artikel "Verkohlte Papyri in der Sammlung des Instituts für Altertumskunde der Universität Köln", in *Festschrift zum 100-jährigen Bestehen der Papyrussammlung der Österreichischen Nationalbibliothek Papyrus Erzherzog Rainer* (Wien 1983) 107–11.

οὐσιακὸς λόγος wohl unter den Flaviern eingerichtet worden.[10] Die Institution des ἴδιος λόγος haben die Römer dagegen gleich zu Beginn ihrer Herrschaft im wesentlichen unverändert von den Ptolemäern übernommen; in die Zuständigkeit des ἴδιος λόγος, der, wie der Name besagt, eine "Spezialkasse" für unregelmässig zu erwartende Einnahmen war,[11] fiel, um nur einige Beispiele zu nennen, die Verwaltung desjenigen staatlichen Besitzes, der durch die Einziehung herrenloser oder widerrechtlich erworbener Güter zustande gekommen war, ferner zumindest zeitweilig der Verkauf von unproduktivem Staatsland, sowie die Einziehung von Geldern, die dem Staat von Priestern und Tempeln zuflossen. Alle Finanzangelegenheiten, die nicht in die Zuständigkeit eines dieser beiden letztgenannten Ressorts fielen, gehörten in den Bereich der Diokesis.

Die Oberaufsicht in dieser wichtigen Behörde führte also der Dioiket, und es versteht sich ganz von selbst, dass der Chef nicht in allen Bagatellangelegenheiten persönlich tätig geworden ist, vielmehr wurden die meisten Vorgänge vor Ort von subalternen Beamten erledigt. Man denke etwa an die immense Verwaltungsarbeit, die laufend im Zusammenhang mit der Steuererhebung entstand und von den lokalen Behörden weitgehend in eigener Regie erledigt wurde. Dennoch ist für heutiges Empfinden überraschend, mit wie vergleichsweise unbedeutenden Fragen der Procurator behelligt wurde, Angelegenheiten von wie geringer Tragweite er zu entscheiden hatte. Einige solcher Fälle werde ich weiter unten referieren.

Es sind bis heute – allzu fragmentarische Texte nicht mitgerechnet – rund 35 Urkunden bekannt geworden, in denen der Dioiket uns bei der Ausübung seines Amtes gegenübertritt. Naturgemäss überwiegen die Fälle, die auf schriftlichem Wege erledigt wurden: Der Dioiket empfängt Eingaben von Bürgern, die deren eigene Angelegenheiten[12] oder solche des Fiskus betreffen,[13]

10. Vgl. Parássoglou, a.a.O. (Fussn. 6). Die frühere Ansicht, der οὐσιακὸς λόγος sei nur ein Unterressort des ἴδιος λόγος gewesen, wird ebenda 86f. zurückgewiesen.

11. Die ältere Auffassung, derzufolge der ἴδιος λόγος die "Privatkasse" der Könige bzw. der Kaiser war, ist überholt; vgl. die in Fussn. 5 genannte Literatur.

12. *BGU* xi 2060.9ff.; *P. Oxy.* vi 899; *P. Flor.* i 6. Vgl. *P. Leit.* 5.12f. = *SB* viii 10196; *P. Oxy.* iii 533.24–26; *P. Oxy.* x 1264.7ff. = *FIRA²* iii 9.

13. Vgl. *P. Petaus* 10.6f. und 11.5f. Interessen sowohl des Fiskus als auch

und gibt in Zirkularen oder in Briefen an einzelne Beamte, meist an Strategen, Anweisung, wie in bestimmten Fragen zu verfahren sei.[14] Nicht alle diese Vorgänge sind uns in Originalurkunden erhalten; meist kennen wir sie nur durch Zitate in anderen Dokumenten.

Sieht man ab vom Erlass und dem Empfang schriftlicher Mitteilungen, so sind es nur wenige Tätigkeiten des Dioiketen, von denen die Papyri zeugen. Wir finden ihn einmal als Mitglied des συμβούλιον, d.i. des Beratungsausschusses des Präfekten beim Konvent,[15] und erfahren einige andere Male, dass er ein Gerichtsverfahren geleitet hat,[16] wobei nicht immer klar wird, ob er das kraft eigener Jurisdiktion, im Auftrag des Präfekten oder als Stellvertreter des *iuridicus* getan hat. Vertretung des *iuridicus* gehörte nämlich zu den regelmässigen Aufgaben des Dioiketen. Wir werden unten unter (II) darauf zurückkommen.

Unter den Gegenständen, mit denen der Dioiket sich bei der Ausübung seiner Amtsgeschäfte zu befassen hatte, lassen sich Bereiche ausmachen, die häufiger in Erscheinung treten, während andere Themen nur in einzelnen Urkunden auftauchen. Einige Beispiele aus häufigeren Themenkreisen will ich zunächst etwas detaillierter beschreiben.

Die Liturgen, die Zwangsbeamten der Kaiserzeit, waren bekanntlich mit ihrem Privatvermögen für alle Einbussen verantwortlich, die der Staatskasse durch ihre Amtsführung eventuell entstanden;[17] dadurch wollte der Staat sich vor jedem Risiko

private betreffen die Anträge auf Kauf aus dem Staatsbesitz in *P. Ross.–Georg.* v 25 und den *P. Colon.* inv. carbon. B.

14. Zirkulare: *P. Oxy.* XII 1409.7ff. = *Sel. Pap.* 225; vgl. *P. Mich.* XI 623.7–10. Briefe an einzelne Strategen: *P. Oxy.* XXIV 2411.43ff.; *BGU* XI 2060.3ff.; *P. Flor.* I 89 (vgl. *CE* 46 (1971) 155–57); vgl. *P. Mich.* VIII 479.10–12; *P. Oxy.* III 513.28–31 = *W. Chr.* 183 = *Sel. Pap.* 77; *P. Oxy.* III 533.20–22; *P. Oxy.* VI 899 Einl. (S.225 unten); *P. Oxy.* VIII 1115.3–5 = *Sel. Pap.* 426; *P. Leit.* 5.14f. = *SB* VIII 10196; *P. Petaus* 10.5f. und 11.4f.; *P. Strassb.* ined. in *W. Chr.* 363 Einl.; *P. Flor.* I 6.3–4; viele Beispiele enthalten die Kölner carbonisierten Papyri. Brief an den ἐπίτροπος Νέας πόλεως: *BGU* I 8 ii 29ff. = *W. Chr.* 170. Ein Schreiben des Dioiketen an die βουλή von Oxyrhynchos wird in *P. Oxy.* XII 1412.8 = *Sel. Pap.* 237 erwähnt.

15. *P. Strassb.* 179. Ein um neue Fragmente erweiterter Neudruck dieses Textes ist von S. Daris im *Aegyptus* publiziert, 63 (1983) 123–28.

16. Vgl. unten Fussn. 42.

17. Vgl. nur Oertel, a.a.O. (Fussn. 1) 357ff.; N. Lewis, *The Compulsory Public Services of Roman Egypt* (= *Papyrologica Florentina* 11, Firenze 1982) 65ff.

schützen. Besassen die Liturgen aber kein ausreichendes Vermögen, dann konnten sie im Ernstfall natürlich auch nicht zum Regress herangezogen werden. Die Benennung eines liturgischen Beamten mit unzureichendem Vermögen bedeutete daher für die Staatskasse ein finanzielles Risiko und musste verhindert werden. Jeder, der einen Liturgen zu bestellen hatte, sei es ein Dorfschreiber, sei es ein Stratege, musste darauf achten, weil er nämlich möglicherweise sonst selbst zum Ersatz des Defizits herangezogen wurde. In den beiden Urkunden *P. Petaus* 10 und 11 (2.5.184 n.Chr.) erfahren wir von zwei Dorfschreibern, die von Delatoren beim Dioiketen angezeigt worden waren mit der Behauptung, sie seien χρεῶσται, also Schuldner, höchstwahrscheinlich Schuldner gegenüber der Staatskasse, und ἄποροι; ἄπορος ist ein terminus technicus, der in diesem Zusammenhang bedeutet, dass die Beamten nicht das für die spezielle Liturgie erforderliche Mindestvermögen besitzen.[18] Der Dioiket veranlasste auf die Anzeige hin die Klärung der Vorwürfe auf dem Dienstwege, wie wir heute sagen würden, d.h. er delegierte die Fälle an den zuständigen Strategen, der wiederum vom κωμογραμματεύς des Heimatdorfes der beschuldigten Dorfschreiber einen Bericht anforderte. Die Antwort, die uns in den genannten Papyri erhalten ist, lautete in beiden Fällen, die Vorwürfe seien unzutreffend, das erforderliche Vermögen von 3000 Drachmen sei vorhanden. Offensichtlich waren die falschen Beschuldigungen in diesen beiden Fällen von persönlichen Gegnern der Dorfschreiber vorgebracht worden, die auf diese Weise vielleicht ihnen unbequeme Beamte beseitigen wollten.

Erheblich häufiger ist der umgekehrte Fall, dass nämlich jemand, der zu einer Liturgie benannt worden war, selbst durch eine Eingabe an einen höheren Beamten versuchte, der Last des Zwangsamtes zu entgehen,[19] sofern er es nicht sogar vorzog, unter Aufgabe von Hab und Gut das Weite zu suchen.[20] *P. Leit.*

18. Vgl. *P. Petaus* 10.10 Anm.; N. Lewis, a.a.O. (Fussn. 17) 74–76.

19. Vgl. Lewis, a.a.O. (Fussn. 17) 99–103 und die weit über 70 Beispiele enthaltende "Table 5: Protest" ebenda S.122–27.

20. In dem von E. G. Turner, *The Papyrologist at Work*, 44f. mitgeteilten Papyrus hören wir von nicht weniger als 120 Liturgen, die um 147/8 ihre Heimat verlassen hatten, um liturgischen Verpflichtungen zu entgehen. Ihr Vermögen (πόρος) wurde von Staats wegen verkauft, der Dioiket (Julius Amyntianus)

5 = *SB* VIII 10196 enthält ein Beispiel für eine derartige Petition aus dem Jahre 167/8 n.Chr.: Orsenuphis, ein Einwohner des Ἀρσινοίτης νομός, wendet sich an den Dioiketen Aurelius Ptolemaeus und macht seine Aporia gegen seine Bestellung zum πρεσβύτερος κώμης geltend. Wiederum verfährt der Dioiket in derselben Weise: Er delegiert die Untersuchung an den zuständigen Strategen, der ebenfalls die Angelegenheit wieder an den Dorfschreiber des Heimatdorfes weitergibt.

Bittschriften, mit deren Hilfe die Menschen die Übernahme eines Zwangsamtes abzuwenden hofften, sind – wie schon gesagt – in den Papyri nicht selten anzutreffen, doch liefert der soeben geschilderte Fall das einzige uns erhaltene sichere Beispiel dafür, dass man sich direkt an den Dioiketen gewandt hat.[21] Der normalerweise unter solschen Umständen gewählte Adressat war der Epistratege; gut über 20 Beispiele für an ihn gerichtete Petitionen gegen die Benennung zu einem liturgischen Amt lassen sich zitieren.[22] Warum mag Orsenuphis sich stattdessen an den Dioiketen gewandt haben? Ein naheliegender Grund ist der, dass auch er in der Bittschrift seine Aporia herausgestellt hat. Damit

natürlich von dem Vorgang in Kenntnis gesetzt. Vgl. auch Lewis, a.a.O. (Fussn. 17) 103 Anm. 60 (Bibliographie); *P. Wisc.* II 81.

21. Ein weiterer, nicht ganz sicherer Fall ist *P. Strassb.* I 57, wo in Z. 1 das Amt des Adressaten der Petition, Aelius Mamertinus, ungelesen geblieben war; Thomas hat jetzt a.a.O. (Fussn. 3) 215f. wahrscheinlich gemacht, dass am Ende der Zeile [διο]ι̣[κ]η̣τῆι zu lesen ist. Erwähnt wird ein derartiges ὑπόμνημα an den Dioiketen in *P. Oxy.* X 1264 (272 n.Chr.); der Schreiber hatte vom Dioiketen Liturgiebefreiung wegen seines Kinderreichtums erhalten (vgl. dazu jetzt den parallelen Fall in *P. Mich.* XIV 675 mit *ZPE* 49 (1982) 76–78). Der fragmentarische *P. Flor.* III 312 aus dem Jahre 91 n.Chr. ist von Lewis, a.a.O. (Fussn. 17) 122, ebenfalls als ein dem Dioiketen eingereichtes ὑπόμνημα aufgeführt worden, weil in Z.7–9 dieses Papyrus ein Kollationsvermerk eines διοικητικὸς ὑπηρέτης erhalten ist. Da ich weiter unten dafür plädieren werde, dass das Dioiketenamt zu dieser Zeit noch nicht mit so weitreichenden Kompetenzen ausgestattet war, nehme ich an, dass diese Eingabe dem Präfekten oder einem anderen höheren Beamten eingereicht worden ist und die Abschrift nur zufällig von dem Amtsdiener eines διοικητής niedrigeren Ranges kontrolliert worden ist, wie wir ihn in *P. Fouad* 21 kennen lernen werden; vgl. auch die vorsichtige Formulierung von Thomas, a.a.O. (Fussn. 3) 87f. Ein διοικητικὸς ὑπηρέτης begegnet in *P. Oxy.* II 259.13f. schon im Jahre 23 n.Chr. Mit *P. Leit.* 5 vergleichbar ist *P. Oxy.* VI 899r (s. dazu weiter unten), allerdings geht es dort nicht um eine Liturgie im engeren Sinne, sondern um erzwungene Bearbeitung von δημοσία γῆ.

22. Thomas hat a.a.O. (Fussn. 3) in dem Kapitel "Appeals against Liturgies", 83–93, das einschlägige Material untersucht; vgl. auch ebenda S.143–49 "Table A. Petitions to the epistrategos".

war impliziert, dass bei eventuell auftretenden Defiziten die Staatskasse keine direkte Sicherheit besass, und ein solcher Fall musste den Dioiketen natürlich interessieren.[23]

Sicher ist diese Erklärung jedoch nicht. Von der Einschaltung des Dioiketen lesen wir nämlich auch in einem Privatbrief aus Oxyrhynchos (*P. Oxy.* III 533; 2./3. Jhdt.), in dem die Hintergründe der Affäre jedoch unklar bleiben. Ein Vater schreibt hier seinem Sohn und erteilt ihm verschiedene Aufträge. Unter anderem soll er im Büro des Strategen einen Brief des Dioiketen an den Strategen einsehen (Z.20–22), ἐπιστολὴν γραφεῖσαν περὶ τοῦ ὀνόματα πεμφθῆναι ἀντ' ἐμοῦ εἰς κλῆρον τῆς πρακτορείας, d.h. einen Brief des Inhalts, dass statt seiner andere für die Auslosung zum Praktorenamt vorgesehen werden sollen. Vermutlich war der Name des Vaters auf eine Liste von Leuten gesetzt worden, aus denen die Steuereinnehmer ausgelost werden sollten.[24] Dagegen hatte er beim Dioiketen, so vermuten wir, protestiert, und dieser gab, vielleicht nachdem er auf dem Dienstwege weitere Informationen eingeholt hatte, dem Strategen die Anweisung, den Namen unseres Mannes durch einen anderen zu ersetzen. Von Aporia ist hier nicht die Rede, was in einem Privatbriefe auch nicht zu verwundern brauchte, aber aus den übrigen Details des Briefes gewinnt man eher den Eindruck, dass der Vater in wirtschaftlich guten oder sogar sehr guten Verhältnissen lebte. Sollte dieser Eindruck zutreffen, dann wäre ein Interesse des Fiskus nicht so auf der Hand liegend und der Dioiket möglicherweise aus einem anderen Grunde eingeschaltet worden.

Deutliche Belange der Staatskasse sind dagegen wieder in dem Fall der Apollonarion aus Oxyrhynchos tangiert (*P. Oxy.* VI 899r), die um das Jahr 200 n.Chr. den Dioiketen in einer Eingabe bittet, von der Verpflichtung zur Bearbeitung von Staatsland befreit zu werden. Die γεωργία δημοσίας γῆς wurde vielfach als eine schwere Last empfunden, die der Belastung durch Liturgien durchaus gleichzustellen war. Unsere Apollonarion war beim Tode ihres

23. In *PSI* x 1103, einer an den Epistrategen gerichteten Petition gegen Benennung zu einer Liturgie aus dem 2. Jhdt., spielt ἀπορία ebenfalls eine Rolle, ist jedoch nur ein Nebenargument. Im Vordergrund steht das zu hohe Alter des Petenten.

24. Zum Losverfahren bei der Bestellung gewisser liturgischer Ämter s. zuletzt N. Lewis, a.a.O. (Fussn. 17) 86–88; Thomas, a.a.O. (Fussn. 3) 86–88. Beispiele solcher Listen sind etwa *P. Petaus* 60; 62 und 65.

Vaters von den lokalen Behörden gezwungen worden, in demselben Umfang Staatsland weiter zu bearbeiten, wie es ihrem Vater auferlegt gewesen war. Sie betont nun, dass sie als Frau der Arbeit nicht gewachsen sei und auch aufgrund von Entscheidungen von Präfekten und Epistrategen, die diese in zahlreichen Präzedenzfällen getroffen hätten, nicht dazu verpflichtet sei. Stossrichtung ihrer Argumentation gegenüber dem Dioiketen scheint das Risiko für den Fiskus gewesen zu sein.[25]

War ein Bürger erst einmal zu einem liturgischen Amt bestellt, dann drohten ihm verschiedene finanzielle Lasten. Zum Beispiel konnte er für Versäumnisse, durch die dem Staat nicht einmal direkt ein finanzieller Schaden entstanden war, mit einer Busse belegt werden, die an die Staatskasse abzuführen war. Den Befehl zur Zahlung einer solchen Busse erteilte der Dioiket, jedenfalls in dem Fall des Strategen Sarapion alias Apollonianos in *P. Oxy.* I 61 (18.11.221 n.Chr.). Das Versäumnis dieses Strategen hatte darin bestanden, gewisse Aktenstücke, die zur Einsichtnahme und Kontrolle nach Alexandria gebracht werden mussten, vermutlich die monatlich abzuliefernden Rechenschaftsberichte, nicht rechtzeitig eingereicht zu haben.[26]

War jemand durch Verfehlungen dieser Art oder auch auf andere Weise dem Staat gegenüber in Verschuldung geraten, dann fiel die Behandlung dieser Angelegenheit erst recht in die Kompetenz des Dioiketen. In *BGU* I 8, Kol. II 26–III 4 = *W. Chr.* 170 (um 248 n.Chr.) hören wir von einem Schiffsspediteur, der zum Schuldner des Fiskus geworden war, möglicherweise dadurch, dass er eine zum Transport anvertraute Ladung Steuergetreide nicht unversehrt am Bestimmungsort abgeliefert hatte. Der Dioiket ordnete daraufhin eine Überprüfung seiner Vermögensverhältnisse an, was wahrscheinlich der erste Schritt zur Konfiskation seines Besitzes war. Der Amtsweg ist in diesem Fall gegenüber den bisher erwähnten Beispielen um eine Station

25. Ein vergleichbarer Fall ist *BGU* II 648, wo jedoch das Amt des um Hilfe angegangenen Beamten nicht genannt wird; vgl. auch Thomas, a.a.O. (Fussn. 3) 91 mit Anm. 159.

26. Die uns zur Verfügung stehenden Informationen über die verschiedenen Amtszeiten des Strategen Sarapion alias Apollonianos hat G. Bastianini, "La carriera di Sarapion alias Apollonianus", *Aegyptus* 49 (1969) 149–82 zusammengetragen; zu *P. Oxy.* I 61s. ebenda S.172f. und schon U. Wilcken, *APF* 4 (1907) 126–28.

erweitert, insofern als der Dioiket zuerst den *procurator Neaspoleos* wegen seiner Zuständigkeit für den staatlichen Getreidetransport einschaltete, der seinerseits die Angelegenheit an den Strategen des betroffenen Gaues zur Bearbeitung weiterreichte. Der Papyrus ist auch für die Stellung des Dioiketen in der alexandrinischen Verwaltungshierarchie von Interesse, weil er deutlich zeigt, dass der Dioiket gegenüber dem *procurator Neaspoleos* eine Art Weisungsbefugnis besass.

Wenn Hab und Gut eines Staatsschuldners erst einmal durch Konfiskation in den Besitz des Staates übergegangen waren, dann versuchte der Fiskus, die Immobilien durch Verkauf so schnell wie möglich wieder abzustossen. Zu diesem Zweck wurden sie öffentlich zum Kauf feilgeboten, und jeder Kaufwillige konnte ein Angebot einreichen. Eine Serie solcher Kaufangebote besitzen wir in den schon erwähnten Kölner carbonisierten Papyri.[27] Die Angebote sind alle an den Dioiketen adressiert, der sie – wir sind mit dem Verfahren inzwischen bestens vertraut – zur Bearbeitung an den Strategen, in unserem Falle den Strategen des Bubastites, weitergeleitet hat. Dass man dem Dioiketen als Haupt des Ressorts die Kaufanträge persönlich einreichen musste, ist möglicherweise eine Neuerung des 3. Jhdts. n.Chr. Noch am Ende des 2. Jhdts. war es nämlich anscheinend üblich, die Anträge bei einer deutlich niedrigeren Instanz, nämlich beim Gaustrategen, zu stellen.[28]

Von besonderem Interesse für das Verfahren bei der Konfiskation ist *P. Oxy.* xxiv 2411, weil wir aus dieser Urkunde erkennen können, wie sorgsam eventuelle private Ansprüche an den Staatsschuldner gegen die des Staates abgewogen wurden.[29] In dem Papyrus wird eine Entscheidung des Dioiketen Mallius Crassus aus

27. Vgl. oben S.170 mit Fussn. 9. Ein Fragment aus einer recht ähnlichen Rolle ist *P. Ross.–Georg.* v 25.

28. Z.B. in *P. Amh.* ii 97 und *P. Petaus* 13–16. Auch andere Procuratoren, nämlich der Epistratege und der Procurator des Idios Logos, haben hin und wieder Funktionen beim Auktionsverfahren ausgeübt; ob allein chronologische Gründe oder bestimmte, uns nicht erkennbare Kompetenzverteilungen für die unterschiedliche Handhabung des Verfahrens verantwortlich waren, oder ob überhaupt kein System dahinter stand, lässt sich noch nicht sagen; vgl. dazu auch Thomas, a.a.O. (Fussn. 3) 178f.

29. Vgl. zu diesem Papyrus N. Lewis, "Notes on Two Documents from Oxyrhynchos", *APF* 21 (1971) 83–89, bes. 85ff., und von juristischer Seite G. Purpura, "Il concorso tra fisco e creditore ipotecario in Pap. Oxy. xxiv 2411", *SDHI* 44 (1978) 452–60.

dem Jahre 159 n.Chr. zitiert, die folgendes besagt: Wenn ein Privatmann gegenüber einem Staatsschuldner Ansprüche geltend macht, die nachweislich älter sind als die des Staates, dann soll die private Forderung Vorrang haben. Im konkreten Beispiel hatte ein Privatmann einem anderen ein Darlehen gewährt, der danach ein Amt, nämlich die Strategie, hatte übernehmen müssen und in seiner Eigenschaft als Stratege in die Schuld des Fiskus geraten war. Wenn nachweisbar sei, so entschied der Dioiket, dass der Darlehensvertrag tatsächlich vor der Bestellung des Schuldners zum Strategen abgeschlossen worden sei, solle der Gläubiger beim Verkauf der inzwischen konfiszierten Güter des Schuldners das Vorkaufsrecht haben, und geliehenes Kapital zuzüglich der Zinsen sollten auf den Preis angerechnet werden. Wenn aber von dritter Seite ein höheres Kaufangebot gemacht werde, solle der Höherbietende zwar den Zuschlag erhalten, dem Gläubiger aber müssten seine Forderungen erstattet werden. Ähnliche Regelungen kennen wir auch aus juristischen Quellen für eine etwas spätere Zeit; beispielsweise hat ein Reskript Caracallas im Codex Justinianus einen ganz ähnlichen Tenor.[30] *P. Oxy.* xxiv 2411 ist für das Dioiketenamt insofern besonders wichtig, als er, soweit ich sehe, das einzige Beispiel dafür liefert, dass der Dioiket eine Frage von prinzipieller Bedeutung entscheidet und sein Spruch als Präzedens zitiert wird.

Es muss übrigens angemerkt werden, dass das, was ich hier Kauf aus dem Staatsbesitz nenne, nur mit Einschränkungen die Bezeichnung "Kauf" verdient; besser würde man von "Versteigerung" sprechen. In den Kölner verkohlten Papyri gibt der Dioiket nämlich regelmässig die Anordnung, der Stratege solle eine Abschrift des Kaufangebots und der Bearbeitungsakten öffentlich aushängen lassen, damit Leute, die eventuell bereit seien, ein höheres Angebot zu unterbreiten, sich melden könnten. Tatsächlich besitzen wir zwei Urkunden, aus denen hervorgeht, dass Personen, die aus dem Staatsbesitz gekauft hatten, durch das höhere Angebot eines Konkurrenten aus diesem Besitz wieder verdrängt werden konnten. Es handelte sich also – zumindest für

---

30. *Codex Iustinianus* 7.73.4: *Si debitor, cuius fundum fuisse et ipse confiteris, prius eum distraxit quam fisco aliquid debuit, inquietandum te non esse procurator meus cognoscet. Nam etsi postea debitor extitit, non ideo tamen ea, quae de dominio eius excesserunt, pignoris iure fisco potuerunt obligari.* Vgl. auch Purpura, a.a.O. (Fussn. 29) 457f.

eine begrenzte Zeit – nur um eine eingeschränkte Form von Eigentum. In beiden genannten Urkunden sind ausdrücklich Entscheidungen von Dioiketen erwähnt.

Die erste Urkunde, *P. Oxy.* XIV 1633 aus dem Jahre 275 n.Chr., ist das Angebot eines Bürgers der Stadt Oxyrhynchos, einen anderen beim Kauf ἀπὸ ἀπράτων τῆς διοικήσεως zu überbieten.[31] "Ich bin bereit", erklärt er, "den Aurelius Serenos im Angebot zu übertreffen", und er gibt genau an, wieviel mehr er zu zahlen gewillt ist als dieser Aurelius Serenos.[32] In seinem Angebot beruft er sich auf Anordnungen des Dioiketen, vermutlich ähnliche Anweisungen zur Publikation des Aktenmakterials, wie die, die ich soeben aus den Kölner verkohlten Papyri erwähnt habe.

Der andere Text ist *P. Oxy.* III 513 = *W. Chr.* 183. Diogenes alias Dionysios aus Oxyrhynchos hatte ἀπὸ ἀπράτων τῆς διοικήσεως ein Haus mit Nebengebäuden zu kaufen angeboten und hatte im November/Dezember 181 n.Chr. auch den Zuschlag erhalten und anschliessend den Preis und die anfallenden Nebenkosten auf die Staatsbank überwiesen. Unwiderruflich in sein Eigentum übergegangen war das Objekt damit aber noch nicht, denn etwa zwei Jahre später musste er es wieder aufgeben, weil ein gewisser Serenos aus derselben Stadt dafür den dreifachen Preis geboten hatte und das besagte Objekt auf Anweisung des Dioiketen auch in Besitz nehmen durfte. Der erste Käufer erhielt den Kaufpreis, den er ja bereits gezahlt hatte, vom zweiten Käufer erstattet; in der Urkunde liegt uns die Quittung des ersten Käufers über den Erhalt dieser Zahlung vor.[33]

Mit diesen ausführlicheren Beschreibungen einzelner Urkunden will ich es bewenden lassen und andere Gegenstände, mit denen der Dioiket sich nach Ausweis der Papyri zu befassen hatte, nur kurz andeuten. Wir sehen ihn tätig werden im Zusammenhang mit der Umwandlung von normalem Ackerland zu Weinland, die

---

31. Der Adressat des Angebots ist nicht erhalten, aber aus τοῦδε τοῦ νομοῦ in Z.11 kann man vielleicht schliessen, dass er ein Gaubeamter, am ehesten also der Stratege war.

32. Vgl. Z.5f. βού[λομαι ὑπερ]βαλεῖν Αὐρήλιον Σερῆν[ον... und Z.17–20 προ[σ]φέρων μ[εθ᾽ ἃς ὑπέ]σχετο ὑπὲρ τιμῆς δραχμὰ[ς ἑξακοσίας] ἑξή[κοντα τὰς τ]οῦ ὑπερβ[ολίου] δρα[χ]μὰς ἑκα[τ]ὸ[ν τεσσ]αράκοντ[α.

33. Vgl. hierzu M. Talamanca, *Contributi allo studio delle vendite all'asta nel mondo classico* (Roma 1954) 212ff.

gewissen Restriktionen unterlag;[34] er gibt Order, das für die Bewässerung der Felder notwendige System von Kanälen und Deichen zu reparieren;[35] er überwacht die Lebensmittelversorgung der Soldaten;[36] als aus dem Gau von Oxyrhynchos zu einer Festlichkeit eine Anzahl von Stieren abgeliefert werden musste, diese Auflage dann aber anscheinend nicht erfüllt worden war, ordnete er eine Ersatzzahlung von 400 Drachmen pro Tier an, die dem κυριακὸς λόγος gutzuschreiben war;[37] in einem Fall von privaten Grenzstreitigkeiten veranlasste er eine Ortsbesichtigung und Neuvermessung der Grundstücke, vermutlich durch den Strategen, und nach *P. Oxy.* x 1264 = *FIRA*[2] iii 9 gewährte er einem Kinderreichen ἀσυλία.[38]

Dreierlei scheint mir nach diesem Überblick über die Urkunden hervorhebenswert. Erstens: In den allermeisten Fällen von persönlicher Aktivität des Dioiketen, die uns begegnet sind, war das Interesse des Fiskus an dem Vorgang deutlich ersichtlich. Bei nur wenigen Gelegenheiten fällt die Relevanz für die Staatskasse nicht direkt in die Augen,[39] was nicht bedeuten muss, dass sie wirklich nicht vorliegt. Es wird vielmehr eher der Schluss nahegelegt, dass

---

34. *BGU* xi 2060 (13.9.180), ein Antrag auf Umwandlung von Weizenland in Weinland, den der Dioiket Julius Crispinus routinemässig an den zuständigen Strategen zur Bearbeitung weiterleitet. Mit der Prüfung eines solchen Vorganges war der Dioiket Vernasius Facundus im Juni/Juli 161 n.Chr, befasst (*P. Oxy.* vii 1032).

35. *P. Oxy.* xii 1409.7ff. ( = *Sel. Pap.* 225; März/April 278), ein Rundschreiben des Dioiketen Ulpius Aurelius an die Strategen und Dekaproten der Heptanomia und des Arsinoites. Ein inhaltlich verwandtes und ebenfalls dem späteren 3. Jhdt. angehörendes Rundschreiben ist *P. Yale* inv. 447 (*CE* 49 (1974) 338 = *SB* xiv 11349), dessen Absender bedauerlicherweise nicht erhalten ist, möglicherweise aber ebenfalls der Dioiket war.

36. *P. Oxy.* viii 1115 = *Sel. Pap.* 426 (21.5.284) und *P. Oxy.* xii 1412 = *Sel. Pap.* 237 (etwa gleichzeitig). Es ist in beiden Fällen derselbe Dioiket, Aurelius Proteas, der sich um die annona der Soldaten kümmert.

37. *P. Mich.* xi 623 (um 190 n.Chr.; vgl. *ZPE* 29 (1978) 190). Der Dioiket hiess vielleicht Ummidius Pius (vgl. J. Rea, *JEA* 60 (1974) 297).

38. Vgl. *P. Oxy.* xlvi 3288 (252/3 n.Chr.). Die Hintergründe, weswegen der Dioiket (Septimius Apollonius) in dieser Privatsache tätig geworden ist, bleiben im Dunkeln. Immerhin begründet der Petent in Z.9–11 (ὅπως δυνηθῶ τὰ ὑπὲρ τούτων δημόσια εἰσενεγκεῖν τῷ ἱερωτάτῳ ταμείῳ) seine erneute Eingabe (an den Strategen?) mit fiskalischem Interesse.
In *P. Oxy.* 1264 handelt es sich wohl um Befreiung von Liturgieverpflichtungen aufgrund von Kinderreichtum; vgl. auch oben Fussn. 21.

39. *P. Oxy.* iii 533; *P. Oxy.* xlvi 3288.

bei jeglichem persönlichen Eingreifen des Dioiketen die Staatsfinanzen unmittelbar tangiert waren.

Dieses Ergebnis hätte man von vorneherein postulieren können. Degegen ist der zweite Punkt vielleicht überraschender: Es waren in erstaunlich hohem Masse ganz banale Dinge, Vorgänge von geringer Tragweite, mit denen der Dioiket befasst war, Verwaltungsakte, die auch ohne sein Eingreifen auf niedrigerer Ebene hätten entschieden werden können.[40] Welche Flut von Akten in seinem Büro verarbeitet werden musste, kann man ahnen, wenn man erfährt, dass die Zahl der Kaufanträge für Objekte aus dem Staatsbesitz allein aus dem Bubastites innerhalb etwa eines Jahres sich nach Ausweis der erwähnten Kölner carbonisierten Papyri[41] auf mindestens ca. 30 belief. Dabei wurde die eigentliche Bearbeitung dieser Akten, wie wir gesehen haben, regelmässig untergebenen Instanzen, gewöhnlich dem Strategen, überlassen. Der Dioiket gab nicht einmal konkrete Anweisung, was zu geschehen habe, sondern steckte normalerweise nur den Rahmen ab, innerhalb dessen der Vorgang abzuwickeln war. Die Verantwortung für die Details überliess er dem Strategen, der beispielsweise bei den Verkäufen aus Staatsbesitz zu entscheiden hatte, ob die Objekte wirklich zum Verkauf standen, ob der gebotene Preis ausreichte und nicht geringer war als die Rendite, die das Objekt auch so erbrachte, und schliesslich auch noch dafür verantwortlich war, dass der Kaufpreis wirklich an den Fiskus überwiesen wurde. Kaum einmal hatte der Dioiket Fragen von prinzipieller Bedeutung zu entscheiden oder Urteile zu fällen, die etwa als Präzedens in künftigen, ähnlich gelagerten Fällen hätten dienen können. Kurz gesagt: Die Aktivitäten des Dioiketen lagen hauptsächlich auf dem Felde der Administration, nur ausnahmsweise im Bereich der Jurisdiktion und Rechtsetzung.[42]

40. G. Alföldy macht darauf aufmerksam, dass dies selbst für Statthalter gilt, wie man z.B. aus Plinius' Briefwechsel mit Trajan (Plin. *Ep.* x) entnehmen kann; Plinius ist mit Bagatellangelegenheiten überlastet, mit denen er sogar auch noch den Kaiser selbst belästigt.

41. Vgl. Fussn. 9.

42. Hier sind nicht diejenigen Fälle heranzuziehen, bei denen der Dioiket als Vertreter des Iuridicus zu Gericht gesessen hat; vgl. dazu unten unter II. Wirkliche Zeugnisse für Gerichtsverhandlungen vor dem Dioiketen sind folgende: *P. Oxy.* vii 1032; es geht um die Umwandlung von Ackerland in Weinland (vgl. oben Fussn. 34); dass eine mündliche Verhandlung stattgefunden hat, beweist Z.51 [Oὐηρνά]σιος Φακοῦντος εἶπεν. *P. Teb.* ii 287 = *W. Chr.* 251; eine

Und schliesslich drittens: Ordnet man die Urkunden, die Informationen über das Amt des Dioiketen enthalten, chronologisch, so ergibt sich ein zahlenmässiges Übergewicht für das 3. Jhdt. gegenüber dem 2. Jhdt., und das, obwohl doch generell das 2. Jhdt. in den Papyri erheblich dichter repräsentiert ist als das dritte. Sicherlich spielt hier auch die Frage der Einführung und des Verschwindens des Amtes eine Rolle, auf die ich weiter unten eingehen werde, aber allein durch diese Daten wird man das Phänomen nicht erklären können. Ich erwähnte bereits oben, dass noch gegen Ende des zweiten Jahrhunderts Leute, die vom Staate kaufen wollten, ihre Angebote den Strategen einreichten; rund 40 Jahre später werden die Verkäufe, wie die Kölner verkohlten Papyri zeigen, zentral über das Büro des Dioiketen und unter seiner Kontrolle durchgeführt. Es scheint, als habe zu Beginn des dritten Jahrhunderts Hand in Hand mit einem auch sonst zu beobachtenden Schwinden der Kompetenz der Gaustrategen eine Stärkung der zentralen Verwaltungsorgane, u.a. des Dioiketen, stattgefunden.[43] Dabei ist Stärkung möglicherweise nicht einmal das richtige Wort; denn ob durch die Zentralisierung auch eine höhere Effizienz der Verwaltung erreicht wurde, darf sehr bezweifelt werden. Eher resultierte daraus nur ein Plus an Bürokratie, welches den reibungslosen und wirkungsvollen Ablauf der Verwaltung womöglich noch behinderte.

Verhandlung findet unter Annius Severianus statt, eine frühere, deren Vorsitz Mallius Crassus geführt hatte, wird erwähnt (vgl. unten den prosopographischen Anhang); Walker und Weber des Arsinoites klagen, dass ihnen ein überhöhtes χειρωνάξιον abverlangt worden sei. Auch die Formulierung τὰ λ[εγ]όμενα ὑπὸ...τοῦ κρατίστου διοικ[ητο]ῦ in *BGU* III 925 lässt auf eine mündliche Verhandlung schliessen. *P. Flor.* I 6 ist eine Eingabe an den Dioiketen Calventius Adiutor, eingereicht von einem Manne, den dieser Dioiket aufgrund einer Anzeige zu einer Gerichtsverhandlung nach Alexandria geladen hatte. Eine ebensolche Vorladung vor das Tribunal des Dioiketen scheint in der Subscription von *P. Strassb.* I 57.18 erhalten zu sein; vgl. *ZPE* 53 (1983) 238.

43. Man vergleiche die Erscheinung, die Thomas, a.a.O. (Fussn. 3) 93, beobachtet hat, dass im Laufe des 3. Jhdts. immer mehr Petitionen in Liturgieangelegenheiten direkt an den Präfekten statt wie früher an den Epistrategen gerichtet wurden.

## II. Die Stellung des Dioiketen innerhalb der alexandrinischen Beamtenhierarchie

Bekanntlich wurden die ritterlichen Procuratoren für ihre Tätigkeit entlohnt, und zwar – je nach ihrem Rang – in fixen "Gehaltsklassen" von 60000, 100000 oder 200000, später auch 300000 Sesterzen jährlich. Dieses System ist voll ausgeprägt zwar erst in severischer Zeit bezeugt, geht aber auf ältere Regelungen zurück. H.-G. Pflaum vermutet, dass die Gehaltsklassen in dieser Weise mindestens seit Hadrian existierten.[44]

Was nun das Gehalt des Dioiketen angeht, so wissen wir aus zwei in Ephesos gefundenen, griechisch abgefassten Cursusinschriften, dass der Ritter M. Aurelius Mindius Matidianus Pollio vermutlich unter Commodus als Dioiket den Rang eines *ducenarius* besass, also ein Gehalt von 200000 Sesterzen erhielt; Rat und Demos der Stadt Ephesos bezeichnen ihn in diesen Inschriften mit den Worten ἐπίτροπος διοικητὴς Αἰγύπτου δουκηνάριος.[45] Wie ferner aus den Inschriften hervorgeht, hatte Matidianus Pollio vor seiner Ernennung zum Dioiketen schon zwei Posten derselben Gehaltsstufe innegehabt, nämlich als *procurator (praefectus) vehiculorum* und als *procurator patrimonii*. Daraus erhellt zweifellos der relativ hohe Rang des Dioiketen auch innerhalb der ducenaren Ämter. Dennoch sagt das Zeugnis nichts aus über die Stellung des Dioiketen im Vergleich zu anderen höheren alexandrinischen Procuratoren. Ebenso wie der Dioiket gehörten nämlich auch der *iuridicus* (δικαιοδότης) und der *procurator idiu logu* (griechisch ἐπίτροπος τοῦ ἰδίου λόγου oder einfach ὁ πρὸς τῷ ἰδίῳ λόγῳ) der ducenaren Gehaltsklasse an; genauer gesagt: so war die Situation am Ende des 2. Jhdts. und im 3 Jhdt., wo allein wir Zeugnisse über die Gehälter dieser Procuratoren haben.[46]

44. Vgl. z.B. H.-G. Pflaum, *Abrégé des procurateurs équestres* (Paris 1974) 55f. Weitere Literatur etwa bei G. Alföldy, "Die Stellung der Ritter in der Führungsschicht des Imperium Romanum", *Chiron* 11 (1981) 184 Anm. 81.

45. Die Inschriften sind: (a) Keil, *JÖAI* 23 (1926) Beibl. 269 = *SEG* IV 520 = *AE* 1928, Nr. 97 = *IK* XIII (Ephesos) 627; (b) Keil, *Forsch. in Ephesos* III 56 = *IK* XVII 1 (Ephesos) 3056. Vgl. dazu H.-G. Pflaum, *Les carrières procuratoriennes équestres* (Paris 1960) 523–31 Nr. 193.

46. Man vergleiche z.B. für den *iuridicus AE* 1908, Nr. 400; für den *procurator idiu logu CIL* III 6757 = *ILS* 1413 (vgl. Pflaum, *Carrières*, 700) und *CIG* II 3751 (vgl. Pflaum, *Carrières*, 715). S. ferner die Übersichten bei Pflaum, *Carrières*, 1083–92.

Einen verlässlicheren Hinweis auf die Rangordnung der alexandrinischen Procuratoren mag daher vielleicht das System der Vertretungen geben. Es war eine allgemeine Praxis in der Verwaltung des Landes, dass im Falle der Abwesenheit oder Verhinderung eines Beamten sein Posten durch einen auf der nächstniederen Stufe stehenden Kollegen ausgefüllt wurde. So nahm etwa der βασιλικὸς γραμματεύς die Aufgaben des Strategen wahr oder vertraten die Dorfältesten den Dorfschreiber, wenn diese Ämter vakant waren. An der Spitze der Verwaltung wurde nun ganz entsprechend der *praefectus Aegypti* üblicherweise durch den *iuridicus* vertreten, was durch zahlreiche Zeugnisse gesichert ist,[47] und die Aufgaben des *iuridicus* wiederum nahm während dessen Abwesenheit der Dioiket wahr. Dafür besitzen wir jetzt zwei Zeugnisse: Schon lange war bekannt, dass der Dioiket Julianus um 141 n.Chr. den *iuridicus* als Richter in dem berühmten Drusilla-prozess vertreten hat;[48] dazu ist jüngst das Beispiel des Dioiketen Herakleides getreten, der im Jahre 217 den *iuridicus* vertreten hat.[49] Aus diesen Vertretungsregeln könnte man also folgern, dass dem Dioiketen in der alexandrinischen Hierarchie ungefähr der dritte Platz zugestanden habe, gleichsam als Stellvertreter des Stellvertreters des Präfekten.

Es existieren jedoch auch zwei Zeugnisse für die umgekehrte Regelung, dass nämlich nicht der Dioiket den *iuridicus*, sondern dieser den Dioiketen vertreten hat. Davon ist eines der schon lange bekannte *P. Flor.* I 89 aus dem 3. Jhdt.,[50] das andere der noch unveröffentlichte *P. Thmouis* I.[51] Man wird daher eher beide

47. Man findet die Belege in Bastianinis "Lista dei prefetti d'Egitto", *ZPE* 17 (1975) 263–328; vgl. dazu auch J. Schwartz, "Préfecture d'Egypte et intérim", *ZPE* 20 (1976) 101–7; ferner *BGU* VII 1578.5 (dazu P. Parsons, *JRS* 57 (1967) 138 Anm. 46). Zu *CIL* VI 1638 = *ILS* 1331 s. Bastianini, a.a.O. 313 Anm. 2.

48. *M. Chr.* 88 i 1f.; *BGU* XI 2070.12. Zu dem Prozess vergleiche man H. Maehler, "Neue Documente zum Drusilla-Prozess", *Proceedings of the XII Intern. Congress of Papyrology* (= *American Studies in Papyrology* 7, Toronto 1970) 263–71; *idem*, "Neues vom Prozess der Drusilla gegen Agrippinus", *Symposion 1977. Vorträge zur griechischen und hellenistischen Rechtsgeschichte* (Köln-Wien 1982) 325–33.

49. *P. Oxy.* XLIII 3093.5–6 und 8–9.

50. Der Juridicus heisst Flavius Rufus; vgl. den prosopographischen Anhang.

51. Um 165/6 vertritt der Juridicus Ulpius Marcellus den Dioiketen Annius Severianus. Ich verdanke diese Information einer freundlichen Mitteilung von S. Kambitsis.

Ämter als gleichrangig nebeneinander stehend einstufen wollen – ein Schluss, den so auch schon Wilcken gezogen hat.[52] Allerdings wird das Zeugnis der beiden letztgenannten Texte dadurch ein wenig relativiert, dass, wie wir aus *P. Oxy.* XLIII 3092 wissen, bei Abwesenheit des Dioiketen auch ein anderer Beamter als der *iuridicus* als dessen Vertreter einspringen konnte, nämlich der Procurator des ούσιακὸς λόγος, der mit Sicherheit einen niedrigeren Rang als der Dioiket besass und bisweilen gar nur kaiserlicher Freigelassener war.[53]

Für beide Möglichkeiten der Vertretung des Dioiketen, die durch den *iuridicus* und die durch den rangniedrigen *procurator usiacus*, besitzen wir also Beispiele, und es scheint schwierig zu entscheiden, was von beiden Regel und was Ausnahme war. Ich glaube indes wahrscheinlich machen zu können, dass die Vertretung durch den *procurator usiacus* durch ungewöhnliche Umstände begründet und daher wohl die Ausnahme war. Die Urkunde, durch die diese Möglichkeit der Vertretung bezeugt wird, ist zwar nicht auf den Tag datiert, stammt aber aus dem Jahre 216/17 und ist ganz offenbar gegen Ende dieses Jahres niedergeschrieben worden, d.h. im Sommer des Jahres 217, denn sie enthält Vereinbarungen für das folgende Jahr 217/18. Am 21. September 217, also vermutlich nur wenige Monate nach der Abfassung von *P. Oxy.* XLIII 3092, musste der Dioiket den *iuridicus* vertreten, wie wir aus *P. Oxy.* XLIII 3093 wissen. Was liegt nun näher als die Annahme, dass der Dioiket durch diese Vertretung auch schon einige Zeit früher in Beschlag enommen war, und zwar in solchem Masse, dass er sein eigenes Amt nicht mehr ausüben konnte und sich deshalb ebenfalls vertreten lassen musste? Durch den *iuridicus* konnte er nicht vertreten werden, denn dessen Amt hatte er ja selbst zu verwalten. Daher musste ein Procurator einer niedrigeren Rangstufe, aber mit verwandten Aufgaben einspringen, der ἐπίτροπος ούσιακῶν.[54]

52. *APF* 4 (1907) 453 und *Grundzüge* 156. In *ZPE* 54 (1984) 87–90 habe ich mich dafür ausgesprochen, *P. Ryl.* II 84 und *P. Wash. Univ.* I 3.26ff. als mögliche Zeugnisse dafür anzusehen, dass der Dioiket gelegentlich sogar einmal die Amtsgeschäfte des Präfekten übernehmen konnte, wenn dieser vorübergehend von Alexandria abwesend oder aus anderen Gründen verhindert war. Falls man mir darin folgen will, wäre das ein weiterer, sehr deutlicher Hinweis darauf, dass Juridicus und Dioiket ungefähr gleichen Ranges waren.

53. Vgl. G. M. Parássoglou, a.a.O. (Fussn. 6) 84–90.

54. So vermutet ebenfalls schon vorsichtig J. Rea in *P. Oxy.* XLIII 3092.5 Anm.

Möglicherweise können wir sogar erklären, weswegen der Dioiket in diesem Augenblick den *iuridicus* vertreten musste: Der Grund könnte sein, dass der *iuridicus* gleichzeitig das Amt des *praefectus Aegypti* stellvertretend ausübte. In den Sommer des Jahres 217 fallen nämlich die Wirren, die durch die Ermordung Caracallas Anfang April 217 hervorgerufen worden waren. Den damaligen Präfekten Valerius Datus, einen Parteigänger Caracallas, hatte Macrinus hinrichten lassen, und so war mit Sicherheit eine Vakanz im Amte des Präfekten zu überbrücken. Möglicherweise kennen wir sogar den Namen des *iuridicus*, der den Präfekten in dieser Situation zu verteten hatte.[55] Denkbar ist jedenfalls, dass wir im Sommer 217 in Ägypten folgende Konstellation vorfinden: Der Präfekt wurde vom *iuridicus* vertreten, der *iuridicus* vom Dioiketen, der Dioiket vom *procurator usiacus*.[56] Wie immer es sich aber mit dieser speziellen Frage verhalten mag, wir können sicherlich bei der Annahme bleiben, dass *iuridicus* und Dioiket sich, sofern möglich, gegenseitig vertraten und folglich auch ungefähr gleichen Rang besassen.

Im Zusammenhang mit der Frage nach der Stellung des Dioiketen muss auch ein Wort zu dem Rangprädikat gesagt werden, das ihm zukam. Es ist dasjenige, das ursprünglich alle Inhaber ritterlicher Ämter führten, nämlich κράτιστος; das ist die Ensprechung für das lateinische *vir egregius*.[57] Während aber der Rangtitel des Präfekten sich im Laufe der Zeit änderte – aus κράτιστος wurde über das ursprünglich senatorische λαμπρότατος (*vir clarissimus*) ein διασημότατος (*vir perfectissimus*) – blieb der der übrigen alexandrinischen Procuratoren bis zum Ende des 3. Jhdts. gleich. Für den Dioiketen finden wir den Titel κράτιστος während praktisch der gesamten Zeit der Existenz dieses Amtes bezeugt.

55. Callistianus, bekannt aus *P. Oxy.* XLIII 3117.18.21.24; vgl. hierzu Bastianini in *ZPE* 38 (1980) 86 Anm. 5.

56. Meine Rekonstruktion der Verhältnisse setzt voraus, dass *P. Oxy.* XLIII 3092 zu einem Zeitpunkt nach der Ermordung Caracallas (8.4.217) geschrieben worden ist, zu dem zwar Valerius Datus wenn auch nicht ermordet, so doch wenigstens schon abberufen war, zu dem aber in Unkenntnis der Titulatur des Macrinus in Ägypten noch weiterhin nach Caracalla datiert wurde.

57. Literaturangaben beispielsweise bei G. Alföldy, *Chiron* 11 (1981) 191 Anm. 107. Nach A. Stein, a.a.O. (Fussn. 4) 34 mit Anm. 94, wurde der *praefectus Aegypti* seit Nero so bezeichnet; Thomas, a.a.O. (Fussn. 3) 44–47, nennt als früheste Beispiele für die Verwendung dieses Titels für den Epistrategen solche aus der Regierungszeit Trajans.

Nur zwei Zeugen nennen ihn διασημότατος. Der eine ist *P. Thead.* 14 = *P. Sakaon* 32.18, der den um 253 n.Chr. tätigen Dioiketen Septimius Apollonios so nennt und aus kaum viel späterer Zeit stammt (vgl. unten den Anhang S.205), der andere *P. Oxy.* VIII 1115 = *Sel. Pap.* 426.5 vom 21.5.284 mit einer Erwähnung des letzten uns namentlich bekannten Dioiketen Aurelius Proteas. Bemerkenswerterweise heissen beide Dioiketen in anderen Urkunden jedoch noch κράτιστος, nämlich Septimius Apollonius in *P. Oxy.* XLVI 3288.3 und Aurelius Proteas in *P. Oxy.* XII 1412.9. Ja sogar dieselbe Urkunde, die Aurelius Proteas διασημότατος nennt, verwendet im Zitat eines um etwas mehr als drei Jahre älteren Dokuments vom 11.1.281 den alten Titel κράτιστος (*P. Oxy.* VIII 1115 Z. 11). Wenngleich der Nachfolger des Dioiketen, der seit Diokletian bezeugte Katholikos (s. unten), von Anfang an den Rangtitel διασημότατος trug,[58] wird man nicht schliessen dürfen, dass in dem genannten Zeitraum von rund drei Jahren zwischen dem 11.1.281 und dem 21.5.284 unmittelbar vor dem Verschwinden des Dioiketen eine offizielle Anhebung seines Ranges erfolgt ist, vielmehr geht das Schwanken in der Verwendung der Rangtitel sicherlich auf eine Unsicherheit im Gebrauch der Titel in dieser späten Zeit zurück.

## III. Die zeitlichen Begrenzungen der Bezeugung des Dioiketenamtes

In vorrömischer Zeit trug einer der höchsten Verwaltungsbeamten der Ptolemäer ebenfalls die Bezeichnung διοικητής.[59] Da nicht nur der Name übereinstimmt, sondern auch die Aufgaben verwandt sind (man bezeichnet den ptolemäischen Dioiketen häufig als den Finanzminister der Könige), könnte man glauben, die Römer hätten den Posten bei der Übernahme des Landes einfach beibehalten. Mit allergrösster Wahrscheinlichkeit ist dies

---

58. Als erster Ulpius Cyrillus am 11.6.286 in *P. Oxy.* x 1260; für die weiteren s. J. Lallemand, *L'administration civile d'Egypte de l'avènement de Dioclétien à la création du diocèse (284–382)* (Bruxelles 1964) 257ff. Zu Claudius Marcellus, dem *rationalis* unter Philippus Arabs, der ebenfalls schon διασημότατος war, s. unten 197.

59. Vgl. Wilcken, *Grundzüge*, 148f.; R. Seider, *Beiträge zur ptolemäischen Verwaltungsgeschichte* (Heidelberg 1938) 43–73; J. D. Thomas, "Aspects of the Ptolemaic Civil Service: The Dioiketes and the Nomarch", in: H. Maehler und V. M. Strocka, *Das ptolemäische Ägypten* (Mainz 1978) 187–94.

aber nicht so, vielmehr spricht alles dafür, dass das hohe Procuratorenamt mit der Bezeichnung διοικητής, um das es uns hier geht, erst im 2. Jhdt. n.Chr. geschaffen worden ist. Wir besitzen aus dem ersten Jahrhundert unserer Zeitrechnung zwar sechs Zeugnisse für das Wort διοικητής in den Papyri Ägyptens, aber fünf von ihnen haben mit Sicherheit nichts mit dem Procuratorenamt zu tun, das wir hier untersuchen. Es handelt sich in allen Fällen um Privatbriefe, deren Empfänger in den Adressen als Dioiketen bezeichnet sind.[60] Nichts im Inhalt der Briefe deutet darauf hin, dass die Empfänger eine höhere Verwaltungsfunktion ausübten, und die Namen sind nicht die römischer Ritter, sondern griechisch. In einem Fall lässt ein solcher Dioiket sich mit einiger Wahrscheinlichkeit mit einem Mann gleichen Namens identifizieren, der einige Jahre später als Toparch bezeugt ist.[61] Sollte diese Identifikation zutreffen, dann müsste der Dioiket des frühen 1. Jhdts. noch unter dem Toparchen rangieren, falls es sich überhaupt um ein öffentliches Amt handelt. Denn selbst, dass mit dem Wort διοικητής in dieser Zeit private Verwalter bezeichnet wurden, lässt sich nach den Quellen nicht ausschliessen.[62]

60. Die Belege sind: *P. Teb.* II 408.19 (3 n.Chr.; Ἀκουσίλαος); *P. Teb.* II 409.1f. 14 (5 n.Chr.; derselbe); *P. Oxy.* II 291.15 (25/6 n.Chr.; Τύραννος); *P. Oxy.* II 292.14 (um dieselbe Zeit; derselbe); *P. Oxy.* XIV 1661.1.11 (74 n.Chr.; Ἡρακλείδης); *P. Bonon.* 43.1 = *SB* V 7615 (1. Jhdt. n.Chr.; Δίδυμος). Mit diesen Dioiketen vergleicht Stein auch den bei Plutarch, *Apophthegm.*, Aug. 4 (p. 207B) erwähnten Eros ὁ τὰ ἐν Αἰγύπτῳ διοικῶν (unter Augustus), auf den mich J. D. Thomas aufmerksam macht (*RE* VI.1 543 Eros 9). In *PIR*² E 86 wird Eros dagegen als Procurator bezeichnet, und G. W. Bowersock, *Augustus and the Greek World* (Oxford 1965) 40, möchte in ihm sogar speziell einen Procurator des ἴδιος λόγος sehen, mit der Begründung, das Amt des Dioiketen habe in frührömischer Zeit in Ägypten nicht existiert. Das ist sicherlich richtig, wenn man das hohe Procuratorenamt meint, das wir hier untersuchen, aber einen διοικητής vom Range des Claudius Heracleides, dem wir sogleich in *P. Fouad* 21 begegnen werden, könnte es auch schon unter Augustus gegeben haben; denn das Finanzressort διοίκησις existierte mit Sicherheit bereits um diese Zeit, vgl. nur *WO* 359 (11/10 v.Chr.); *P. Fouad* 67 (39 n.Chr.); *WO* 1325 (67 n.Chr.). Über die Leitung dieses Ressorts wissen wir jedoch praktisch nichts, und es lohnt sich meines Erachtens nicht, darüber zu spekulieren, solange die Quellen fehlen. Was nun Eros angeht, so ist die Formulierung bei Plutarch so vage, dass man kaum Konkretes daraus entnehmen kann, ganz zu schweigen davon, dass die Art literarischen Genres, um die es sich dort handelt, überhaupt nicht sehr geeignet scheint, als historische Quelle zu dienen.

61. Akusilaos; vgl. *P. Teb.* II 408 Einl.

62. An die erste Möglichkeit dachten die Herausgeber von *P. Oxy.* XIV 1661: "Heraclides was evidently not the high finance-official at Alexandria, and that

### Zum Amt des διοικητής im römischen Aegypten

Bei einem weiteren Text des 1. Jhdts. n.Chr. mit der sechsten Bezeugung für die Bezeichnung διοικητής aus dieser Zeit fällt die Entscheidung weniger leicht. Es handelt sich um *P. Fouad* 21, das Protokoll einer Verhandlung, die im Jahre 63 unter dem *praefectus Aegypti*, vermutlich Caecina Tuscus,[63] stattgefunden und sich mit den Privilegien von Veteranen beschäftigt hat.[64] Zu Beginn des Textes werden die Mitglieder des *consilium* des Präfekten, die Beisitzer, genannt: An erster Stelle der *iuridicus*, der zu diesem Zeitpunkt, wohl zufälligerweise, in Personalunion auch Procurator des Idios Logos war,[65] danach vermutlich fünf Militärtribune,[66] ferner ein Julius Lysimachus, dessen Funktion nicht angegeben ist, der aber mit dem aus etwas späterer Zeit bekannten *procurator idiu logu* gleichen Namens identisch sein dürfte,[67] und dann erst ein

he was the administrator of a private estate is unlikely. Probably he was a subordinate local dioecetes similar to the dioecetae who are known in the reign of Augustus from [*P. Oxy.*] 291 and *P. Tebt.* 408–9, and were no doubt a survival from Ptolemaic times", wozu anzumerken ist, dass diese lokalen ptolemäischen Dioiketen, wie J. D. Thomas, a.a.O. (Fussn. 59), gezeigt hat, ὑποδιοικητής hiessen. Demgegenüber meint O. Montevecchi in *P. Bonon.* 43.1–2 Anm.: "Suppongo che qui abbia il significato di 'amministratore' di beni privati." Der Inhalt aller dieser Briefe scheint auch mir sehr deutlich für diese letztere Interpretation zu sprechen.

63. Vgl. zu ihm *ZPE* 17 (1975) 274 und 38 (1980) 77.

64. Der Text ist mehrfach abgedruckt worden: *FIRA*² III 171a; E. M. Smallwood, *Documents Illustrating the Principates of Gaius and Nero* (Cambridge 1967) Nr. 297; S. Daris, *Documenti per la storia dell'esercito romano in Egitto* (Milano 1964) Nr. 101; vgl. auch E. Balogh und H.-G. Pflaum, "Le 'consilium' du préfet d'Egypte. Sa composition", *Rev. hist. droit français et étranger* 30 (1952) 117–24 = H.-G. Pflaum, *Gaule et l'empire romain: Scripta varia* II (Paris 1981) 250–57.

65. C. Norbanus Ptolemaeus. Er wird ohne Angabe des Amtstitels und ohne genaues Datum auch in *BGU* v §50, *BGU* XI 2059 ii 1 und *P. Oxy.* XLV 3250.4 erwähnt.

66. Vgl. H. Devijver, *De Aegypto et Exercitu Romano sive Prosopographia Militiarum Equestrium quae ab Augusto ad Gallienum seu statione seu origine ad Aegyptum pertinebant* (= *Studia Hellenistica* 22, Louvain 1975) Nr. 16, 18, 21, 89 und 113. Vgl. auch H.-G. Pflaum, *Les carrières procuratoriennes équestres sous le Haut-Empire romain*, Supplément (Paris 1982) 40 Nr. 121.

67. Vgl. *P. Fouad* inv. 211 = *SB* VI 9016.9–24 (29.1.69 und 29.1.70) und *P. Oxy.* XLIX 3508 (16.4.70). In der jüngsten Liste von Inhabern dieses Amtes (Pflaum, a.a.O. (Fussn. 66) 135–37) wird Iulius Lysimachus immer noch eine zweite Amtszeit im Jahre 88 zugewiesen, obwohl R. Hübner in *ZPE* 24 (1977) 51 wahrscheinlich gemacht hat, dass diese Annahme nur auf einem Lesefehler beruht (vgl. auch J. D. Thomas, *ZPE* 56 (1984) 107–12). Lysimachus begegnet auch in *SB* XII 11044 = XIV 11640.3. In der genannten Liste fehlen die Procuratoren des Idios Logos -crates (*P. Merton* II 73.3; vor 163/4 n.Chr., vielleicht identisch mit Timocrates; vgl. *ZPE* 4 (1969) 65–68), ein Anonymus in *SB* VIII

Claudius Heracleides mit dem Titel διοικητής. Der Name ist mit Nomen und Cognomen römisch gebildet,[68] und schon die Tatsache, dass dieser Dioiket zusammen mit dem Präfekten im *consilium* sitzt, beweist hinreichend, dass wir es hier mit einer höher gestellten Persönlichkeit zu tun haben, nicht vergleichbar den vorher erwähnten lokalen διοικηταί. Kann es sich aber wirklich um das hohe Procuratorenamt handeln, das wir hier untersuchen?

Einiges scheint dagegen zu sprechen; das wichtigste Argument ist schon von anderen vorgebracht worden:[69] Wir haben oben erwähnt, dass der Procurator διοικητής einen ducenaren Posten innehatte, zumindest am Ende des 2. Jhdts. Hier in *P. Fouad* 21 aber wird Claudius Heracleides erst nach den *tribuni militum* aufgeführt, die, wie gewöhnlich angenommen wird, nur 50000 Sesterzen Gehalt erhielten. Das kann nur bedeuten, dass er rangmässig noch unter ihnen stand. In einem vergleichbaren Text dagegen, der ebenfalls die Mitglieder des *consilium* des Präfekten aufführt (*P. Strassb.* 179), steht der Dioiket Iulius Crispinus an der Spitze der Liste vor den militärischen Chargen, so wie es dem Inhaber eines ducenaren Amtes zukommt.

Aber noch etwas lässt sich gegen die Gleichsetzung des Dioiketen in *P. Fouad* 21 mit dem Procurator der späteren Zeit ins Feld führen; das ist die Tatsache, dass dieses Zeugnis so vereinzelt da steht. Wir werden sogleich sehen, dass der Dioiket als Procurator mit voller Sicherheit erst gegen 141 n.Chr. bezeugt ist, ein Datum, das sich möglicherweise um rund 20 Jahre auf die Zeit um 120 vorziehen lässt, aber bis zu diesem Zeitpunkt wäre *P. Fouad* 21 der einzige Beleg aus römischer Zeit. Dagegen besitzen wir für andere procuratorische Ämter Ägyptens, etwa den *iuridicus* und den ἐπίτροπος ἰδίου λόγου, Zeugnisse auch aus dem ersten Jahrhundert in relativ dichter Folge, so wie für den Dioiketen in der Zeit nach

9905.8f. (3.3.171 n.Chr.) und der letzte bekannte Inhaber des Amtes, Geminius Valerianus, der durch *CPR* v 4.12–13 und *P. Oxy.* xlvi 3287.1 für die Zeit um 238 n.Chr. bezeugt ist. Für andere dort aufgeführte ἐπίτροποι τοῦ ἰδίου λόγου lassen sich die Belegstellen vermehren, z.B. für A. Prifernius Augurinus (*P. Ryl.* ii 291.1; vgl. *P. Oxy.* 3287 Einl.), für Claudius Iustus (*P. Oxy.* xlix 3472.4) und Modestus (*SB* viii 9658 = xiv 11342.23.48). Ob die aufgeführten Claudius Calvinus und Septimius Serenus Procuratoren des Idios Logos waren, ist mehr als unsicher; vgl. auch unten S.207f.

68. Das Gentiliz Claudius könnte um diese Zeit ein Hinweis darauf sein, dass er kaiserlicher Freigelassener war.

69. E. Balogh und H.-G. Pflaum, a.a.O. (Fussn. 64) 123f.

140. Das kann in meinen Augen nicht auf Zufall beruhen, sondern kann nur bedeuten, dass ein Amt mit vergleichbarer Kompetenz überhaupt nicht existierte.

Vielleicht darf man in dem in P. *Fouad* 21 bezeugten Dioiketen einen Vorläufer des späteren Procurators sehen, einen Beamten ebenfalls der Finanzverwaltung, aber mit begrenzter Kompetenz, der möglicherweise vom Präfekten bestellt und ihm persönlich verantwortlich war, während die Procuratoren ja vom Kaiser eingesetzt wurden. Ein solcher subalterner Beamter hätte nie persönlich Eingaben aus der Bevölkerung erhalten und auch nie in eigenem Namen mit Beamten der χώρα Korrespondenz ausgetauscht, was gut erklären würde, weswegen er in den Papyri praktisch nicht erscheint. Auf der anderen Seite wäre klar, dass er vom Präfekten immer zu Rate gezogen wurde, wenn es galt, Entscheidungen zu treffen, die Konsequenzen für die Kasse des Staates mit sich brachten.

Wann genau aber soll man die Einführung des Amtes mit der erweiterten Kompetenz als Leiter eines selbständigen Ressorts ansetzen? Wie schon erwähnt, stammen die frühesten sicher datierten Belege dafür aus den Jahren um 140/141; es sind einige Papyri des Drusillaprozesses, in denen der Dioiket Julianus in seiner Eigenschaft als Vertreter des *iuridicus* mehrfach in Erscheinung tritt.[70] Möglicherweise kann man aber noch etwa 20 Jahre zurückgehen. Das hängt wesentlich von der Beantwortung der Frage ab, ob man in der Bezeichnung *procurator ad dioecesin Alexandreae* oder griechisch ἐπίτροπος ἐπὶ διοικήσεως ['Αλεξανδρείας] dasselbe Amt sehen will wie das des Dioiketen oder ein anderes. Die genannten Bezeichnungen begegnen in vier Cursusinschriften als Bestandteil procuratorischer Laufbahnen. Die Inschriften betreffen zwei Personen,[71] einmal höchst wahrscheinlich den späteren *praefectus Aegypti* Valerius Eudaemon,[72] jedenfalls

---

70. Vgl. oben Fussn. 48 und unten den prosopographischen Anhang S. 199.

71. Der von Pflaum, *Carrières*, 243f. und 1087, ebenfalls als *procurator ad dioecesin Alexandriae* angesehene Ser. Sulpicius Serenus gehört wohl nicht hierhin, denn der Text, den Pflaum dafür in Anspruch nimmt (*P. Lond.* II 482 = *ChLA* III 203 = *CPL* 114 = R. O. Fink, *Roman Military Records on Papyrus* (Cleveland 1971) Nr. 80) erwähnt nur einen Serenus (ohne Praenomen und Nomen), der trotz seines Titels *procurator* eher eine militärische Funktion gehabt hat; vgl. Fink a.a.O.

72. Vgl. zu ihm Bastianini, *ZPE* 17 (1975) 289 und 38 (1980) 81 und den prosopographischen Anhang unten S. 198.

aber einen Ritter, der die Tätigkeit des *procurator ad dioecesin Alexandreae* in den ersten Regierungsjahren Hadrians ausgeübt hat,[73] und zum anderen einen Anonymus, dessen ritterliche Ämterlaufbahn Pflaum in severische Zeit setzen zu müssen geglaubt hat.[74]

Auf die Frage, ob dieses procuratorische Amt mit dem Dioiketen gleichzusetzen sei, ist auch Pflaum verschiedentlich eingegangen, und er hat dabei folgende Ansicht verteten:[75] Der *procurator ad dioecesin Alexandréae* könne nicht wie der Dioiket ein ducenarer Posten gewesen sein, da der Anonymus, der, wie gesagt, von Pflaum in die Zeit der Severer gesetzt wird, bevor er diesen Posten bekommen habe, zuletzt *procurator ad censos accipiendos* dreier Städte in Gallien gewesen sei, was nur ein sexagenares Amt war, wie sicher bezeugt ist. Der Sprung von einem sexagenaren zu einem ducenaren Amt aber wäre in einer procuratorischen Laufbahn äusserst ungewöhnlich. Valerius Eudaemon, der andere uns bekannte *proc. ad dioecesin Alexandreae*, begann gar seine Laufbahn mit diesem Amt, woraus man ebenfalls schliessen könne, dass die Stellung nur sexagenaren Rang hatte. Allerdings war Valerius Eudaemon ein Vertrauter Hadrians, und deswegen könne er sogleich als erstes Amt eine höher dotierte Procuratur erhalten haben. Dennoch spreche alles dafür, so Pflaum, dass der *procurator ad dioecesin Alexandreae* höchstens ein centenarer Posten war und somit vom Dioiketen verschieden.

Folgende Entwicklung denkt sich Pflaum: Zu Beginn der Römerzeit wurden die Aufgaben der Finanzverwaltung Ägyptens von einem rangniedrigen Funktionär mit einem Gehalt von 40000 Sesterzen wahrgenommen, den wir möglicherweise in *P. Fouad* 21 unter der Bezeichnung διοικητής erwähnt finden (leicht abweichend hiervon führt Pflaum in *Carrières*, 1087, Claudius Heracleides unter den *procuratores ad dioecesin Alexandreae* auf). Unter Titus war das Amt schon sexagenar und erscheint in lateinischen

---

73. *CIL* III 431 = *ILS* 1449 = *IK* XIII (Ephesos) 666 und *IGR* III 1077 = E. Breccia, *Iscrizioni greche e latine*, 48 Nr. 65 = *SB* I 3998; vgl. dazu Pflaum, *Carrières*, 264–71 (Nr. 110).

74. *AE* 1913, Nr. 213 = *ILS* 9501 = *CIL* XIV 4468/70 = *AE* 1960, Nr. 163 und *AE* 1946, Nr. 95 = *AE* 1950, Nr. 183 = *AE* 1960, Nr. 164; vgl. unten den prosopographischen Anhang S.203.

75. *Les procurateurs équestres sous le Haut-Empire romain* (Paris 1950) 48 und 73; ferner *Carrières* 244, 267, 528 und 720.

Inschriften als *procurator Alexandreae*,[76] während seit Hadrian der Posten *procurator ad dioecesin Alexandreae* hiess und mit einem Gehalt von 100000 Sesterzen entlohnt wurde; die Bezeichnung dürfe zu dieser Zeit nicht so verstanden werden, als werde dadurch die Kompetenz auf Alexandria beschränkt, vielmehr seien der *procurator Alexandreae* und der *procurator ad dioecesin Alexandreae* für ganz Ägypten zuständig gewesen. Unter Antoninus Pius sei dann schliesslich daneben das ducenare Amt des διοικητὴς Αἰγύπτου mit Zuständigkeit für die χώρα eingeführt worden, während der weiterhin existierende *procurator ad dioecesin Alexandreae* auf Alexandria beschränkte Befugnisse gehabt habe.

Gegen diese Sicht der Dinge lassen sich, wie mir scheint, Bedenken vorbringen, insbesondere gegen die These der Aufspaltung des Postens des *procurator ad dioecesin Alexandreae*, die doch offensichtlich nur eingeführt worden ist, um die Existenz des anonymen *procurator ad dioecesin Alexandreae* in severischer Zeit erklären zu können, ohne ihn doch mit dem Dioiketen gleichsetzen zu müssen. Eine Identifikation der beiden Bezeichnungen scheint mir da viel näher zu liegen. Zwar könnte man auf den ersten Blick meinen, gerade durch die Wörter *ad dioecesin Alexandreae* solle zum Ausdruck gebracht werden, dass die Befugnisse des Procurators auf die Stadt Alexandria beschränkt waren, aber dieser Eindruck trügt. Auch andere procuratorische Ämter mit eindeutiger Zuständigkeit für ganz Ägypten erfahren in inschriftlichen Belegen gelegentlich eine scheinbare Beschränkung auf Alexandria. Ich begnüge mich mit ein paar Beispielen: Der *iuridicus* heisst in den

---

76. *CIL* II 4136 = *ILS* 1399 = G. Alföldy, *Inschr. Tarraco* (Berlin 1975) 159 (dazu Pflaum, *Carrières*, 113f. (Nr. 49)) und *AE* 1937, Nr. 87 (dazu Pflaum, *Carrières*, 701f. (Nr. 262bis)). Vgl. auch *CIL* XIV 2932 = *ILS* 1509; *AE* 1972, Nr. 574 = Pflaum, *Carrières*, 27 (Nr. 70) = *IK* XIII (Ephesos) 852; *AE* 1974, Nr. 415 (*proc. divi Titi Alexandreae*) und den ἐπίτροπος Ἀλεξανδρείας in *P. Oxy.* XLII 3031.1 (302 n.Chr.). Mir scheint dies nur eine sehr vage und allgemeine Bezeichnung für in Alexandria tätige Procuratoren zu sein; dass sie Finanzprocuratoren mit Zuständigkeit für ganz Ägypten waren, ist wenig glaubhaft. Schwierig ist die Trennung von dem Amt des *procurator fisci Alexandrini* (*AE* 1888, Nr. 130 = *ILS* 1518), das ein kaiserlicher Freigelassener ausüben konnte (vgl. dazu G. Boulvert, *Esclaves et affranchis impériaux sous le haut-empire romain* (Napoli 1970) 231; P. R. C. Weaver, *Familia Caesaris* (Cambridge 1972) 244f.). In der Inschrift *Corinth* VIII, 1 75 (vgl. Pflaum, *Carrières*, 174 (Nr. 77)) ist in dem Titel ἐπί]-τροπον... [το]ῦ ἐν Ἀλεξανδρείᾳ φ[ίσκο]υ statt φ[ίσκο]υ möglicherweise auch Φ[άρο]υ zu ergänzen; zum *procurator Phari* vgl. *P. Oxy.* XLIII 3118.2–3 Anm.

Inschriften meist *iuridicus Alexandreae*[77] bzw. griechisch δικαιοδότης τῆς λαμπροτάτης ᾽Αλεξανδρέων πόλεως,[78] daneben aber auch *iuridicus Aegypti*,[79] und H. Kupiszewski hat eindeutig nachgewiesen, dass seine Zuständigkeit sich auf Alexandria wie auch auf das übrige Ägypten erstreckte.[80] Ein Vorsteher des Idios Logos heisst in einer lateinischen Inschrift *proc(urator) (ducenarius) Alexandria[e] idiu logu*,[81] ein anderer in einer griechischen ἐπίτροπος δουκηνάριος ᾽Αλεξανδρείας τοῦ ἰδίου λόγου, dagegen derselbe Mann in einer zweiten griechischen Inschrift ἐπίτροπος Αἰγύπτου ἰδίου λόγου.[82] Auch der Procurator des Idios Logos war mit Sicherheit für ganz Ägypten zuständig. Die Bestimmungen *Alexandreae* und *Aegypti* konnten demnach wahlweise ohne eigentlichen Bedeutungsunterschied verwendet werden. Man muss daher fragen, wie wohl, insbesondere ausserhalb Ägyptens, zwei gleichzeitig existierende Ämter, nämlich einmal der διοικητής mit Kompetenz für Ägypten ohne Alexandria und zweitens der *procurator ad dioecesin Alexandreae* mit Zuständigkeit nur für Alexandria, hätten auseinandergehalten werden können, zumal der Inhaber des letzteren vor der Einführung des διοικητὴς Αἰγύπτου auch die Finanzen ganz Ägyptens verwaltet haben soll. Mir scheint das wenig glaubhaft, und ich möchte daher auch schon in dem Amt, das vermutlich Valerius Eudaemon innegehabt hat, das des Dioiketen sehen.

Möglicherweise gibt es jedoch auch in den Papyri ein Zeugnis für den Dioiketen als Procurator mit vollen Kompetenzen aus der Zeit vor Antoninus Pius. Es handelt sich dabei um einen undatierten Privatbrief der Sammlung in Michigan, der zu dem lateinisch-griechischen Tiberianusarchiv gehört.[83] Claudius Terentianus, wohl der Sohn des Tiberianus, bittet diesen, er möge doch einen Brief, den der Dioiket an den Strategen geschrieben

77. *Forsch. in Ephesos* IV 1 S.89f. = *AE* 1935, Nr. 167 = *IK* XVII 2 (Ephesos) 4112 (vgl. dazu Pflaum, *Carrières*, 281); *CIL* VIII 8925 und 8934 = *ILS* 1400 (vgl. Pflaum, *Carrières*, 323); *CIL* VI 1564 = *ILS* 1452 (vgl. Pflaum, *Carrières*, 445).

78. *AE* 1908, Nr. 400 (Pflaum, *Carrières*, 832 Text V).

79. *CIL* X 6967 = *ILS* 1434 (Pflaum, *Carrières*, 295).

80. A.a.O. (Fussn. 7) 194–96. Zum Titel ebenda 189f.

81. *CIL* III 6757 = *ILS* 1413 (Pflaum, *Carrières*, 700 Text 2).

82. Vgl. die Texte bei Pflaum, *Carrières*, 715; *CIG* II 3751 ist jetzt = *IK* IX (Nikaia) Nr. 58.

83. *P. Mich.* VIII 479 = G. B. Pighi, *Lettere latine d'un soldato di Traiano* (Bologna 1964) Nr. XII.

habe, an den Strategen weiterleiten, damit er bald antworte. Korrespondenz mit Gaustrategen ist, wie wir weiter oben gesehen haben, eine der häufigsten Tätigkeiten des procuratorischen Dioiketen,[84] und es ist kaum zu bestreiten, dass wir es mit diesem auch in dem Brief des Tiberianusarchivs zu tun haben. Jedenfalls war es kaum ein Dioiket mit dem niedrigen Rang des Claudius Heracleides aus *P. Fouad* 21.

Leider ist nun kein einziger der Briefe des Tiberianusarchivs genau datiert, aber aufgrund paläographischer Kriterien wird ihre Entstehung gewöhnlich in das erste Viertel des 2. Jhdts. gesetzt.[85] In einem von ihnen hat man geglaubt, Anspielungen auf Ereignisse des Jahres 115 n.Chr. entdecken zu können,[86] und nach der Ansicht von N. Lewis gibt es einen Beweis dafür, dass die Briefe mit Sicherheit vor 136 geschrieben worden sind.[87] Sollte das zutreffen, so besässen wir in *P. Mich.* viii 479 tatsächlich einen recht tragfähigen Beweis dafür, dass der Dioiket schon vor Antoninus Pius existierte und die vollen Kompetenzen eines hohen Procurators besass.

An dieser Stelle muss daran erinnert werden, dass auch die Cursusinschriften des anonymen Ritters, die Pflaum als Beweis für das Vorhandensein eines *procurator ad dioecesin Alexandreae* neben dem Dioiketen in severischer Zeit angesehen hat, ohne absolute Datierung sind. Pflaum hat sie nur deshalb in die Zeit der Severer gesetzt, weil der Anonymus Ämter sowohl im Osten wie im Westen des Reiches bekleidet hat; das sei, sagt Pflaum, vor Septimius Severus ungewöhnlich. Doch vielleicht ist dieses Argument allein nicht ausreichend. Wären die Inschriften einige Jahrzehnte älter (in *AE* 1969, 163/4 wird als Entstehungszeit Mark Aurel–Severus angegeben), so hinderte nichts daran, den *procurator ad dioecesin Alexandreae* mit dem διοικητής zu identifizieren und anzunehmen,

84. Vgl. oben Fussn. 14 und die Anm. der Herausgeber zu *P. Mich.* viii 479.11 mit Verweis auf *W. Chr.* 363 Einl.; *P. Ryl.* ii 84 und *P. Flor.* i 6.3–4.

85. S. *P. Mich.* viii S.16; O. Montevecchi, *La papirologia* (Torino 1973) 253 Nr. 32.

86. *P. Mich.* viii 467 = *CPL* 250 = Pighi, a.a.O. (Fussn. 83) Nr. IV; vgl. die Anmerkung der Herausgeber zu Z. 8.

87. *TAPA* 90 (1959) 139–46; der dort publizierte *P. Cornell* inv. i 64 (= *SB* vi 9636) aus dem Jahre 136 scheint zu beweisen, dass Terentianus (falls es sich wirklich um denselben Terentianus handelt) in diesem Jahr aus dem Militärdienst ausgeschieden ist, während die Korrespondenz aus seiner Dienstzeit in Alexandria stammt.

dass der Posten zu dieser Zeit noch mit einem Gehalt von 100000 Sesterzen entlohnt worden ist. In den Jahren bis zur Zeit des M. Aurelius Mindius Matidianus Pollio, der vielleicht unter Commodus Dioiket war, müsste der Posten dann auf 200000 Sesterzen erhöht worden sein. Solche Aufstockungen sind auch sonst durchaus bekannt.[88]

Ich möchte mich also dafür entscheiden, dass die Ämter *procurator ad dioecesin Alexandreae* und διοικητής dasselbe sind. Damit besässen wir den frühesten einigermassen sicher datierten Beleg in den Cursusinschriften des Valerius Eudaemon, der das Amt um 120 bekleidet haben muss.[89] Strenggenommen wäre dieses Datum nur der *terminus ante quem* für die Einführung des procuratorischen Dioiketen; sie könnte theoretisch auch noch einige Jahre früher stattgefunden haben. Seit aber vor wenigen Jahren der Beginn eines Ediktes des Präfekten Haterius Nepos aus ebenfalls der Zeit um 120 bekannt geworden ist, in welchem dieser mit klaren Worten zum Ausdruck bringt, dass ein dem Dioiketen im Rang vergleichbares anderes procuratorisches Amt, das des ἀρχιερεύς, soeben von Hadrian neu eingerichet worden sei,[90] liegt es nahe, beide Daten zueinander in Beziehung zu setzen. Es wäre gut denkbar, dass Hadrian zu Beginn seiner Regierungszeit in Verbindung mit anderen Verwaltungsreformen auch diese beiden ägyptischen Procuraturen neu geschaffen hat, die des Archiereus durch Abspaltung von Kompetenzen, die vorher vom Ressort des Idios Logos mitverwaltet wurden, die des Dioiketen durch Aufwertung eines Amtes, dessen Inhaber bis zu diesem Zeitpunkt in stärkerer Abhängigkeit vom Präfekten die Finanzangelegenheiten der Provinz überwacht hatte. Valerius Eudaemon, der Vertraute des Kaisers, könnte unter diesen Umständen der erste Dioiket mit den erweiterten Kompetenzen gewesen sein.

Weniger verwickelt als die Frage der Einführung des Dioi-

88. Es ist z.B. bemerkenswert, dass der einzige Text, der das Gehalt des Epistrategen angibt (*P. Oxy.* XVII 2130 von 267 n.Chr.), ihn als δουκηνάριος bezeichnet, während Pflaum das Amt als ein sexagenares einstuft; vgl. dazu Thomas, a.a.O. (Fussn. 3) 51f. Grundsätzliche Bedenken gegen zu grosse Starrheit bei der Ansetzung der Gehaltsklassen hat F. G. B. Millar in *JRS* 53 (1963) 194–200 angemeldet.

89. Vgl. oben Fussn. 73 und Pflaum, *Carrières*, 264–71 (Nr. 110).

90. *P. Yale* inv. 1394v = *SB* XII 11236, ediert von G. M. Parássoglou in *ZPE* 13 (1974) 21–37.

ketenamtes ist die, wann es aufgehört hat zu bestehen. Man hat immer schon gesehen, dass mit dem Beginn des 4. Jhdts. die Aufgaben, die vorher der Dioiket wahrgenommen hatte, in die Zuständigkeit des καθολικός oder *rationalis* übergegangen waren. Zu klären bleibt nur noch, wann der Wechsel stattgefunden hat. Noch vor wenigen Jahren bot sich dem Forscher, der sich dieser Frage zuwandte, ein verwirrendes Bild, weil nämlich mehrere καθολικοί schon seit dem Beginn des 3. Jhdts. bezeugt zu sein schienen, zu einer Zeit, zu der Dioiketen noch zahlreich und sicher belegt sind. Das schien zu bedeuten, dass der Dioiket nicht einfach vom Katholikos abgelöst worden ist, sondern vorübergehend beide nebeneinander existiert haben.[91] P. Parsons hat aber zeigen können,[92] dass von den angenommenen mehreren Katholikoi des früheren 3. Jhdts. nur ein einziger real ist; bei den anderen handelt es sich um Missverständnisse und falsche Lesungen. Dieser eine Katholikos war Claudius Marcellus, der gemeinsam mit Marcius Salutaris von Philippus Arabs zur Neuordnung der Verwaltung nach Ägypten entsandt worden ist. Seine Aufgaben waren ausserordentlicher Art und mit denen des Finanzbeamten der diokletianischen und nachdiokletianischen Zeit überhaupt nicht vergleichbar.

Wenn man von Claudius Marcellus absieht, kommt man zu einer klaren zeitlichen Aufeinanderfolge der Ämter διοικητής und καθολικός. Die letzte Bezeugung für einen Dioiketen stammt vom 21. Mai 284,[93] der erste Katholikos ist rund zwei Jahre später am 11. Juni 286 belegt.[94] Der Wechsel dürfte also gleichzeitig mit dem Regierungsantritt Diokeletians bzw. seiner Anerkennung in Ägypten stattgefunden haben, die in den Winter 284/5 fällt.[95]

Die Geschichte des ägyptischen Dioiketenamtes in römischer Zeit stellt sich demnach folgendermassen dar. Vom Beginn der Römerherrschaft bis etwa zum Jahre 120 gab es keinen höheren Procuratorenposten mit der Bezeichnung διοικητής, sondern die Verwaltung der διοίκησις wurde von einem im Rang niedrig stehenden Beamten, möglicherweise einem kaiserlichen Freigelas-

91. So äussert sich z.B. J. Lallemand, a.a.O. (Fussn. 58) 81f.
92. "Philippus Arabs and Egypt", *JRS* 57 (1967) 134–41, bes. 138f.
93. *P. Oxy.* VIII 1115.
94. Vgl. oben Fussn. 58.
95. Vgl. zu dieser Frage *P. Oxy.* XLII 3055–56 Einl.

senen, unter der direkten Aufsicht des *praefectus Aegypti* ausgeübt. Erster Dioiket des avancierten Typs war vermutlich Valerius Eudaemon, der Freund Hadrians. Zu seiner Zeit dürfte das Amt centenaren Rang gehabt haben, war aber später, vielleicht unter Commodus, zu einem ducenaren Posten aufgestockt worden. Um das Jahr 285 scheint das Dioiketenamt eines der ersten Opfer des Reformeifers gewesen zu sein, mit dem Diokletian auch die Verwaltungstrukturen Ägyptens völlig umgestaltet hat.[96]

### PROSOPOGRAPHISCHER ANHANG

Die zuletzt publizierte Liste der bisher bekannt gewordenen Dioiketen (H.-G. Pflaum, *Les carrières procuratoriennes équestres sous le Haut-Empire romain*, Supplément (Paris 1982) 134f.) ist nicht vollständig und enthält zudem einige Ungenauigkeiten. Ich veröffentliche daher hier ebenfalls eine solche Liste, wobei ich zwischen sicher bezeugten Dioiketen und Procuratoren, in denen man nur Dioiketen vermutet hat, unterscheide. Aufgenommen worden sind als Bezeugungen nur diejenigen Papyri und Inschriften, die eine namentliche Nennung eines Dioiketen enthalten oder doch erkennbar früher einmal enthalten haben, nicht dagegen blosse Erwähnungen des Amtes. Die angegebenen Daten sind die der Wirksamkeit des Dioiketen, nicht die Abfassungszeit der zitierten Urkunde.

### A. Sicher bezeugte Dioiketen

VALERIUS EUDAEMON (?)

um 120   *IGR* III 1077 = *SB* I 3998.2ff. Εὐδα]ίμονι ἐπιτρόπῳ [Αὐτο-
κράτορος Κ]αίσαρος Τραιανοῦ ['Αδριανοῦ Σεβασ]τοῦ ἐπὶ
διοικήσεως ['Αλεξανδρείας
*CIL* III 431 = *ILS* 1449 = *IK* XIII (Ephesos) 666.1–3 *proc(uratori)*
[*Imp(eratoris)*] *Caesaris Tra(ia)ni Hadriani* [*Aug(usti)*] *ad di-*
*oecesin Alexandr(eae)* (kein Name erhalten)

Lit.: *R-E* VI 884 Eudaimon 4 (Stein); *R-E* VIIA.2 2496 Valerius 149 (Hanslik); Pflaum, *Carrières*, 264–71 (Nr. 110), 1087; H. Pavis d'Escurac, *La préfecture de l'annone*, 341; Bastianini, *ZPE* 17 (1975) 289 und 38 (1980) 81.

---

96. In byzantinischer Zeit kommt das Wort διοικητής in verschiedenen Bedeutungen wieder in Gebrauch; vgl. z.B. Wilcken, *Grundzüge* 233; E. Wipszycka, *Les ressources et les activités économiques des églises en Egypte du IV^e au VIII^e siècle* (= *Papyrologica Bruxellensia* 10, Bruxelles 1972) 141f. Mit dem Amt, das wir hier untersucht haben, hat das nicht das Geringste zu tun.

## Zum Amt des διοικητής im römischen Aegypten

Zu der Frage, ob der *procurator ad dioecesin Alexandreae* mit dem Dioiketen gleichzusetzen ïst, s. oben S.191–96.

ḄAN. . .IUS IULIANUS

um 141    *BGU* IV 1019.11f. Ḅạν[. . . Ἰουλι]ανῷ διọικητῇ. Vgl. *BL* I 88,
zur Lesung des Nomen ebenda Anm.10

um 141    *P. Lond.* II 196 (S.152f.) = *M. Chr.* 87: mehrfach Ἰουλιανός

später    *P. Cattaoui* = *M. Chr.* 88 I 1f. ὁ κράτιστος διοικητὴς Ἰουλιανὸς ὁ
διέπων τὰ κατὰ τὴν δικαι[ο]δοσίαν

danach    *BGU* XI 2012.24 Ἰọυλ[ι]ạνὸς ὁ γενόμενος διοικητής

ebenso    *BGU* XI 2070.12f. ___]ιος Ἰουλ[ι]ạνὸς ὁ γενόμενος διοικητὴς
[ὁ διαδεχ]όμεν[ος τὰ κατὰ τὴν δικαιοδοσίαν; Z.21 Ἰουλιανοῦ

Lit.: *R-E* x.1 23 Iulianus 19 (Stein); der Eintrag lautet *Ṛan . . . Iulianus*; vgl. *BL* I 88 Anm.10. Die Lesung ist sehr unsicher.

IULIUS AMYNTIANUS

146/7    *P. Oxy.* ined. bei E. G. Turner, *The Papyrologist at Work*
(Durham N.C. 1973) 44f. Z.16 τῷ διοικητῇ Ἰουλίῳ
Ἀμυντιανῷ

Lit.: *R-E* Suppl. xv 123 Iulius 65aa (Eck).

Der Dioiket ist nicht unbedingt identisch mit Iulius Amyntianus, dem Bruder des Konsuls Iulius Severus (s. *PIR*² I 147; *R-E* x.1 159 Iulius 65), gehört aber wahrscheinlich in diese (nicht senatorische) Familie. Vgl. auch *IK* XIII (Ephesos) 930, Komm. zu Z.2.

MALLIUS CRASSUS

27.12.158    *P. Oxy.* XXIV 2411.41f. Μαλλίου Κράσσου γενομένου δι-
οι[κητο]ῦ; Z.43 Μάλλιος Κρạ[σσο]ς

o.D.    *P. Teb.* II 287 = *W. Chr.* 251.6f. Κράσσον τὸν κράτιστον
[διοικητ]ήν; Z.12 Κρ[άσσῳ

Lit.: Pflaum, *Carrières*, 1107, Suppl. 134; *R-E* Suppl. xv 129 Mallius 11a (Eck); Bastianini, *ZPE* 17 (1975) 293 Anm. 5; Thomas, *Roman Epistrategos*, 217; *PIR*² M 111 (Datum fälschlich Dez. 159).

VERNASIUS FACUNDUS

um 160    *P. Thmouis* 1 (ined.; vgl. Bastianini, *ZPE* 17 (1975) 300 Anm.
4)

8.7.161    *P. Oxy.* VII 1032.44f. Οὐηρνασίῳ Φακούνδῳ τῷ κρατίστῳ
διοικητῇ; Z.51 [Οὐηρνά]σιος Φακοῦντος (vgl. *BL* I 330)

o.D.    *BGU* III 786 I 5 ὑ]πὸ Οὐηρνασίου Φακούνδου

o.D.    *P. Wash. Univ.* I 3.26 Οὐηρνασίου Φακού[νδου

Dieter Hagedorn

Lit.: Pflaum, *Carrières*, 1107 (Vonasius), Suppl. 50 (Nr. 179A) (Vernasius, aber S.134 Vonasius); *R-E* VIIIA.2 1558 (Stiglitz); *R-E* Suppl. XV 898 (Eck); C. A. Nelson, *BASP* 9 (1972) 49–52; Bastianini, *ZPE* 17 (1975) 300 mit Anm. 4; Thomas, *Roman Epistrategos*, 212; *P. Wash. Univ.* I 3.26 Anm.; D. Hagedorn, *ZPE* 54 (1984) 87–90.

Aufgrund von *P. Wash. Univ.* I 3.26ff. war geschlossen worden, Vernasius Facundus sei in späterer Zeit zum Praefectus Aegypti avanciert; in *ZPE* 54 (1984) 87–90 wird demgegenüber vorgeschlagen, dass Vernasius Facundus während seiner Amtszeit als Dioiket nur den Präfekten vertreten hat. Es gibt dann auch keinen Grund mehr, *BGU* III 786 in eine andere Zeit als die Jahre um 161 zu datieren; vgl. dazu Thomas a.a.O.

ANNIUS SEVERIANUS

165/6   *P. Thmouis* I (ined.; für die folgenden Angaben danke ich S. Kambitsis) Kol.84.7f. Ἄννιος Σεουηριανὸς ὁ γενό(μενος) διοικητής; Kol.83.16 ]τῷ Σεουηριανῷ; Kol.86.7 τῷ αὐτῷ Σεουηριανῷ; Kol.90.3 Ἀνν[ίου] Σεουηριανοῦ τοῦ γενο[μένου] διοικητοῦ; Kol.90. 16f. Ἀννίῳ Σεουηριανῷ γενο(μένῳ) [διοικ]ητῇ

Dez./Jan.165/6 *P. Thmouis* I Kol.88.15f. τῷ α(ὐτῷ) [δι]οικητῇ τῷ αὐτῷ ς (ἔτει) Τῦβι

o.D.     *P. Teb.* II 287 = *W. Chr.* 251.13 Σευηρ]ιανός; Z.20 Σευηριανός (der Text stammt aus der Zeit von Mark Aurel und Verus)

Lit.: *R-E* IIA.2 1929 Severianus I (Stein); Bastianini, *ZPE* 17 (1975) 293 Anm. 5.

Annius Severianus war früher vermutungsweise für einen Praefectus Aegypti gehalten worden; vgl. Bastianini a.a.O.

ULPIUS MARCELLUS

165/6   *P. Thmouis* I (ined.; die folgenden Angaben verdanke ich S. Kambitsis) Kol.68.2ff. Οὐλπίῳ Μαρκέλλῳ τῷ [γ]ενο(μένῳ) δικαιοδότῃ διαδεχο(μένῳ) τότε καὶ τὰ τῇ διοικήσει διεφέροντα; Kol.84.8ff. Οὔλπιος Μαρκέλλος ὁ γενόμενος δικαιοδότ(ης) διαδεξάμενος τὸν Σεουηριανόν; Kol.90.1ff. Οὐλπίῳ Μ[αρκέλλῳ τῷ γενομένῳ] δικαι[οδότῃ] διαδεχο(μένῳ) ἀπο-[δημίαν] Ἀνν[ίου] Σεουηριανοῦ

Dez./Jan. 166/7 Kol.68.15ff. ὁ Μαρκέλλος ἔ[γρ]αψεν [τῇ. μ]ηνὸς Τῦβι τοῦ ζ (ἔτους)

*Zum Amt des* διοικητής *im römischen Aegypten*

Ausserhalb der *P. Thmouis* ist Ulpius Marcellus in den Papyri nicht bezeugt. Es liegt sehr nahe, ihn mit dem bekannten Juristen gleichen Namens zu identifizieren, der dem *consilium* des Antoninus Pius und des Mark Aurel angehört hat, doch wird man Sicherheit nicht erzielen können. Das Amt des δικαιοδότης Ägyptens wäre für einen Juristen zwar sehr passend, für einen so engen Vertrauten der Kaiser aber möglicherweise doch nicht bedeutend genug gewesen. Zu dem Juristen vgl. W. Kunkel, *Herkunft und soziale Stellung der römischen Juristen*[2] (Graz-Wien 1967) 213f., wo auch Informationen über andere Träger desselben Namens zusammengestellt sind; *R-E* IXA.1 570 Ulpius 4 (Mayer–Maly); vgl. *R-E* Suppl. XIV 941 Ulpius 42 (Eck). Zu Ulpii Marcelli vgl. auch A. R. Birley, *The* Fasti *of Roman Britain* (Oxford 1981) 140–42 (Hinweis von G. Alföldy).

AURELIUS PTOLEMAEUS

1.7.168    *P. Leit.* 5 = *SB* VIII 10196.21f. τ]ῶι κρατίστῳ δι[οι]κητῇ Αὐρηλίῳ Πτολεμα[ί]ῳ; Z.12f. τῷ τότε διοικητῇ Αὐρηλίῳ Πτολεμαί[ῳ]

Lit.: Pflaum, *Carrières*, Suppl. 134; *R-E* Suppl. XV 78 Aurelius 199a (Eck).

FULVIUS F...

um 175    *PSI* III 235.29 τῷ κρατίστ]ῳ διοικητῷ Φουλουίῳ Φ.....; vgl. Z.9 und 18 und *PSI* III 323.26, wo überall nur der Titel διοικητής erhalten ist

Lit.: Pflaum, *Carrières*, 1084, Suppl. 134; *PIR*[2] F 537; *R-E* Suppl. XV 106 Fulvius 48a (Eck).

JULIUS CRISPINUS

176–180    *P. Strassb.* 179.5 ᾽Ιο]υλί[ου] Κρισπε[ίνο]υ (vgl. *P. Strassb.* IV S.187)

13.9.180    *BGU* XI 2060.3 [᾽Ιο]ύλιος Κρησπεῖνος; Z.9 ᾽Ιουλίῳ Κρησπείνῳ τῷ κρα(τίστῳ) διοικητῆι

Litt.: *R-E* Suppl. XV 123 Iulius 203a (Eck); Pflaum, *Carrières*, Suppl. 134.

Der Strassburger Papyrus stammt noch aus der Zeit vor dem Tode Mark Aurels. Eine um neue Fragmente erweiterte Publikation des Textes gibt S. Daris, *Aegyptus* 63 (1983) 123–28.

VESSIDIUS (VESTIDIUS) RUFINUS

182/3    *P. Strassb.* inv. 31 + 32 bei Wilcken, *APF* 4 (1907) 124 Anm. 1 (Οὐεστίδιος ῾Ρουφεῖνος)

25.2.184  *P. Oxy.* III 513 = *W. Chr.* 183 = *Sel. Pap.* 77.29 τ]οῦ κρατίστου
διοικητοῦ Οὐεσσιδίου ῾Ρ[ο]υφείν[ο]υ

2.5.184  *P. Petaus* 10.6 Ο<u>ὐε</u>[σσιδίου] ῾Ρ[ο]υφίνου τοῦ κρατίστου
διοικητοῦ

2.5.184  *P. Petaus* 11.4f. Οὐεσσιδίου [῾Ρουφ]είνου τοῦ κρα(τίστου)
διοικητοῦ

Lit.: *R-E* VIIIA.2 1778 (Stiglitz); *R-E* Suppl. XV 908 (Eck); Pflaum,
*Carrières*, Suppl. 134.

Zu den verschiedenen Schreibungen des Nomen s. *P. Petaus* 10.6 Anm.


M. AURELIUS MINDIUS MATIDIANUS POLLIO

unter Commodus?  Keil, *JÖAI* 23 (1926) Beibl. Sp. 269 = *IK* XIII
(Ephesos) 627 Μ(ᾶρκον) Αὐρήλι(ον) Μίνδιον
Ματτιδιανὸν  τὸν  κράτιστον---ἐπίτροπον
διοικητὴν Αἰγύπτου δουκηνάριον
Keil, *Forsch. in Ephesos* III (1923) 141 Nr. 56 = *IK*
XVII 1 (Ephesos) 3056 (lückenhaft, nach vorigem
ergänzt)

Lit.: *PIR*[2] A 1559; *R-E* XIV.2 2203 s.v. Matidianus (Stein); Pflaum,
*Carrières*, 523–31 (Nr. 193), 1084, Suppl. 134.


UMMIDIUS PIUS

um 190  *P. Mich.* XI 623.8 ὑπὸ Οὐμμιδί[ο]<u>υ</u> Πίου τοῦ κρατίστου
διοικητοῦ

Lit.: *R-E* Suppl. XV 934 Ummidius 1a (Eck); geht noch von dem falschen
Datum aus.

Zur Lesung des Cognomens s. J. Rea in *JEA* 60 (1974) 296f.; zum Datum
von *P. Mich.* XI 623 s. D. Hagedorn in *ZPE* 29 (1978) 190.


SUILLIUS SATURNINUS

7./8.–10./11.194  *P. Strassb.* inv. 31 + 32 bei Wilcken, *APF* 4 (1907) 124
Anm. 1

Lit.: *R-E* IVA.1 722 Suillius 6 (Stein); Pflaum, *Carrières*, 1084, Suppl. 134.


FLAVIUS STUDIOSUS

2.3.199  *P. Oxy.* VI 899 = *W. Chr.* 361.1 (Name und Titel ergänzt; vgl.
*P. Oxy.* VI S.225); vgl. Z.37f.

28.8.200  *P. Oxy.* VI 899 verso (Einl. S.225 unten) Φλαυίου Στουδιώσου
τοῦ κρα(τίστου) διοικ(ητοῦ)

## Zum Amt des διοικητής im römischen Aegypten

24.9.203? *P. Flor.* II 278 = Daris, a.a.O. (Fussn. 64) 64 Kol.4.26
Φλαουίῳ Στ[ουδιώσῳ (?); vgl. *APF* 6 (1920) 216

Lit.: *PIR*² F 372; *R-E* Supp. VII 202 Flavius 184a (Stein); Pflaum,
*Carrières*, 62of. (Nr. 232), 1084, Suppl. 134.

--- --- (?)

2./.3. Jh.   *CIL* XIV 4468/70 = *AE* 1913, Nr.213 = *ILS* 9501 = *AE* 1960,
Nr.163 Z. 4 *proc(uratori) ad dioecesin Alexandr[eae*
*AE* 1946, Nr.95 = *AE* 1950, Nr.183 = *AE* 1960, Nr.164 Z.4f.
*proc(uratori) dioeces(eos) [Alexa]ndr(eae)*

Lit.: Pflaum, *Carrières*, 719–25 (Nr.271), Add. 994, 1087; G. Barbieri,
*Epigraphica* 19 (1957) 93–105; H. Devijver, *Prosopographia Militiarum
Equestrium*, 990 Incert. 255.

G. Barbieri a.a.O. erwägt eine Identifikation mit C. Fulvius Plautianus,
dem Prätorianerpräfekten unter Septimius Severus. Zur Frage, ob der
*procurator ad dioecesin Alexandreae* mit dem Dioiketen zu gleichzusetzen ist,
s. oben S.191–96.

### AELIUS MAMERTINUS

31.12.207 ? *P. Strassb.* I 57.1 Αἰλίωι Μαμερτείνωι τῷ κρατίστωι
[διο]ι[κ]ητῆι (vgl. Thomas, *Roman Epistrategos*, 215f.)

Lit.: *PIR*² A 212 als Epistratege; Pflaum, *Carrières*, 1090 als Epistratege;
M. Vandoni, *Gli epistrategi nell'Egitto romano*, 38; Thomas, a.a.O.

J. Schwartz liest das Datum in *P. Strassb.* I 57.17 jetzt (ἔτους) ις Τῦ[β]ι
δ (vgl. Thomas a.a.O.); da das Verso (= *P. Strassb.* 452) in der Zeit des
Severus Alexander wiederbenutzt worden ist, ist 207 ein passenderes
Datum für das Rekto als 175. Vgl. auch den Kommentar zu *P. Strassb.*
452.

### CALVENTIUS ADIUTOR

3.7.210   *P. Flor.* I 6.1 Καλουεντίῳ Ἀδιούτορι τῷ κρατίστῳ διοικητῇ

Lit.: *PIR*² C 337; Pflaum, *Carrières*, 1084, Suppl. 134.

### AURELIUS TERPSILAUS

Anf. 217   *P. Oxy.* XLIII 3092.3f. Αὐρηλίῳ Τερψιλάῳ ἐπιτρόπῳ οὐσι-
ακῶ(ν) [διαδεχομένῳ] καὶ τὰ κ[ατ]ὰ τὴν διοίκη[σι]ν

Lit.: *R-E* Suppl. XV 78 Aurelius 225b (Eck); Pflaum, *Carrières*, Suppl. 134.

## Dieter Hagedorn

--- HERACLIDES

ca. 21.9.217    P. Oxy. XLIII 3093.5–6 Ἡρ]ακλίδη τῷ κρατίστῳ διαδεχομέ[νῳ (καὶ?) τὰ κατὰ τὴν δικαιοδοσία]ν; Ζ.8–9 Ἡρα-
κλίδη τῷ κρα]τίστῳ διοικητῇ διαδεχομέ[νῳ (καὶ?) τὰ
κατὰ τὴν δικαιοδοσί]αν

Lit.: R-E Suppl. xv 111 Herakleides 34a; Pflaum, Carrières, Suppl. 134.

### SEPTIMIUS ARRIANUS

19.11.221    P. Oxy. 1 61.14f. Σεπτιμίου Ἀρριανοῦ τοῦ κρατίστου
διοικητοῦ

Lit.: R-E IIA.2 1564 Septimius 24 (Stein); Pflaum, Carrières, 1084, Suppl.
135

Septimius Arrianus wird mehrfach in den noch unpublizierten, von
J. Frösén bearbeiteten carbonisierten Papyri aus dem Bubastites erwähnt
(Mitteilung von J. Frösén). Möglicherweise erscheint Septimius Arrianus
auch in P. Flor. III 382.27 (kurz vor 3.11.222 n.Chr.), wo der Name eines
Dioiketen, den Vitelli nicht zu entziffern wagte (vgl. P. Flor. III S.105),
getilgt und durch den des Präfekten Aedinius Julianus ersetzt worden ist.
R. Pintaudi schreibt mir in einem Brief vom 6.1.1984, dass zu Beginn
der Zeile vor der Lücke Σεπτιμίῳ eine vertretbare Lesung ist, und
denselben Eindruck habe ich an einem von Pintaudi freundlicherweise
übersandten Photo. Man wird daher mit gutem Gewissen Σεπτιμίῳ
[Ἀρριανῶι τῶι κρατίστωι δ]ιοικητῆι ergänzen dürfen, was auch schon
Vitelli erwogen hatte. Das danach von Vitelli mit Bedenken in den Text
gesetzte Αἰ[γύπτ]ου ist kaum richtig, da innerhalb Ägyptens dieser
Zusatz nicht üblich ist. Mir scheint am Photo Μ[άρκ]ῳι, d.h. das
Praenomen des Präfekten Aedinius Julianus, durchaus auch in Frage zu
kommen.

### CLAUDIUS SEVERIANUS

7./8.223–6.4.224  P. Colon. inv. carbon. B, zahlreiche Bezeugungen in der
Form Κλαύδιος Σεουηριανὸς (ὁ κράτιστος διοικητής)
6./7.225        P. Oxy. ined. (Mitteilung von J. Rea)

Lit.: PIR² c 1020; R-E II.2 2867 Claudius 343 (Stein); R-E Suppl. xv
91 Claudius 343 (Eck); Pflaum, Carrières, 1039, Suppl. 8of. (Nr. 317A);
115 und 135; D. Hagedorn, a.a.O. (oben Fussn. 9).

### VELLEIUS MAXIMUS

24.8.248 (?)    BGU 1 8 II = W. Chr. 170.29 [Οὐ]ελλη[ίου Μ]αξίμου τοῦ
κρατίστου δι[οι]κητοῦ

## Zum Amt des διοικητής im römischen Aegypten

Lit.: *R-E* VIIIA.1 660 Velleius 9 (Hanslik); Pflaum, *Carrières*, 1084, Suppl. 135.

SEPTIMIUS APOLLONIUS

252/3     *P. Oxy.* XLVI 3288.3f. τοῦ κρατίστου διοικητοῦ Σεπτιμίου Ἀπολλωνίου

8./10.253   *P. Flor.* I 88.10 Σεπτιμίωι [Ἀπολλωνίῳ (?); zum Datum vgl. R. Pintaudi, *ZPE* 27 (1977) 118–20

o.D.        *P. Thead.* 14 = *P. Sakaon* 32.18f. τοῦ διασημοτάτου Σεπτιμίου Ἀπολλωνίου κοσμήσαντος τὴν δι[οί]κησιν (der Pap. lässt sich wegen der Nennung des Septimius Apollonios in Verbindung mit Z.20f. τῷ πρώτῳ ἔτει τῆς εὐτυχεστάτης ταύτης βασιλεί[ας] (wohl = 253/4) jetzt mit Sicherheit in die Regierung Galliens datieren; vgl. *Gnomon* 53 (1981) 806f.).

Lit.: *PLRE* I Apollonius 4; Pflaum, *Carrières*, Suppl. 135.

Durch die Publikation von *P. Oxy.* XLVI 3288 sind alle früheren Datierungs- und Identifikationsversuche hinfällig geworden (vgl. z.B. Lallemand, *L'administration civile*, 262). In *ZPE* 38 (1980) 87 mit Anm. 3 hält Bastianini an der Möglichkeit fest, dass mit Σεπτιμίωι [ in *P. Flor.* I 88.10 ein Praefectus Aegypti gemeint sein könne, während Thomas, *Roman Epistrategos*, 210f. an den Epistrategen denkt. Mir scheint jedoch, dass auch der Dioiket Septimius Apollonius eine gute Chance hat.

FLAVIUS RUFUS

ca. 260/268 *P. Flor.* I 89.1f. Φλάυιος Ῥοῦφος ὁ κράτι[στ]ος δικαιοδότ[ης διέ]πων τὰ μέρη τῆς διοικήσεως (vgl. J. Rea, *CE* 46 (1971) 155–57)

Lit.: *PIR*² F 349; *R-E* VI.2 2610 Flavius 162 (Stein); Pflaum, *Carrières*, 1084, Suppl. 135; *PLRE* I Rufus 6.

Ein ungefähres Datum ist dadurch gegeben, dass auf der Rückseite in derselben Hand ein Brief des Heroninos-Archivs (*P. Flor.* II 158) steht.

--- ANDROMACHUS

vor 4.3.272 *P. Oxy.* X 1264 = *FIRA*² III 9.8f. ἐπὶ τοῦ κρα(τίστου) γενομένου διοικητοῦ Ἀνδρομάχου

Lit.: *PIR*² A 587; Pflaum, *Carrières*, 952f. (Nr. 357b) und 1084, Suppl. 135; *PLRE* I Andromachus 1.

# Dieter Hagedorn

IULIUS MONIMUS

23.8.275  *P. Oxy.* XIV 1633.16f. ὑπὸ ᾿Ιουλ[ί]ου Μονίμου τ[οῦ κρατίστου]
διοικητοῦ

Lit.: *PIR²* I 433; Pflaum, *Carrières*, Suppl. 135; *PLRE* I Monimus.

ULPIUS AURELIUS

1.4.278  *P. Oxy.* XII 1409.3 ὑπὸ Οὐλπίου Αὐρηλίου τοῦ κρατ[ίσ]του
διοικητοῦ

Lit.: *PLRE* I Aurelius 8; *R-E* Suppl. XV 931 Ulpius 28a; Pflaum, *Carrières*,
Suppl. 135.

AURELIUS PROTEAS

11.1.281  *P. Oxy.* VIII 1115 = *Sel. Pap.* 426.11 Αὐρηλίου Πρ[ω]τέα τοῦ
κρατίστου διοικητοῦ
21.5.284  ebenda Z.5 τοῦ δι[α]σημοτάτου διοικητοῦ Αὐρηλίου
[Πρωτέα]
o.D.  *P. Oxy.* XII 1412.9 τοῦ κρατίστου διοικητοῦ Αὐρηλίου
Π[ρ]ωτέα

Lit.: *PIR²* A 1589; *PLRE* I Proteas.

AURELIUS ---

3. Jhdt.  *BGU* III 925.2 ὑπὸ Αὐρηλί⟨ου⟩ .... τοῦ κρατίστου διοικητοῦ

Lit.: Pflaum, *Carrières*, 1084, Suppl. 135; *R-E* Suppl. XV 76 Aurelius 8a
(Eck).

Das Original ist verbrannt. Eine erste Abschrift hatte Αὐρηλίας statt
Αὐρηλί⟨ου⟩.

--- ---

3. Jhdt.  *P. Ross.–Georg.* V 25.6  ]ι τῶι κρατίστωι διοικητῇ

## B. Unsichere Fälle und fälschlich für Dioiketen gehaltene Procuratoren

Vielfach erscheinen in den Papyri Procuratoren ohne genaue Angabe
ihres Amtes. In einigen von ihnen hat man Dioiketen vermutet. Die
folgende Liste enthält sowohl solche Fälle, bei denen es sich wirklich um
Dioiketen handeln kann, als auch andere, bei denen dies aus unter-
schiedlichen Gründen unmöglich ist. Die Liste erhebt keinen Anspruch
auf Vollständigkeit.

## Zum Amt des διοικητής im römischen Aegypten

MOENATIDES (?)

1.8.146(?)    *P. Ryl.* II 84.1 Μοιν̣ατ[ί]δης. Schreibt als διαδεχόμενος τὴν Πρόκλου τοῦ κρατίστου (d.i. der Präfekt Valerius Proculus?) εἰς Αἴγυπτον ἀποδημίαν an den Strategen des Hermopolites

*P. Ryl.* II 84.6 Anm.: "The writer of the letter is very likely the διοικητής." Ähnlich *PIR²* M 673 (Name: Moenatides vel Munatides); *R-E* XV.2 2343 (Stein). Vgl. auch G. Foti Talamanca, *Ricerche sul processo nell'Egitto greco-romano* I (Milano 1974) 116–19; D. Hagedorn, *ZPE* 54 (1984) 89f.


L. SILIUS SATRIANUS

12.5.164 und 165   *P. Warren* I = *SB* IV 7472.1 Λουκίωι Σειλίω[ι] Σ[α-τριανῶι; Z.16 Σειλίωι Σατριανῶι τῷ κρατί[στῳ

*P. Warren* S.7: "Satrianus is certainly not an idiologus... The fisc being interested, it is perhaps better to think of a διοικητής or of a δικαιοδότης." Ähnlich *R-E* Suppl. XV 567 Silius 23a (Eck). Vgl. Pflaum, *Carrières*, 1085 (Idios Logos), Suppl. 134 (Dioiketes), 136 (Idios Logos), 139 (Dikaiodotes).

Falls Silius Satrianus Dioiket war, müsste er zwischen Vernasius Facundus und Annius Severianus amtiert haben. Annius Severianus ist schon im Jahre 165/6 bezeugt; mir ist daher eher unwahrscheinlich, dass Silius Satrianus Dioiket war.


--- ---

10.9.164 oder 196   *BGU* II 648 = *W. Chr.* 360 = Meyer, *Jur. Pap.* 58.1 τῶι κρ[α]τίσ[τ]ωι (Name verloren, Titel nie geschrieben)

Wilcken und Meyer vermuten, dass der Dioiket gemeint ist. Vgl. J. D. Thomas, *Roman Epistrategos*, 91 mit Anm. 159 (Dioiket oder Epistratege).


SEPTIMIUS SERENUS

1.4.174(?)   *P. Mich.* XI 616.21f. ὑπὸ [Σε]πτιμίου Σερήνου τοῦ τότε ἐπιτρόπου

*P. Mich.* XI 616.3–4 Anm.: "διοικητής rather than the procurator usiacus". *R-E* Suppl. XV 567 Septimius 51b (Eck): "wahrscheinlich Dioiket'; Parássoglou, *Imperial Estates*, 68: Idios Logos; Pflaum, *Carrières*, Suppl. 134 (Dioiket) und 136 (Idios Logos).

Septimius Serenus hatte dasselbe Amt wie Claudius Calvinus (s. den nächsten Eintrag). Da dieser kaum Dioiket gewesen sein kann, trifft dasselbe auch für Septimius Serenus zu.

Das Datum der Amtsführung des Septimius Serenus ist im Papyrus vermutlich fehlerhaft angegeben, das oben vermerkte ist das von Shelton konjizierte; vgl. *P. Mich.* XI 616.18 Anm.

CLAUDIUS CALVINUS

März/Apr. 181 oder 182  *P. Mich.* XI 616.3f. Κλαύδιος Καλουῖν[ος] ὁ
γενόμενος ἐπίτροπος

*P. Mich.* XI 616.3–4 Anm.: "διοικητής rather than the procurator usiacus"; ebenso *R-E* Suppl. XV 90 Claudius 95a (Eck). Parássoglou, *Imperial Estates*, 68: Idios Logos; Pflaum, *Carrières*, Suppl. 136 (Idios Logos) und 137 (Procurator in Aegypto).

Zwischen Julius Crispinus und Vessidius Rufinus ist kaum noch Platz für einen weiteren Dioiketen (s. oben); Claudius Calvinus hatte daher vermutlich ein anderes Amt.

PLAUTIUS ITALUS

16.12.184 oder 216  *P. Oxy.* III 474.1 Πλαύτιο[ς] Ἴταλος
*CIL* VIII 12428.1f. *L(ucio) Plautio Ita[lo] proc(uratori)
Aug(usti)*

*P. Oxy.* III 474 Einl. "It is...probable that Plautius Italus was διοικητής or perhaps ἴδιος λόγος". Ebenso Thomas, *Roman Epistrategos*, 210. Pflaum, *Carrières*, 514f. (Nr. 190) (Dioiket), Suppl. 134 (Dioiket); *R-E* Suppl. XV 309 Italus 56a (Eck): "Möglicherweise war er in Ägypten διοικητής"; Wilcken, *APF* 4 (1907) 127 Anm. 1: "Sollte vielleicht auch er procurator Neaspoleos sein?"

Im Mai 184 war Vessidius Rufinus Dioiket; falls Plautius Italus wirklich ebenfalls dieses Amt innehatte, passt er 216 (vor der Vertretung durch Aurelius Terpsilaus, s. oben) besser in die Fasten.

ANTONIUS AELIANUS

27.10.188  *P. Oxy.* IV 708 = *W. Chr.* 432.2 ['Αντ]ώνιος Αἰλιανός; Z.15
'Αντώνιος Αἰλιανός

*P. Oxy.* IV 708 Einl.: "probably epistrategus or dioecetes". Wilcken, *Chr.* 432 Einl.: Procurator Neaspoleos; ebenso Pflaum, *Carrières*, 1089, Suppl. 141; *PIR*[2] A 808; H. Pavis d'Escurac, *La préfecture de l'annone*, 443. J. D. Thomas, *Roman Epistrategos*, 208: "perhaps procurator ad Mercurium".

# Zum Amt des διοικητής im römischen Aegypten

**AURELIUS VICTOR**

27.5.199       *BGU* I 106 = *W. Chr.* 174.1 Αὐρήλιος Οὐίκτωρ

o.D.          *P. Coll. Youtie* I 32 = *P. Oxy.* XLVII 3363.1f. Α[ὐρ]ηλίωι
Οὐίκτορι ἐπιτρόπωι Ἑρμοῦ

*PIR*² A 1632 "dioecetes Aegypti et Alexandriae potius quam idiologus".
Pflaum, *Carrières*, 1084 (Dioiket), Suppl. 134 (Dioiket).

Nach der Publikation von *P. Coll. Youtie* I 32 = *P. Oxy.* XLVII 3363 kann
kein Zweifel mehr über das Amt des Aurelius Victor bestehen: Er war
Procurator ad Mercurium.

**AURELIUS FELIX**

6./7.201    *BGU* I 156 = *W. Chr.* 175.3f. Αὐρηλίου Φήλικος το[ῦ] κρατίστου ἐπιτρόπου

M. Rostowzew, *Studien zur Geschichte des römischen Kolonats*, 142: Procurator
usiacus. Dagegen Wilcken, *Chr.* 175 Einl., ohne eigenen Vorschlag.
Pflaum, *Carrières*, 1085 und Suppl. 137: Procurator in Aegypto; Parássoglou, *Imperial Estates*, 89: Viell. Dioiket.

Man könnte erwägen, Aurelius Felix mit dem aus *CIL* III 53 = *ILS* 8759g
bekannten *Felix Augg(ustorum) libertus procurator usiacus* zu identifizieren (s.
dazu G. Boulvert, *Esclaves et affranchis impériaux*, 225 Anm. 136), wodurch
er als Procurator usiacus bestimmt wäre. Falls er wirklich Dioiket war,
käme eine Identifikation mit dem Αὐρήλιος Φῆλιξ von *IG* XIV 1480 = *IGR*
I 227 = *ILS* 8854 (Pflaum, *Carrières*, 696f. Nr. 260; H. Devijver, *Prosopographia Militiarum Equestrium* A 226) in Frage; vgl. *PIR*² 1503. Allerdings
dauerte die Amtszeit von Flavius Studiosus möglicherweise von 199 bis
203, so dass für Aurelius Felix als Dioiketen keine Zeit bliebe; s. oben.

--- --- (?)

ca. 161–211?     *CIL* 14195³⁷ = *IK* XIII (Ephesos) 818.4 *dioecete]s Aegypti*

Lit.: Pflaum, *Carrières*, 415f. (Nr. 169), 1084, Suppl. 134; H. Devijver,
*Prosopographia Militiarum Equestrium*, 902 Incert. 20–21.

Die Ergänzung des Amtes ist sehr unsicher; auch *iuridicu]s* kommt in
Frage, vgl. oben Fussn. 79.

**AURELIUS MERCURIUS**

8./9.283 oder 285   *P. Oxy.* XIX 2228.27.37 Αὐρήλιος Μερκούριος

*P. Oxy.* XIX 2228 Einl.: Praefectus Aegypti, ebenso noch Bastianini, *ZPE*
17 (1975) 319. A. K. Bowman, *BASP* 6 (1969) 35–40: Epistratege.

## Dieter Hagedorn

Thomas, *Roman Epistrategos*, 168f. mit Anm. 63: Epistratege oder, wenn das Datum 283 ist, Dioiket, bzw. wenn 285, Katholikos.

Da 283 allem Anschein nach Aurelius Proteas als Dioiket im Amt war (s. oben), kann Aurelius Mercurius nicht Dioiket gewesen sein.

SERVAEUS (NERVAEUS ?) AFRICANUS

13.9.288   *P. Oxy.* I 58 = *W. Chr.* 378 = *Sel. Pap.* 226.1 [Σ]ερβαῖος
                  Ἀφρικανός (in *BL* II 2 S.92 wird als Nomen [N]ερβαῖος
                  vorgeschlagen)

*P. Oxy.* I 58 Einl.: "either prefect of Egypt or, more probably, epistrategus". Wilcken, *Chr.* 378 Einl.: Viell. Procurator usiacus. *P. Oxy.* XII S.16: Dioiket. Thomas, *Roman Epistrategos*, 211: "the katholikos must be a possible candidate". Vgl. *R-E* IIA.2 1754 Servaeus 4 (Stein); *PLRE* I Africanus 8.

Um 288 war der Dioiket schon vom Katholikos abgelöst; vgl. oben S.197.

# House and household in Roman Egypt[1]

DEBORAH W. HOBSON

This paper addresses itself to a very simple question, and that is: how many people were likely to have lived under one roof in an Egyptian village of the Roman period? My interest in this question emerges from the fact that there occur, in the numerous Greek papyri which we have from Egypt in the Roman period, many references of all sorts to the houses that people own and live in, but more often than not the property involved is only a fraction of a house rather than a whole building. We know that such fragmentation of property results primarily from the Egyptian system of partible inheritance,[2] but it seems important to establish the relationship between these fractional properties and the conditions under which the Egyptians actually lived. Did people really occupy fractional parts of houses, and if so, how were households organized, and how many occupants were there to an individual house?

1. Earlier versions of this paper were presented at the University of Toronto in December 1982, and at a colloquium on Social History and the Papyri held at Columbia University in April 1983. I thank the organizers of both of these events for affording me an occasion on which to explore this subject. I am particularly pleased to be able to offer this contribution to *Yale Classical Studies*, since it was as a graduate student at Yale, under the inspiring and benevolent guidance of the late Professor C. Bradford Welles, that I first learned of the importance of papyri as incomparable source material for the social history of the ancient world. I would like also to express my appreciation to Professor Naphtali Lewis, not only for initiating and editing the present volume, but also for his countless acts of professional generosity to me and other scholars of my generation.

2. On partible inheritance see R. Taubenschlag, *The Law of Greco-Roman Egypt in the Light of the Papyri, 332 BC–640 AD*[2] (Warsaw 1955) 239f., and the references cited therein, esp. Kreller, *Erbrechtlich Untersuchungen auf Grund der graeco-aegyptischer Papyrusurkunden* (Leipzig–Berlin 1919), and E. Weiss, 'Communio pro diviso und pro indiviso in den Papyri', *APF* 4 (1908) 330–65. For comparative purposes a useful and interesting collection of studies is to be found in *Family and Inheritance; Rural Society in Western Europe, 1200–1800*, eds. J. Goody, J. Thirsk, E. P. Thompson (Cambridge 1976).

Answers to these questions can, I believe, be deduced through the juxtaposition of information provided by a variety of different sources. Admittedly, it is difficult to use our written Greek sources as a means of gaining some insight into the peasant's existence. In a fundamentally non-literate society only the most formal and official aspects of life are recorded, and mundane questions of how many people lived in one room and who did the cooking are not immediately accessible. However, bringing together some indirect reflections of the conditions of life can, I think, show that the concept of living space which the Egyptians had was, as we might expect, rather different from our own. Houses were extremely small by our standards, many people were crowded into a few rooms, there was a great deal of communal living and very little notion of privacy. There is perhaps nothing surprising about this observation, but it has never, to my knowledge, been demonstrated before, and it is a point which needs to be established if we are going to have any realistic understanding of what daily life was like for the average Egyptian peasant in the Roman period.

Although I suspect that what is going to be presented here on the subject of peasant housing is likely to have been true both before and after the Roman period – indeed, probably for most of Egypt's long history – nevertheless, the period which particularly concerns me, and for which our evidence is especially abundant and fruitful, is the early Roman period, and that will be the chronological limit of the present paper. My interest is in the everyday life of the Egyptian peasant, and the discussion here will center around housing conditions in the little villages where Greek and Roman influences were least obtrusive in the lives of the inhabitants. The evidence which forms the basis of this investigation is drawn from the villages of the Arsinoite nome, where sites like Karanis and Tebtunis, Soknopaiou Nesos and Philadelphia are well known to us from the papyri, and have yielded a great deal of material, archeological as well as papyrological, which is relevant to the matter at hand.

There are many types of Greek documents which provide evidence about Egyptian housing arrangements in the Roman period. Among property transactions we have sales of houses, contracts of rental, divisions of property, registrations of property; there are, too, many loans secured against property owned by the debtor, as well as loans where a right of habitation is given in lieu of interest. Wills and marriage contracts also record transmission of real property. Most importantly, there are census lists and numerous individual census declarations for the house-to-house census which was conducted every fourteen years in Roman Egypt in order to establish an accurate list of those liable for the poll tax. Since the householder records all of the occupants of his/her household, as well as all of the property holdings of household members, census declarations are an invaluable source of information about the number of members of a household and its social structure.[3] In addition to these Greek papyri, we also have

3. Given the range of evidence at our disposal, it is perhaps surprising that so little scholarly attention has been paid to such a fundamental question as the everyday living conditions of the native population of Egypt during the Roman period. Fritz Luckhard, in his doctoral dissertation *Das Privathaus im ptolemäischen und römischen Aegypten* (Giessen 1914), collected all of the papyrological documentation about houses that was then available (only a few houses had been excavated at that time, so the archeological evidence was very limited), and from this was able to give a preliminary but still very useful account of what could then be known about housing in Greco-Roman Egypt. In 1924 Aristide Calderini was the first to grasp the potential importance of census declarations as a source of information about the size and composition of households, and the analysis he made of this subject in his small monograph, *La composizione della famiglia secondo le schede di censimento dell'Egitto romano* (Milan 1924), forms the basis of the sociological aspect of the definitive work on the census by Marcel Hombert and Claire Préaux, *Recherches sur le recensement dans l'Egypte romaine* ( = P. Lugd.-Bat. v, Leiden 1952). Cf. also A. Calderini, *Le schede di censimento dell'Egitto Romano secondo le scoperte più recenti* (Rome 1932) and 'Nuove schede del censimento romano d'Egitto', *Aegyptus* 12 (1932) 346–54. Orsolina Montevecchi in 1941 published a lengthy article in *Aegyptus* 21 (1941) in which she collected, listed and analysed all of the sales of houses in the papyri ('Ricerche di sociologia nei documenti dell'Egitto greco-romano III. I contratti di compravendita', 93–151; cf. 287–90 of the same volume, where, in another article, 'Affitto di una casa', she lists all of the rentals of houses; cf. also *eadem, La papirologia*, 217f.). These few works are not only the *loci classici* of the subject at hand, but they remain virtually the only scholarly works which deal in any way with the sociological aspects of housing in Egypt, despite the fact that the amount of evidence has grown considerably since all of these standard works were completed. A recent article by Genevieve Husson, 'La maison privée à Oxyrhynchos aux trois premiers siècles de notre ère', *Ktema* I (1976) 5–27, discusses the architectural features of houses at Oxyrhynchos and elsewhere primarily from a philological perspective. She points to the question of the number of occupants of a house as a problem for which no conclusion can be established (25f.). Jurists have of course taken an interest in the legal implications of fractional property ownership (see above, n. 2), but they tend not to be concerned with the practicalities of everyday life, which are quite a different matter from the theoretical provisions of the law.

a growing body of archeological information about houses in Egyptian villages during the Roman period.[4] We can even get a vivid appreciation for the flavour of real life in Egyptian villages through the writings of scholars and journalists who describe modern villages, where the basic conditions of life appear to have remained astonishingly unchanged since the Pharaonic period.[5]

Today's general image of Egyptian architecture is undoubtedly shaped by the great monuments of the Pharaonic period, the pyramids of Giza or the temples at Luxor. But there is a stark contrast between housing which is fit for gods and kings, made of stone and enormous in size, built to last for eternity, and that of the humble peasant, which is as ephemeral as the man himself.[6] In reality Egypt was a country where agricultural land was at such a premium that it could not be squandered for housing purposes.[7] In Soknopaiou Nesos and Karanis, for example, the outside walls of the outer perimeter of houses constituted, in effect, the wall of the village, and access to the town was through a gate. Streets were very narrow (about $1\frac{1}{2}$ m) and the houses themselves were made, in most cases, of crude mud bricks, with wooden frames and doors.[8]

4. For Karanis see esp. A. E. R. Boak and E. E. Peterson, *Karanis: Topographical and Architectural Report of Excavations during the Seasons 1924–8* (University of Michigan Studies, Humanistic Series xxv, Ann Arbor 1931), and E. M. Husselman, *Karanis: Topography and Architecture* (University of Michigan Kelsey Museum of Archeology Series v, Ann Arbor 1979). For Soknopaiou Nesos see A. E. R. Boak, *Soknopaiou Nesos* (University of Michigan Studies, Humanistic Series xxxix, Ann Arbor 1935). For other Fayum sites, see D. J. Crawford, *Kerkeosiris: An Egyptian Village in the Ptolemaic Period* (Cambridge 1971) ch. 3 and notes.

5. For this purpose I have found the following books interesting: H. H. Ayrout, *The Egyptian Peasant* (Boston 1963); H. Ammar, *Growing up in an Egyptian Village* (New York 1966): H. Fakhouri, *Kafr El-Elow: An Egyptian Village in Transition* (New York 1966); V. Gornick, *In Search of Ali Mahmoud* (New York 1973); U. Wikan, *Life Among the Poor in Cairo* (New York 1980); R. Critchfield, *Shahhat, An Egyptian* (New York 1980).

6. This contrast is very neatly encapsulated by Eric Turner, in *Greek Papyri: An Introduction* (London and Princeton 1968) 18f., where he points out that the decipherment of the first documentary papyrus which was brought to Europe from Egypt in the late 18th century and which proved to be merely a list of men eligible for the dike corvée in A.D. 192, occurred in the same decade as Mozart's production of the Magic Flute, where Egypt is celebrated as the mysterious land of Isis and Osiris, the embodiment of wisdom and eternal truth.

7. On this point see D. J. Crawford, *Kerkeosiris*, 46.

8. Boak, *Soknopaiou Nesos*, 5–21; Husselman, *Karanis*, 67–73.

The houses appear to have been very small; from the papyrological references to house dimensions which he collected, Luckhard[9] estimated that the average size of an Egyptian house must have been between 50 and 62 m² of floor space in the villages, and even smaller in the nome metropoleis. This is about the size of a small townhouse in downtown Toronto or a one-bedroom apartment in New York.

Grenfell and Hunt, in describing the various villages of the Fayum which they excavated around the turn of the century in search of papyri, wrote in the introduction of *Fayum Towns*,[10] in a description of the village of Bakchias, that the houses of the poor were small and that they seemed to have consisted of three to six rooms, on no particular plan, one room opening onto the street and the other rooms leading into that room. This accords very well with the material presented in a recent study of housing in modern Egypt,[11] where an example is given of the typical house of the landless peasant, which is 75 m² and has three finished rooms, one more or less in back of another, with an unfinished unroofed room at the back and a long narrow yard in which the family made its own bricks for the house.

The University of Michigan excavation reports on Karanis and Soknopaiou Nesos provide much more extensive documentation about house sizes in Roman Egypt, but nothing which does not corroborate the descriptions of private houses made by these earlier scholars. At Soknopaiou Nesos the University of Michigan conducted a brief excavation in 1931/2, concentrating on two areas of private houses; in one area they unearthed four houses, and in the other an insula which contained, at its maximum level of construction in the first century, a total of eleven houses.[12] The entire insula measures only 28 by 24 m, and the largest individual house[13] occupies only 80 m² including its courtyard, with the house itself occupying only 56 m² of the property. In fact, the average

9. Luckhard, *Das Privathaus*, 16ff. and 23.
10. *Fayum Towns and Their Papyri*, eds. B. P. Grenfell, A. S. Hunt, D. G. Hogarth (London 1900) 40.
11. Mohsen Bayad, *Housing and Urban Development in Egypt* (The Royal Danish Academy of Art, School of Architecture, Foreign Students Department, FSD Publication, Series A, no. 12, Copenhagen 1979) 120f.
12. See Boak, *Soknopaiou Nesos*, Plan VI.
13. House 101.

size of the eleven houses in this insula is 57.9 m² including a court
(or 45.7 m² without the court), which is exactly within the range
suggested seventy years ago by Luckhard on the basis of the then
much more limited evidence. Many houses had second or even
third storeys; if the documents from Soknopaiou Nesos give us a
representative sample, of the houses in that village of which we
have descriptions, six are two-storeyed, three are three-storeyed,
and two are single-storeyed.[14] This shows that the most common
type of house, at least in this one village, is a structure with two
storeys. It is said[15] that the crude mud bricks which are used in
the construction of peasant housing in Egypt still today are not
strong enough to support more than two storeys, and it is likely
that the same problem existed in antiquity. A house of 46 m² which
had a second storey would still have only 92 m² of living space in
total, a rather cramped house by our standards.

The excavation report from Soknopaiou Nesos shows that three
rooms per house floor seems to have been the norm for that village,
just as it was in Bakchias according to Grenfell and Hunt's
description. The houses are not arranged in any clear plan, and
their access to the street seems to vary haphazardly according to
their location. Courtyards seem to face on the street in some cases,
and elsewhere to be situated between several houses.

The number and variety of houses at Karanis was much greater
than at Soknopaiou Nesos, partly because the village was a much
larger one (and the excavation of it more extensive), and also
because it was in existence for about two centuries after the demise
of Soknopaiou Nesos. Although it is harder to establish an average
house size for Karanis because of the variety, many of the houses
shown in the plans given in the excavation reports are similar to

14. Here and elsewhere throughout this paper I use illustrative examples
drawn from Soknopaiou Nesos because I have made a comprehensive study of
all of the papyri from this village and can therefore feel confident of the reliability
of my evidence. Although there are numerous papyri which contain references
to houses in Soknopaiou Nesos, I find only eleven houses which are specifically
described in terms of the number of storeys they have; of these there are
one-storeyed houses referred to in *P. Ryl.* II 160c and *SB* I 5247 = *P. Vind. Tand.*
25 (the same house in these two different documents), two-storeyed houses in *SB*
I 5246, *P. Ryl.* II 160a/*SB* I 5108, *SB* I 5109, *BGU* III 854, *SB* V 8950, *BGU* I 184/
*P. Strassb.* IV 208, and three-storeyed houses in *P. Ryl.* II 160b, *P. Ryl.* II 155.12f.,
*P. Ryl.* II 155.13f.

15. Bayad, *Housing and Urban Development*, 110, 215.

the houses of Soknopaiou Nesos.[16] An indication of the generally small scale of the dwellings is reflected in the final archeological report put together by Elinor Husselman from the notebooks of Enoch Peterson, the excavation director. Here she describes[17] as a '*large* [italics mine] rectangular building' a structure which measures only 15 by 9 m, including its several courtyards.

The amount of archeological evidence which is now available seems to me sufficient to justify a general statement that most private houses in Roman Egypt were extremely small. We may now proceed to consider how many people were likely to have lived together in a house which had about 60 m² of floor space per storey, or a possible total of about 120 m² for a typical two-storey dwelling.

Hombert and Préaux, in their definitive study of the census, added up the number of individuals mentioned in all the census returns available to them (a total of 688) and divided this figure by the number of households for which they had declarations (117), arriving thereby at an average household size of six people.[18] Although this statistic is valid for determining the size of individual households, as a means of establishing the number of people living under one roof it tells only part of the story.

When the head of a household made a census declaration, he not only declared the members of his household, but also listed all of their property holdings, including, in most cases, a statement of which house they lived in. In many cases, unfortunately, not all of this information is available, either because the document is fragmentary or because the text is incomplete and ambiguous. But in those cases where the declarant clearly states his living situation, it is often the case that the building in which the household lives is only part of a house, a fact of which Hombert and Préaux take no account in arriving at their estimates of household populations. For instance, in *BGU* I 154 (A.D. 159/60) the declarant is a sixteen-year-old girl who owns a half of a house and court and exedra in Karanis where she lives with her father,

16. On Karanis see Husselman, *Karanis*, esp. 67–73, 'Private Houses', and Maps 9–14. Unfortunately the printing of the plates in this volume is of such poor quality that it is virtually impossible to read the scale on most of the maps.

17. Husselman, *Karanis*, 14 and Map 11.

18. Hombert and Préaux, *Recherches*, 154.

mother, and sister, four people living in half of a house, and this despite the fact that her mother owns two houses elsewhere in the village. In *P. Lugd.-Bat.* XIII ( = *P. Select.*) 12 (A.D. 105) the declarant is a twenty-year-old man who lives with his two younger sisters in a share (*meros*), the proportion unspecified, of a house. How many other people lived in the same house? Individual census declarations do not provide this kind of information, and thus they are of limited use in establishing the living conditions of the villagers.

A more enlightening source for this purpose comes from the testimony provided by census lists, which record inhabitants house by house and thereby give an indication of how many households might have been contained under a single roof. There are about twenty-five such lists extant,[19] and of these the most lengthy and interesting documents come from a series of papyrus rolls in the collection of the British Library, published as numbers 257, 258 and 259 of *P. Lond.* II. These three rolls were all written in the same hand, and appear to have been part of the same record, although they are distinct rolls. Number 259 bears the date of year 14 of Domitian, A.D. 94/5, and the latest month named in the three rolls is Hathyr ( = 28 October–27 November), so the rolls were written in the latter part of 94. They are a series of lists giving the names, ages, and occupations, household by household, of male occupants of households of some unnamed villages in the division of Herakleides of the Arsinoite nome. Ann Hanson has, from her unpublished prosopography of Philadelphia in the first century, been able to identify the names in *P. Lond.* II 257 as coming from Philadelphia.[20] However, for our purposes here the exact identification of the location is not critical, since what is clear is that the names are those of native Egyptians, and it is also obvious from the occupations given that they are peasants, in that most of the men are identified as weavers or state farmers. The editors of the volume comment that 'the only interesting points of detail [in these rolls] relate to the occupations of the various individuals'.[21]

19. A list of these is given by Hombert and Préaux, *Recherches*, 135ff.
20. I would like to express my appreciation to Ann Ellis Hanson for this piece of information, derived from her unpublished prosopography of Philadelphia in the first century.
21. *P. Lond.* II 21.

From my point of view the most significant aspect of these rolls is that they list all of the male occupants of households between the ages of 14 and 60 (the years during which men were liable for the poll tax), and thus these documents provide an incomparable source of information about the size of households in Egyptian villages in the first century.[22] Furthermore, since each household entry is labeled by house – the heading is either οἰκία ἰδ(ία) or οἰκία(ς) μέρο(ς) ἴδ(ιον) or a specified fraction such as $\frac{1}{2}$, $\frac{1}{4}$ or $\frac{1}{3}$ of a house – by tabulating the sizes of the households in relation to the proportion of the house occupied, we are in a position to arrive at some conclusions about the density of housing occupancy in the village.

Our first step is to extrapolate from the list of males given in the London papyri some figures as to the total size of the households. A. E. R. Boak, in his article, 'The Population of Roman and Byzantine Karanis',[23] used the Egyptian census statistics for the years 1907, 1917 and 1927 to establish the relationship between men of the ages between 14 and 60 and the rest of the population. The ratios in these three census years were, respectively, 1:3.276, 1:3.163, and 1:2.862. He used the median of these, 1:3.163, as the basis for calculating the probable population of Karanis in the second century from the tax rolls published in *P. Mich.* IV. More recently, Hanna Geremek, in her monograph on Karanis in the second century,[24] which is based on a study of these same tax rolls, found that an analysis of the relation between adult men and total households in the twelve second-century census declarations from Karanis yielded the slightly higher ratio of 1:3.8, which she used as her basis for the estimation of the population of Karanis at that time. For my calculations here of the total size of households represented by the male taxpayers in the London documents I have used a middle figure of 1:3.5, between Boak's figure and Geremek's, since Geremek's ratio is

22. For the use of these London census lists as evidence for 'The Life Cycle of An Egyptian Household', see Keith Hopkins, 'Brother–Sister Marriage in Roman Egypt', *Comparative Studies in Society and History* 22 (1980) 332f. He does not, however, attempt to extrapolate the total size of the household from the numbers of adult males.

23. *Historia* 4 (1955) 159.

24. *Karanis: Communauté rurale de l'Egypte romaine au II–IIIe siècle de notre ère* (Warsaw 1969) 37ff.

based on a very small number of documents.[25] In the analysis which follows my figures are derived from *P. Lond.* II 257 alone, since it has many more complete entries than either of the two papyri which follow it. In *P. Lond.* II 257 there are 112 households listed in readable entries, and in these there are 235 men between the ages of 14 and 60. Multiplying 235 by 3.5 we arrive at a total of 822.5 people in these 112 households, which is an average of 7.34 people per household. This is slightly higher than the average figure of six per household given by Hombert/Préaux,[26] but I think the discrepancy can be accounted for by the fact that the census declarations which have survived have tended to come from slightly more prosperous families than the average, since the conditions of preservation would favour the family which had some reason to keep its papers in good order. Thus we would expect to find that families which were better off might live under somewhat less crowded conditions. In this respect again the London papyri are particularly useful, because they presumably include all households without reference to economic status, and therefore should be an accurate reflection of the population of the village at that particular moment in time.

Using our figure of 7.34 people living in an average household, let us proceed to examine the possible accommodation in which these 7.34 people were housed. As I have already indicated, each entry in *P. Lond.* II 257 is labeled to indicate whether the household occupies a house, part of a house or a specified fraction of a house.

25. The figure of 3.5 people per ancient household is also used by James E. Packer in attempting to estimate the population of ancient Ostia in 'Housing and Population in Imperial Ostia and Rome', *JRS* 57 (1967) 81–95, esp. 86 n. 55, following J. C. Russell, 'Late Ancient and Medieval Population', *Transactions of the American Philosophical Society* 48 (1958) 65 (where, incidentally, the figure of 3.5 is used not of a household, but of the average size of an ancient family). Cf. also A. R. Burn, '*Hic breve vivitur*', *Past and Present* (Nov. 1953) 2–31 and Table III p. 24, where the population of Roman Africa is estimated at 1 adult male → 3.6 total population on the basis of analogies in census data from India in 1901–10. Cf. also R. P. Duncan-Jones, 'City Population in Roman Africa', *JRS* 53 (1963) 87, making use of Burn's statistics. Bayad, *Housing and Urban Development*, 107, gives 5.2 as the national average size of a family in present-day Egypt. For comparisons with other societies see *Household and Family in Past Time*, eds. P. Laslett and R. Wall (Cambridge 1977).

26. Hombert and Préaux, *Recherches*, 154. Cf. Hopkins, 'Brother–Sister Marriage', 328f., who arrives at a figure of 5.1 people per average household, using an updated list of census documents as given by him at 312 n. 31.

When we tabulate these data, we find a total of 33 labels specifying private houses (that is, presumably, whole houses), as compared with 61 (almost double that number) indicating shares (unspecified percentages) of private houses. In addition, there is one entry for half a house, five for a quarter of a house and five for a third of a house, and there are six entries where the heading is lost in a lacuna.[27] The difference between the unspecified shares (*meros...*) and the specific fractions $(\frac{1}{2}, \frac{1}{4}, \frac{1}{3})$ is, I believe, the distinction between *communio pro indiviso* (that is, the legal designation of a portion of a physically undivided house) and *communio pro diviso* (a physically separate portion of a house).[28] In other words, in this London papyrus we see that by far the greatest number of households are situated in unspecified shares of houses, living presumably in some sort of communal arrangement with the other households under the same roof. Though we have a total of 112 households in our list, we have no way of establishing precisely the total number of houses represented by these 112 households, since we do not know how many of these unspecified shares were grouped in one house. However, if we assume that at the very least every household which occupies a *meros* must share the whole house with at least one other household, we can see that our 112 households could not represent more than 73 houses, i.e. 33 (whole houses) $+ 30\frac{1}{2}$ (half of the 61 unspecified fractions of houses) $+ 3\frac{5}{12}$ (total of specified fractions) $+ 6$ (houses with headings lost). If one compares the number of men listed for shared houses with the number listed for whole houses, one sees that shared houses have smaller households: the average number of men in shared houses is 1.8, which would represent a total household size of 6.33, whereas for whole houses the figure is 2.63, which means an average of 9.2 people per household. However, the overall occupancy of a *house* (as distinct from a household) could not have been lower than 11.27 ($= 822.5$ people divided by 73 houses). This is

27. Note that there are only 106 (of our total of 112 identifiably distinct households) which preserve the heading intact such that we can be sure whether it is a whole house or a fraction of one. Household entries with a lacuna at the critical point in the heading (i.e. where one would find the designation of a whole house or a fraction of one) occur at lines 81, 93, 219, 229, and 283 of *P. Lond.* II 257.

28. On the legal distinction between these two types of fractional ownership the *locus classicus* is E. Weiss, *APF* 4 (1908) 330–65.

a figure remarkably consistent with the figures given for Egypt in 1979,[29] which show that in rural areas the average occupancy is 3.5 people per room, or 10.5 people per average three-room house.

When one examines the names and relationships given for the males listed, one sees the same pattern of household formation that is amply attested in the census declarations, patriarchal households where grown brothers live together, with their father if he is still living, and presumably with their own wives and children.[30] Assuming that the list was drawn up in some sort of topographic sequence, then the order of households listed reflects their actual physical proximity, and we can see that similar names occur within particular sections of the list.[31] This shows that families lived close to one another, perhaps in compounds with shared facilities. Certainly a high degree of shared activity is implied by the coexistence of two households within one small six-room house with a common court which would have served as both a kitchen and a stable.[32]

A further kind of evidence for the communal life of Egyptian peasants is furnished by the documents from Soknopaiou Nesos. The information provided by all of the documents relating to property holdings in this village corroborates the picture presented by the London census rolls. Of 25 domiciles which are described in property transactions in these papyri, 8 appear to have been occupied by single owners,[33] whereas 17 have shared ownership

---

29. Bayad, *Housing and Urban Development*, 101.

30. On this point see Hopkins, 'Brother–Sister Marriage', 332f.

31. So, for example, even a common name like Herakles occurs nine times in lines 236–49, seven times in lines 44–66, four times in lines 87–95, but only a few other times throughout the long document. This points to three different family groups with members named Herakles, but suggests that family members are not scattered generally throughout the village.

32. On the use of courtyards see Boak, *Soknopaiou Nesos*, 8f.; Boak and Peterson, *Karanis*, 34f.; Husselman, *Karanis*, 49f., 67. The flavour of family life in modern Egypt is very well conveyed by V. Gornick in her journalistic account of modern Egypt (cited above, n. 5); see esp. 303f., where she describes a building in Giza where ten out of fifteen flats are occupied by members of one family.

33. Soknopaiou Nesos properties which appear to have been owned wholly by one person: *SB* I 5246 (house is sold by two brothers to one person), *SB* I 5231, *P. Ryl.* II 160c (actually a loan/mortgage where two owners sell/borrow), *P. Ryl.* II 160b (one owner sells to two brothers), *BGU* III 854, *SB* I 5117 (the description of this property is lost in a lacuna but it is a sale by one person to one other), *SB* X 10571, *P. Ryl.* II 155.13f.

(i.e. a sale of a property is not for a whole house, but for a fraction of it).[34] This is very close to the ratio of shared to wholly-occupied houses in *P. Lond.* II 257, indicating once again that it was much less common for a nuclear family to occupy a whole structure than for several extended family units to cohabit. In sales of real estate the names of the occupants of the adjacent properties are usually given. Among the 25 property descriptions from Soknopaiou Nesos, where the contiguous properties are not designated by the name of a single person they are always said to belong to a person and his siblings, or to the children of someone. There is no instance where a house is described as having two unrelated owners or occupants. This indicates just what was observed in *P. Lond.* II 257, that the basis of house occupancy was familial – and for the most part patrilinear – and that the partition of property resulting from the system of inheritance led to shared households of siblings. Further evidence of shared households may, I think, be detected in the fact that when a portion of a commonly owned property is being sold, the property is always described in terms of the neighbours of the *whole* house, and there is never any indication of the other owners or occupants of the shared house. This, I believe, reflects the fact that the house as a whole is owned by a group of related households or individuals, bound to one another by ties of kinship through common parents or grandparents. The house is not perceived as a divided entity, though individuals may own partial shares of it.

Thus far I have dealt only with the relatively straightforward question of house size and occupancy; the evidence seems clear that a great many individuals must have been accommodated in very small spaces. I turn now briefly to the more complicated but related question of shared ownership and its connection with house occupancy.[35]

34. Soknopaiou Nesos property transactions involving shares of houses: *P. Ryl.* II 160a.1–3 / *SB* I 5108 (same property in both papyri), *SB* I 5109 i 4–6, *SB* I 5109 i 6–8, *SB* I 5247.9–11 / *P. Vind. Tand.* 25.6ff. / *CPR* I 4 = *MChr.* 159 (same property in three documents), *P. Vind. Tand.* 25.4ff. / *SB* I 5247.7–9 (same property in two documents), *BGU* I 184/*P. Strassb.* IV 208 (same property), *SB* V 8952, *P. Ryl.* II 161, *SB* V 8950, *BGU* I 350, *CPR* I 11.11ff., *CPR* I 11.17ff., *P. Vind. Tand.* 26, *P. Ryl.* II 162, *P. Ryl.* II 155.12f., *P. Lond.* II 334 (p. 211), *P. Amh.* II 97.7ff., *P. Vind. Tand.* 25a.

35. The scope of the present paper does not allow me to do justice to this important topic, but I intend to make it the subject of a subsequent study. For

In a system of partible inheritance, where women can inherit equally with men, the possibilities for division of property are virtually infinite. A person could only live in one house (or part of one house) at a time, but he or she might well own parts of numerous other houses, since he/she could have inherited portions of houses through both male and female forebears on both sides of the family. What would one do with all of these fractions of properties?

One practical thing to do with dispersed real estate holdings would be to trade shares, so that partial shares in two different houses could be converted to a larger portion of a single house. There are certainly documents which attest to this kind of activity: in *CPR* I 11 (A.D. 108), for example, two brothers, Horion and Stotoëtis, trade their quarter-shares in two different houses, and Stotoëtis gives his brother 220 drachmas as well, presumably because his house share (which contained an oil works) was worth more than Horion's.

A second method of consolidating one's real estate holdings would be to marry a person whose family owned part of the same house. The high number of consanguinous marriages in Roman Egypt suggests that this practise was followed.[36]

Selling or renting a property of which you were only a partial owner would have been distinctly more complicated, since presumably the living conditions would not have been entirely appropriate for the cohabitation of totally unrelated families. In fact, there is virtually no rental market for housing in the villages of the Fayum during the early Roman period, a situation which still pertains in the rural areas of Egypt today.[37] There are, to be sure, a certain number of contracts for house rental,[38] but these

the purpose at hand I wish only to suggest some of the most obvious implications behind commonly-owned property.

36. The statistics adduced by Hombert and Préaux indicate that as many as 25% of Egyptian marriages were consanguinous (149ff.). Cf. Hopkins, 'Brother–Sister Marriage', esp. 322, who is disinclined to accept the view that property considerations could offer an explanation for brother–sister marriages in Egypt, though he does not take into account the possibility that the census declarations from which he draws his evidence would be biased in favour of property-owning families (on this point, see above, p. 220). See now also N. Lewis, *Life in Egypt under Roman Rule* (Oxford 1983) 43 and 216 n. 8.

37. Bayad, *Housing and Urban Development*, 109, 113.

38. See Montevecchi, *Aegyptus* 21 (1941) 287ff. and *La papirologia*, 217f.

are mostly for commercial structures – an oil works or a granary or a laundry, any of which would have encompassed a whole building. The absence of rental housing can best be seen by examining the entries recorded in the archives of the Tebtunis grapheion in the first century, those papyri which were published in *P. Mich.* II and V. Here, in a complete record of all of the transactions which occurred in this record office during twenty months in the years A.D. 42–46 (*P. Mich.* II 121v, 123, 238), which presumably reflect the whole spectrum of the contractual life of the village, we find only two possible entries (among a total of some 1,200 transactions) for rental of houses, and in both of these the texts are undoubtedly incorrectly restored.[39]

Among sales of portions of houses it is very hard to establish conclusively the extent to which sales are between relatives, except in cases where it is stated explicitly. Among the 17 Soknopaiou Nesos contracts which involve the sale of shared property, four are sold by one relative to another,[40] at least one is actually a mortgage (i.e., a loan secured against a property),[41] and in a further seven cases two of the contracting parties have a name in common and are very likely to belong to the same family.[42] It may well be that many of the apparent sales of partial properties, particularly in cases where the fraction is small, are in fact mortgages of which we have not received the loan portion of the document, a possibility suggested by Montevecchi many years ago.[43] It is hard to imagine how one could either occupy or rent out $\frac{1}{27}$th of a property in any real sense, but one can imagine converting that theoretical share into an amount of cash. In this way women especially would have been able to apply their inherited property toward the everyday cash needs of their husband's household. So, for example, we find in a well-known census declaration from

39. *P. Mich.* II 123r xvi 36: [μίσθωσις]...ψιλοῦ τόπου and *P. Mich.* II 123r xvii 6: [μισ]θό(σεως) οἰκία(ς).
40. *P. Ryl.* II 161, *CPR* I 11.11f., *CPR* I 11.17f., *P. Ryl.* II 155.12f.
41. *SB* I 5109 i 4–6.
42. E.g. *SB* v 8952 where Thaësis daughter of Pisais sells her share of a house to Pisais son of Kalatytes; the two are undoubtedly of the same family, but their relationship is not stated in the contract. See also *SB* I 5109, *P. Lond.* II 334 (p. 211), *SB* I 5246, *P. Vind. Tand.* 25 / *SB* I 5247.4ff., *P. Vind. Tand.* 25.6ff. / *SB* I 5247.9ff. / *CPR* I 4, *P. Ryl.* II 160 d i 4f.
43. Montevecchi, *Aegyptus* 21 (1941) 105f.

Bakchias, that Tapekusis the wife of Horos, whose husband and brother-in-law together own merely one-quarter of the house in which they all live in A.D. 119, manages somehow to garner financial resources that enable her in the following year to lend 300 drachmas,[44] secured against a relatively large property of 120 m²,[45] a property probably larger than the space in which she herself lives with her own extended family.

A further indication of the function of property holdings as a means of securing ready cash is, I think, to be found in the large number of loans where a right of habitation (*enoikesis*) in the house of the debtor is given in lieu of the usual interest. There are a number of these contracts extant,[46] but the proportion of such contracts in the grapheion records from Tebtunis is striking, particularly in the absence of any contracts for house rental in the same archive. Among 800 contracts of all kinds registered in *P. Mich.* II 123 there are 35 *enoikesis* contracts, in *P. Mich.* II 238 there are 17 such documents among 239 entries, and in *P. Mich.* II 121v there are 11 among 247 entries. Although the grapheion entries do not contain further information about the property involved, an examination of the extant contracts for *enoikesis* suggests that such transactions most often involved portions of commonly-owned properties: *P. Oxy.* VIII 1105 is a loan of 400 dr. secured against *enoikesis* in ⅗ of a commonly-owned house; in *P. Hamb.* I 30 the borrower of 600 dr. grants *enoikesis* for five years in two-thirds of the three-fourths of a property that she owns.

A single commonly-owned property in Bakchias is the subject of five different *enoikesis* loans over a period of fifty years (A.D. 71–123) through which we can trace its history.[47]

We know that *enoikesis* loans generally contained the provision that the property in question would pass to the lender if the debt

44. The documents are *P. Mich.* III 178 (one of three consecutive census returns from the same family) and 188.

45. See *P. Mich.* X 584.

46. On *enoikesis* see Taubenschlag, *Law of Greco-Roman Egypt*, 288; *BASP* 7 (1970) 13f. = *SB* XII 10779; *P. Mich.* X 585; *P. Mich.* XI 605, with their respective introductions and the references contained therein.

47. The five are: *SB* XII 10779 (A.D. 71), *P. Mich.* X 585 (A.D. 87), *P. Mich.* XI 605 (A.D. 117), *P. Mich.* III 188 (A.D. 120) and *P. Mich.* III 189 (A.D. 123). A full discussion of this interesting and important archive would take me far beyond the bounds of this paper. See also above, nn. 44, 45.

were not paid within a specified period of time. What we do not know is whether the right of habitation was actually exercised by the lender, and if so, what implications such temporary occupation of premises might have had for housing conditions. Was the *enoikesis* loan a *de facto* lease in which the rental money was provided when the contract was drawn up, or was it in effect a lease with the option to buy? It seems significant that such contracts often relate to partial properties or small portions of buildings, rather than to separate premises.[48] Perhaps the borrower simply loaned out whatever portion of his property was of the value of the money he needed to borrow. In this way he could take several loans on a single property at different times. Or perhaps he simply provided a temporary lodging in his own household to a creditor. On the basis of available evidence it is difficult to obtain any certain picture of the relationship between these *enoikesis* contracts and the actual living arrangements of Egyptian villagers, and I can do little more for the moment than point to some of the possibilities which the contracts suggest.

It remains to comment on the value of these small and crowded Egyptian houses. House prices are remarkably inconsistent, but of course we have no way of knowing the size of the property in most cases, which might perhaps explain the variations in amounts.[49] The range at Soknopaiou Nesos is from a low of 60 drachmas for half a house in A.D. 159 (*P. Ryl.* II 162) to a high of 500 dr. for ⅓ of a house, court and atrium (*BGU* I 350, Trajan). Among the thirteen documents of the first two centuries which contain information about house prices at Soknopaiou Nesos,[50] the mean

48. For example, in *P. Oslo* III 118 (A.D. 111/12) *enoikesis* is given for occupancy of a οἰκίδιον μονόστεγον, in *SB* v 7664 (A.D. 109) it is for a οἰκίδιον and αὐλύδριον, in *BGU* VI 1273 and 1280 (both 3rd c. B.C.) there are references to a πύργον.

49. For a list of house prices, see A. C. Johnson, *Roman Egypt to the Reign of Diocletian*, vol. II of *An Economic Survey of Ancient Rome*, ed. T. Frank (Baltimore 1936) 257ff. The list of house sales given there is supplemented at *P. Mich.* x 22.

50. The following is a list of house sales from Soknopaiou Nesos which include prices: *BGU* I (A.D. 72), ⅑ house/court for 60 dr.; *SPP* XXII 175 (A.D. 78), ½ house for 140 dr.; *BGU* XI 2098 (A.D. 83), ½ of one-storey house/court for 160 dr.; *P. Ryl.* II 107 (*ca* A.D. 84) ¾ of ½ house/court for 200 dr.; *SB* v 8950 (A.D. 82–96), ½ house for 160 dr.; *BGU* I 350 (A.D. 98–117), ⅓ of house/court/atrium for 500 dr.; *P. Fay.* 100 (A.D. 99), ½ of house/court/rooms (τόποι) for 600 dr.; *P. Vind. Tand.* 26 (A.D. 143), ⅓ of house/court for 80 dr.; *BGU* II 446 (after A.D. 158/9), ⅓ of court and 1½ arouras for 800 dr.; *P. Ryl.* II 162 (A.D. 159), ½ of house/court

price is 360 drachmas for a whole house. When one compares this figure with the mean sum of 200 drachmas for a loan with habitation rights in the entries recorded in the Tebtunis grapheion of the first century, one might conclude that it was relatively more lucrative, at least in the short run, to take a loan secured against a part of a property than to sell the whole house.

An interesting context within which to place housing prices at Soknopaiou Nesos is to compare them with the cost of camels, another frequently sold possession. In the twenty sales at Sokno-paiou Nesos which state the price,[51] we find an average cost of 600 drachmas for a camel. Camels were only occasionally owned jointly by several people, whereas with houses this was the common situation. Thus it is clear that more people could afford to own a piece of real estate than a camel. The mere fact that state farmers, the lowest element on the social scale, were able to afford even a part of a house is in itself a testimony to the low value of ordinary real estate.[52]

The evidence I have presented here enables us to understand more clearly the relationship between house and household in villages of Roman Egypt, and thus to gain some appreciation of the living conditions of the native peasants at least during the first two centuries of Roman rule. The average Egyptian peasant was likely to share a house and its attached court/stable/kitchen with other branches of his family; he might also rent space in his house to non-relatives in order to generate some cash. At the same time he or she might own shares in other houses in the neighbourhood, which would probably be occupied by other relatives.[53] But he lived mostly out of doors, and his sense of place was not therefore bound by the confines of a single building, just as his land, if he

for 60 dr.; *P. Lond.* II 334 (A.D. 166) $\frac{1}{42}$ of house for 20 dr.; *P. Amh.* II 97 (A.D. 180–92), $\frac{1}{3}$ of house/court/oil press for 120 dr.; *SB* X 10571 (A.D. 194), house/court for 500 dr.

51. A list of all camel sales in papyri is given at *P. Vindob. Worp.* 9.

52. On this point see Montevecchi, *Aegyptus* 21 (1941) 104f. In this connection it is probably significant that women owned a great deal of real estate in Roman Egypt (on which see my article, 'Women as Property Owners in Roman Egypt', *TAPA* 113 (1983) 311–21), whereas they appear less prominently as camel owners.

53. See Lee Horne, 'The Household in Space: Dispersed Holdings in an Iranian Village', *American Behavioral Scientist* 25.6 (July/August 1982) 677–85.

had any, was outside the village wall, and not connected to the place where he slept at night. When he identified himself for official purposes he might give his name, the names of his father and mother and paternal grandfather, but he did not refer to the house where he lived. Family and village were integral units and they might extend indefinitely in time, but house properties were fractional and ephemeral, vulnerable to decay and dissolution. An individual house might provide shelter for a household, or even for two, and it might perhaps serve as a visible symbol of a family's worth, but it was a far cry from our idea of home.

# Donatio ante nuptias and Jewish dowry additions

RANON KATZOFF

About half a century ago it was suggested by A. Gulak that the rules in Jewish legal texts of the early centuries of this era requiring husbands to add to their wives' dowries could be identified with analogous arrangements known from non-Jewish sources, including contemporary papyri. In particular the Jewish rules could be seen as part of the background for the rules on *donatio ante nuptias* laid down by Justinian in *Novella* 97.[1] The possibility Gulak raises has implications in various directions. For the study of Roman law it would demonstrate a specific oriental influence precisely in an institution where such influence has been the subject of considerable debate.[2] For the study of Jewish law it would represent an instance of foreign influence, as Gulak puts it, or, stated more conservatively, an instance where a Jewish legal institution is supported by the practice of neighboring gentiles.[3] For the study

1. Asher Gulak, 'Ältere talmudische Parallelen zur Novelle 97 des Kaisers Justinian', *Zeitschrift für vergleichende Rechtswissenschaft* 47 (1933) 241–55; repeated with some change in emphasis in *Das Urkundenwesen im Talmud in Lichte der griechisch-aegyptischen Papyri und des griechischen und roemischen Rechts* (Jerusalem 1935) 63–75.

Much of the material in the present study is found in a different form in my Hebrew supplementary notes to the Hebrew translation of the Gulak article due to appear in the forthcoming volume of *Shenaton Hamishpat Ha'ivri. Annual of the Institute for Research in Jewish Law, The Hebrew University of Jerusalem*, hereunder referred to as 'Hebrew Notes'. The study was undertaken under the auspices of the Institute for Research in Jewish Law, and supported in part by the Memorial Foundation for Jewish Culture. I wish to express here my gratitude to both.

2. Standard accounts of the development of *donatio ante nuptias* in Roman law, and of the controversy concerning it, are Max Kaser, *Das römische Privatrecht*[2] (Handbuch der Altertumswissenschaft 10.3.3) II (Munich 1975) 193–201; Percy Ellwood Corbett, *The Roman Law of Marriage* (Oxford 1930) 205–10.

3. The standard detailed English account of the relevant Jewish institutions is Louis M. Epstein *The Jewish Marriage Contract. A Study in the Status of the Woman in Jewish Law* (New York 1927), particularly 102–6. A recent summary account with bibliography is Ben-Zion Schereschewsky, s.v. Dowry, *Encyclopedia Judaica* VI (Jerusalem 1971) 185–89, reprinted in Menachem Elon (ed.), *The Principles*

of papyrology this would afford an opportunity to assess the degree
to which conclusions drawn from papyri found in Egypt are
generalizable to neighboring provinces of the Roman empire.[4]
Though Gulak's suggestion has been noted from time to time,[5] it
does not seem to have undergone a critical review. It is the purpose
of the present study to attempt such an examination. It is not
intended to address the more general issues raised above, but
rather to assess the degree to which the texts cited by Gulak
support his thesis.

# I

Gulak's thesis can be summarized thus. Justinian established in
*Novella* 97, dated 539,[6] that in every marriage the *donatio ante nuptias*
must equal the dowry. The *donatio ante nuptias*, it will be recalled,
is a settlement the husband makes on the wife, a sum of money
or goods which he gives or promises her at the time of the marriage
on the understanding that the disposition of these goods at the time
of the dissolution of the marriage will be the same as that of the
dowry which she gives him. Like the dowry, the *donatio ante nuptias*
may come from the parent rather than from the spouse. Justinian
also provided that such a *donatio* may also be set up during the
course of the marriage, forming an exception to the general rule
voiding gifts between spouses, and accordingly changed the name
of the institution to *donatio propter nuptias*.[7] The institution of *donatio
ante nuptias* itself, though not classical, was not an invention of
Justinian, but rather was in use for at least two centuries before
his time. More to the point here is that the rule requiring parity

*of Jewish Law* (Jerusalem 1974) 390–94. Much valuable information particularly
pointing to later periods is found in Mordechai Friedman, *Jewish Marriage in
Palestine. A Cairo Geniza Study* 1: *The* Ketubba *Traditions of Eretz Israel* (Tel Aviv
1980).

4. For the papyri, Raphael Taubenschlag, *The Law of Greco-Roman Egypt in
Light of the Papyri, 332* B.C.*–640* A.D.[2] (Warsaw 1955, repr. Milan 1972) 127–29.

5. E.g. A. Steinwenter, *ZSav* 56 (1936) 383; Eduardo Volterra, *Diritto romano
e diritti orientali* (Bologna 1937) 248; Saul Lieberman, *Tosefta Ki-Fshutah. A
Comprehensive Commentary to the Tosefta* VI (New York 1967) 251; Kaser, *op. cit.*
(n. 2) 199 n. 54.

6. All dates given are A.D.

7. For brevity's sake, I will use the term *donatio ante nuptias* for both *donatio ante*
and *donatio propter nuptias*.

of dowry and *donatio ante nuptias* is not entirely an invention of Justinian either.

Of particular interest to Gulak's thesis is a passage which appears in some of the versions of the Syro-Roman Law Book, enunciating the same rule of parity. Here we are told that a law of the king requires that the husband bring the same amount in his wedding gift[8] as the wife brings in dowry,[9] in money or in goods of any sort. While parity is the custom in the West, the custom in the East is that the husband brings half of what the wife brings as dowry.[10]

Both these customs, says Gulak, are attested in rabbinic literature. The traditional Jewish practice, he says, is that of a statutorily required increase of 50%. This appears in *Mishna Ketubot* 6.3.[11] 'If the woman undertook to bring in to her husband one thousand denars, over against this he must assign to her (as her *ketubah*)[12] fifteen minas [i.e. 1,500 denars], but over against goods (which she undertakes to bring in), estimated to be of a certain value, he rates it at one fifth less... 4. If she undertook to

8. *dōreā* transliterated into Syriac.

9. *phernē* transliterated into Syriac.

10. The manuscripts vary somewhat in their expressions for West and East. P40 and R11 51: 'In the city of the kingdom [i.e. in the capital] and all places in the West...In the land of the realm of the East.' R1 31: 'In the land of the Romans.... In the land of the realm of the East.' This East–West division has been variously interpreted as that between the Western and Eastern Empires, between the two prefectures of the Eastern Empire, and between the Byzantine and Sassanid Empires. E. Sachau, *Syrische Rechtsbücher* 1: *Leges Constantini Theodosii Leonis* (Berlin 1907) 187. The geographical interpretation is related to the dating of the original Greek work and of its Syriac translation. Gulak does not discuss the interpretation of East–West, and appears to assume the conventional dating to 476–77. He mentions Mitteis' urging of post-Justinian interpolations, but not the possibility of substantial revisions in the eighth century suggested by Nallino and Volterra. For this see Eduardo Volterra, 'Il libro siro-romano nelle recenti ricerche', *Atti del convegno internazionale sul tema: l'Oriente cristiano nella storia della civiltà* (Rome 1964) 297–328.

11. The dissenting, or interpreting, opinion of Rabban Shimeon ben Gamliel, second third of the second century, if originally said in this context, serves as a *terminus ad quem*. In the absence of evidence to the contrary the anonymous opinion may be ascribed to the contemporary Rabbi Meir.

12. *Ketubah* may mean the marriage document, the financial obligations at the termination of the marriage which the husband undertakes therein, or the statutory one hundred or two hundred *zuz* which form the kernel of these obligations, but are usually overshadowed by the dowry. In the translation of the *Mishna* quoted here the second meaning is intended.

bring him in ready money, one silver sela [i.e. four denars] shall count as six denars. The bridegroom undertakes to give her ten denars as pin-money for every mina (that she brings in). Rabban Shimeon ben Gamliel says: In all things they should follow local custom.'[13] That such 'fictive' dowries, or dowry evaluations, were customary in the orient is evidenced, Gulak says, by clauses in papyrus dowry documents[14] specifying that 'nothing has been added', and that they were known to Roman law from efforts taken to void such arrangements.

On the other hand, Gulak believes, a custom of requiring a 100% dowry increase by the husband entered the Jewish community later and is evidenced by a polemical statement against it in a *beraita* by Rabbi Yossi which appears in several places.[15] 'Where the local custom is to make the *ketuba* a loan, it is collected as a loan; where the custom is to double it, half is collected.'[16] The second half of the *beraita* implies that some localities had a custom of doubling the dowry, in other words, that the husband increased the amount of the dowry he received by 100% rather than by the 50% prescribed by the *Mishna*. Rabbi Yossi so objected to this deviation that he voided the arrangement entirely.

Since fictitiously high recording of a dowry can be juristically resolved as a gift on the part of the husband on the same terms as the dowry, Gulak is able to find in rabbinic literature both practices recorded in the Syro-Roman Law Book – gifts equalling 50% and 100% of the dowry.

## II

A re-examination of the evidence, however, leads to some misgivings. How similar are the institutions which Gulak compares, and do all the texts indeed say what he took them to mean?

13. Translation adapted from Danby.

14. *P. Oxy.* II 267.8 = *M. Chr.* 281 (A.D. 36); *P. Oxy.* X 1273.16 = *Sel. Pap.* I 5 (A.D. 260).

15. *Tosefta Ketubot* 4.13 *Yerushalmi Yevamot* 15.3.14d *Yerushalmi Ketubot* 4.8.29a *Bavli Bava Metzia* 104b. Rabbi Yossi *floruit* second third of the second century. In the first reference cited the author is given as Rabbi Yossi the Galilean, *floruit* first third of the second century.

16. I have translated the version with impersonal plural verbs which appear in two manuscripts of the *Tosefta* to avoid prejudicing Gulak's argument.

First there appears to be a significant difference between the economic functions of the Roman *donatio ante nuptias* and the Jewish dowry increases. The Roman *donatio ante nuptias* in principle is delivered at the beginning of the marriage. Admittedly, variations are possible. The husband may promise to deliver the *donatio* at some later date. The family of the bride may lend him the money to give her as *donatio*.[17] This, however, does not detract from the main purpose of the *donatio*, to specify the husband's, or his family's, contribution to the wealth of the common household, or, insofar as the payment goes to the bride's family, to serve as payment for the bride.

The Jewish dowry increases, on the other hand, not only are not normally delivered at the beginning of the marriage, but, on the contrary, constitute an obligation to pay only after the dissolution of the marriage. Thus they neither contribute to the standard of living of the household nor are they ever delivered to the wife's family.

What the purpose of the 50% increase required by *Mishna Ketubot* 6.3 is may be ascertained from the context of that rule. Specifically, the increase is only required on such part of the dowry as is given in cash. When, on the other hand, the dowry is given in goods, not only is the husband not obligated to increase it, but on the contrary he may enter it in the document at a fifth less than the assessed value. The explanation for this is given by Rabbi Yossi ben Hanina in the *Talmud Yerushalmi, ad loc.* It is presumed that the woman wishes to use the articles included in the dowry and accepts a depreciation of one fifth: and that the man wishes to invest the money of the dowry and accepts a 50% surcharge (or to put it more precisely, accepts the risk of having to pay a surcharge should the conditions under which the dowry must be paid obtain). The principle that the husband obligates himself to pay the 50% surcharge in return for the ability to use the dowry for his profit, while not stated explicitly, also lies behind the deliberations of the *Talmud Bavli, Ketubot* 67a, in which the surcharge obligation is applied also to such dowry goods other than cash as are normally traded.[18]

17. Something like this appears to have occurred in *P. Lond.* v 1708, dated in the second half of the sixth century.

18. Rashi *ad loc.* The quotations in the Bavli passage date from the mid second to early third centuries.

The 50% increase, then, is a way of charging the husband for the use of the dowry money which nonetheless will not fall under the rules forbidding usury.[19] If this surcharge, as it should now be seen, is to be related to any non-Jewish practice it should be to the *hēmiolion*, the 50% penalty frequently imposed in Greek marriage contracts, as in other contracts, for failure of immediate payment of the obligation.[20]

Secondly, there are juristic differences which may be considered. Despite the possible juristic resolution mentioned above, the degree of similarity may be assessed by the following considerations. The functional goal of providing the wife at the end of the marriage with an obligation on the part of the husband to an extent larger than that given to him as dowry may be achieved by several juristically distinct modes, which include the following:

Mode 1. The marriage document asserts that the bride, or her family, gave the groom more than was in fact given.

Mode 2. The husband (or groom) explicitly adds from his own funds or goods to his wife's (or bride's) dowry.

Mode 3. The husband gives his wife a gift on the understanding that it will be added to the dowry (*donatio ante nuptias in dotem redacta*).

Mode 4. The husband gives his wife a gift and the law applies to it the incidents of dowry (*donatio ante nuptias*).

To these we may add a fifth type of practice: writing in the marriage document an amount which was not in fact given, and with no intention that it functionally increase the dowry. We may term this Mode 0.[21]

When examining the evidence in light of these distinctions we immediately notice that the effective dotal increase in the *donatio ante nuptias* in Justinian's legislation and its Roman antecedents is, of course, Mode 4. The dotal increase in *Mishna Ketubot* 6.3, on the other hand, is Mode 1.

Was Mode 1 common to the Roman and Hellenistic world as

19. For the reason it is indeed not considered usury, see Lieberman, *op. cit.* (n. 5) 251 n. 95 and 276, and the literature cited there.

20. Cf. Mitteis, *Grundzüge*, 226.

21. For illustrations of each mode in rabbinic literature see 'Hebrew Notes', *op. cit.* (n. 1).

well? In Roman law such a fiction would be entirely impossible. That is not to say that there were no attempts to make dowries seem larger than they were in fact. Daube has reconstructed from classical sources a case of a bridegroom who gave his bride a gift on the understanding that it would be added to the dowry, no doubt to make it seem that he succeeded in landing a more richly dowered wife than he in fact did. The second-century jurist Julianus voided the attempt, declaring that there was here neither gift nor dowry (Mode 3 fails).[22] A constitution of Severus and Caracalla allows this sort of transaction, but only if the property actually passed to the wife before the constitution of the dowry (Mode 3 succeeds, Mode 2 fails).[23] If the goods were given by the husband to the wife, for the purpose of increasing the dowry, during the course of the marriage, again the transaction fails, as being contrary to the rule voiding gifts between spouses.[24] In brief, 'Delivery not the writing of the document creates the dowry.'[25] Constitutions to this effect were also issued in the sixth century. The defense, *exceptio non numeratae pecuniae*, will be available to a husband who claims that the dowry was not in fact delivered to him.[26] This defense received its own name *exceptio non numeratae dotis* (Mode 1 fails).[27] In *P. Cair. Isid.* 62, dated 296, the assertion is made that 'the laws' require assessment of the dotal goods by a goldsmith and a tailor. 'The laws' at that period presumably indicates imperial constitutions. If the assertion is true we have yet another indication of the rejection of Mode 1 dowry increases.

In contrast to the clarity of the Roman legal sources, the papyri do not afford a clear picture. This is the result of the paucity of legal literature in Egypt. We do have many marriage documents among the papyri.[28] However, if a dowry is fictive, in whole or

22. David Daube, *Roman Law: Linguistic, Social, and Philosophical Aspects* (Edinburgh 1969) 109–12.

23. *C.*5.3.1, not dated explicitly, but clearly from near the beginning of the third century.

24. *C.*5.15.2, dated 230.

25. *C.*5.15.1, dated 204.

26. *C.*5.15.3, dated 528. The language of the constitution implies that this point in and of itself is not new.

27. *C.* 4.30.14.6, dated 528. Kaser, *op. cit.* (n. 2) 193.

28. For a listing, Orsolina Montevecchi, *Aegyptus* 16 (1936) 4–6, and *La papirologia* (Turin 1973) 203–6.

in part (Mode 1), the document can hardly be expected to say so. Nonetheless, it has been argued from time to time that fictitious dowries were practised in Egypt. This was asserted in the nineteenth century by Wessely and especially by Mitteis.[29] Their argument rested primarily on *CPR* I 23, a fragmentary receipt written by a woman stating that she received her dowry from her husband. The editor, Wessely, restored the lacuna so that the receipt appeared to have been written before the marriage. The husband himself, then, supplied the dowry (Mode 3). It was also argued that this showed continuity from ancient Egyptian practice. At the end of the century, however, Grenfell and Hunt disposed of these arguments entirely, restoring *CPR* I 23 on the analogy of *P. Oxy.* II 266 so that it turned out to have been written at the time of divorce, and raising doubts as to the reliability of the Egyptological evidence.[30] Mitteis himself conceded later that there was no basis for the view that in Egypt fictive dowries were practised.[31]

The issue of fictitious dowries in Roman Egypt was raised again recently by E. Seidl.[32] Seidl claims first that although ancient Egyptian law recognized a defense similar to the Roman *exceptio non numeratae pecuniae*, Demotic marriage documents do not show the same attitude (Mode 1 succeeds). Secondly, a group of Roman documents from Egypt, two prefectural decrees and two imperial, point to a frequent practice of fictitious dowries, which the Romans tried to suppress. The Roman documents are the following: (1) *P. Catt.* r i 5–13: In a trial dated 117, where a woman claims a deposit from the estate of her late husband, a soldier, the prefect decides that the deposit is really a dowry, and, says Seidl, he appoints a *iudex* to examine the facts, suspecting that in fact the deposit was never given to the soldier (Mode 1). (2) The prefect

29. Ludwig Mitteis, *Reichsrecht und Volksrecht in östlichen Provinzen des römischen Kaiserreichs* (Leipzig 1891, repr. Hildesheim 1963) 274–83.

30. *P. Oxy.* II 266, introd. pp. 239–41; *P. Teb.* II 386 introd.

31. Mitteis, *Grundzüge*, 223.

32. Erwin Seidl, *Rechtsgeschichte Ägyptens als römischen Provinz* (Sankt Augustin 1973) 220–21; *idem*, 'Zur Vorgeschichte der Exceptio non Numeratae Dotis', *Festschrift...Kaser* (Munich 1976) 609–14. Seidl cites Gunther Häge, *Eheguterrechtliche Verhältnisse in den griechischen Papyri Ägyptens bis Diokletian* (Gräzistische Abhandlungen 3, Köln–Graz 1968), but I have not found there support for Seidl's thesis.

Tiberius Julius Alexander in the edict *Hibis* 4 = *OGIS* 669, citing imperial and prefectural decrees, establishes that women have a preferred claim (*prōtopraxia*) against the treasury in collecting from their husbands' confiscated property, their dowries 'which belong to others and not to the husbands who received them (τὰς μὲν γὰρ προῖκας ἀλλοτρίας οὔσας καὶ οὐ τῶν εἰληφότων ἄνδρων, 25)'. Seidl considers the implication of 'which belong to others, ἀλλο- τρίας οὔσας' to be that women will have a preferred claim only if the dowry was set up by someone other than the husband. If, however, the dowry was set up by the husband himself (Mode 2), the wife will not have this preferred claim. (3) *P. Cair. Isid.* 62, mentioned above, indicates that such imperial intervention was necessary. (4) *C.* 5.15.1, in which Septimius Severus enunciates the rule that only delivery makes dowry, was published in 204, not long after Severus' return from Egypt, and is addressed to 'Dionysia', a common name in Egypt.

However, in none of these instances is the presence of a fictive dowry demonstrable. (1) In *P. Catt.* the prefect is more likely denying the action, because it concerns a dowry in a soldier's, hence in a forbidden marriage.[33] Even on Seidl's reading that the prefect grants the action, in the absence of any hint in the papyrus of the claims of the defendant it is arbitrary to say that it was a claim of *non numeratae dotis* which concerned the prefect. (2) Nearly all who have written on *OGIS* 669 have understood ἀλλοτρίας οὔσας as a non-restrictive modifier. All dowries are alien to the husbands, whether in the sense that title to the dotal goods is vested in the wife or in the sense that economically they are to serve ultimately the interests of the wives, and for that reason are separable from the rest of the husbands' confiscated property.[34] (3) The requirement recorded in *P. Cair. Isid.* 62 for professional estimates of dotal goods is most naturally interpreted as intended to prevent frauds, disappointed husbands, and subsequent marital strife. It seems less likely that the Roman emperor intervened to prevent a mutually agreed fiction to which none of the parties objected. (4) There is little to connect *C* 5.15.1 with Egypt. The

33. Ranon Katzoff, 'Judicial Reasoning in PCatt: Fraus legi', *Transactions of the American Philological Association* 101 (1971) 241–52.

34. G. Chalon, *L'Édit de Tiberius Julius Alexander* (Olten–Lausanne 1964) 140–43; Häge, *op. cit.* (n. 32) 146–48.

significant impression Severus' visit left on law in Egypt, and the considerable employment its documentation has afforded papyrologists, do not imply that Egyptian legal concerns made an equally lasting impression on Severus. In any case, as Seidl himself observes, Dionysia was a common enough name outside of Egypt as well.

### III

The second rabbinic text quoted by Gulak, the *beraita* of Rabbi Yossi, poses serious problems of interpretation.[35] He interprets the first half – 'Where the local custom is to make the *ketuba* a loan, it is collected as a loan' – as meaning that where the *causa* of the obligation is not phrased as that of a *ketuba* but of a loan, the wife will collect it when it becomes due to her according to the rules applying to loans rather than those applying to *ketuba*. Presumably the result would be that the woman would be in a better position to collect from the better land of the estate, to collect from inheritances due to the estate, and against other creditors in case of insolvency, according to some opinions. It would put her in a worse position vis-à-vis debts due to the estate, according to other opinions, and the debt could be cancelled by the sabbatical year. There are indeed cases in the Talmudic literature in which it is explicit that novation extinguishes the incidences of the original debt, and *a fortiori* one would expect that to be true when the original debt is phrased as a loan. Rav Hai Gaon (939–1038), who offers this interpretation, goes so far as to say that the woman could collect even during the course of the marriage. This last is an eccentric position, which is credible only if it is limited to the dowry and additions, but excludes the basic *ketuba* debt of two hundred *zuz*, since by the time of Rav Hai it was settled law that a couple may not live together without this basic obligation. Admittedly this distinction between the basic *ketuba* debt and all else in the *ketuba* document would fit the wording of the *beraita* as it appears in the *Tosefta* – 'loan is collected, not *ketuba*'.

On the other hand, this interpretation was subjected to severe criticism by medieval commentators. For one thing, the parallel

35. For further details in connection with the discussion of this text, as well as references to the medieval commentators and some modern literature in Hebrew, I refer the reader to 'Hebrew Notes', *op. cit.* (n. 1).

structure of the two parts of the *beraita* would lead one to expect them to be complementary, which they are not in the interpretation of Rav Hai. Secondly, this interpretation is possible only if it is the woman who collects. Now in the version of the *beraita* in two manuscripts of the *Tosefta* the verbs are impersonal plural; in the version in the *Talmud Bavli* the lack of vocalization leaves the gender of the verb indeterminate.[36] These versions, then, can tolerate the interpretation that the wife collects. However, in the versions in a third manuscript of the *Tosefta* and in two separate passages of the *Talmud Yerushalmi* the verb in the second half is unequivocally masculine.[37] The reference can only be to the husband collecting the dowry from the bride's father. Since the verbs of the two halves presumably have the same subject – there is no indication of change of subject – in the first half it must be the husband collecting as well.

These considerations lead to the interpretation given by Rashi[38] and most subsequent commentators, who take the two halves as complementary. Where the local custom is to *treat* the writing of the *ketuba* as that of a loan, that is to say, to write exactly the amount actually given, then the groom will receive the dowry from the bride's father exactly as written. Where, on the other hand, the local custom is to write in the *ketuba* double what is given, the groom will collect from the father of the bride half of what was written.[39]

In some localities, then, it was customary to write in the dowry clause of marriage documents exaggerated sums. Everyone involved understood that these fanciful amounts were part of the festivities, and they were not taken seriously by anyone. The

36. It is apparently the version of the *Talmud Bavli* that Gulak had in mind, though curiously he refers only to the others.

37. See Lieberman, *op. cit.* (n. 5) 250.

38. *Talmud Bavli, ad loc.* It is not clear to me why Epstein ascribes to Rashi the interpretation 'the bride's father offering, instead of a real dowry, a note of indebtedness as his daughter's marriage portion'.

39. A middle position takes the two halves as complementary, the first half as in Rav Hai and the second as in Rashi. Accordingly, if the document is explicitly phrased as a loan it will be collected by the wife at its full face value, even if inflated. So RaBaD, and in modern times Epstein, *op. cit.* (n. 3) 104: Friedman, *op. cit.* (n. 3) 305 n. 64. This interpretation still faces the problem of the gender of the verbs, and is not without theoretical difficulties as well. It does not, however, detract from my thesis.

pericope in *Talmud Bavli Bava Metzia* on this *beraita* records this as a current custom, as well as a custom of multiplying the true sum by three.[40] The custom is well documented in post-Talmudic times, when it understandably caused considerable litigation.[41]

Rabbi Yossi, then, is not forbidding a practice of the groom contributing a 100% increase to the dowry. Rather he is noting the fact that there are localities in which it is customary to write in the marriage documents fanciful sums as dowries which are not intended to be taken literally. He decides that in such localities the amount the groom can claim from the father of the bride, and by implication what the wife will collect at the termination of the marriage, will not be determined by the literal text of the document but by the local customary understanding of it. This decision is therefore a specific application of the general rule stated by Rabban Shimeon ben Gamliel in the *Mishna Ketubot* quoted above. 'In all things they should follow local custom'. This rule is explicitly applied by Rabbi Yossi in *Tosefta Ketubot* 6.6.

The result is that though there is indeed documentation for writing in the marriage document double the amount the groom actually receives as dowry, this doubling is Mode o, and is not at all parallel to the 50% increase in *Mishna Ketubot*. In the *Mishna* the increase is intended to obligate the husband, in the *beraita* the doubling is not intended to obligate the husband. The main evidence for a Jewish *donatio ante nuptias* in the amount equivalent to the dowry thus disappears.

Several other rabbinic passages quoted by Gulak as showing a custom of doubling must also be interpreted in this light. An example is the anecdote, placed at the end of the third century, reported in *Yerushalmi Ketubot* 6.3.30d, *à propos* the *Mishna* quoted above. Three prominent rabbis came to perform the estimate of the dotal goods of the daughter of Rabbi Yossi ben Hanina. They said to him, 'He deducts a fifth and doubles'. He said to them,

40. This shows that the compiler of the pericope also understood the *beraita* in the manner now indicated.

41. Epstein, *op. cit.* (n. 3) 104; Friedman, *op. cit.* (n. 3) 296–97. This is still, or again(?), the practice at weddings in some communities in Israel today. The declaration of fantastic dowry sums during the public reading of the *ketuba* elicits 'oohs' and 'ahs' from the assembled guests and much banter as to how the families will manage to raise such sums. If the documents ever get to the courts the sums are disregarded.

'He deducts a fifth and does not double'. The three rabbis, suggests Gulak, were prepared to go along with the new fashion of 100% increases, but Rabbi Yossi ben Hanina chose conservatively to reject it. Several different interpretations of the interchange are offered by the commentators, *ad loc*. The most likely, by Lieberman, is that the locality where the incident took place had the custom of doubling.[42] The interchange between the three rabbis and Rabbi Yossi ben Hanina has to do with whether or not the law is settled in accordance with the view of Rabban Shimeon ben Gamliel, in *Mishna Ketubot* 6.3–4, that in all things local custom should be followed, or not. The three rabbis believe it is; Rabbi Yossi ben Hanina dissents, holding that only the first view in that *Mishna* is settled law.[43] Homiletical references to grooms doubling their brides' dowry[44] cited by Gulak are too vague to build on in the absence of legal material.

# IV

In summary, we come, it seems, to negative conclusions. There does not appear to be the evidence required to show continuity between the Jewish practices concerning grooms' statutory additions to brides' dowries and the non-Jewish *donatio ante nuptias*. The practice of increasing cash dowries by 50% seems insufficiently similar to be a useful parallel. A practice of requiring the groom to increase the dowry generally by 100% does not appear in the texts at all.

## ADDENDUM

Two attempts to find continuities between the rabbinic sources discussed above and various Aramaic papyri do not seem to have been successful either. In Kraeling, *Brooklyn Museum Aramaic Papyri* 2,[45] an Aramaic

42. The 'doubling' could on the face of it be either Gulak's Mode 1 doubling of cash only, or Rashi's Mode 0 doubling of the entire dowry. Since the latter does not require introducing into the text of the anecdote a distinction not made explicitly, it has the advantage of simplicity.

43. Saul Lieberman, *Hilkhoth Ha-yerushalmi* (New York 1947) 58, section 70.

44. *Canticles Rabbah* 4.25 on *Canticles* 4.13. A second passage with the same languages as the previous, *Yerushalmi Pesahim* 4.9 end.31c, does not illustrate commensurate increases at all, but the contrary.

45. Re-edited by B. Porten, *Jews of Elephantine and Aramaeans of Syene* (Jerusalem 1974) 38–41.

marriage contract of the fifth century B.C., the articles in the dowry are valued at sums totalling about $7\frac{1}{2}$ shekels. On the other hand, the endorsement on the back states that the woman brought a dowry worth 15 shekels. J. Rabinowitz suggested that the dowry was in fact $7\frac{1}{2}$ shekels, and that the doubled figure on the outside was to make a more generous impression (Mode o), thus continuous with the practice indicated in the *beraita* of Rabbi Yossi discussed above.[46] Reactions to this suggestion have been mixed. Porten accepts the suggestion.[47] Yaron rejects it, correctly I believe, suggesting instead that the discrepancy is due to further negotiations. Yaron notes that the text of the papyrus is otherwise characterized by last minute changes.[48]

Lieberman suggested tentatively that *umishlam lireva'in* in *P. Mur.* II 19.10, a divorce document of A.D. 111(?), may refer to a customary increase in the dowry along the line of *Mishna Ketubot* 6.3, though with different amounts.[49] His rejection of the editor's interpretation of the phrase as meaning a fourfold penalty is shared by Lehmann[50] and Yaron.[51] Both, however, point out that the specific amounts of the dowry are not usually mentioned in Jewish divorce documents. The latter suggests with a good deal of probability that what is meant here is time payments.

46. Jacob J. Rabinowitz, *Jewish Law: Its Influence on the Development of Legal Institutions* (New York 1956) 88.

47. Bezalel Porten, *Archives from Elephantine. The Life of an Ancient Jewish Military Colony* (Berkeley 1968) 207 n. 30.

48. Reuven Yaron, *Introduction to the Law of the Aramaic Papyri* (Oxford 1961) 57–58.

49. Lieberman, *op. cit.* (n. 5).

50. Manfred R. Lehmann, 'Studies in the Muraba'at and Nahal Hever Documents', *Revue de Qumran* 4 (1963) 53–81.

51. Reuven Yaron, *JJS* 11 (1960) 159; *Ha'umah* 3 (1964) 337–41. Cf. Volterra, *Iura* 14 (1963) 47 (dissent); Elisabeth Koffmahn, *Die Doppelurkunden aus der Wüste Juda* (Leiden 1968) 154 (assent).

# Village shepherds and social tension in Byzantine Egypt

JAMES G. KEENAN

From the rich vein of evidence that has been yielded by the sixth-century archive of Dioscorus of Aphrodito have come documents ranging in intrinsic interest from the most pedestrian of rent receipts to the most extraordinary of legal and literary documents.[1] Between these are some seemingly average pieces, each with its story to tell, but long lacking interpreter and audience. One such piece is that published by Maspero nearly seventy-five years ago as *P. Cair. Masp.* 1 67087, which, though outwardly concerned only with a specific case of trespass, seems to touch on problems that ran much deeper into Aphrodito's social fabric. The text with which the present paper[2] starts is substantially a reprinting of Maspero's; but it adds the accents and incorporates suggestions (never verified) both by early reviewers of *P. Cair. Masp.* 1 and by later observers. There are, besides, one or two new ideas, and the text has been liberally re-punctuated, resulting (I hope) in a clearer view of the text's sense than Maspero's punctuation allows.[3]

---

1. Lists of Aphrodito papyri: G. Malz, 'The Papyri of Dioscorus: Publications and Emendations', *Studi in onore di Aristide Calderini e Roberto Paribeni* II (Milan 1957) 345–56; A. Calderini, *Dizionario dei nomi geografici e topografici dell' Egitto greco-romano* I.2 (Madrid 1966) 303ff. Major recent additions: *P. Mich.* XIII, *P. Vatic. Aphrod.*

2. First delivered as one of the bi-weekly luncheon talks sponsored by Loyola University's Department of Classical Studies (my thanks to Dr James Daly for this invitation and opportunity), subsequently, on 29 December 1983, presented to the American Society of Papyrologists, meeting in Cincinnati.

3. Problems, of course, remain, in this text as in so many of the other *P. Cair. Masp.* editions, outstanding as they were at their time of publication; cf. R. S. Bagnall, *BASP* 18 (1981) 177.

245

P. Cair. Masp. 1 67087            A.D. 543
38 × 31.5 cm

[† Ἐκσφρ]άγισμα ἐμοῦ Κολλούθου βοηθοῦ τῆς ἐκδικίας τῆς
    Ἀνταιοπολιτῶν, Φλ(αουίῳ) Διοσκόρῳ Ἀπολλῶτος
[τῷ εὐδοκιμ]ωτάτῳ ἀπὸ κώμης Ἀφροδίτης τοῦ Ἀνταιοπολίτου
    νομοῦ. κατὰ τὴν σήμερον ἡμέραν, ἥτις ἐστὶν νεομηνία
[τοῦ παρόντος] μηνὸς Τῦβι τῆς ἐνεστώσ[ης ἑ]βδόμης
    ἰνδ(ικτί)ο(νος), Βασιλείας τοῦ θειοτάτου ἡμῶν δεσπότου
    Φλ(αουίου) Ἰουστινιανοῦ τοῦ
4 [αἰωνίου αὐγούσ]του αὐτοκράτορος ἔτους ἑπτακαιδεκάτου,
    τοῖς μετὰ τὴν ὑπατείαν Φλ(αουίου) βασιλίου
    τοῦ ἐνδοξοτάτου, καταλαβὼν
[τὴν Ἀφροδίτ]ης κώμην δημοσίας χρείας ἕνεκεν καὶ αἰτηθεὶς
    παρὰ τῆς σῆς εὐδοκιμήσεως ἐλθεῖν καὶ ἐπιθεωρῆσαι
[τὰ λήϊα τοῦ] ὑπ' αὐτὴν ὀργάνου τοῦ [ε]ὐαγοῦς μοναστηρίου ἅπα
    Σουροῦτος τοῦ διακειμέν[ου] ἐν τῇ βορινῇ πεδιάδι τῆς
[εἰρημένης κώ]μης, κλήρου Φήνε[ω]ς καλουμένου πρότερον
    ἅπα Ψεντ[υ]σῆτος· κἀκεῖσε οὖν παραγενάμενος ἅμα
8 [τῇ σῇ εὐδοκι]μήσει, ἑώρακα τὰ προειρημένα λήϊα
    λελυμηθέντα παντελῶς πρὸς ἅπασαν αὔξησιν καρποῦ,
[τὰ μὲν κατα]πατηθέντα καὶ πηλοπατηθέντα ὥστε ἀφανῆ
    γενέσθαι, τὰ δὲ [π]αρωθέντα καὶ ἐκριζωθέντα
[ . . . . . . . . ] πρὸς ἀχρήστων εἴδησ[ι]ν. καὶ ταῦτα οὕτως
    θεωρήσας, ἐπερώτησα τὴν αἰτίαν δι' ἣν ἐπὶ τοσοῦτον
[ . . . . . . . . ]ιστως ἐλυμήνοιτο ὁ καρπός· ἔφησέν μοι ἡ
    σὴ εὐδοκίμη[σ]ις ὅτι δὴ ἀνήρ τις λεγόμενος
12 [ . . . . . . . . Μο]υσαίου ἐστὶν ὁ ταῦτα π[οι]ῶν. πρὸ ἡμερῶν γὰρ
    ἦλθεν πρὸς ἐμὲ μέλλων τὰ πρόβατα αὐτοῦ
[ἀγαγεῖν εἰς(?)] τὸ ὄργανον τοῦ Μακαρίου ἀδελφοῦ αὐτοῦ,
    παρακάτω τοῦ ἐμοῦ ὀργάνου, εἰς χλωροφαγίαν.
[ . . . . . . . . ]σατο μοι, βουλόμενος δι[ὰ τ]οῦ ἐμοῦ αὔλακος
    τὴν εἴσοδον τῶν αὐτοῦ προβάτων πο[ι]ήσασθαι, καὶ μαθὼν
[ὅτι . . . . . . . ] ταύτην γενέσθαι οὐ παρεχώρησ[α] ἑκουσίως,
    ἀπῆλθεν τυραννίδι ἐπερειδόμενος, ἀπηλάσας
16 [ . . . . τὰ προρ]ηθέντα αὐτοῦ πρόβατα καὶ ὅσα εἶχεν θρέμματα
    διὰ τῶν ἐμῶν ληΐων, καὶ ο[ὕ]τως ἐλυμήν[ατ]ο
[ . . . . . . . . μ]οι τοιαύτην ζημίαν καὶ ἀνατροπὴν εἰς βλάβην
    τοῦ δημοσίου, καίτοι γε παραγγελθεὶς
[παρ' ἐμοῦ, μι]μνήσκοντος μὴ οὕτω χρήσασθαι τῷ ἐμῷ
    αὔλακι· ὑφορωμένῳ τὸν γενάμενον αἰκισμὸν
[ἔφησεν εἶν]αί(?) ποτε τὸν τόπον ἐν ὁδηπορίας τάξει
    θρεμμάτων ἐπὶ ἡμῶν καὶ ἐπὶ προγόνων.
20 [καὶ πρὸς τ]ὴν τῶν οὕτως εἰρημένων καὶ ἡγημένων
    ἀσφάλειαν, αἰτηθεὶς παρὰ σοῦ καὶ συνθεὶς τόδε

[τὸ ἐκμαρτύ]ριον, ἐξεδόμην σ[ο]ὶ μεθ᾽ ὑπογραφῆς ἐμῆς.
  ⳨ Κολλοῦθος βοηθὸς τῆς ἐκδικίας τῆς
[᾽Ανταιοπολι]τῶν ἐκδέδωκα τοῦτο τὸ ἐκμαρτύριον ὡς
  πρόκ(ειται). ⳨ ⳨ ⳨ ῾Χμγ‾‾᾿

19 ὁδοιπορίας

Authentication of me, Kollouthos, assistant of the office of *defensor* of the (city of) Antaiopolites, to Flavius Dioscorus, Apollos' son, the most excellent, from the village of Aphrodite of the Antaiopolite nome.

On this very day, which is the first day of the present month Tybi, in the current seventh indiction, the seventeenth year in the reign of our most divine ruler, the eternal august emperor, Flavius Justinian, in the post-consulship of Flavius Basilius, the most renowned, I arrived at the village of Aphrodite on public business and was asked by Your Excellency to come and inspect the crops of the field subject to it (*sc.* Your Excellency), belonging to the holy monastery of Apa Sourous, lying in the northern plain of the said village, in the allotment of Phenis, formerly called that of Apa Psentuses. Consequently, on arrival there with Your Excellency, I saw that the aforementioned crops had been utterly ruined so as to inhibit any increase of produce, that some had been trampled down and trampled in the mud so as to have vanished and the rest had been thrust aside and uprooted...to forms(?) of worthlessness(?). And thus after seeing this I asked the reason why to such an extent...the produce had been destroyed. Your Excellency said to me: 'A certain man called..., Mousaios' son, is the perpetrator. For, a few days ago, he came to me intent on driving his sheep to the field of Makarios, his brother, just below my field, for pasturing. He...me, wishing to make entry for his sheep through my "furrow". And upon learning that...I did not willingly concede this to be, he went off, steadfast in his tyrannical behavior, driving his aforesaid sheep and as many lambs as he had through my crops; and thus he destroyed [them?], [inflicting on?] me so great a harm and reversal to the detriment of the public treasury, even though he had been ordered by me, warning him not to use my "furrow". (To me) as (I) was inspecting the damage that had been done, he said that the place was formerly [*or*: sometimes] in a category of thoroughfares for lambs "in our time and in that of our ancestors".' And having been asked by you for a guarantee that these things had thus been said and done, and having composed this authentication, I issued it to you with my subscription.

I, Kollouthos, assistant of the office of *defensor* of the (city of) Antaiopolites, have issued this authentication as aforesaid.

Line **2.** εὐδοκιμ]ωτάτῳ: G. Malz, *op. cit.* (n. 1) 351; cf. *Berichtigungsliste* IV, 13; θαυμασι]ωτάτῳ, *ed.* Although the latter epithet, as applied to Aphroditan village headmen (πρωτοκωμῆται) and contributaries (συντελεσταί), is the more common in these archival documents, it seems, for some purposes at least, to have been interchangeable with the former. In this restoration, harmonizing the epithet with the abstract noun εὐδοκίμησις (lines 5, 8, 11) appears decisively to warrant Malz's emendation: cf., e.g., *P. Cair. Masp.* III 67301.

**2–4.** Maspero prints a comma after νομοῦ, a period after ἐνδοξοτάτου. The preposition κατά, however, appears to prefix the dating indicators to the body of the document instead of appending them to its heading and address. Regnal and indictional datings set the papyrus' year as 543; Basilius' post-consulate year number is not given (see R. S. Bagnall and K. A. Worp, *The Chronological Systems of Byzantine Egypt* (*Studia Amstelodamensia* 7, Zutphen 1978) *passim* and esp. at 124). In the Egyptian leap year 543, Tybi 1 = December 28: Worp, *ZPE* 26 (1977) 272.

**5.** The commas printed by Maspero after ἕνεκεν and ἐλθεῖν are here deleted as superfluous, the latter obscuring the dependency of ἐπιθεωρῆσαι on αἰτηθείς, the former obscuring the co-ordination between αἰτηθείς and καταλαβών.

**6.** ὑπ᾽ αὐτήν: *sc.* εὐδοκίμησιν. Maspero's brief introduction might suggest he believed Dioscorus owned the land in question (cf. line 13: τοῦ ἐμοῦ ὀργάνου). See, however, *P. Cair. Masp.* II 67133 (Dioscorus as lessee of land belonging to Apa Sourous' monastery) and Maspero's note to line 2 of that text (suggesting the same arrangement there as in *P. Cair. Masp.* 67087); in accord, *P. Lond.* V, p. 70 n. 1.

ὀργάνου: For ὄργανον as a 'field' or 'piece of land under cultivation': *P. Lond.* V 1690.9 note; for the monastery of Apa Sourous and its seeming economic oversight of Apa Psentuses' monastery: *P. Mich.* XIII 667 intro.

**7.** Φήνε[ω]ς: Φηνθ[.]ς, *ed.*, but see *Berichtigungsliste* I, 446 (incorporated in A. Calderini, *Dizionario*, 346).

Ψεντ[υ]σῆτος: or Ψεντ[ου]σῆτος. Cf., albeit a bit too tentatively, *P. Mich.* XIII 667.4 and note.

**8.** λελυμηθέντα: a hybrid, with perfect reduplication and aorist

248

ending, cf. F. Gignac, *A Grammar of the Greek Papyri of the Roman and Byzantine Periods* II, 243.

**9.** Line opening restored after *Berichtigungsliste* I, 107, cf. *P. Cair. Masp.* I, p. 206.

**10.** εἴδησ[ι]ν: acc. sing. of εἴδησις; or, for better sense(?), read εἴδεσιν, dat. pl. of εἶδος?

ἐπερώτησα: Gignac, *Grammar* II, 234.

**11.** [τρόπον κακ(?)]ίστως, *ed*. But τρόπον seems gratuitous, and though the supplement as a whole *may* get at the sense of the lacuna, without supportive parallels, it now seems overbold as a representation of the lacuna's precise details, even if queried.

ἐλυμήνοιτο: the form is corrupt though the attempt to achieve an optative may have been genuine. As is well known, the optative in the papyri is usually restricted to stereotypical expressions. Still, some Byzantine Egyptian students of Greek continued to practise its forms, cf. the verb paradigms in *P. Cair. Masp.* II 67176.

**13.** Μακαρίου: the personal name Makarios for the editor's μακαρίου, 'blessed' (and consequently 'deceased').

**14.** αὔλακος: cf. line 18; apparently poetic 'furrow' by synecdoche for 'field'. One may well wonder, if this is so, whether Dioscorus' own poetic diction is at work here and has been taken over by the βοηθὸς τῆς ἐκδικίας (text line 1, and see discussion below). In his epithalamium for Isaac (*P. Cair. Masp.* III 67318, at line 11), Dioscorus uses αὔλακες in connection with 'wheat-bearing earth'.

**15.** Maspero prints την at the lacuna's beginning, but this can hardly be assured. The punctuation for the words that follow is uncertain, as is whether γενέσθαι depends on μαθών or on παρεχώρησα. Perhaps τὴν εἴσοδον filled the lacuna's opening; in which case the sense would have been something like: 'Upon learning that the right of way existed, I did not willingly concede (it).'

τυραννίδι ἐπερειδόμενος: stereotypical? Cf. *P. Lond.* v 1676.43–44.

**16.** τὰ προρ]ηθέντα: Wessely's supplement, cf. *P. Cair. Masp.* II, p. 198.

**17.** εἰς βλάβην τοῦ δημοσίου: same expression, e.g., in *P. Cair. Masp.* I 67078.5.

**19.** The quotation is structurally indirect, but the appropriate adjustment in the apparently stereotypical ἐπὶ ἡμῶν καὶ ἐπὶ προγόνων (cf. *P. Cair. Masp.* 1 67001.11) has not been made. Cf. *P. Oxy.* 1 130.9: ὡς ἐκ πατέρων καὶ προγόνων δουλεύειν.

**20.** [καὶ πρὸς τ]ήν: not absolutely guaranteed, but surely yielding smoother sense than Maspero's [καὶ εἰς εἴδησ]ιν. Maspero seems to have considered ἀσφάλειαν as somehow dependent on αἰτηθείς; but that word is better taken as object of a restored πρός (or εἰς) and the comma should fall after, not before, ἀσφάλειαν.

**22.** Most recently on the Χμγ symbol: A. Gostoli, *Studia Papyrologica* 22 (1983) 9–14.

*Commentary*

To start by attending to the text's general form: it is worth noting that its opening word identifies it as an ἐκσφράγισμα, an authentication or deposition. This identification is reinforced at the text's end when the βοηθὸς τῆς ἐκδικίας, the assistant to the *defensor civitatis* of Antaiopolis,[4] just before and then again in his subscription (ὑπογραφή), makes use of the synonym ἐκμαρτύριον.[5] This type of deposition in the late Byzantine papyri is one drawn up and subscribed to by a competent official, the *defensor civitatis* or (as here) his delegate. It therefore differs from the type of affidavit called a διαμαρτυρία, which was drawn up in advance by a private party and then submitted for the *defensor*'s consideration and signed approval.[6] Noteworthy here in *P. Cair. Masp.* 1 67087 is that the assistant's statement provides both an extensive introduction to, and the frame for, a direct quotation of the plaintiff's own verbal statement of the case's 'facts'.[7] These words of

4. For the *defensor civitatis* at this time, see G. Rouillard, *L'administration civile de l'Egypte byzantine*² (Paris 1928) 153ff.; B. R. Rees, *JJP* 6 (1952) 73–102; V. Dautzenberg, *Die Gesetze des Codex Theodosianus und des Codex Justinianus für Ägypten im Spiegel der Papyri* (diss. Cologne 1971) 165–70; D. Simon, *RIDA*³ 18 (1971) 626–33; J. Keenan, *ZPE* 29 (1978) 191–209, *passim*. Each Egyptian *polis* theoretically had its *defensor* (with authority extending to the surrounding *polis* territory), each *defensor* his staff of assistants (details are sketchy). In the papyri, the *defensor* and his delegates commonly appear in authenticating roles, as in the present case; Justinian (*Nov.* 15.3.2) in A.D. 535 limited the *defensor*'s competence to cases of up to 300 *solidi* in value.

5. *P. Oxy.* XVI 1882.15 note. The word ἐκσφράγισμα regularly appears in the heading and texts of such documents, ἐκμαρτύριον in their subscriptions.

6. *ZPE* 29 (1978) 202.

7. For the practice of such quoting: *P. Lond.* v 1677.49ff. with note.

Dioscorus, the plaintiff, had he decided to proceed in alternate fashion, might have served with little or no change as the text of his own privately drafted *diamartyria*. As things stand, however, Dioscorus would seem to have gotten the best of both worlds: by incorporating Dioscorus' unwritten affidavit[8] into his own statement of authentication, the *defensor*'s assistant would appear to have endorsed Dioscorus' words. The assistant, who was present in Aphrodito on evidently other public business (δημοσίας χρείας ἕνεκεν, line 5), has verified by inspection the alleged damage, Dioscorus has explained the reasons and named the malefactor. Curious, therefore, is that within the quotation from Dioscorus there is quoted in line 19, in a conflation of indirect and direct discourse constructions (see note *ad loc.*), the accused's summary of the legal justification for his own actions.

Those words are important, for they sharply define the immediate issue of the case: the accused claims a right of way similar to what Roman jurists would have classified as a rustic praedial servitude, an easement especially important in those regions where the agrarian architectonic was, as in Egypt, even with the oft-described but poorly known consolidatings of the Byzantine period,[9] one of scattered holdings. Roughly to paraphrase Dioscorus' summary of the accused's claim: this place was classified by ancestral tradition as a thoroughfare for livestock. Dioscorus, for his part, had against this appeal to tradition asserted his own right to oppose what he construed as trespass into the land in question – land, by the way, which he apparently did not own himself (line 6 n.), but which he held in lease or oversaw as its manager: it was '*subject to* His Excellency', but owned by the monastery of Apa Sourous.[10]

In short, and to repeat in slightly different terms, the accused asserts a traditional easement against Dioscorus' insistence on some kind of interdictive possessory authority; but this interpretation, which sets the argument at its extremes, allows of at least two mediative alternatives. One is that there was indeed a customary

8. Cf. *W. Chr.* 471.7: διεμαρτύραντο δὲ ἡμᾶς ἐγγράφως. The word ἐγγράφως would seem to suggest the possibility, and legitimacy, of its opposite.

9. *ZPE* 17 (1975) 239–40, with nn. 4–6.

10. For the entrepreneurial bent of such arrangements, cf. Keenan, *BASP* 17 (1980) 145–54, and *Atti del XVII Congresso Internazionale di Papirologia* III, 957–63.

easement on the land. What made this livestock droving impermissible was its timing. The crops planted a few months ago were at the time of the alleged trespass (the first of Tybi, shortly before December's end) 'standing crops' (λήϊα – line 8, cf. 16) well on their way to harvest growth. Their trampling caused irreparable damage; the crops had been trampled down in the mud, thrust sideways, uprooted (line 9). By this alternative, passage to livestock would have been allowed *sometimes* (ποτε, line 19) during the agricultural year, without objection (say) to their grazing on stubble and with thanks for the fertilizer they might leave behind – but not at this time.[11] Or again: the field could perhaps rightfully be used as a thoroughfare in years when, for one reason or another,[12] it was not successfully planted or was deliberately left fallow, but not in this year, the seventeenth of Justinian's reign, when the crops were apparently doing well.

Another mediative possibility: the quoted summary of the ancestral custom mentions only θρέμματα (line 19), but, according to Dioscorus (line 16), both θρέμματα and πρόβατα were driven through the field. Perhaps the easement was valid, but available only for the flock's lambs, the θρέμματα, not for their more cumbersome and potentially more destructive elders.[13] That the easement may have been personal rather than praedial, and therefore perhaps not available to this particular drover, Mousaios' son, seems unlikely; the possibility, not raised in the papyrus itself, need not be considered here.

Whatever these possibilities, the surface issues of *P. Cair. Masp.*

11. According to the editor (*P. Cair. Masp.* II, p. 60), *P. Cair. Masp.* II 67141 ii verso, lines 23–28, concerns the alternation of responsibility for shepherding a flock between two shepherds; but if ἐγγύς in that excerpt is taken in its more usual sense, the rotation of the flock was not between shepherds, but rather between fields, a movement, given the near coincidence of datings (the first date in the cited lines of 67141 is Tybi 3/December 29), of possibly more than casual connection with the flock movement pictured in *P. Cair. Masp.* 67087.

12. E.g., it was still under water even at this late date; cf. *P. Lond.* v 1688, dated Choiak 28 (December 25), 523.

13. Not a frivolously raised possibility. See Fredrik Barth, *Nomads of South Persia* (Oslo–London–New York 1965) 7: amongst the Basseri tribesmen, '[l]ambs and kids are usually herded separately from the adults'; E. Le Roy Ladurie, *Montaillou: The Promised Land of Error* (trans. B. Bray, New York 1979) 111: two medieval Pyrenees shepherds divide a flock, one caring for the adult sheep, the other for the new lambs and the yearlings. Cf. Polyphemus' sheep (*Od.* 9.219–22), put into segregated pens according to their ages.

67087 are simple enough. Mainly there is a conflict of claims, between a right to drive flocks to pasture and a right to save crops from destruction. The surface issues, however, seem to suggest the outlines of a deeper and wider social tension, one between Aphrodito's landholding elite and the village herders, the shepherds in particular. What brings this concrete case into the larger societal orbit is the statuses and positions of the disputants.

The Dioscorus of *P. Cair. Masp.* 67087 is the famous Dioscorus of the archive. He, as a man destined by birth and education and (shortly) by inheritance to take his place among the village's elite, can readily be taken to stand for the village's landholding interests. Apollos, his father, would die about three years after the present dispute,[14] leaving Dioscorus as principal though not sole heir to an apparently large estate.[15] By the time of his removal to the provincial capital at Antinoopolis around 566, Dioscorus would have run the gamut of village titles, from village headman (πρωτοκωμήτης) to contributary (συντελεστής) to possessor (κτήτωρ), and he would have engaged in the same kinds of entrepreneurial activities that had brought his family and his class to local prominence: land engrossment and the managing and leasing of land belonging to ecclesiastical and monastic institutions and to individual absentee landlords.[16] Although it is true that Dioscorus' colleagues, in other documents,[17] presented themselves to the outside world, in a self-styling too readily accepted by some modern scholars, as 'wretched smallholders' (ἄθλιοι λεπτοκτήτορες), they were, when viewed from within the village framework, themselves the exploiters, not the exploited; they were the moving forces in village life.

14. He died in the 546/47 indictional year: H. I. Bell, *JHS* 64 (1944) 26 and n. 21; J. Gascou, *CE* 52 (1977) 361; *P. Vatic. Aphrod.* 7 intro. and 10.4 note.

15. Plurality of heirs: cf. *P. Cair. Masp.* 1 67103–9, *P. Gen.* inv. 204 (in *Proceedings of the XVIth International Congress of Papyrology*, 487–89).

16. My language here belies a suspicion that there may have been something of a *cursus honorum* at Aphrodito, but this is a hunch that awaits conclusive demonstration, or rejection. Dioscorus held all three titles before his Antinoopolitan 'exile': cf., e.g., *P. Cair. Masp.* II 67128 and 67129 (*protokomētēs*); II 67251 and III 67303 (*syntelestēs*); II 67130 (*ktētor*). Typical entrepreneurial activities: the articles mentioned above, n. 10; a particular Dioscoran example: *P. Cair. Masp.* II 67133.

17. Notably in *P. Cair. Masp.* 1 67002.2 and in *P. Lond.* V 1674.100 (damaged and restored, but cf. line 95).

On the other side, Mousaios' son, the accused in *P. Cair. Masp.* 67087, though not, as were many Aphroditans, explicitly labeled a shepherd (ποίμην),[18] was (quite clearly) the drover and (evidently) the grazier of his own flocks. If in any sense he can be taken as representative of Aphrodito's shepherding community at large, then his dispute with Dioscorus may simply be an instance of the general tension that exists in many traditional communities between the more sedentary portion of the populace, that with a vested interest in real estate, and the less sedentary fringe groups like the shepherds. There can be a symbiosis beneficial to both groups; at the same time, there are often signs that collaboration is not smooth. There may at times not be co-operation so much as pragmatic co-optation of the less propertied by the more propertied; and there may be instances of disruptive behavior on the part of the lesser partners in the bargain. Where the distinction between farmer and shepherd is sharply drawn, there may even be a strong sense of disdain for shepherds by non-shepherds.[19] At Aphrodito, though the distinction between shepherd and farmer tended to be blurred in practice, or at least in some aspects of practice,[20] shepherds were often clearly identified both as individuals and as a group.[21] This must have set them apart in the community's division of labor, without of course conferring any special 'distinction' on them for their specialization.[22]

For the co-optation of Aphrodito's shepherds by the village's landed elite, the most striking text remains *P. Cair. Masp.* 1 67001. In that papyrus, from the very end of the year 514 (2 Tybi/

18. Cf. Calderini, *Dizionario*, 403–4; A. Girgis, *Prosopografia e Aphroditopolis* (Berlin 1938) *passim*. A new list of Aphroditan trades and occupations is being compiled by L. S. B. MacCoull.

19. Cf. LXX *Genesis* 43.32: βδέλυγμα γάρ ἐστιν τοῖς Αἰγυπτίοις πᾶς ποίμην προβάτων (a gloss inserted in the story of Joseph in Egypt).

20. Blurred in practice: e.g., shepherds as tenant farmers in Aphrodito, cf. *P. Cair. Masp.* 1 67106; *P. Michael.* 46; *PSI* VIII 931, among other texts.

21. Individuals: above, n. 18; as a group: *P. Cair. Masp.* 1 67001, cf. 67090.

22. Some shepherds also achieved recognition as shearers (cf. the abbreviation πλοκ/ in *P. Cair. Masp.* III 67328 vii). For shepherds and shearers as specialists: 'Western Sheep Ranchers Fighting to Survive', *The New York Times*, Sunday, 7 August 1983, pp. 1, 15: nowadays shepherds in the western U.S. have to be 'imported from Peru, Mexico and the Basque region of Spain'. These foreign shepherds 'are essential to the industry, since only they seem to possess the gentle and seemingly intuitive skill necessary to keep sheep moving easily over the range'. Their pay remains rather low.

28 December), the representatives of the village '*collegium* (κοινόν) of shepherds and fieldguards' agrees, on oath addressed to 'the *collegium* (κοινότης) of village headmen, contributaries and land-owners', to a lifelong obligation to guard the village's 'estates' (κτήματα) from damage to livestock and to agricultural machinery and from damage to the *ktēmata* in general (cf. lines 17ff.). For this service they are to receive a fixed pay in kind, while taking on themselves responsibility to redeem any future losses in full. So far as I know, no scholar has entered very deeply into discussion of this text, even to the point of remarking how convenient it is to employ shepherds for such purposes.[23] The document's heading has often been cited; its body seems straightforward enough, but it does raise problems, the most urgent of which goes to the very heart of the reason for the text's drafting.

This is because the shepherds/fieldguards, after beginning the body of the document with: 'It is customary (ἔθος ἐστί)', abruptly shift from impersonal to personal constructions: 'We have been accustomed (εἰώθαμεν)', they say, 'from (the time of) our fathers and forefathers (to keep) watch over all the "estates" (κτήματα) of the aforementioned village of Aphrodite with respect to the driving off of livestock and of other property in the stated *ktēmata*.'[24] The question therefore becomes: if this verbal, traditional obligation was already well known and so frankly conceded by the shepherds themselves, what was the need for this new, written covenant, *P. Cair. Masp.* 67001? Was it to establish, as detailed later in the text, a 'pay scale' for the fieldguards[25] and to extract from them an admission of their liability in case of failure in their duty? Had there been problems, slackness or dereliction on the part of *this* generation of shepherds/fieldguards that begged correction?[26] Perhaps the document was drawn up because the custom as conveyed by oral tradition was in danger of lapsing. Or

23. Not only convenient, but wickedly clever: those who are in the best position to damage and steal from the fields are made the fields' custodians.

24. Lines 11–13: Ἔθος ἐστὶ εἰώθαμεν ἐκ πατέρων ἡμῶ[ν κα]ὶ [π]ρ[ογό]νων [ἐκτελέσαι] παραφυλακὴν | ὅλων κτημάτων πάσης τῆς αὐτῆς κώμης Ἀφροδίτης περὶ ἀπελασίαν ζώων καὶ | ἑτέρων σκευῶν ἐν τοῖς εἰρημένοις κτήμασι.

25. Lines 30–31: three artabs of grain, one *kolobion* of wine per 'locality' (τόπος). How many *topoi* were to be under guard is unknown.

26. Derelict fieldguards from another village, Tholthis of the Oxyrhynchite nome: *PSI* I 47 (6th century?).

perhaps the tradition was still vigorous, but, notwithstanding, *P. Cair. Masp.* 67001 was drawn up as part of a wider effort to commit village traditions to written form.[27] Or (finally) *P. Cair. Masp.* 67001 may have been viewed as a vehicle to extend the customary duties, narrowly construed by the shepherds/fieldguards (the prevention of thefts of livestock and equipment from the *ktēmata*), to more general and sweeping responsibilities: not just for *thefts* of livestock and moveables, but for damage to them and to the land in general.

If this last possibility is the right one, then there may perhaps be seen a further development of this trend – extending, formalizing, and writing down the responsibilities of the shepherds/fieldguards – in the series of twelve guarantees submitted to the village police officer (*riparius*) in the year 521, all in the month Epeiph (25 June–24 July), and published as *P. Cair. Masp.* III 67328. The guarantees in the series oblige the shepherds/fieldguards individually 'to remain in service for a year[28] and to stay put,[29] and to work at all public duties, resolutely and unexceptionably, and to keep watch[30] over matters of peace, and to effect the appearance [*sc.* before the competent authorities] of parties being sought'.

The full range of prosopographical links between *P. Cair. Masp.* 67001 and 67328, and between them and other Aphrodito papyri, interesting as they are, cannot be deployed here. It is important to note, however, that several of the shepherds who are sworn for in 67328 had appeared as representatives of the shepherd/

27. A possible analogy: in Aphroditan documents land plots tend not to appear with defined measurements; rather they are identified through an intricate naming system, with boundaries often referred to as 'old' or 'ancient' (παλαιά, ἀρχαῖα). One may well ponder the relationship between this traditional system and the written register of John the *censitor*, also often referred to in the documents; cf. A. Claus, Ὁ ΣΧΟΛΑΣΤΙΚΟΣ (diss. Cologne 1965) 118ff. Another, this time peculiarly Aphroditan, custom: the cheeses, charlock, etc. – the 'grab bag of extras': Bagnall, *BASP* 18 (1981) 178 – that were added on to the base rents in some Aphroditan land leases, e.g., *P. Michael.* 43, *P. Vatic. Aphrod.* 1.

28. On the assumption that the infinitive παραμεῖναι stands in these guarantees as cognate for the technical term παραμονή, cf. the participle παραμένων in *SB* I 5656 = *P. Cair. Masp.* III 67305.

29. If *LSJ* is right in taking προσυδρεύειν as a slip for προσεδρεύειν.

30. τὴν παραφυλακὴν...ποιεῖσθαι.

fieldguard *koinon* six and a half years earlier, in 67001.[31] Such recurrences lead to questions about the links between the yearlong, individual obligations officially required by the *riparius* in the year 521 (as detailed in 67328) and the seemingly more freely concluded, communal, lifelong arrangements of the year 514 (as set forth in 67001). Did 67328 extend[32] and 'bureaucratize' the arrangements of 67001? Or had the shepherds/fieldguards been generally negligent[33] or not living up to something implied in, but not rendered explicit in, 67001 by its use of the term *paraphylakē*, namely, the handing over of fugitives from justice, an issue of concern in Egyptian documents of all periods, but especially critical in the eyes of Egypt's Byzantine officials?[34]

To accept this (there are several more possibilities)[35] as the correct explanation and to take it a step further: if the shepherds/ fieldguards were indeed suspected of harboring parties 'on the lam', the fugitives were all too likely to be of their own ilk. For shepherds, to judge from the papyri, could be a troublesome lot; sometimes victims of violence,[36] they tended also to be its perpetrators.[37] That the shepherds of Aphrodito could be, as

31. Aurelius Psenthaesis, son of Mousaios (67328 iii, 67001.6, 36); Aurelius Victor, son of Hermauos (67328 iv, 67001.9, 41); Aurelius Victor, son of Psaios (67328 v, viii, 67001.7, 37); Aurelius Hermauos, son of Josephius (67328 vii, 67001.7, 36).

32. *P. Cair. Masp.* 67001 speaks insistently, not of fields generally, but of κτήματα, 'estates' or 'vineyards' (unless that word is being used there in an acceptable, broader sense for 'fields').

33. Again, cf. *PSI* I 47.

34. Fugitives from justice, taken in a larger sense to include not only criminals on the run, but all individuals whose absences from their *idiai* were unauthorized. See H. Braunert, *JJP* 9–10 (1955–56) 211ff.; *idem, Die Binnenwanderung (Bonner Historische Forschungen* 26, Bonn 1964) esp. 311ff.

35. Perhaps 67328 was, without inspiration of dereliction or crisis, simply an official police intervention with purposes overlapping the communal purposes of 67001. The one-year terms of the 67328 guarantees raise other questions, again touching on their general purpose. Were they a special, *ad hoc* one-year-only arrangement, or were they to be renewed annually in succeeding years? If so, were the guaranteed parties to remain the same, or somehow to be systematically rotated with other shepherds, or wholly replaced?

36. Victims: see *P. Thead.* 57 = *P. Sakaon* 50 (A.D. 317) for a shepherd who had apparently been a murder victim. Cf. the fieldguard reported murdered in *P. Lond.* III 1309.

37. Perpetrators: *P. Lips.* 38 (A.D. 389), robbery, violence, murder by shepherds of the village of Telbonthis. Palladius, *Historia Lausiaca* 17 (Migne,

mentioned, co-opted as guardians of the peace[38] suggests that they were also in a position to disturb it.

But if Aphrodito's own shepherds could largely be kept in line by arrangements like those documented in *P. Cair. Masp.* 67001 and 67328, and by other, still more particular arrangements,[39] the same control proved hard for Aphroditans to impose over shepherds of the village of Phthla. Phthla was Aphrodito's neighbor to the east,[40] and besides being its neighbor seems to have been something of an economic satellite.[41] Aphroditans appear in the papyri as exerting a certain amount of control over Phthla, sometimes owning land situated in Phthla's arable area (πεδίας), at other times appearing as lessees of Phthla's land and as its managers for outside landlords (residents of the metropolis and the like).[42] As was common with neighboring villages in Egypt,[43] relations between the two were not always harmonious; and there are two papyri of the late 560s,[44] and now a third,[45] which seem to be concerned with a single *cause célèbre*, or with a series of incidents hauntingly alike in nature, timing and *dramatis personae*. Their precise interrelationships are clouded and obscure, but their general substance can be identi'ied with sufficient certitude as having to do with a group of Phthla shepherds whose misdeeds were

*Patrologia Graeca* 34, 1041), tells the story of Macarius, an 18-year-old shepherd who committed an accidental murder while at play. See also the discussion below.

38. In addition to *P. Cair. Masp.* 67001, cf. 1 67090.

39. I.e., guarantees for individual shepherds, cf. *PSI* VIII 932; *P. Michael.* 48.

40. Cf., though damaged and obscure where critical, *PSI* IV 283.

41. *P. Flor.* III 296; *P. Cair. Masp.* 1 67105; Keenan, *Atti del XVII Congresso Internazionale di Papirologia* III, 957–63.

42. Texts and Keenan art. cited in preceding note (with reliance on *P. Lond.* V 1702, *P. Cair. Masp.* II 67134–35, III 67326–27).

43. Numerous Byzantine examples of a perennial Egyptian (and agrarian) problem: *BGU* IV 1035 (= *Sel. Pap.* II 429); *P. Hafn.* inv. 318 (discussion by D. Bonneau, *Hommages à la mémoire de Serge Sauneron* II (Cairo 1979) 3–23, with plate); *P. Cair. Goodsp.* 15; *P. Oxy.* VIII 1106, 1165; XVI 1831, 1853, 1866–67, 1897; XIX 2233; *P. Princ.* III 120; *P. Ryl.* IV 653; Palladius, *Historia Lausiaca* 36 (Migne, *Patrologia Graeca* 34, 1098); *Historia monachorum*, ed. Festugière (*Subsidia hagiographica* 53, Brussels 1971) 8.30ff. and 36ff.; M. Gelzer, *Studien zur byzantinischen Verwaltung Ägyptens* (*Leipz. Hist. Abhand.* 13, Leipzig 1909) 66–67.

44. *P. Cair. Masp.* 1 67002; *P. Lond.* V 1677.

45. Egyptian Museum inv. 3733, presented by A. Hanafi Hassanein at the XVII Congresso Internazionale di Papirologia in Naples (see, for now, *Il libro delle communicazioni* of the Congress, 45–46). *P. Cair. Masp.* III 67322 and *P. Lond.* V 1682 are seemingly related documents.

aided and abetted by their own village assistant (βοηθός), blessed and encouraged by the new – and to the Aphroditans infamous – pagarch, Menas.

Menas, it is charged, had allowed the Phthla shepherds, with their village's βοηθός, to occupy and to enjoy, taxfree, the fruits of land that was claimed as belonging to an Aphroditan who had paid, and was continuing to pay, its taxes. From the texts, however puzzling in sense, however physically damaged, it appears that the shepherds committed assorted acts of violence and generally engaged in harassing the Aphroditan's own tenant farmers.[46] Menas' part in the hullabaloo gives an otherwise socio-economic issue something of a political tinge, for Aphrodito was an autopract village, entitled to collect its own taxes and deliver them direct to the provincial treasury. Land beyond Aphrodito's pale was not autopract, its taxation proceeding through the office of the pagarch. That the land in dispute here may have been Phthla-Aphrodito borderland and that its occupation by the Phthla shepherds was a preamble to its transfer from Aphroditan auto-pragia to pagarchic control are seeming possibilities.[47] That the aggrieved party, whose name I have withheld till now, turns out to be none other than Dioscorus, with others of his family and with his tenant farmers joining his suffering, is perhaps not surprising, given his earlier dilemma as outlined in the papyrus with which this article began: *P. Cair. Masp.* 67087. Whether he satisfactorily resolved either of his 'shepherd problems', the earlier, easier one, which was simply another example of 'an endemic phenomenon of the agricultural scene',[48] or the later, and apparently more troublesome one, is unknown.[49]

46. Cf. *P. Lond.* v 1682, seemingly a small piece in the large puzzle: a shepherd has been officially ordered to cease harassing certain farmers.

47. Cf. *P. Lond.* v 1677. 15. Peaceful transfers of land from one village's responsibility to another's were possible: *P. Cair. Masp.* III 67329.

48. N. Lewis, *Life in Egypt under Roman Rule* (Oxford 1983) 121.

49. For some valuable comments and references I am grateful to my Loyola colleague, Dr Robert F. Sutton, Jr.

# Χάρτης ἔληξε

GIOVANNA MENCI

Si legge al foglio 8 *verso* di *P. Brit. Libr.* 2562, commentario tachigrafico del III/IVᵖ (tetrade 287):[1]

χαρτης
εληξε
μηκινει (*l.* μηκυνει)
βιβλον

È un'interessante attestazione, passata finora inosservata, di due termini, χάρτης e βίβλος, sul cui significato si è discusso a lungo.[2] Segnalarla mi è parso utile per almeno due aspetti della *querelle* sul papiro:[3] il primo è l'aspetto terminologico, per il quale la

1. Questo codice papiraceo è pubblicato, insieme con *P. Brit. Libr.* 2561 (che contiene lo stesso testo del 2562 e anzi subentra nell'edizione laddove il 2562 si interrompe), in H. J. M. Milne, *Greek Shorthand Manuals, Syllabary and Commentary* (London 1934) 21–67.

2. Bibliografia reperibile in N. Lewis, *Papyrus in Classical Antiquity* (Oxford 1974) 70–79, *passim*.

3. Con questa denominazione alludo agli innumerevoli problemi suscitati dall'indagine sul papiro dal punto di vista materiale, che è stata motivo di moltissimi articoli, libri o parti di manuali. Dopo l'opera del Lewis sopra citata, che utilizza in pratica tutta la bibliografia precedente, si trovano riferimenti alla bibliografia successiva in I. H. M. Hendriks, "Pliny, Historia Naturalis XIII, 74–82 and the Manufacture of Papyrus", *ZPE* 37 (1980) 121–36; sulla riutilizzazione dei rotoli nell'archivio di Eronino, E. G. Turner, "Writing Material for Businessmen", *BASP* 15 (1978) 163–69. In seguito sono usciti i seguenti studi: H. C. Youtie, "P. Mich. Inv. 1665: χαρτάριν εἰς τοὺς λόγους", *ZPE* 35 (1979) 105–7; H. Ragab, *Contribution à l'étude du papyrus* (Cyperus papyrus L.) *et à sa transformation en support de l'écriture* (*papyrus des anciens*) (Le Caire 1980); E. G. Turner, "An Open Letter to Dr. I. Hendriks", *ZPE* 39 (1980) 113–14; N. Lewis, "Open Letter to I. H. M. Hendriks and E. G. Turner", *ZPE* 42 (1981) 293–94; T. C. Skeat, "Two Notes on Papyrus", in *Scritti in onore di O. Montevecchi* (Bologna 1981) 373–78; T. C. Skeat, "The Length of the Standard Papyrus Roll and the Cost-Advantage of the Codex", *ZPE* 45 (1982) 169–75; D. Holwerda, "Plinius über die Anfertigung von 'charta'", *ZPE* 45 (1982) 257–62; T. Dorandi, "Lucilio fr. 798 Krenkel", *SIFC* 54 (1982) 216–18; M. Manfredi, "Opistografo", *Parola del Passato* 208 (1983) 44–54; T. Dorandi, "Glutinatores", *ZPE* 50 (1983) 25–28; E. G. Turner, "Sniffing Glue", *Cron. Erc.* 13 (1983) 7–14.

261

"tetrade", anche se non porta sostanziali novità, offre tuttavia delle conferme; il secondo riguarda le modalità di confezione di rotoli più lunghi di quella che sembra essere l'unità standard di fabbricazione, il τόμος/*scapus* di 20 fogli al massimo: a questo proposito la "tetrade" suggerisce qualche cosa di nuovo.

(i) Quale necessaria premessa, è opportuno ricordare che nei commentari tachigrafici in genere, e in questo in particolare, le parole di ogni gruppo tetradico sono spesso legate da associazione di idee, quando non formino addirittura una o due frasette di senso compiuto. In questa "tetrade" credo possibile riconoscere un brevissimo periodo con una intonazione quasi proverbiale:

> Il rotolo
> è finito:
> allunga
> il papiro.[4]

Sotto l'aspetto terminologico, il dato più rilevante è che questa è l'unica testimonianza, tra quelle che provengono dai papiri, in cui χάρτης e βίβλος compaiono simultaneamente in un contesto dal quale è possibile derivare una distinzione di significato tra i due termini.

Le prime due parole, χάρτης ἔληξε, lasciano intravedere una

4. Si può immaginare sottinteso a μηκύνει un soggetto indefinito (τις) e tradurre in italiano con un impersonale "si allunga". Riferito a materiale librario, il verbo è attestato una sola volta, e in connessione con un termine più generico di βίβλος: Philod. *de poem.* 5.26.21 ἤδη μεμηκυσμένον τὸ σύγγραμμα καταπαύσομεν. Ma si noti in Du Cange, *Glossarium ad Scriptores Mediae et Infimae Graecitatis* (Lugduni 1688) *s.v.* μῆκος: "pro libri seu voluminis forma in Indice Ms. Bibliothecae Monasterii S. Trinitatis Insulae Chalces: Μῆκος πρῶτον, Μῆκος πάμπρωτον, Μῆκος κατάπρωτον, Μῆκος πρωτοδεύτερον, Μῆκος δευτερόπρωτον, Μῆκος τρίτον μικρόν."

In assenza di qualsiasi nesso coordinante o subordinante (impossibile, del resto, e inconcepibile all'interno di una struttura tetradica), si potrebbe obiettare che il "senso compiuto" della "tetrade" sia in realtà un risultato del tutto casuale – un mero effetto apparente, non voluto – di un'ordinata elencazione di parole, connesse, tutt'al più, da forte associazione di idee. Eppure si dovrà ammettere che nella "tetrade" è insito anche un certo ordine logico, rispondente al succedersi di due situazioni, rappresentate – come in altri casi nello stesso Commentario – dai due *cola* della "tetrade" (χάρτης ἔληξε/μηκύνει βίβλον). Inoltre mi pare che sciolga ogni dubbio il fatto che βίβλος sia all'accusativo, mentre nelle tetradi costituite da semplice elencazione di quattro parole, i nomi sono lemmatizzati al nominativo. Per più ampi ragguagli sulla struttura e il contenuto delle tetradi, cfr. Milne, *Greek Shorthand*, 3–4, e H. Boge, *Griechische Tachygraphie und Tironische Noten* (Berlin 1973) 110 e ss.

situazione in cui il rotolo che era stato preparato per la trascrizione di un testo è finito, cioè non è stato sufficiente a contenere tutto ciò che si intendeva scrivere. Il rimedio a questo inconveniente è subito indicato: allungare il papiro. Fino ad ora potevamo immaginare un intervento del genere – benché non ve ne siano accenni negli studi più recenti – ma non ne avevamo le prove.

Χάρτης, dunque, ha in questo contesto non tanto il significato generico di carta fatta con la pianta di papiro, quanto quello specifico di rotolo papiraceo di lunghezza prestabilita o programmata dallo scrivente: è la "technical designation" indicata da Naphtali Lewis "of a standard unit, or quantity, in the manufacture and sale of the product".[5]

Βίβλος non mi pare che qui possa equivalere a βιβλίον = rotolo scritto, libro, "the finished product, as it were, made from a papyrus roll";[6] infatti, se si parla di prolungare, s'intende che si ha a che fare con qualche cosa che è ancora in fase di produzione, con un prodotto librario ancora incompleto.

Βίβλος sarà, se mai, da interpretare in questo contesto come "the finished product made from the plant",[7] ma senza alcuna connotazione né limitazione quantitativa; in opposizione a χάρτης, rotolo di lunghezza fissata in anticipo, βίβλος esprime qui il concetto generico di supporto scrittorio in forma di rotolo, superficie scrittoria di estensione variabile, in relazione al testo che deve contenere.

(ii) Interviene, a questo punto, il secondo aspetto. Sull'esistenza di un rotolo standard e sulla confezione di rotoli di varie lunghezze per esigenze di mercato, esiste una divergenza di vedute tra coloro che in passato si sono occupati del problema. Ma, fra gli studiosi più recenti, fa eccezione l'accordo esplicito di Skeat con Lewis nel ritenere che la frase di Plinio *numquam plures scapo quam vicenae* (*scil. plagulae*) si riferisce all'unità standard di fabbricazione (cioè un rotolo composto da non più di venti fogli),[8] non certo al prodotto librario finito, perché, come si sa, numerosissimi sono i rotoli superstiti che sorpassano notevolmente questa lunghezza.

Sir Eric Turner, nell'ultimo suo lavoro, non si è pronunciato sul numero di fogli della unità standard, forse anche perché era sua opinione che il rotolo uscisse dalla fabbrica già nella misura

5. Lewis, *Papyrus*, 70.  6. Lewis, *Papyrus*, 78 e 79 nota 16.
7. Lewis, *Papyrus*, 78.  8. Skeat, "The Length...", 169.

richiesta dal cliente, composto cioè di un numero di fogli variabile, che i *glutinatores*, operanti all'interno della fabbrica, avevano il compito di unire.[9]

Skeat, al contrario, ha ritenuto perfettamente concepibile che il papiro lasciasse la fabbrica in rotoli di venti fogli (τόμοι) e che intermediari o dettaglianti attaccassero insieme rotoli o parti di rotoli su richiesta dei clienti, come è dimostrato dalla pratica di età faraonica e perfino araba[10] e come si desume, per l'età greco-romana, dalle designazioni χάρτης τρίτομος, τετράτομος, πεντηκοντάκολλος, ecc., testimoniate dai papiri stessi.[11]

In conclusione, χάρτης poteva designare, per usare le parole di Lewis, "the larger unit, sometimes encompassing three, four, and even eight τόμοι".[12]

(iii) Resta comunque controverso un punto molto importante: in quale fase della produzione il rotolo-libro raggiungeva la lunghezza desiderata o, meglio, la sua estensione definitiva? nella fabbricazione (Turner, Lewis), nel commercio (Lewis, Skeat), oppure, come riteneva Kenyon, nel corso della stesura di un testo?[13] A mio parere, in tutte e tre le fasi poteva verificarsi la necessità di modificare una data lunghezza originaria; dell'ultima fase è testimone la "tetrade".

Un utile indizio è la constatazione che i rotoli di 50 o 70 fogli non hanno designazione analoga (χάρτης πεντηκοντάκολλος, ἑβδομηκοντάκολλος) a quella dei rotoli risultanti dall'unione di

9. Turner, "Sniffing Glue", 12–13.

10. Lewis, *Papyrus*, 54–55.

11. Lewis, *Papyrus*, 77 nota 9; Skeat, "The Length...", 169–170 e note 2–3.

12. Lewis, *Papyrus*, 76–77.

13. Cfr. F. J. Kenyon, *The Palaeography of Greek Papyri* (Oxford 1899) 18; *The Papyrus Book* (London 1926) 126; *Books and Readers in Ancient Greece and Rome*[2] (Oxford 1951) 52.
Per evitare equivoci, vorrei chiarire che qui non è in discussione la fase di "montaggio" dei singoli fogli in τόμος, sulla cui anteriorità rispetto all'atto della vendita o della scrittura non dovrebbero più sussistere dubbi di sorta (cfr. Dorandi, "Glutinatores", 27); si tratta invece di ammettere che il massimo standard del prodotto librario finito, cioè il rotolo letterario di 10–11 metri (cfr. G. Cavallo, *Libri scritture scribi a Ercolano* (Napoli 1983) 15–16), possa derivare dal "montaggio" di più unità di fabbrica, composte ciascuna da un massimo di 20 fogli e lunghe, secondo i calcoli di Skeat ("The Length", 170), non più di cm 360; e infine accettare il dato di fatto che ci viene dal contenuto della "tetrade": la possibilità che un rotolo venisse prolungato, se necessario, anche dopo il suo acquisto.

più τόμοι, cioè composti probabilmente da un numero di fogli multiplo di venti (secondo Skeat, χάρτης τρίτομος = 60 fogli; χ. τετράτομος = 80 fogli; χ. ἑπτάτομος = 140 fogli; χ. ὀκτάτομος = 160 fogli).[14] Ciò suggerisce l'ipotesi che i χάρται multipli di τόμοι si trovassero già pronti sul mercato, in quanto confezionati in fabbrica in varie "pezzature" multiple dell'unità di venti, mentre i χάρται composti di una o più unità con l'aggiunta di parti di un altro rotolo (forse ritagli o "scampoli": infatti 50 fogli = 2 τόμοι da 20 fogli + mezzo τόμος; 70 fogli = 3 τόμοι + mezzo τόμος) fossero approntati su ordinazione del cliente presso la fabbrica stessa o dal rivenditore (o dai κολληταί/ *glutinatores* presso di lui?).[15] Essendo impossibile denominare questi χάρται con un composto di τόμος, si usava designarli in base al numero di fogli (κολλήματα) che contenevano.

Ma la misura del rotolo acquistato o programmato poteva anche rivelarsi insufficiente per le reali necessità. Ce ne dà una prova la "tetrade" del Commentario, che allude ad una aggiunta, un prolungamento della superficie scrittoria, un rimedio, insomma, che sembrerebbe del tutto estemporaneo. E doveva anche essere un caso molto comune – forse per edizioni non particolarmente impegnative o per rotoli documentari – se ne abbiamo traccia in questo testo di ambito scolastico, e in una frase che suona quasi come un proverbio.

Resto nel dubbio se supporre la presenza, anche presso i centri di copia, di κολληταί/*glutinatores*, a disposizione per simili eventualità;[16] altrimenti gli scribi stessi avrebbero dovuto com-

14. Forse già Skeat intendeva far notare questa differenza terminologica in "The Length...", 170, ma nella stampa deve essere saltato un rigo.

15. Non è un caso che per il rotolo da 50 fogli si usi un verbo che adombra un'ordinazione particolare: χάρτας ἐγδοῦναι πεντηκοντακόλλους ν (*P. Cairo Zen.* 59054.46–47; questa osservazione si deve a Lewis, *Papyrus*, 55 nota 29).
Di un commercio diretto del papiro dalla fabbrica al "consumatore" si ha il sospetto per l'età tolemaica: in *P. Teb.* 112.22 (112 a.C.) χαρτ[ο]πο(ιῶι) sembra più accettabile di χαρτ[ο]πό(ληι) (Lewis, *L'industrie du papyrus dans l'Egypte gréco-romaine* (Paris 1934) 127 e ss.; *Papyrus*, 117 e ss., in particolare 118 nota 7). In età romana, si può arguire l'esistenza di una vendita al dettaglio da due ricorrenze di un termine abbreviato, χαρτοπ( ) (*P. Flor.* 388.22, I/II[9]; *P. Wisc.* 29 *v.* 28, III[p]), interpretabile come χαρτοπώλης. Nessun'altra testimonianza fino al VII secolo, con il χαρτοπράτης di *BGU* 319.7.

16. Un'ipotesi del genere, per l'ambito latino, fu espressa da Lewis nel 1934 con queste parole: "...on nommait *glutinatores* les employés dans les ateliers des éditeurs romains qui collaient des pages supplémentaires aux rouleaux trop courts

piere, se necessario, l'incollatura di un altro rotolo, o di parte di un rotolo, al χάρτης originario.[17]

E questo è proprio quanto riteneva Kenyon, il quale più volte espresse il parere che non sempre si potesse (o si volesse?) prevedere con esattezza la lunghezza del rotolo necessaria:

The true interpretation of Pliny's statement [*numquam plures scapo quam vicenae*], no doubt, is that in practice the sellers of papyrus kept and sold it in lengths (Pliny's *scapi*) consisting of twenty sheets. Egyptian rolls have been observed in which the number 20 is marked at the end of each twentieth κόλλημα, and this no doubt indicates the end of each length of papyrus as purchased by the author from the stationer. But the author was no more limited by this fact than the modern writer is limited by the fact that he purchases his foolscap by the quire or the packet. He could join one length of papyrus on to another, and when he had finished his work he could cut off whatever papyrus was left blank.[18]

E ancora:

If his work did not extend to the length of a roll of twenty sheets, he could cut off the superfluous material. If it was of greater length, he could glue on a second roll to the first.[19]

Le parole di Kenyon, per lungo tempo dimenticate,[20] riacquistano ora piena validità alla luce della "tetrade" del Commentario, tratteggiando una pratica libraria che varrebbe la pena tentare di verificare autopticamente sui papiri.

pour contenir l'oeuvre qu'on était en train d'éditer" (*L'industrie*, 54). Questo tipo di mansione non risulta dalle testimonianze di *glutinatores*; tanto meno da quelle dei corrispondenti greci κολληταί, che sono estremamente incerte o per nulla indicative (cfr. Dorandi, "Glutinatores", 28 e nota 23); ma non può essere esclusa in via ipotetica.

17. Ma Skeat ritiene che l'unione di rotoli o porzioni di rotoli da parte dell'acquirente "might not have been convenient" e così prosegue: "We should in any case remember that the making of neat joins between sheets of papyrus, as described in detail by Turner [*The Typology of the Early Codex*, 47], clearly required skill and care" (Skeat, "The Length...", 172). Ma effettivamente non tutti i *joins* risultano essere *neat*.

18. F. J. Kenyon, *Palaeography*, 18.

19. F. J. Kenyon, *Books and Readers*, 52.

20. Ma, per la verità, Lewis cita il passo di *Books and Readers*, a sostegno della inopportunità di emendare *vicenae* della frase di Plinio con *ducenae* o *VIcenae* (= 600) (*Papyrus*, 55 nota 29).

# Problemi di datazione: Tiberio

## ORSOLINA MONTEVECCHI

In Egitto il primo anno di Tiberio dovrebbe decorrere dal 19 al 28 agosto 14[p] e coincidere con l'ultimo anno di Augusto; tuttavia è certo che il primo anno di Tiberio nei documenti egiziani è il 14/5.[1] Egittologi e papirologi, dal Wessely al Wilcken al Gauthier al Grenfell all'Hunt al Pestman...e a chi scrive,[2] hanno addotto come motivo di questa anomalia il fatto che la notizia dell'avvento di Tiberio giunse più tardi, ad anno incominciato. Una spiegazione che non regge, se si considera il modo tradizionale di datare in Egitto.[3]

Eppure della datazione egiziana di Tiberio si era occupato nel 1941 il Pippidi,[4] che, dopo aver riassunto le opinioni degli studiosi precedenti, aveva risolto la difficoltà in altro modo, adducendo valide ragioni di ordine storico-politico. Ma, come si vede, il suo scritto è rimasto ignorato proprio dai papirologi. Anche fra i moderni storici dell'antichità non tutti ne tengono conto; e alcuni, pur menzionandolo, non presentano il problema in termini esatti.[5]

---

1. Cf. P. W. Pestman, *Chronologie égyptienne d'après les textes démotiques* (Lugdunum Batavorum 1967) 90.
2. C. Wessely, "Das erste Jahr des Tiberius in Aegypten", *Wiener St.* 24 (1902) 391–93; U. Wilcken, *Grundzüge* (Leipzig 1912) lviii; H. Gauthier, *Le livre des rois d'Egypte* v: *Les empereurs romains* (*Mém. de l'IFAO* xxi, Le Caire 1917) 26 n. 3; Grenfell and Hunt, *P. Oxy.* xii 1453, introduzione; P. W. Pestman, *Chronologie*, *loc. cit.*; O. Montevecchi, *La papirologia* (Torino 1973) 67.
3. Cf. lo stesso Pestman, *Chronologie*, 5.
4. D. M. Pippidi, "L'avènement officiel de Tibère en Egypte", *Rev. hist. du sud européen* 18 (1941) 87–94 (= *Autour de Tibère* (Bucarest 1944) 125–32); A. Piganiol ne diede notizia in *Rev. Et. Lat.* 24 (1946) 376, ma, pur giudicando importante l'articolo, gli dedicò poche righe, da cui non risulta che avesse compreso il significato delle testimonianze papirologiche e il valore delle argomentazioni del Pippidi.
5. Lo ignora E. Kornemann, *Tiberius* (Stuttgart 1960), che pure ha un capitolo intitolato "Das einmonatige Interregnum beim Übergang des Prinzipates auf Tiberius" (59ss.); lo ignora D. Timpe, *Untersuchungen zur Kontinuität des frühen Prinzipats* (*Historia* Einzelschriften, Heft 5, Wiesbaden 1962), che ha un

Ritengo perciò non inutile riprendere la questione, valendomi di tutti gli elementi che oggi possediamo.

E' ovvio che la notizia della morte di Augusto sia arrivata in Egitto con un certo ritardo: un breve ritardo, poichè si era nel colmo dell'estate (19 agosto), nella stagione più propizia alla navigazione.[6] Si può supporre con buone probabilità che ad Alessandria sia giunta negli ultimi giorni dell'anno egiziano, nell'interno del paese nei primi giorni del nuovo anno, più o meno tardi a seconda della distanza da Alessandria. In agosto da Roma ad Alessandria si potevano impiegare da 7 a 10 giorni. Per le comunicazioni ufficiali si usavano per mare i mezzi più celeri e sicuri; per terra vi era un servizio organizzato di corrieri a cavallo. La notizia della morte di Galba e dell'avvento di Otone (15 gennaio), nel colmo dell'inverno e nella stagione più avversa alla navigazione (*mare clausum*), arrivò nell'interno, a Menfi, il 10 febbraio: ne abbiamo la certezza dal biglietto scritto a Menfi dal prefetto Tiberio Giulio Alessandro appena ricevuto l'annuncio.[7] Durante il primo secolo le comunicazioni sono regolari e celeri: Augusto stesso aveva riorganizzato il sistema delle poste imperiali.[8]

Che si trovino in Egitto documenti posteriori al 28 agosto del 14[p] datati con un inesistente 44° anno di Augusto,[9] è normale: un fatto analogo si ripeterà per altri imperatori. Nei documenti greci la data più arretrata in cui compare Tiberio è il 29 ottobre (*P. Teb.* II 561 iii), a cui seguono un ostracon del 7 novembre (*O. Edfu*

capitolo "Der Regierungswechsel des Jahres 14 n.Chr.". Cita Pippidi K. Wellesley, "The *dies imperii* of Tiberius", *JRS* (1967) 23 note 2 e 3, sorvolando, perchè non serve alla sua tesi. A. Garzetti, *L'Impero da Tiberio agli Antonini* (Bologna 1960), ne tiene conto (15) e cita Pippidi (581), ma non spiega in che consista la testimonianza dei papiri. Ancor più concisa B. Levick, *Tiberius the Politician* (London 1976) 79 e nota 30 a p. 249. J. Béranger, *Recherches sur l'aspect idéologique du principat* (Basel 1953), è forse il solo a valersi ampiamente del Pippidi e dei documenti papiracei, pur con qualche inesattezza nella valutazione dei documenti (20–21). P. Petit, *Histoire générale de l'Empire romain* (Paris 1974), 70 nota 2, fa dire al Pippidi esattamente il contrario di quanto aveva affermato (errore di stampa?).

  6. Cf. J. Rougé, *Recherches sur l'organisation du commerce maritime en Méditerranée sous l'Empire romain* (Paris 1966) 101–2.

  7. *P. Med.* inv. 69.66 *Verso*; cf. G. Geraci, *Aegyptus* 57 (1977) 145–50.

  8. Cf. Suet. *Aug.* 49.3.

  9. 44° anno di Augusto: *O. Med. Habou* 113, del 21 agosto; *O. Bodl.* 273 (= *O. Mattha* n. 13), del 30 agosto; *SB* III 6845 (17 ottobre).

401) e uno del 15 dicembre (*SB* 1 4519). Dei documenti demotici i più antichi sono due ostraca del dicembre (*O. Edfu*, ed. Menu, *BIFAO* 79 (1979) 131 n. 22, del 18 dic., e *O. Bodl.* 1370 = *O. Mattha* 93, del 27 dic.). Il 17 ottobre a Gebel Silsile, nell'Alto Egitto, si data ancora con Augusto (iscrizione votiva *SB* III 6845). Strano che il 17 ottobre si ignorasse l'avvento di Tiberio, sia pure a Gebel Silsile, e che le prime datazioni di Tiberio imperatore siano della fine di quel mese. Ma queste costatazioni non hanno un grande peso: il dedicante di *SB* III 6845, in una località sperduta dell'Alto Egitto, poteva non essere al corrente degli ultimi avvenimenti, e d'altra parte il vuoto di documenti, dagli ultimi di Augusto al primo di Tiberio, potrebbe essere colmato da nuove scoperte. *Ciò che conta è il fatto che l'anno primo di Tiberio è il 14/5.* La notizia ufficiale mandata da Roma ad Alessandria, e da Alessandria trasmessa a tutta la *chora*, doveva portare l'indicazione precisa del giorno in cui Tiberio aveva assunto il potere,[10] e se questo giorno fosse stato il 19 o il 20 agosto, o altro giorno prima del 29 agosto, anche ammesso che la comunicazione fosse arrivata in Egitto dopo l'inizio del nuovo anno, si sarebbe tenuto conto dei giorni trascorsi come di anno 1°, e da quel momento si sarebbe incominciato a datare anno 2°, come avverrà per Adriano, che, salito al trono l'11 agosto, non ha in Egitto alcun documento datato anno 1° (il suo primo anno è citato però in documenti posteriori, e si riferisce a quei pochi giorni di agosto).[11]

In Egitto questo modo di datare è consuetudine antica, che anche i Tolemei finirono per adottare, e che viene applicata quasi automaticamente: una consuetudine che ha permesso di spiegare perchè in Egitto si arrivi all'anno settimo di Aureliano. Disconoscendo Quintillo e ricollegandosi a Claudio il Gotico, Aureliano, consolidato il suo potere dopo la vittoria su Palmira, retrodata il

10. L'annuncio della morte di Claudio e dell'avvento di Nerone (*P. Oxy.* VII 1021 = *W. Chr.* 113 = *Sel. Pap.* II 235) non è, come pensa il Béranger (*Recherches*, 21), una comunicazione ufficiale venuta da Roma, ma la minuta di una circolare o di un annuncio alla popolazione preparata da un funzionario locale, probabilmente lo stratego, dopo aver ricevuto la comunicazione da Alessandria. Per l'avvento di Nerone il tempo impiegato per l'arrivo della comunicazione dovette essere necessariamente maggiore (siamo in ottobre–novembre). Su *P. Oxy.* VII 1021 cf. O. Montevecchi, "L'ascesa al trono di Nerone e le tribù alessandrine", in *I canali della propaganda nel mondo antico* (Contributi dell'Istituto di Storia antica, Milano 1976) 200–19.

11. *BGU* 1 19 i.18 (del 135ᵖ); *P. Oxy.* VII 1023.8 (data imprecisata del IIᵖ).

suo *dies imperii* anteriormente al 29 agosto 270, e con quei pochi giorni (o mesi, secondo alcuni studiosi) nelle datazioni egiziane "guadagna" un anno; e poichè muore dopo il 28 agosto 275, ha documenti datati 7° anno.[12]

Pertanto, poichè è certo che il primo anno di Tiberio in Egitto è il 14/5, resta da spiegare perchè quei giorni prima del 29 agosto non siano stati computati come anno 1° (almeno a posteriori, se la notizia arrivò troppo tardi). *Le ragioni non vanno cercate in eventuali ritardi di trasmissione della notizia, bensì in quello che accadde a Roma e nelle disposizioni che di là vennero inviate ad Alessandria.*

Occorre tener presente l'importanza eccezionale del trapasso da Augusto a Tiberio, che formalmente segna la fine della repubblica e il definitivo consolidarsi del principato. Momento critico, di cui Tiberio ha coscienza, come dimostra il suo rifiuto iniziale di accettare tutta intera l'eredità di Augusto e quella sua riluttanza ad arrivare ad una decisione in questo senso, che Tacito, Svetonio e Cassio Dione[13] interpretano come irresolutezza e ipocrisia. Ipocrisia o no, di fatto egli volle che la questione fosse aggiornata a dopo i funerali di Augusto. Almeno in teoria – osserva il Pippidi –[14] la dignità del *princeps* era stata creata per Augusto e per una durata limitata e, sempre in teoria, dopo la sua morte spettava al senato e al popolo romano abolire questa dignità oppure offrirla a un altro; Tiberio, rispettoso della legalità e dei privilegi del senato, era tenuto ad un atteggiamento di massimo riserbo.

Per quanto riguarda i suoi primi atti dopo la morte di Augusto, Tacito[15] dice che i consoli *primi in verba Tiberii Caesaris iuravere* e *apud eos* giurarono il prefetto del pretorio e il prefetto dell'annona, e tosto il senato, l'esercito e il popolo, *nam Tiberius cuncta per consules incipiebat tamquam vetere re publica et ambiguus imperandi.* Aggiunge poi che nell'editto di convocazione del senato Tiberio si qualificò solo con la potestà tribunicia conferitagli da Augusto. Però, prosegue Tacito, aveva dato la parola d'ordine alle coorti come *imperator*, e mandò lettere agli eserciti *tamquam adepto principatu, nusquam cunctabundus nisi cum in senatu loqueretur.* Più breve ma più preciso Cassio Dione:[16]

12. Cf. la fondamentale introduzione a *P. Oxy.* XL di J. R. Rea.
13. Tac. *Ann.* I 7–13; Suet. *Tib.* 24; Dio Cass. LVII 2.
14. *Autour de Tibère*, 131–32.
15. Tac. *Ann.* I 7.  16. Dio Cass. LVII 2.1.

ἔς τε τὰ στρατόπεδα καὶ ἐς τὰ ἔθνη πάντα ὡς αὐτοκράτωρ εὐθὺς ἀπὸ τῆς Νώλης ἐπέστειλε, μὴ λέγων αὐτοκράτωρ εἶναι.

Dunque mandò comunicazioni e ordini all'esercito e alle provincie come *imperator*, pur "dichiarando di non essere *imperator*" (μὴ λέγων αὐτοκράτωρ εἶναι).[17] Vale a dire, si comportò come chi esercita il potere interinalmente, ma formalmente non lo assume. E' in gioco l'ambiguità del titolo di *imperator*,[18] che cominciava a caricarsi di un significato nuovo, non più limitato all'esercito: e Tiberio lo rifiuta. Dione, che scrive quando il processo evolutivo è compiuto e superato, e all'*imperator* si è sostituito il *dominus*, coglie il significato di quell'apparente contraddizione? Certo non l'avverte Tacito, più vicino ai fatti ma ancor meno attento alle distinzioni di natura giuridica e più portato a interpretazioni psicologiche – e per di più esponente della corrente senatoria avversa a Tiberio.

Cassio Dione afferma che questi primi ordini e messaggi furono inviati subito, da Nola: dunque il 19 o al più il 20 agosto Tiberio notificò la morte di Augusto alle legioni e alle provincie; ma poichè non voleva accettarne la somma dei poteri nè assumere il titolo di *imperator*, dovette dare *disposizioni di carattere transitorio* per varie occorrenze e formalità immediate, tra cui, per le provincie in cui non si datava mediante i consoli, anche per la datazione. Delle altre provincie ci mancano i documenti; per l'Egitto pare si debba dedurre che ivi si continuò a datare da Augusto, pur conoscendosi la sua morte, certo per disposizioni venute da Roma. La datazione con l'anno di regno è una forma di riconoscimento della sovranità: il prefetto d'Egitto non poteva arrogarsi il diritto di prendere iniziative in merito.[19] Per questo l'omissione di quei 10 giorni ha un'importanza decisiva per valutare il significato che Tiberio volle dare alla sua posizione in quel preciso momento.

17. "Dichiarando di non essere imperatore" (οὔ φημι, μή φημι = *nego*): non già, come talora viene tradotto, "senza dirsi imperatore" (L. Pareti, *Storia di Roma* IV (Torino 1955) 694), nè "though he did not claim to be emperor" (Dio's *Roman History* VII, trad. E. Cary (London 1924)). L'uso di μή anzichè οὔ indica la volontà di Tiberio di non essere ritenuto imperatore.

18. Cf. in proposito Béranger, *Recherches*, 36ss.

19. Il Béranger (*Recherches*, 21) sembra sottovalutare l'importanza della datazione, e attribuire alle autorità provinciali la facoltà di prendere decisioni e la possibilità di arbitrî, impensabili in quest'epoca, e soprattutto in Egitto, provincia "a statuto speciale" dipendente direttamente dall'imperatore.

Sappiamo che il problema della successione, per espressa volontà di Tiberio, fu posto solo dopo l'apoteosi di Augusto, che fu celebrata il 17 settembre.[20] E la discussione in senato dovette probabilmente protrarsi ancora, come fanno pensare Tacito, Svetonio e Cassio Dione (*diu... recusavit*, dice Svetonio):[21] Pippidi ritiene "fin verso la fine di settembre, forse i primi giorni di ottobre".[22] Ignoriamo il *dies imperii* di Tiberio: certo non fu anteriore al 17 settembre, forse fu posteriore di qualche giorno.[23] Il che concorda con i dati dei documenti egiziani, nei quali il Pippidi vede la prova che il comportamento di Tiberio fu coerente con l'atteggiamento di riserva da lui assunto di fronte al senato.[24]

L'interregno tra Augusto e Tiberio, ammesso ormai dagli storici più recenti, è dunque confermato dai documenti papiracei (i quali però ci danno, per il suo scadere, solo un *terminus post quem*, 28 agosto), e con esso si chiarisce pienamente il motivo della datazione egiziana di Tiberio.

20. Tac. *Ann.* 1 8 e 11.

21. Suet. *loc. cit.*

22. *Autour de Tibère*, 129.

23. B. Levick (*Tiberius the Politician*, 79), considerando il protrarsi delle discussioni in senato – e i poteri che Tiberio aveva ricevuto da Augusto – conclude: "On this view, the problem of Tiberius' *dies imperii* and the date he 'took over' the Principate dissolves. He had not *dies imperii*, except in the sense that Augustus' death left him alone in a position of overwhelming strength, guaranteed by his official powers, *imperium* and *potestas*, and confirmed by his personal relationship to the dead Princeps." Non è qui il caso di discutere questa interpretazione, che potrebbe essere accettata, fino a un certo punto, se si considera la sostanza delle cose. Ma vi sono aspetti formali dei quali è necessario pure tener conto. E' vero che – come prosegue la Levick – "historians writing a century or more later naturally thought in terms of a *dies imperii*", ma anche il prefetto d'Egitto, nell'agosto–settembre del 14, "naturally thought in terms of *dies imperii*", aspettando direttive da Roma: la datazione dei documenti richiede un preciso *terminus a quo*. Al primo annuncio di Tiberio, subito dopo la morte di Augusto, dovette seguirne un altro, in cui si fissava il giorno in cui a ἔτους...Καίσαρος si sostituiva ἔτους...Τιβερίου Καίσαρος.

24. *Autour de Tibère*, 132.

# A roll upon his knees

G. M. PARÁSSOGLOU

In his justly celebrated inaugural lecture, Jaroslav Černý summarized our knowledge regarding the posture of the ancient Egyptian scribe in the following manner:

When writing on a roll, the Egyptian always sat and this is the position displayed by statues of scribes.... Egyptians sat either with the hind part of the body on the ground with the legs crossed in front or with the body resting on the crossed legs.... In a squatting position the loin cloth of the scribe is tightly stretched so as to provide a firm support for the papyrus.... He never uses a table of any kind.[1]

A few years ago Professor Naphtali Lewis suggested that I undertake an examination of the corresponding evidence pertaining to the position of the ancient Greeks and Romans. The results have been published elsewhere,[2] and I will give only a brief summary of them here. The artistic evidence on the subject, although disconcertingly scant and late, points to a picture that differs in some important details from the one painted by Černý. When writing on a roll, the Greeks and the Romans did not sit on the ground with their legs crossed beneath them in the Oriental way but sat on a seat of some kind. Like the Egyptians, they did not use tables or writing desks; instead, they held the roll spread upon their lap or placed upon one knee or one thigh only.

The literary evidence is even more exiguous but it, too, testifies to a close connection between the act of writing and the knees. At the time of my earlier publication I had searched in vain for an unequivocal description of a person engaged in the act of committing his, or someone else's, thoughts to a papyrus roll. By

---

1. J. Černý, *Paper and Books in Ancient Egypt* (London 1952) 13–14.
2. 'Δεξιὰ χεὶρ καὶ γόνυ. Some Thoughts on the Postures of the Ancient Greeks and Romans when Writing on Papyrus Rolls', *Scrittura e Civiltà* 3 (1979) 5–21, with six plates.

pure chance, and while casting my nets for a completely different kind of fish, I came upon my elusive objective; and I trust that my readers will allow me to offer it to the person who had encouraged me to undertake the original labor:

> *destinat hoc monstrum cumbae linique magister*
> *pontifici summo.*

The portrait I am referring to is found in that neglected opusculum going under the name of 'Hippocratic Epistles'. Since the discovery of *P. Oxy.* 1184, a renewed and determined investigation of the ideas expounded in the pseudepigraphical collection has led modern pundits to date it sometime in the first century before our era and to consider it the work of a learned doctor of the Coan school of medicine.[3] A number of these letters deal with the question whether Democritus, given as he was to fits of maniacal and inopportune laughter, was mad or not. According to our author, the Abderites, notwithstanding their proverbial simplemindedness, were worried about the mental stability of their most illustrious son so deeply that they summoned Hippocrates to restore him to normality. In the seventeenth epistle, the best of the lot, Hippocrates describes his first encounter with the 'mad scientist' (IX 350 and 352 L.):[4]

καὶ αὐτὸς ὁ Δημόκριτος καθῆστο ὑπό τινι ἀμφιλαφεῖ καὶ χθαμαλῆι πλατανίσκωι ἐν ἐξωμίδι παχείηι, μοῦνος, ἀνήλιπος, ἐπὶ λιθίνωι θώκωι, ὠχριακὼς πάνυ καὶ λιπόσαρκος, κουριῶν τὰ γένεια. παρ' αὐτὸν δ' ἐπὶ δεξιῆς λεπτόρρυτον ὕδωρ κατὰ πρηνοῦς τοῦ λόφου ἠρεμαίως ἐκελάρυζεν. ἦν δέ τι τέμενος ὑπὲρ ἐκεῖνον τὸν λόφον, ὡς ἐν ὑπονοίηι κατεικάζοντι, νυμφέων ἱδρυμένον, αὐτοφύτοις ἐπηρεφὲς ἀμπέλοις. ὁ δ' εἶχεν ἐν εὐκοσμίηι πολλῆι ἐπὶ τοῖν γονάτοιν βιβλίον, καὶ ἕτερα δέ τινα

---

3. For the date see especially R. Philippson, 'Verfasser und Abfassungszeit der Sogennanten Hippokratesbriefe', *Rheinisches Museum*, N.F. 77 (1928) 293–328, with the previous bibliography; see also K. Svoboda, 'Mravní tendence a společenská kritika v hippokratovských listech', *Listy Filologické*, N.F. 1 (1953) 55–64, with a French summary on pp. 312–13; D. Th. Sakalis, 'Beiträge zu den pseudo-hippokratischen Briefen', in F. Lasserre and Ph. Mudry (ed.), *Formes de pensée dans la collection hippocratique. Actes du IVᵉ colloque international hippocratique* (Geneva 1983) 499–514.

4. I quote from W. Putzger's edition, *Hippocratis quae feruntur epistulae ad codicum fidem recensitae* (*Wiss. Beilage zum Jahresbericht des Gymnasiums in Wurzen*, 1914). It may well be the 'erste kritische' edition of the letters (so Gossen in *R-E* Suppl. III 1154), but 'ihre Textgestaltung ist nicht immer glücklich' (Philippson, 'Verfasser...', 293). Professor Sakalis is preparing a new edition.

ἐξ ἀμφοῖν τοῖν μεροῖν αὐτέωι παρεβέβλητο· σεσώρευντο δὲ καὶ ζῶια συχνὰ ἀνατετμημένα δι' ὅλων. ὁ δὲ ὁτὲ μὲν ξυντόνως ἔγραφεν ἐγκείμενος, ὁτὲ δὲ ἠρέμει πάμπολύ τι ἐπέχων καὶ ἐν ἑωυτῶι μερμηρίζων. εἶτα μετ' οὐ πολὺ τουτέων ἐρδομένων ἐξαναστὰς περιεπάτει καὶ τὰ σπλάχνα τῶν ζῶιων ἐπεσκόπει καὶ καταθεὶς αὐτὰ μετελθὼν ἐκαθέζετο.[5]... ἐπεὶ δ' ἐπλησίαζον, ἔτυχεν ἐπελθὸν αὐτέωι ὅ τι δήποτε γράφειν ἐνθουσιωδῶς καὶ μεθ' ὁρμῆς· εἱστήκειν οὖν περιμένων αὐτέου τὸν καιρὸν τῆς ἀναπαύσιος· ὁ δὲ μετὰ σμικρὸν τῆς φορῆς λήξας τοῦ γραφείου ἀνέβλεψέν τε εἰς ἐμὲ προσιόντα καί φησιν· χαῖρε, ξένε.

It is a charming and a vivid depiction, so sufficiently self-explanatory that I prefer not to spoil it with exegetical comments. Let me only add a parting detail from a few lines farther on. After the necessary introductions, Democritus invites Hippocrates to sit down and inform him of the purpose of his visit (ix 354 L.):

τί δὲ χρέος, ἑταῖρε, δεῦρό σε ἤγαγε; μᾶλλον δὲ πρὸ πάντων κάθησο. ὁρῆις δέ, ὡς ἔστιν οὗτος οὐκ ἀηδὴς φύλλων θῶκος, ὅ τι χλοερὸς καὶ μαλθακὸς ἐγκαθίσαι προσηνέστερος τῶν τῆς τύχης ἐπιφθόνων θώκων.

The courteous Democritus, the philosopher who goes on to condemn the aspirations to riches and to glorify the sagacity of the simple life, invites his guest to sit on a humble and natural seat, a heap of fresh leaves. The author of the epistle, however, must have felt that to portray Democritus *writing* while seated on the ground would not have sounded verisimilar; in fact it might have been taken as a symptom of his μανίη, while, as Hippocrates himself diagnoses (ix 348 L.),

τοῦτ' ἐκεῖνο, Δαμάγητε, ὅπερ εἰκάζομεν, οὐ παρέκοπτε Δημόκριτος, ἀλλὰ πάντα ὑπερεφρόνεε καὶ ἡμέας ἐσωφρόνιζε καὶ δι' ἡμέων πάντας ἀνθρώπους.

With the above description in mind, it is easy to understand how it is possible for a written papyrus roll to declare that κάλαμος μ' ἔγραψε, δεξιὰ χεὶρ καὶ γόνυ.[6]

5. As becomes clear later on (ix 356 L.), Democritus is writing a treatise... περὶ μανίης; he is dissecting the carcasses χολῆς διζήμενος φύσιν καὶ θέσιν.
6. *P. Lond.* inv. 136 = *P. Lit. Lond.* 11. See pp. 18–19 of my article cited above for discussion and bibliography.
I am greatly obliged to Professors D. Lipourlis and D. Hagedorn for their assistance with the bibliography.

# Aurelios Apollonios alias Dionysios, ginnasiarco ad Ossirinco

PAOLA PRUNETI

La recente pubblicazione di tre testi documentari[1] provenienti da Ossirinco nei quali viene nominato il ginnasiarco Aurelios Apollonios alias Dionysios[2] fornisce l'occasione per dare uno sguardo d'insieme ad un gruppo di papiri che attestano la presenza attiva di questo personaggio nella vita pubblica della città.[3] Purtroppo, mancando per alcuni di questi documenti la possibilità di una collocazione cronologica precisa (o perché la data è perduta in lacuna, o perché eventuali elementi di datazione, sia diretta che indiretta, anche se presenti nel testo non hanno un valore determinante), non solo è difficile stabilire con esattezza la successione delle cariche ricoperte da Aurelios Apollonios alias Dionysios, ma risulta impossibile anche delimitare con precisione il periodo di tempo al quale si riferiscono le attestazioni della sua attività pubblica.

I papiri che fanno menzione di Aurelios Apollonios alias Dionysios sono:

| | |
|---|---|
| *P. Ups. Frid.* 6 | 273[p] |
| *P. Berol.* 11314 (= *SB* x 10555) | 281/82[p] |
| *P. Oxy.* I 55 | 283[p] |
| *P. Oxy.* I 59 | 292[p] |
| *P. Flor.* I 63 | ? |
| *PSI* VI 705 | ? |
| *PSI* inv. 1145 | ? |
| *P. Laur.* IV 155 | ? |

1. *PSI* inv. 1145 (in *Anagennesis* 1 (1981) 255–65), *P. Ups. Frid.* 6, *P. Laur.* IV 155.

2. In *PSI* inv. 1145 il nome è conservato solo parzialmente: in proposito si veda, più avanti, il commento al papiro.

3. Cfr. P. J. Sijpesteijn, *Liste des gymnasiarques des métropoles de l'Egypte romaine* (Amsterdam 1967) ai nn. 262, 383, 391, e A. K. Bowman, *The Town Councils of Roman Egypt* (Toronto 1971) 133 e 136.

In *P. Ups. Frid.* 6, contenente una richiesta di registrazione di un fanciullo datata al mese di Mesorè del 4° anno di Aureliano (luglio–agosto del 273ᵖ), Aurelios Apollonios alias Dionysios è il proprietario della casa, situata nell'*amphodon* Παμμένου Παραδείσου di Ossirinco, nella quale viene registrato il fanciullo. La definizione attribuitagli, cioè γυμνασίαρχος βουλευτής, sembrerebbe indicare, rispetto a quanto si legge in altri documenti, che l'attività pubblica di Aurelios Apollonios alias Dionysios come appartenente alla classe senatoria è ancora relativamente limitata; tuttavia, poiché egli compare nel papiro non in veste di pubblico funzionario, ma come privato cittadino, non si può escludere l'eventualità di una menzione solo parziale e approssimativa delle cariche ricoperte.

L'elenco dei πρυτάνεις (in successione cronologica) restituito da *P. Berol.* 11314 assegna al 7° anno di un imperatore non nominato (ma che secondo l'editore sarebbe da identificare con Probo, per cui il 7° anno corrisponderebbe al 281/82ᵖ), un Ἀπολλώνιος ὁ καὶ Διονύσιος.[4] La mancanza del *nomen* Aurelios non appare sufficiente per dubitare che Apollonios alias Dionysios sia la stessa persona che negli altri papiri è chiamata Aurelios Apollonios alias Dionysios. Qui egli viene indicato semplicemente come πρύτανις, senza menzione delle altre cariche, essendo la pritania l'ufficio connesso al documento stesso (si tratta di una lista di persone addette ai bagni pubblici, anno per anno, sotto i rispettivi pritani).[5] Ciò che si legge riguardo ad Apollonios alias Dionysios, analogamente a quanto avviene per gli altri πρυτάνεις citati nel papiro, si limita all'anno e alla funzione esercitata:

3 (ἔτους) πρυτ(ανεύοντος ?) Ἀπολλωνίου τοῦ κ(αὶ) Διονυσίου (r. 15).

Una lunga serie di appellativi, riferiti a cariche già ricoperte o ancora in atto, accompagna invece il nome di Aurelios Apollonios alias Dionysios in *P. Oxy.* 1 55, che è di poco posteriore al documento precedente, essendo datato al 1° anno di Caro, Carino e Numeriano.[6] Due fratelli, rivolgendosi ad Aurelios Apollonios

4. Circa i problemi connessi alla datazione del papiro, si rimanda all' *ed. pr.* in *Chr. d'Eg.* 43 (1968) 325–31. La ricostruzione cronologica viene accolta anche da Bowman, *Town Councils*, 132–33.

5. Le competenze dei pritani si estendevano anche alle opere pubbliche e, in particolare, ai bagni: cfr. Bowman, *Town Councils*, 87–90.

6. Il documento reca la data del 12 Pharmouthi, corrispondente al 7 aprile del 283ᵖ.

alias Dionysios per ottenere il pagamento di lavori effettuati ad una strada in costruzione,[7] lo definiscono (rr. 1–4)

γενομένῳ ὑπομνηματογράφῳ κ[αὶ] ὡς χρηματίζει γυμνασιαρχήσαν[τ]ι βουλευτῇ ἐνάρχῳ π[ρ]υτάνι τῆς λαμπρᾶς καὶ λαμπροτάτ[ης Ὀ]ξ(υ-ρυγχιτῶν) πόλεως διέποντι καὶ τὰ πολιτικά.[8]

In *P. Oxy.* 1 59, documento con il quale la κρατίστη βουλή di Ossirinco, tramite il suo presidente Aurelios Apollonios alias Dionysios,[9] comunica ufficialmente allo stratego la nomina di un sostituto per un incarico liturgico, la carriera di questo personaggio non è più ristretta a sole cariche municipali, ma appare chiaramente estesa anche a magistrature Alessandrine.[10] Il papiro, che è del 292[p],[11] riporta per Aurelios Apollonios alias Dionysios questi attributi:

γενομένου ὑπομν(ηματογράφου) βουλευτοῦ τῆς λαμπροτάτης πόλεως τῶν Ἀλεξανδρέων γυμν(ασιαρχήσαντος) πρυτ(ανεύσαντος) βουλευτοῦ ἐνάρχου πρυτάν[ε]ως (rr. 3–5).

Una successione di titoli abbastanza simile, anche se non identica, si ritrova in *P. Laur.* IV 155, contenente una richiesta della corporazione τῶν χαλκέων relativa al pagamento di lavori in un bagno cittadino.[12] Purtroppo, essendo perduta in lacuna la data, risulta impossibile una collocazione cronologica sicura, ed anche gli elementi interni non sono abbastanza significativi: l'appellativo λαμπρὰ καὶ λαμπροτάτη che accompagna il nome della città di Ossirinco può solo costituire un probabile *terminus post quem*;[13]

7. Per la competenza dei pritani sulle opere pubbliche, cfr. nota 5.

8. E' probabile che in questa serie di titoli la carica di *hypomnematographos* sia relativa alla città di Alessandria, come avviene in *P. Oxy.* 1 59, *P. Laur.* IV 155 e, verosimilmente, in *PSI* VI 705. Tuttavia, mancando un chiaro e sicuro riferimento ad Alessandria, non si può escludere che si alluda – invece – a una magistratura metropolitana: cfr., in proposito, N. Lewis, *The Compulsory Public Services of Roman Egypt* (Firenze 1982) 77 n. 64. Quanto al significato della espressione διέπων καὶ τὰ πολιτικά, cfr. Bowman, *Town Councils*, 59.

9. Il nome sembrerebbe presentarsi nella forma Αὐρήλιος Ἀπόλλων: ai rr. 2–3 si legge infatti διὰ Αὐρηλίου Ἀπόλλωνο[ς / τοῦ καὶ Διονυσίου κτλ. (Cfr. anche Sijpesteijn, *Gymnasiarques*, no. 391).

10. Per attestazioni analoghe, relative a πρυτάνεις della città di Ossirinco che ricoprirono uffici anche in Alessandria, cfr. Bowman, *Town Councils*, 58.

11. Il documento è datato al 16 Mechir dell'anno 8° di Diocleziano e 7° di Massimiano.

12. Cfr. nota 5.

13. Il *terminus post quem* sarebbe il 272[p]: si veda D. Hagedorn in *ZPE* 12 (1973) 285.

quanto alla titolatura di Aurelios Apollonios alias Dionysios, testimonianza di un *cursus honorum* ormai avanzato (cfr. rr. 1–4:

Ἀὐρηλίῳ Ἀπολλωνίῳ τῷ καὶ Διονυσίῳ [γενομένῳ] ὑπομνη(ματο-γράφῳ) τῆς λαμπρο(τάτης) πό[λε]ω[ς] τῶν Ἀ[λεξανδρέων] γυμ(νασι-αρχήσαντι) βουλευτῇ καὶ ῷ[ς] χρημ(ατίζει) [τῆς λαμπρᾶς καὶ] λαμπ[ρ]ο(τάτης) Ὀξ(υρυγχιτῶν) π[όλ]εως ἐνάρχῳ πρυτάνει)

sembrerebbe rispecchiare una situazione intermedia fra le cariche elencate in *P. Oxy.* I 55 (283ᵖ) e quelle ricordate in *P. Oxy.* I 59 (292ᵖ). Tuttavia anche questo è un indizio troppo vago e troppo incerto per poter essere considerato un utile elemento di datazione, sia pure relativa.

*PSI* VI 705, in cui Aurelios Apollonios alias Dionysios agisce privatamente, in veste di compratore della sesta parte di una stalla, presenta un testo lacunoso che, pur non permettendo di ricostruire l'insieme degli uffici che vi erano citati, è però sufficiente a stabilire che Aurelios Apollonios alias Dionysios ricopre (o ha ricoperto) cariche in Alessandria, è ginnasiarca, ex-pritane e senatore (vero-similmente di Ossirinco). Ciò che rimane dei titoli che lo qualificavano è, infatti, leggibile ai rr. 3–4:

Αὐρηλίῳ Ἀπολλωνίῳ τῷ καὶ Διονυσί[ῳ . . . . . . . . . . . . . . . . . πόλεως τῶν
Ἀλεξ]ανδρέων γυμνασιάρχῳ πρυτανεύσαντι βουλευτῇ τῆ[ς . . . .¹⁴

Anche per questo papiro, non essendo conservata la data, bisogna limitarsi ad accogliere una datazione generica alla fine del secolo IIIᵖ.¹⁵

Pure *P. Flor.* I 63, nonostante rechi la data del 3 Phamenoth "del quinto anno", presenta difficoltà di datazione, dal momento che il nome dell'imperatore non vi è espresso. Infatti, se è vero che alla luce delle conoscenze attuali può essere meno discutibile l'ipotesi che si tratti del 5° anno di Probo (280ᵖ), così come l'eventuale attribuzione al 5° anno di Aureliano (274ᵖ), risulta tuttavia impossibile stabilire la data precisa.¹⁶ Nel documento, che

14. Sulla base di *P. Oxy.* I 59 e *P. Laur.* IV 155, si potrebbe suggerire, fra la fine del r. 3 e l'inizio del r. 4, una integrazione in cui, dopo il nome, com-paia (forse con qualche termine abbreviato?) una qualifica del tipo Αὐρηλίῳ Ἀπολλωνίῳ τῷ καὶ Διονυσί[ῳ γενομένῳ ὑπομνηματογράφῳ τῆς λαμπροτάτης πόλεως τῶν Ἀλεξ]ανδρέων κτλ.

15. Per la datazione di *PSI* VI 705, cfr. Bowman, *Town Councils*, 136 n. 24.

16. Oltre a Bowman, *Town Councils*, 136 n. 24, e alle le osservazioni di J. Rea, che ripubblica il documento in *Chr. d'Eg.* 46 (1971) 153–55, si veda quanto dice lo stesso Rea nella introduzione a *P. Oxy.* LI 3606, pag. 13.

*Aurelios Apollonios alias Dionysios, ginnasiarco ad Ossirinco*

contiene una ricevuta rilasciata a un καψάριος, Aurelios Apollonios alias Dionysios è detto essere (rr. 2–3)

γυμνασιαρχήσ[ας] βουλ(ευτὴς) ἔναρχος πρύτανις τῆς Ὀξυρυγχ( ) πόλ(εως).[17]

Rimane ancora da prendere in considerazione *PSI* inv. 1145, nel quale la lacuna parziale del nome e delle cariche lascia un margine di incertezza circa la possibilità di riconoscere Aurelios Apollonios alias Dionysios[18] nella persona che, insieme ad altri, dà in affitto – a decorrere dal 1° Phamenoth τοῦ ἐνεστῶτος ε (ἔτους)[19] – una casa situata nell'*amphodon* Βορρᾶ Δρόμου di Ossirinco. Ai rr. 2–4, mutili nella metà destra, si legge soltanto

ὁ καὶ Διονύσιο[ς . . . . . . . . . . . . / καὶ πρυτανε[ύσας . . . . . . . . / Ὀξυ-ρυγχειτῶ[ν πόλεως . . . . . . . . . .

ma non sembra troppo azzardato supporre che nelle lacune dei rr. 2–3 si alludesse anche alla qualifica di ginnasiarco e di buleuta.[20]

Non sarà inutile, infine, segnalare che *P. Oxy.* LI 3610 (datato *ante* 30.8.251ᵖ) attesta, ai rr. 4–5, un Αὐρήλιος Ἀπολλώνιος ὁ καὶ Διονύσιος ὁ ἱερεὺς καὶ ἀρχι[δικαστής, del quale però, come osserva anche l'editore, non si può dire se sia la stessa persona del ginnasiarco.

17. La mancanza dell'appellativo λαμπρὰ καὶ λαμπροτάτη per Ossirinco potrebbe far orientare verso una datazione anteriore al 272ᵖ (cfr. anche nota 13), tuttavia i titoli che qualificano Aurelios Apollonios alias Dionysios apparentemente attestano un *cursus honorum* più avanzato rispetto a *P. Ups. Frid.* 6, che è del 273ᵖ.

18. L'ipotesi della probabile identificazione con Aurelios Apollonios alias Dionysios è ampiamente discussa nell'*ed. pr.* del documento.

19. La data non è, tuttavia, precisabile, poiché il papiro manca della parte finale dove – presumibilmente – erano indicati per esteso il giorno, il mese e l'anno con la relativa titolatura imperiale.

20. Ancora una volta si rimanda all'*ed. pr.* per le possibili integrazioni.

# Furlough in the Roman army

M. P. SPEIDEL

To the Roman soldier furlough must have been particularly welcome since he spent his twenty-five years of service largely in garrison duty at outlying forts, sometimes far from his parents and his possessions. Yet whether and when he could get furlough depended on the army commanders and the troop officers and their often conflicting interests.

The army commanders wanted a strong and disciplined army, hence they strove to reduce furlough to a minimum. The troop officers, by contrast, wanted to profit from selling furlough grants and from pocketing the absent soldiers' rations, hence they sought to have as many men on leave as possible. Since the troop officers were the backbone of the army, their interests, however selfish, could not be overlooked. The soldiers, in turn, eager for leave but not wanting to pay for it, pressured the High Command to bear the cost. Thus compromises had to be found and enforced.

Any fair system of granting leave in keeping with the needs and means of the army required documentation in order to check how much furlough was taken by each man and when, and how many men were on leave simultaneously in each unit. How was this accomplished? Papyri and ostraca, next to stone inscriptions our best documentary sources, can be drawn upon to answer this question. Indeed, when it comes to furlough in the Roman army, inscriptions leave us in the dark, while papyri and ostraca add enough fresh and telling detail to warrant a look at just how they fill in the picture drawn from the legal and literary sources.

The High Command's policy of curbing the issue of furlough in order to keep the army strong and well trained remained the same under the emperors. Under Nero, Caesennius Paetus is blamed for weakening his legions through indiscriminate furloughs even though a Parthian attack was looming; Galba, as commander of the Upper German army, forbade his men even to apply for leave.[1] In the Severan period, Paternus advised that furlough should be given only very sparingly.[2] Of Diocletian's old order Vegetius says 'when, and for how many days, anyone received furlough, was written down in the rosters. For at that time little furlough was given and only for the most just and approved reasons.' Likewise for his own time in the later fourth century, Vegetius still suggests barring all furlough if the army's discipline is endangered.[3]

Unlimited furlough (*liber commeatus*) was, in the view of the staff officer Ammianus Marcellinus, one of the reasons for the weakness and lack of battle-readiness of the troops in Gaul. Even as late as the reign of Anastasius (491–518) the number of soldiers on furlough was limited by law to no more than thirty per unit. The High Command's policy in restricting furlough is further reflected in the Codes' stern punishments prescribed for *emansores* and *desertores* and, in a more general way, in Trajan's maxim that as few men as possible should be away from the standards (*quam paucissimos a signi avocandos esse*).[4]

The troop officers' machinations are exposed by Tacitus: 'A demand was made that the fees for leave usually paid to the centurions should be abolished; these the common soldiers had paid like a yearly tribute. One fourth of a company could be scattered on furlough, or even loitering in the camp, as long as they paid the fees to the centurions.'[5] Tacitus goes on to say that since the reign of Otho these yearly furlough fees (*vacationes annuae*) were

1. Tacitus, *Annals* 15.9 (A.D. 62): *reliquas (legiones) promiscuis militum commeatibus infirmaverat.* Suetonius, *Galba* 6.2: *Pari severitate interdixit commeatus peti.* Cf. SHA, *Hadr.* 10: *Numquam passus aliquem a castris iniuste abesse.* For discussions of furlough in the Roman army see especially M. Rostovtzeff, *Commeatus, R-E* IV (1901) 718–20; A. Müller, 'Excurs zu Tacitus' *Histor.* 1.46, *Philologus* 65 (1906) 289–306; R. Grosse, *Römische Militärgeschichte* (Berlin 1920) 246–48; R. S. Bagnall, *The Florida Ostraca* (Durham/N.C. 1976) 19f. and 40f.

2. *Dig.* 49.16.12: *parcissime commeatum dare.*

3. Vegetius 2.19: *Quando quis commeatum acceperit vel quot dierum, adnotatur in brevibus. Tunc enim difficile commeatus dabatur nisi causis iustissimis adprobatis. Idem,* 3.4: (in the case of *tumultus*) *nullis commeatibus vacent.*

4. Pliny, *Ep.* 10.20; also 10.22: *quantum fieri potest, curandum, ne milites a signis absint. Dig.* 49.16.3ff.; *Cod. Iust.* 1.27.2.9; Ammianus Marcellinus 27.8.9f.

5. *Histories* 1.46: *Flagitatum ut vacationes praestari centurionibus solitae remitterentur; namque gregarius miles ut tributum annuum pendebat. Quarta pars manipuli sparsa per commeatus aut in ipsis castris vaga, dum mercedem centurioni exsolveret.* Cf. *Annals* 1.17: *Saevitiam centurionum et vacationes munerum redimi.* Cf. *Annals* 1.35.1.

paid by the imperial fisc – a passage from which one may infer that a soldier then had the right to get furlough at least once a year.[6]

During the first three centuries centurions and decurions were authorized to grant furlough, as is obvious from Tacitus' report just quoted. As to the decurions, the equivalent of the centurions in cavalry units, one would surmise likewise, and indeed a law passed by Constantine in A.D. 323 expressly forbids *praepositi*, decurions, and tribunes to grant furlough. This they obviously had done up to then.[7] The law has been called into question with the argument that by this time decurions no longer existed as cavalry officers.[8] But here the papyri decide the question clearly, for they attest cavalry decurions as late as A.D. 349.[9]

With the right to grant furlough in the hands of low-ranking company and squadron leaders (a centurion was set over 80 men, a decurion over 30 horsemen), the road to abuse was wide open. While the efficient discipline of the early and high empire may have helped in curbing such abuse, the breakdown of discipline from the third century A.D. onwards made it necessary to restrict the right of issuing furlough. Constantine's law deprived even regimental commanders of it, which left the power to grant furlough in the hands of the *duces*.[10] In practice, of course, the unit commanders (*tribuni*) continued to issue furlough,[11] all the more since the temptation to scrounge a profit from the soldiers' furloughs by pocketing their pay and rations proved irresistible

6. *Histories* 1.46: *Sed Otho, ne volgi largitione centurionum animos averteret, fiscum suum vacationes annuas exsoluturum promisit, rem haud dubie utilem et a bonis postea principibus perpetuitate disciplinae firmatam.* Also *ibid.* 58.1.

7. *Cod. Theod.* 7.12.1: *Ne cui liceat praepositorum vel decurionum vel tribunorum cohortium quocumque genere cuiquam de militibus a castris atque signis vel his etiam locibus quibus praetendant discedendi commeatum dare.* Cf. *Cod. Theod.* 7.1.2.

8. Müller, *op. cit.* (n. 1) *loc. cit.*, followed by Grosse, *op. cit.* (n. 1) *loc. cit.*

9. E.g. *P. Abinn.* 59 and see *ibid.* p. 15.

10. See n. 7. Grosse, *op. cit.* (n. 1) 115 and 246f., suggests *tribuni* and *praepositi* had the right to issue furlough in the fourth, fifth, and sixth century, but the sources he adduces (*Cod. Theod.* 7.12.1, 7.1.2; *Cod. Iust.* 1.27 and 2.9; SHA, *Pescen. Nig.* 3.8, *Alex. Sev.* 15.5 and 54.7) state that it is *against* the law for them to grant furlough. In *Cod. Iust.* 12.37.16, quoted below, the thirty men allowed to receive furlough seem to receive it from on high rather than from the tribune. *Cod. Iust.* 1.27.2.9 (A.D. 534) even deprives the *duces* of the right to issue furlough: *nullum audeant duces aut tribuni commeatalem de ipsis dimittere.* Cf. A. H. M. Jones, *The Later Roman Empire, 284–602* (Oxford 1973) 633. For *commeatales* see also *SB* VI 9613.

11. *Cod. Iust.* 12.37.16.2ff.

even for *duces*. Thus Synesios of Kyrene, in the early fifth century, complains that a certain *dux* Cerialis, 'as if it were the law that the pay of the rank and file belongs to the generals, pocketed what they all used to get and in return gave them immunity from service, so that they need not stay in their units, letting them go where each thought he would make his living'.[12] That this was not an isolated case is clear from the fact that laws had to be passed against such abuses.[13]

How does our documentation of papyri and ostraca reflect the soldiers' furloughs? Entries in the duty roster of *legio III Cyrenaica* in A.D. 90–96, and in that of another unit in A.D. 312, prove Vegetius right in reporting that formerly furloughs used to be entered in the papers of a unit.[14] Likewise, failing to return might be entered on the records as *non comparet*.[15] A third-century papyrus from Oxyrhynchus shows that in the case of a soldier being transferred from one unit to another, the army commander of the province (here the *praefectus Aegypti*) would grant the furlough.[16] A papyrus letter written in A.D. 107 by a soldier at Petra in Arabia reads 'I shall take pains, as soon as the governor begins to grant furloughs, to come to you immediately.'[17] If, as is likely, furlough for legionaries at that time was still issued by the centurions, the governor's restriction on leaves must have been due to special circumstances. These are not hard to find: the legion had just come to occupy Arabia and, obviously, during the initial stages of the occupation no furlough could be given. However, since the writer

---

12. Jones, *op. cit.* (n. 10) 645.

13. *Cod. Iust.* 1.27.2.9: *et nullum audeant duces aut tribuni commeatalem de ipsis dimittere, ne, dum sibi lucrum studeant conficere, incustoditas nostras relinquant provincias. Nam si usurpaverint memorati duces vel officia eorum seu tribuni commeatalem de militibus relinquere aut aliquod lucrum de eorum emolumentis subripere...*

14. R. O. Fink, *Roman Military Records on Papyrus* (Cleveland, Ohio 1971) 9.2. For Vegetius 2.19 see above, n. 3. As for the inferences from these annotations by A. von Premerstein, ('Die Buchführung einer ägyptischen Legionsabteilung', *Klio* 3, Beiheft 1 (1903) 1–46) see the healthy scepticism of J. Lesquier in his *L'armée romaine d'Egypte* (Cairo 1918) 247. See also *P. Mich.* x 593 ii 10 and iii 9.

15. *P. Dura* 82 ii 20 = Fink, *Roman Military Records*, 47 = *ChLA* VII 337 *q.v. ad loc.*

16. *P. Oxy.* XIV 1666.1–15 = *Sel. Pap.* 1.149 = S. Daris, *Documenti per la storia dell'esercito Romano in Egitto* (Milan 1964) no. 8.

17. *P. Mich.* VIII 466.

of the letter expected that after a while furloughs would be available, the papyrus neatly illustrates the fact that the issue of furlough depended on the overall strategic situation.[18]

Indeed, from about the same time and concerning the same legion a mobilization order has become known recently, enjoining the curtailment of furlough. The preserved fragment reads as follows:[19]

```
              ]PIENDAS EX E[PISTULA
              ]APOLLONIATAE V[
              ]şulari        ..[
              ].AE    EX EPISTUL[A
5                   ].ONE P(RAE)P(OSIT-)   [
              ]        ITEM[
              ]  GERENDAM LEG(ION-)  ·  III[
              ]MELLONIAE SEDATU.[
              ]M COMMEATUM        [
10            ]DEDUCENDOS EX EPISTULA[
              ]S DEDUCENDAS             [
              ]EDUCENDOS               [
              ]EX CLASSE PRAETORIAE M[ISENATIUM
        EX CLASSE PR]AETORIAE RAUENNATIUM[
15            ].  DEPUTARI              [
              ]ERAE FINITUM COMMEATUM[

                        ]  C...[

              ]....NIUM CUM..TU[
              ]FL(AUIA) · CILICUM AEDI..IU[
20      ]AE FINE                   EX FORMA[
        ].A COGENDA IMFERIOR.[
```

Since the word *commeatus* means 'supply shipments' as well as 'furlough', the editors wondered whether the document was not an order for supply transports. *Finitus*, however, is the opposite of *liber*,[20] and *liber commeatus* is known as the technical term for unrestricted furlough;[21] *finitus commeatus*, therefore, must mean

---

18. The editor's suggestion that the writer may perhaps not have received furlough because he had only recently joined the legion must be rejected if furlough was then still issued by the centurions, for here it is the governor that denies it. A soldier could not know in advance whether he would get furlough, hence Question 78 of the *Sortes Astrampsychi* (ed. G. M. Browne, Leipzig 1983), εἰ λαμβάνω κομιᾶτον.

19. R. Seider, 'Eine Heidelberger lateinische Militärurkunde. (P. Heid. Lat. 7)', *ZPE* 29 (1978) 241–51 = *ChLA* x 500.

20. Quint. *Inst.* 9.4.50: *Rhythmis libera spatia, metris finita sunt.*

21. Above, p. 284; below, pp. 290–91.

'limited furlough'. Thus we learn a new technical army term and see that the document is indeed a mobilization order, possibly for the conquest of Arabia in A.D. 106, or for the quelling of the Jewish revolt in Egypt in A.D. 115–16. Unfortunately it is not clear whether it is intended that only limited furlough be given, or whether even limited furlough is to be suspended. There is no doubt, though, that we have here a mobilization order curtailing furlough.

Apparently from the same *legio III Cyrenaica* in Arabia comes a mid second-century application for furlough:[22]

. . . . . . . . . . . . .
. .

```
    Ịdịb(us) Febṛuarị[is] . . . . . . .
    . . . cụras . . . . . . . ẹ . . . . commẹ-
    ạtum dare . [ . . . . ]ụsụm decem
5   [ . . . ]poṣṣim[ . . ]bẹṇeficio huma-
    nitatis tuae . . . ḍebịtum mẹ-
    um pẹrcipẹṛẹ . . . effeṛci . . .
    er . . . . age[r]e . . e . . . . emẹra
    rṭ manifest . . . . . s . . . ṛium
10  meum . . . ḷịb[e]llum seṛụi
```

The rank of the applicant is not known, but since he addresses his letter to a high-ranking person (*humanitas tua*), presumably the governor, he may have been a centurion, for had he been a simple soldier he might have got furlough from his own centurion. It is noteworthy that the purpose of the leave, financial dealings, had to be declared, and that the granting of the leave was considered a *beneficium*.

For the actual recording of furlough two ostraca are of particular interest. One (*O. Flor.* 1) has the following text written on the upper half of the potsherd:

ἔχεις δέκα ἡμέρας κο-
μιᾶτεν 'Αμμωνᾶς·
ἔχεις δύο ἡμέρας κομι-
ᾶτεν καὶ coì ἀπάγαθαι.

1, 3 *l.* κομιᾶτον    4 *l.* ἀπάγεcθαι

You have ten days' furlough, Ammonas; you have two days' furlough also to return.

22. *P. Berol.* 21652 = *ChLA* xi 467. The legion is mentioned on another part of the same papyrus.

Remarkably, this had been a blank form, with the name of Ammonas filled in later; the documentation of furlough thus followed a strict procedure. The second ostracon (*O. Price* 2) reads:

Μάρκος Ἰουλίωι τῶι ἀδελφῶι
χαίρειν.
καλῶς ποήσεις ἱς τὴν αὔ-
ριον λαβεῖν μοι κομ[ί]ᾳτο(ν)
5      καταβῆναι καὶ ταχέως
ἀνηβαναι. ἔπεμψά σοι
καὶ διὰ τοῦ οὐεστιγάτορος
ἀλλὰ ἐπίδες σήμερον τὸ
πιτάκκιον ἱς τὴν αὔριον.
10               ἔρρωσσοι

3 *l.* εἰς, also in 9    6 *l.* ἀναβῆναι    8 *l.* ἐπίθες?    9 *l.* πιττάκιον    10 *l.* ἔρρωσο

Marcus to Julius his brother greeting. For tomorrow kindly get me leave to come down and return at once. I also sent to you through the *vestigator*; so, hand in the chit today for tomorrow. Farewell.

The editor of the Florida ostraca quite convincingly suggested that the first ostracon was such a chit (πιττάκιον) as the one here mentioned. But both editors were mistaken, I believe, in assuming that the soldier would carry the chit with him as his furlough pass in case he was questioned by someone in authority. The reading of *O. Price* 2, ἐπίδες, is not ἐπίθες, dispatch, but rather ἐπίδος, hand in.[23] The chit, one may understand, would be handed in to the unit's administrative office the day before the furlough was due to begin. Headquarters would thus have documentation for any leave taken, which was particularly important in the never ending struggle against the machinations of the troop officers described above. That this was indeed so is confirmed by the law of Anastasius already mentioned. The law prescribes that each soldier must receive his pay personally, into his own hand. It also requires that pay for soldiers on furlough not be handed over to the officers but be held at headquarters until they return. And this must be done for no more than thirty men, the maximum allowed on furlough, and only for those of whom the *actarius* 'can produce

23. For a similar official handing in (ἐπιδιδόναι) of *pittacia* see *P. Yale* inv. 1528 = *SB* v 8247 = Daris, *op. cit.* (n. 16) no. 103.

the chits he has by agreement' (*quorum . . . actarius . . . pittacia utpote habita super pactione protulerit*).[24]

The word *pittacium* meant, indeed, a chit or a warrant, a document used for checking, and on which check marks could be added.[25] The Florida ostracon seems to be made for just such a purpose, for its text is only written on the upper half of the shard, which leaves the lower half for checking entries such as the dates of the beginning and the end of the leave and its purpose. The law and the ostraca thus explain each other.

To be sure, the ostraca date from the second or third century A.D., while Anastasius' law belongs to the beginning of the sixth century. However, the law still uses the same technical terms (*commeatus, pittacium, actarius*) as those current at the time of the ostraca, and it is aimed against the same abuses as those branded by Tacitus. The three-hundred-year gap between the two documents thus is not a compelling argument against the chit having the same function in the law and in the ostraca; it rather is evidence for the great staying power of Roman institutions.

Officers also needed permission for leave. A career inscription of an equestrian officer records that he was prefect of the first Breuci cohort, *libero commeatu*, i.e. with the right to spend his time where he pleased, a privilege thought worth pointing out in the record of his career.[26] As for troop officers, a papyrus of the early second century A.D. preserves a letter to a decurion of an unknown Egyptian auxiliary cohort concerning his furlough (*P. Wisc.* II 70):

```
[. . . . . .]s              Téri              decurióni
                                            salútem
[. . . . .]ṣtermus . strategus . Coptitú . petí-
[vit a me u]ṭ tibi . commeátum . darem
[dierum] XXX . ad . intervisendás . possessió-
[nes tuas] quás . habés . nomo . Arsinoité.
[me sati]ṣfacere . scripsi . nón . sólum
[illi sed] etiam . Pétronió . Fidó . centu-
[rioni . . .]'e.[´. . .]ọgo . dié . suó . acce-
[p        ±15        ]ṭem . bis[´]
```

[. . .] to the decurion Teres, greetings. [. . .]stermus, strategus of the

24. *Cod. Iust.* 12.37.16.2.
25. E.g. *OGIS* 674. 21ff., with commentary (= *IGRR* I 1183).
26. *CIL* v 6478, cf. H. Devijver, *Prosopographia Militarium Equestrium* I (Leuven 1976) 407, no. G16, Suetonius, *Claudius* 25, Tacitus, *Agricola* 5; contrast *P. Giss.* 41.

Coptite nome has asked me to grant you 30 days' leave so that you may visit your possessions which you have in the Arsinoite nome. I have written not only to him but also to the centurion Petronius Fidus that I grant this [...]

The name and rank of the officer who granted the decurion's furlough is lost, but if centurions and decurions could grant leave to the men, one expects that their own furlough was issued by the officers next in rank, i.e. the tribunes and prefects of the units.[27] Teres, it seems, was assigned to service with the *strategos* of the Coptite nome which is why that official had applied for Teres' furlough. Until now no soldiers in the service of a *strategos* have been known, but such an employment of soldiers may be expected, all the more, since we know that a fair number of men were seconded, for example, to the *epistrategos* at Coptos.[28]

Like *O. Price* 2, and the application quoted above, the letter to Teres indicates the purpose of the leave and the man's destination. The three documents thus confirm what has been inferred from the literary and legal sources, namely that not only the time, but also the purpose and destination were essential considerations in the granting or refusing of furlough, and that such information was recorded.[29] Apparently the army command wanted to keep track of the men so that they could be recalled when needed. This might prevent a situation like that of Count Theodosius, who in the reign of Valentinian had to recall by edict the many men dispersed everywhere on unspecified furlough (*multos per diversa libero commeatu dispersos*).[30]

Furlough, however, was not the only way to see one's family. A curious letter written during Trajan's reign by a soldier at Pselkis in Nubia to his mother at Karanis in the Fayum reads as follows:

27. The editor suggested the *praefectus castrorum* at Alexandria.

28. Fink, *op. cit.* (n. 14) 11.2.9 and 81 iii 10. J. D. Thomas and R. W. Davies, 'A New Military Strength Report on Papyrus', *JRS* 67 (1977) 50–61. See also *O. Latopolis* 9 in the new reading of R. S. Bagnall, 'The Roman Garrison of Latopolis', *BASP* 12 (1975) 135–44, and cf. now *SB* XIV 11641.25.

29. Rostovtzeff, *op. cit.* (n. 1) 719.29ff. See Vegetius' remark (above, n. 3) that furlough used to be given only *causis iustissimis*; reasons had also to be given in the case of the civilian *strategos*, *P. Giss.* 41, and of the provincial governor, Pliny, *Ep.* 10.8–9. The *Digest* (50.1.22) defines *liber commeatus* as the free choice of tarrying where one wanted (*ubi velint morandi arbitrium*).

30. Ammianus Marcellinus 27.8.9.

Saturnilus to Aphrodous, his mother, very many greetings. Before all things I pray for your health and prosperity. I wish you to know that I sent you three letters this month. I have received in full the monthly allowances which you sent to me by Julius and a basket of olives by the lad Julius. I wish you to know that another male child has been born to me, whose name is Agathos Daimon.

If, the gods willing, I find an opportunity of putting my plan into effect I am coming to you with letters. I wish you to know that it is now three months since I came to Pselkis, and I have not yet found an opportunity to come to you. I was afraid to come just now because they say, 'The prefect is on the route', lest he take the letters from me and send me back to the standards and I incur the expense in vain. But I wish you to know that if another two months pass and I do not come to you before the month of Hathur I have eighteen more months of sitting in garrison until I enter Pselkis again and come to you. All those who come will bear witness to you how I seek daily to come. If you wish to see me a little, I wish it greatly and pray daily to the gods that they may quickly give me a good chance to come. In the army everything depends on the right opportunity. If I have an opportunity I am coming to you.

Take care of my children's pigs....[31]

It was not understood until now why the letters which Saturnilus hoped to carry 'seem to be the cause of some anxiety to the writer; why the presence of the prefect somewhere en route should inspire fear; why the prefect should seize the letters and send Saturnilus back to his division; why the seizure should involve financial loss to the bearer; and why the prefect should concern himself with the absence and journey of a mere soldier'.[32] All these questions are answered if one assumes that Saturnilus hoped to carry official letters from his unit at Pselkis to the Egyptian army command, i.e. to the *praefectus Aegypti* at Alexandria. Regular furlough may have been too short for travel from Nubia to the Fayum and back, but if Saturnilus went as courier to Alexandria, he would be able to stop by at Karanis.

If this was indeed what Saturnilus hoped for, he would of course not want to go when the prefect was in the upcountry, for he would have to bring the letters to the prefect's *officium* there. If the letters reached their destination in this way, Saturnilus might

---

31. *P. Mich.* III 203, see *Berichtigungsliste* 3, p. 111.
32. J. G. Winter, editing *P. Mich.* III, p. 258, 10–11.

be sent back to his unit.[33] The wording clearly shows that Saturnilus did not expect punishment in case the prefect took the letters; hence their content cannot have been compromising.[34] What Saturnilus did fear was that his expenses would be lost – surely the bribe he would have to pay in order to obtain such a desirable task as to travel to Alexandria on official business. Such bribes were required at every step in the army, to judge from a *cri-de-coeur* of another soldier, writing to his father *Hic autem sine aere nihil fiet.*[35]

Saturnilus has a similar sad piece of wisdom about the army to share with his reader: 'In the army everything depends on the right opportunity' (πάντα εἰς τὴν στρατείαν [μετ᾽ εὐκ]αιρείας [γ]είνεται). This has been translated as 'everything is ready for the expedition, awaiting an opportunity'. Historians have taken this as evidence for expeditions under Trajan, leaving from Pselkis, or even as the beginning of the raids by the Blemmyes.[36] Saturnilus' sentence, however, must mean that in the army everything had to await the right opportunity, for only so does it fit the train of thought expressed before and after it, i.e. Saturnilus' hope for an opportunity to come and see his mother. Headquarters, of course, would not have letters ready every day to be carried to Alexandria, and there were no doubt others, too, who wanted to be entrusted with such missions.

Thus, while regular furlough may have been paid for by the emperors from Otho onwards, other forms of 'leave' still required bribes. With soldiers like Saturnilus able and willing to pay, the troop officers simply could not resist the temptation of carrying on that age-old tradition.

33. Just such a case of being sent back to one's unit after having served as a courier has now become known in *O. Latopolis* 13 in the very perceptive reading and interpretation by J. F. Gilliam, 'Three Ostraca from Latopolis', *BASP* 13 (1976) 55–61: *Domitio Respecto praef(ecto) suo, Severus (centurio) salutem. Onnuphrin Panamea eq(uitem) turma Procli dismisi ex cursu, VIII K. Ianuarias.* See also *O. Skeat* 11 (= *SB* vi 9118) as explained by S. Daris, 'Su alcuni ostraca militari', *Aegyptus* 43 (1963) 264–68, and *P. Dura* 82 ii 7.

34. Contra: Winter, *op. cit.* (n. 32) *Ad signa* is the technical term for being at one's unit as opposed to being on furlough or being detached to some task elsewhere; see above, nn. 4 and 7 and *Cod. Theod.* 7.1.2; Livy 3.24.5 and 28.24.9.

35. *P. Mich.* viii 468.38–39.

36. A. M. Demicheli, *Rapporti di pace e di guerra dell'Egitto Romano con le popolazioni dei deserti Africani* (Milan 1976) 44f.